Between Generations

Between Generations

Collaborative Authorship in the Golden Age of Children's Literature

Victoria Ford Smith

UNIVERSITY PRESS OF MISSISSIPPI ✕ JACKSON

Children's Literature Association Series

www.upress.state.ms.us

Designed by Peter D. Halverson
Frontis illustration by D. G. Smith

The University Press of Mississippi is a member of the
Association of American University Presses.

Copyright © 2017 by University Press of Mississippi
All rights reserved

First printing 2017

∞

A substantially revised version of chapter 2 was first published in *Children's Literature Association Quarterly* 35.1 (2010), 26–54. Reprinted with permission by Johns Hopkins University Press.

Library of Congress Cataloging-in-Publication Data

Names: Smith, Victoria Ford, author.
Title: Between generations : collaborative authorship in the golden age of children's literature / Victoria Ford Smith.
Description: Jackson : University Press of Mississippi, 2017. | Series: Children's Literature Association series | Includes bibliographical references and index. |
Identifiers: LCCN 2017007705 (print) | LCCN 2017025037 (ebook) |
ISBN 9781496813381 (epub single) | ISBN 9781496813398 (epub institutional) | ISBN 9781496813404 (pdf single) | ISBN 9781496813411 (pdf institutional) | ISBN 9781496813374 (hardcover : alk. paper)
Subjects: LCSH: Children's literature, English—History and criticism. | English literature—19th century—History and criticism. | English literature—20th century—History and criticism. | Child authors—Great Britain—History—19th century. | Child authors—Great Britain—History—20th century. | Children—Writing. | Authorship—Collaboration.
Classification: LCC PR990 (ebook) | LCC PR990 .S63 2017 (print) | DDC 820.9/9282—dc23
LC record available at https://lccn.loc.gov/2017007705

British Library Cataloging-in-Publication Data available

in memory of my mother,
Susan Ford

Contents

ACKNOWLEDGMENTS - IX -

INTRODUCTION
A Child's Story - 3 -

CHAPTER ONE
Active Listeners
Child Auditors as Creative Collaborators - 37 -

CHAPTER TWO
Family Dynamics
The Strange Case of Robert Louis Stevenson and Lloyd Osbourne - 92 -

CHAPTER THREE
Collaborating with the Authorities
Children as Authors, Experts, and Critics - 142 -

CHAPTER FOUR
Pictures of Partnership
Art Education, Children's Literature, and the Rise of the Child Artist - 190 -

CONCLUSION
Mentors and Muses
Why the Collaborative Child Matters - 239 -

NOTES - 263 -
WORKS CITED - 292 -
INDEX - 317 -

Acknowledgments

Between Generations is about collaboration, so I have reflected for many hours on how claims of sole authorship hide the vast networks of individuals and support systems that surround the person holding the pen—or, in this case, the person at the laptop. Many brilliant people have helped make this book happen. It turns out all their names won't fit on the title page, so I will name them here.

I am grateful to Richard C. Sha, who introduced me to the Victorians, led me to the archives, and first suggested that writing about and teaching literature might be something I should pursue as a career. I also was lucky to sit in on discussions led by Marianne Noble, who modeled for me the intellectual curiosity I want to instill in my students, and Henry Taylor, in whose poetry workshops I discovered I loved words even more than I had previously imagined.

I feel profoundly lucky to have written the earliest versions of *Between Generations* at Rice University. I benefited from Robert L. Patten's encyclopedic knowledge of everything Victorian and, as I drafted this book, came to admire his genuine enthusiasm, his creativity as a thinker and teacher, and his reliability and warmth. This book surely would not have happened without Helena Michie, who asked tough and important questions, helped me revise my terrible chapter titles, and taught me the indispensable building blocks of navigating academia—everything from mapping paragraphs to conference presentations. Thad Logan demonstrated through example that a genuine love of my material, an appreciation for its beauty, could enrich my work. Martin J. Wiener and Elizabeth Long were generous with their time and expertise. These scholars—at the most trying and the most triumphant moments of my work—reassured me through their calm confidence that I would succeed.

I could name here all of my colleagues and friends at the University of Connecticut at Storrs. I am especially fortunate that I work down the hall from Katharine Capshaw. She writes beautiful and important scholarship and helps others do the same, champions me and my work, and ensures that UConn is one of the best places to study children's literature. She's also seriously fun. Thank you to Margaret Higonnet—a mentor who made me feel welcome and valued as soon as I stepped on campus and who has the enviable talent of nuancing and refining the ideas of everyone around her with grace. And I have so many colleagues and friends in Storrs whose advice, feedback, and support have inspired me, especially Margaret Breen, Dwight Codr, Lindsay Cummings, Cora-Lynn Deibler, Anna Mae Duane, Clare Eby, Wendy Glenn, Bob Hasenfratz, Kathy Knapp, Charles Mahoney, Anne Oeldorf-Hirsch, Samantha Olschan, Tom Recchio, Cathy Schlund-Vials, Chris Vials, and Sarah Winter. Thanks as well to those inimitable UConn graduate students I have encountered thus far, especially my advisees, who challenge me with new ideas every year: Sara Austin; Emma Burris-Janssen; Kathryn Coto; Amanda Greenwell; Katie Nunnery; Rebecca Rowe; and Michelle Resene, who lent me her expertise in disability studies by reading parts of this book's conclusion.

I am grateful as well to the children's literature community, which is the friendliest academic family I know. Thank you to my anonymous reviewers, whose insightful comments helped me refine my ideas, and to the Children's Literature Association Publications Advisory Board—Jackie Horne, Kenneth Kidd, Maria Nikolajeva, Marek Oziewicz, and Michelle Martin—for supporting this project. Additional thanks to those children's literature scholars whose friendship makes my disciplinary home a welcoming one. There are far too many of you to name, but I would like to extend special thanks to Michelle Abate, who with her usual humor soothed my first-book anxiety; Derritt Mason, whose GIFs keep me going; K Cummings Pipes, who is always a willing editor and a delightful fellow lover of literature; Alexandra Valint, whose feedback on this book's introduction was extraordinarily helpful and smart; and Marah Gubar, whose work on child agency and commitment to talking about real children in children's literature scholarship inspires my own research and indeed makes it possible. Marah's unflagging support for this book, her generous comments on my writing, and her encouragement to be daring and joyful as a scholar were invaluable, and continue to be.

I cannot express how much I appreciate my fearless writing group. Little did I know, when I first met Susan Cook and Ryan Fong at the

Dickens Universe, a powerful alliance was forming. Thank you for reading all of my drafts with compassion and attention, for sharing with me the victories and frustrations of academic work, and for being Fancy in your own ways. It was only through your friendship and our many hours online that this book came together.

Thanks to all of my family—Todd, Amy, Andrew, Matt, Tracey, and Linda—and above all to my dad, Mike "Boots" Ford. He is seriously the best. He is always up for a friendly bowling tournament, and whenever I'm nervous about my next big endeavor, he shows up with a high five and a moving truck. He teaches me every day how to be a good person, and his love for me is unwavering. This book is a testament to his support, and I'm sure he will read it, even though he jokes that he's going to wait for the movie adaptation. And, of course, I will always be thankful to my mom, Susan Ford, to whom this book is dedicated. I love reading, writing, and teaching because I saw her do all three with such love—for me, for my family, and for generations of students. She gave me *Mousekin's Golden House* and *Anne of Green Gables*. She celebrated my victories as her own. It's hard for me to think about publishing this book without her here to read it, but I know she's been watching it happen and cheering me on.

My husband, Danny Smith, never doubted that this book would be published (even when I insisted stubbornly that it was a lost cause). He's been by my side in Charlotte, Houston, and Storrs from my senior year of high school to my first years as a professor. He patiently listened to me talk about the obscure relations of Victorian authors, helped out with his tech skills, tolerated the full repertoire of songs I sing to the cats, and cooked me delicious steak and butterloo chicken. When I feel uncertain about my own projects, I need only look to his own dedication as an illustrator, because he works with unmatched resolution, creativity, and purpose. He has built with me a partnership in work and in life, and he is the best collaborator I could ask for.

Between Generations

INTRODUCTION

A Child's Story

In May of 1842, a young, aspiring artist asked Robert Browning to send him a poem to illustrate. Browning, who knew the young artist but was unsure of his talents, obliged with a brief piece he had written a few years before but had not published: "The Cardinal and the Dog." The poem is short, only fifteen lines, but offers a compelling plot: it narrates the death of the Pope's legate, a man tortured by hallucinations of a "black Dog of vast bigness, eyes flaming, ears that hung / Down to the very ground almost" (41). It was perhaps with curiosity that Browning opened the artist's response—three pencil illustrations and the following letter, written in careful, slanting script:

> My dear Mr Browning
>   I was very much obliged to you, for your kind letter. I liked exceedingly the Cardinal and the dog. I have tried to illustrate the poem, and I hope that you will like my attempt. I cannot go to school because my cough is so bad.
>   I remain your affectionate friend
>   W. C. Macready. (Macready 329)[1]

Most illustrators need not worry about spoiling their attendance records due to a chest cold, but W. C. Macready—son of the famous tragedian William Charles Macready and called Willie by friends and family—was only ten years old in 1842, while Browning was thirty. Browning corresponded with Macready Sr. throughout the 1830s and 1840s, sending the noted actor a series of plays that were met with varying degrees of enthusiasm, but the poet may have found a more willing collaborator in the younger Macready.[2] Willie's drawings for "The Cardinal and the Dog" are executed with seriousness and dense with detail. The poem offers the barest descriptions of the scene: a reference to the legate's table, his weariness, his deathbed. Macready expanded artfully upon those sparse details. Likely inspired by a family life saturated with the trappings of the theater, he provided drawings that resemble staged scenes or elaborate set designs; Willie decorated the legate's chamber with tapered candles, ornate chairs, and art hung gallery-style. A door on the right dramatically opens to reveal the entrance of the terrible dog. Browning provided almost a journalistic report in verse, and Macready responded with a fully realized staging of the legate's fate.

Decades later, Browning recalled how Willie's drawings changed his approach to the partnership, transforming it from a casual lark to a collaboration that was, while playful, also quite earnest. Willie "had a talent for drawing," Browning wrote in 1881 to friend Frederick James Furnivall, "and asked me to give him some little thing to illustrate, so I made him a bit of a poem out of an old account of the death of the Pope's legate at the Council of Trent—which he made such clever drawings for, that I tried a more picturesque subject, the piper" (Peterson 27). Browning transformed this "picturesque subject" into "The Pied Piper of Hamelin; A Child's Story," and Macready responded with four new pencil illustrations. The first depicts the Piper's bold entrance into Hamelin's council chamber, another finds him herding rats into the River Weser, a third reveals the town's children marching toward Koppelberg Hill, and the final shows a mourning Hamelin citizen painting a placard in remembrance of the children's fate. Upon completing the final illustrations for the poem, Willie sent another letter, addressed to "R. Browning Esqr":

> *My dear Mr Browning*
> *I have finished the rest of the illustrations of the Pied Piper, which I hope you will like as well as the others but I am sorry to say that I do not think them so good as the Council chamber, or the other one that I did. Hoping that they will be as great a success as the others*
> *I remain your affect. friend*
> *William C. Macready Jun.*
> *May 18th 1842* (Macready 350)

Willie's illustrations were not printed with Browning's "Pied Piper" when it was first published in *Dramatic Lyrics* in 1842, and in the multiple editions of the poem published for child audiences in the 1880s and beyond his drawings are passed over in favor of the work of established adult artists such Kate Greenaway and Arthur Rackham. However, after Browning's death, his sister Sarianna carefully archived Willie's pivotal role in the poem's composition, saving the boy's letters and illustrations in a single envelope and writing on its exterior a short account of the brief collaboration between "W. C. Macready Jun." and his "affectionate friend," Robert Browning.[3]

The "Pied Piper" is a "Child's Story," then, in more ways than one. It is a child's story in the way that children's literature can be said to belong to young people; while Browning's poem first appeared in a volume intended for older readers, today it is more likely to be found on children's bookshelves than anywhere else. But "The Pied Piper" is also a child's story in that it belongs not only to Browning but also to a real child—to Macready, who was in many ways responsible for its composition. The letters and other documents referenced above work together to suggest that the pair recognized their relationship as, in part, a working partnership between adult poet and child artist. When Browning wrote of the collaboration to Furnivall, he reversed what might be common assumptions about the production of children's literature and the creative agency adults and children enjoy—the assumption that adults produce texts and children consume them. He notes that it was Macready who initiated the collaboration—the boy "asked [Browning] to give him some little thing to illustrate"—and while Browning's language signals that he approached the partnership off-handedly at first, sending a "bit of a poem," the drawings Macready created in response reframed the project for the poet. Browning composed "The Pied Piper" not to humor Macready or develop his drawing toward adult standards but instead to respond to the talents the young artist already possessed. And Macready responded by selecting sedate scenes from Browning's work and drawing in a style that seems perhaps more serious than playful. He sent vistas of Hamelin: for example, a meadow that seems barren but, upon closer examination, is carpeted with rats and a landscape that would be serene if its edge did not reveal a mob of doomed children. These drawings are in some ways unexpected. They disrupt the cultural construct of the child muse so engrained in the origin stories of Golden Age texts—idealizations that rely on sentimental portraits of imaginative children.

When Browning published "The Pied Piper" in *Dramatic Lyrics*, he appended a dedication to Willie—"written for, and inscribed to, W. M. the Younger" (209)—and while some might read this as an affectionate gesture to a child friend, it seems just as likely that it refers to the fact that the poem was *written for* Macready, at the child's request. Willie merits such a gesture, as his correspondence with Browning makes clear the gravity with which he approached his work. While his letters are written with the run-on quality of a ten-year-old's literacy, they also demonstrate his canny knowledge of more formal communications, and Willie voices serious concerns about the quality of his art—his sincere wish that the illustrations of the Piper will be "as great a success as the others." His letters do not document a commission leading to publication, of course, but they do convey the tenor of the pair's work together. The friendship between "William C. Macready Jun." and "R. Browning Esqr" did not necessarily assume the authority of the older creative partner and may not have followed traditional adult and child or teacher and student dynamics. Macready uses his letter to frame a professional partnership.

Despite the preservation of Willie Macready's letters and drawings, his role in the composition of Browning's "Pied Piper" largely has been forgotten. In fact, the Macready-Browning partnership is one of many adult-child collaborations that critical histories of Golden Age children's literature have ignored, underexamined, or undervalued.[4] Even a partial list of these collaborations makes apparent how many real children have been elided in such histories. For example, among those children are the young people William Thackeray consulted, from Edith Story to Thackeray's own daughters, Anny and Minny, while composing *The Rose and the Ring* (1854). Similar adult-child partnerships inspired Margaret Gatty's popular *Aunt Judy's Tales* (1859), a collection that in its pages fictionalizes the network of children and family members who contributed to its stories. That circle of creative collaborators predates the more famous Liddell sisters—Alice, Edith, and Lorina—who plied Lewis Carroll for the tale that would become *Alice's Adventures in Wonderland* (1865) and who feature in that novel's opening poem. J. M. Barrie begins his dedication to *Peter Pan* (1904) by stating he wants "to give Peter to the Five without whom he never would have existed," the Llewelyn Davies brothers.[5] Rudyard Kipling's daughter Josephine and A. A. Milne's son Christopher Robin weave in and out of the *Just So Stories* (1897–1902) and *Winnie-the-Pooh* (1926), respectively, their influence on those canonical texts registering in fictional characters, historical documents, and dedications and prefaces that blend the real and imagined. These children are joined by others who participated in lesser known but once popular texts for children. For example, David Starr Jordan's *The Book of Knight and*

Barbara appeared in 1899 with the subtitle "Being a Series of Stories Told to Children, Corrected and Illustrated by the Children."

In *Between Generations*, I recuperate this tradition of adult-child collaborations in nineteenth- and early twentieth-century British children's literature and culture.[6] I term such adult-child creative relationships intergenerational collaborations, and I demonstrate how these partnerships transform the literature they generate—literature that often portrays the sometimes joyful, sometimes vexed negotiations between generations. I do not fully explore all of the creative partnerships listed above, although most of them do appear in the chapters that follow; instead, I have chosen to explore those texts, both familiar and obscure, that most clearly represent the variety of ways adults and children collaborate and, in doing so, negotiate questions of child agency and discourses of Victorian childhood. In other words, while I do not seek to provide a thorough history of the Golden Age of children's literature, the partnerships I examine, taken separately and read together, elucidate the contours of real children's participation in their own literature and culture and challenge popular narratives of children's literature that read actual young people solely as idealized listeners or passive muses. As I will demonstrate, children's contributions to literary and visual culture are recoverable through the careful examination of letters, dedications, memoirs, and other archival traces as well as through attentive readings of the texts themselves.

As the examples I've sketched out thus far imply, the intergenerational collaborations I consider in this book engage with both the real and the imaginary, and the boundary between fictive collaborations and lived partnerships was not firm. Imaginative and material practices were, in fact, mutually constitutive, each transforming the other—especially during the nineteenth century, a pivotal moment in the history of childhood and children's publishing—and considering the real and fictive side by side offers new insights into how authors wrestled with the place and status of children's voices in children's literature. Fictional representations of adult-child relationships—for example, the uneasy alliance between Jim Hawkins and Long John Silver in Robert Louis Stevenson's *Treasure Island* (1881–1882)—signal on an individual scale a cultural interest in the possibilities of child agency. These representations provided authors such as Stevenson imaginative space to rehearse new paradigms of childhood. However, authors also collaborated with living children. *Treasure Island*, for instance, was a product in part of Stevenson's collaboration with his stepson, Samuel Lloyd Osbourne. Adults' partnerships with young writers, illustrators, and co-conspirators reveal that the agentic, creative child was not only a figure but also an actor, vital to authorial practice; the texts that adult writers produced with children, and their accounts of working with young people, revised models of childhood and authorship in material as well as figurative ways.

These collaborations were part of a larger investigation of the limits and possibilities of child agency taking place in a range of discourses and cultural venues, from educational reform to psychology to librarianship. In other words, many Victorians were revising familiar paradigms of adult-child relationships both in books and in life, and I therefore situate adult-child partnerships forged over the creation of literature alongside other historical examples of intergenerational collaboration. For example, in Chapter One, I explore theories of language acquisition proposed by Child Study scholars at the end of the nineteenth century that suggest children's creative misappropriations of adult speech might transform the English language—a hypothesis reflected in popular children's literature that represents young listeners' influence on told tales. Similarly, shifting theories of art education, outlined in Chapter Four, transformed popular conceptions of the child artist in the nineteenth and early twentieth centuries; as modernism and its celebration of childlike ways of seeing the world approached, classroom practices began to accommodate collaborative curricula that engaged students' as well as their teachers' expertise, and illustrators for children started to consider how they could access childlike ways of making images, sometimes by turning to children themselves. Together, these adult-child partnerships, in literature and beyond, reveal the varied ways adults explored the nature of child agency and the wide-ranging discourses—cultural, social, and scientific—where that exploration took place. In the following pages, I introduce the many writers and thinkers who question the assumed authority of adults, who write about children as both passive and subversive subjects, and who self-consciously negotiate, alongside real children, the ideological and ethical difficulties of listening to and representing children's perspectives.

Why did these collaborative children disappear from the critical stories we tell about childhood and children's literature? Macready's drawings of Hamelin were unpublished, and Browning's dedication to "W. M. the Younger" has very rarely been printed above the poem after its first appearance in *Dramatic Lyrics*, which partially explains why his stake in the poem remains relatively invisible and continues to fade as the poem is reprinted and re-illustrated over time.[7] However, his disappearance is also—and I would argue more importantly—a consequence of critical conventions in the study of children's literature that often look with paralyzing suspicion upon references to an author's biography, devalue the work of children, and underestimate the agency of young people. These critical assumptions can warp our understanding of children's literature and adjacent paradigms of childhood. Without a careful account of Macready's relationship to Browning, after all, "The Pied Piper" coalesces into a story about the exceptionally seductive adult artist who manipulates the town's children, and Macready himself recedes into just another passive child listener. Perhaps this version of "The Pied Piper," a story *without* Macready's participation, is more readily recognizable as children's literature, because the participation of children in a text's creation prevents that text from fitting easily into dominant conceptions of the genre—indeed, conceptions of childhood itself—that assume adult authority.

These conceptions originate from a tradition of children's literature scholarship that reads children as passive or powerless, receivers rather than creators or negotiators of texts, and legible primarily as constructs of adult desire—a tradition largely inspired by Jacqueline Rose's 1984 study *The Case of Peter Pan, or the Impossibility of Children's Fiction*. Rose famously argues that "there is no child behind the category of 'children's fiction,' other than the one which it needs to believe is there for its own purposes" (10). She posits that this child figure not only represents an adult fantasy of linguistic and sexual innocence but also plays a vital role in an extratextual project by adults to manage their anxieties about real children, "to secure the child who is outside the book, the one who does not come so easily within its grasp" (2). "Children's fiction," Rose writes, "sets up the child as an outsider to its own process, and then aims, unashamedly, to take that child *in*" (2). In Rose's work, then, the fictional child and the real child often seem to collapse into one another; both are idealized, eroticized, and slippery constructs, products of an adult imagination characterized as anxious at best and malevolent at worst. While admittedly Rose does not set out to consider real children's relationship with literature written for them—"I am not, of course, talking here of the child's own experience of the book," she writes, "which, despite all the attempts which have been made, I consider more or less impossible to gauge" (9)—those real, reading children always are implicated in her argument, which purposefully considers children both inside and outside the book to insinuate that the difference between the two is tellingly one of degree, not kind. She would not argue, of course, that real children do not exist; rather, she suggests that such children are obscured by the uses to which adults put them.

Rose's work continues to reverberate through studies of children's literature and culture, shaping some of the most persistent questions in the field. Scholars who align with Rose deploy her ideas in diverse ways, but most are alike in that they foster skepticism when it comes to thinking about real children in children's literature scholarship. Rose's legacy, in other words, has resulted in an assumption that scholarship about actual young people is too troubled by the omnipresent machinery of adult desire to succeed in a critical approach to the genre; many scholars focus instead, or insist that we focus almost exclusively, on evidence of adults' ideologies in texts written for young people. Perry Nodelman's work is the most visible example of this critical move. In his touchstone essay "The Other: Orientalism, Colonialism, and Children's Literature" (1992), he argues that "our descriptions of childhood . . . purport to see and speak for children" but instead reinforce adults' authority over young people, replicating the power imbalances of colonizer-colonized relationships (29). Later, in *The Hidden Adult: Defining Children's Literature* (2008), Nodelman frames children's literature as "an adult practice with intentions for child readers" (4).[8] Throughout his ongoing critical reflections about children's literature and child agency, Nodelman has gestured toward the possibility of child agency—and, in fact, he frames *The Hidden Adult* as a call for child agency, as implicit in his work is a dedication to educating children in the interests and agendas of children's literature ("Hidden" 267–68); however, as Richard Flynn has pointed out, the "once-useful hermeneutics of suspicion" often located in Nodelman's work "has devolved into a series of increasingly rote critical gestures that [are] implicated in an overemphasis on children's alterity, in a model of children as helpless or even as victims, implying that children exercise little to no agency in participating in and creating their culture" ("What" 255).[9] Other scholarship demonstrates how adults' investment in ideal childhood varies according to history, culture, class, and gender. James Kincaid takes on this project in *Child-Loving: The Erotic Child in Victorian Culture* (1992), in which he interrogates how "what we think of as 'the child' has been assembled in reference to desire, built up in erotic manufactories," tracing that desire from the Victorian period to the present (4). Catherine Robson is similarly interested in the genesis of powerful figures of childhood, exploring in *Men in Wonderland: The Lost Girlhood of the Victorian Gentleman* (2001) how, for many Victorian authors, "girls represent not just the true essence of childhood, but an adult male's best opportunity of reconnecting with his own lost self" (3). Such scholarship is valuable, making apparent how the child figure's cultural, psychological, and ideological freight shapes children's literature and culture and our own ways, as scholars, of talking about young people.

Fewer studies, however, consider how this figure of the child might exist alongside, or in conversation with, the lived experiences of real children, and how considering the two side by side might change our perception of both—in part because the field has been troubled by the assumption that theorizations of the figure of the child cannot accommodate the real child, and vice versa. The tenacious authority of Rose's critical approach and its dominance in subsequent decades of children's literature studies therefore has resulted in significant blind spots in the field. When Rose and others argue that the figure of the child is a fiction that conceals those things that adults do not want to acknowledge, such as the ruptures of sexuality and language—when they exclude the experiences of actual children as unrecoverable or irrelevant—they endorse an approach to childhood that, ironically, obscures a fuller, richer view of children's literature and culture. In the words of David Rudd, "Insight into the child as a cultural trope . . . has led to a neglect of the child as a social being, with a voice" (30). That child appears, I argue, in facets of children's literature and culture that remain inadequately explored. What texts, authors, and cultural artifacts have been hidden from view by a narrow focus on the figure of the child and its roots in adult desire? What do we miss, and what types of knowledge are inaccessible to us, when we deem the project of thinking about actual young people impossible, misguided, or naïve?

First, as the case of Willie Macready makes clear, scholars often dismiss evidence of children's participation in literature and culture even when that evidence is readily accessible or familiar. Children's literature criticism and histories of the genre might mention in passing young people such as Willie Macready, Lloyd Osbourne, or the Llewelyn Davies brothers, but their place in such criticism is tenuous. Working from the assumption that children's literature is an "adult practice," many scholars reject evidence of a real child's contributions as unreliable or sentimental, and explorations of real children as creative subjects risk characterization as unsophisticated biographical criticism. To avoid such naïveté, scholarship that aligns with Rose tends to avoid altogether the question of the real children who populate the history of Golden Age children's literature or reads them as disembodied constructs who, despite the traces they leave behind, have little to do with material authorial practice. For example, in *Kipling's Children's Literature* (2010), Sue Walsh finds fault with interpretations of the *Just So Stories* that trace the author's relationship with his daughter Josephine, who died at six years old, in characters often considered fictionalizations of her: Effie, Best Beloved, or Taffy. "The dead Josephine weighs down on the interpretive possibility of the text," she writes. "Everything founders in the face of the 'real'" (84). Walsh posits the biographical "real," carefully quarantined in quotation marks, as the opponent of critical complexity, suggesting that allowing Josephine into our consideration of Kipling's oeuvre will likely lead to one-dimensional readings seeking an inarguably true account of a once-living child. While she suggests that Kipling's canon has been particularly subject to such readings, she cautions children's literature scholars in particular and literary scholars as a whole against "biographically informed narratives" in which "fiction becomes a kind of mystery to be unraveled in order to discover the 'true' childhood already existing 'behind' the story" (71).

Certainly relying on biography without recognizing its constructedness according to cultural ideologies or idiosyncratic individual motives is a near-sighted methodology; however, Walsh underestimates and oversimplifies the potentially productive practice of considering real children in our readings of children's literature and culture—a practice that, as I will show below, can be critically self-conscious and complex, eschewing a quest for the truth of an individual child in favor of a critical practice informed by but not limited to considerations of that child as a living, social being. "The dead Josephine" and her many counterparts in Golden Age children's literature do not stymie the interpretive possibilities of a text but instead exist alongside a spectrum of rich, attentive readings. Indeed, recognizing children as authoring subjects opens up *new* avenues for children's literature scholarship. For example, establishing Willie Macready as Browning's collaborator in the creation of "The Pied Piper" is not a limiting but a critically generative move. While scholarship on the poem often undermines or underplays Willie's role—he frequently appears as a stray biographical detail to be recognized but dispensed with as quickly as possible—introducing his illustrations into the critical conversations surrounding "The Pied Piper" and even arguing that the poem bears evidence of him in its very content, as I will in Chapter Four, invites readings that take into account other historical, cultural, and formal influences.[10] Scholars might consider, for example, the poem's connections to the history of child art or Browning's ideas about the broader nature of authors and artists, which the poet interrogates in many of his dramatic monologues.

In fact, reframing children's literature as a discursive realm in which both adults and children participate expands the purview of children's literature scholarship to address underexamined forms. Critics have neglected texts and genres that foreground the participation of real children because, as Marah Gubar argues, "the critical story we have been telling about children's literature rules out the possibility that young people can function as artistic agents, participants in the production of culture" ("Risky" 452). Texts that explicitly feature real children as creative collaborators, or that invite children to participate, are less approachable or even invisible for those who theorize children's literature primarily, if not solely, as evidence of adults' use of the *figure* of the child—those who agree with Nodelman that "children's literature criticism becomes valuable exactly at the point at which the constructedness of the child readers implied by children's literature becomes a focus of attention" (*Hidden* 161). However, when the constructedness of the child is read *alongside rather than in contradiction with* the child as "a social being with a voice" (to use Rudd's phrase)—when we use what Gubar calls a "both-and" approach to childhood ("Hermeneutics" 305)—texts that simultaneously invite child agency and register the social function of figures of childhood become both visible and valuable. We should interrogate, of course, children's literature that makes clear the constructedness of the child, but we should also study texts that through their form, paratextual material, or uses reveal the fissures in the adult project of children's literature and allow real children to complicate those constructions. In *Between Generations*, I consider such cultural artifacts: for example, children's newspapers, early painting and coloring books, books written by adults and illustrated by children, stories that fictionalize the oral participation of young listeners, and regular features in children's periodicals that invite reader response, among other things. While none of these texts is free from the ideological weight of the child-figure, all make space for the possibility of the agentic, creative child, inside and outside the book.

It is challenging to recuperate this real creative child when the construct of nineteenth-century childhood is so saturated with ideals of creativity and imagination. When Victorian studies scholars recognize children as imaginative or creative subjects, they often do so to limn how that creative child served adult agendas. Christopher Parkes, for instance, tracks the evolution through the nineteenth century of a child-figure "defined by an innate curiosity and invention, the kind that leads to capitalist innovation" (1). Fiction such as E. Nesbit's *The Treasure Seekers* and Frances Hodgson Burnett's *A Little Princess* produced "the imaginative child . . . as a figure who could dissolve the boundary between the child's playroom and the nation's industrial landscapes such that they became a part of the same imaginative project" (188). According to Parkes, these children, because they purportedly naturally possessed the creativity required to succeed in England's capitalist systems, assuaged adults' guilt regarding industrialism's costs for young people and maintained a fiction of social mobility, especially for the middle classes. Sally Shuttleworth takes a different approach to the creative child; she finds that a mid-Victorian anxiety over the child with an overactive imagination, who was read as a disturbing figure of Romantic excess, transformed by the fin-de-siècle into a figure whose "imaginative creations . . . were to be treasured as a form of lost wisdom," a perspective bolstered by theories of recapitulation and primitivism. The creative child, then, reflected and reified adult anxieties about the cultural import of childhood.[11] I am attentive to this figure of the creative child—a construct that is, in the words of art historian Amy F. Ogata, "unequivocally an invention of adults" and that is "implied in the schemes that . . . adults have created"—while insisting that the culturally pervasive construction of the creative child does not, and should not, exclude the study of real children who participate in the production of culture (22, xvi).[12]

In *Between Generations*, I recuperate the actual child as creative collaborator by turning a growing and lively body of scholarship on child agency and embodied childhood that has developed in response to scholars such as Rose and Nodelman. Some of this scholarship draws upon theories of cross-writing forwarded by U. C. Knoepflmacher, Mitzi Myers, and Sandra L. Beckett, among others.[13] Cross-writing, in fact, is an authorial practice that hinges on the possibility of adult-child collaboration. As Knoepflmacher and Myers explain, cross-writing involves "a dialogic mix of older and younger voices . . . in texts too often read as univocal" (vii). While some cross-writing reveals "fissures as much as coalitions," Knoepflmacher and Myers "stress creative cooperation" and foreground texts that "involve interplay and cross-fertilization rather than a hostile internal cross fire" (vii). Many of the earliest iterations of scholarship about cross-writing outline adult-child collaborations best characterized as textual or fictional, in which an adult author interpolates adult and child subjectivities into a single text. Knoepflmacher, for instance, identifies Kipling's *Just So Stories* as a cross-written text, and while (to Walsh's dismay) he considers Kipling's blending of adult and child voices in light of the real child Josephine Kipling, he emphasizes that author's fictionalization of the father-daughter relationship, especially the partnership between the child character Taffy and her father Tegumai. Several of the Taffy stories, Knoepflmacher writes, "can be read as dramatizing an alliance or collaboration designed to counter not only the separation between adult and child, but also gaps between the sexes and between the living and the dead" ("Kipling's" 25).

Scholarship exploring cross-writing has not remained tethered to the textual child. My own theorizations of the child collaborator are indebted to critics who interpret cross-writing as a practice that indexes real children's political, social, and creative agency. Katharine Capshaw, for example, argues that African American children's literature published during the Harlem Renaissance—which was "complicated, intertextual, and directed at a heterogeneous audience"—reveals authors' "awareness of the child's position of cultural leadership" and therefore requires us to revise passive models of children's literature forwarded by Nodelman and others (xx). Flynn also identifies cross-writing as evidence of the social agency of real children. He examines the cross-writing of twentieth-century American poet June Jordan, noting her "success as a cross-writer lies first in her exploration of adult and child concerns dialogically (in writing for both adults and children), [but] it is also articulated in her conscious theorizing about actual children in relation to historical and material concerns." Flynn traces the interplay between Jordan's poetry, her own remembered childhood, and her interactions with and respect for child writers, arguing that Jordan's writings "remind us that children's cultural studies should concern itself with actual children as well as with literature and culture" ("Affirmative" 162). Rachel Conrad—who, like Flynn, is interested in tracing child agency in poetry—stretches the limits of cross-writing in her article on childhood, time, and agency. She does not "limit discussion to cross-currents of address within a single text," as Knoepflmacher and Myers suggest, and instead brings "poems written by adults for or about children into the same critical conversation alongside poems written by young people" (129).

I find that Conrad's decision to expand the purview of cross-writing as an authorial practice to include child-authored as well as adult-authored texts emphasizes both the fertility and the limitations of cross-writing as a critical lens. While scholars often use cross-writing as a springboard into conversations about child agency, that term maintains an emphasis on the ways writing by adults gestures toward children, real and textual, and does not privilege the ways children themselves participate in the creation of literature and culture. In response, Conrad and others have developed methodologies that offer more direct means of addressing real children and young people's creative agency, including evidence of the ways those children understand and negotiate the cultural freight of childhood itself. Conrad, for example, reads poetry by children that acknowledges, navigates, and even revises adult-scripted norms of age and agency—a scholarly project that "provides another angle from which to view the complex relationships between children and representations of childhood" (125). I join Conrad and other scholars who read familiar scripts about passive or powerless childhood not as insurmountable cultural narratives but instead as evidence that must be read alongside the creative and cultural work of real children.

For example, my research is animated by Gubar's work, which like *Between Generations* is attentive to adult authority and child agency in the Golden Age of children's literature, a moment burdened with critical assumptions about the Victorians' idealizations of childhood. Gubar resists these assumptions. In *Artful Dodgers: Reconceiving the Golden Age of Children's Literature* (2009), for example, she argues that authors from Dickens to Carroll to Burnett were "interest[ed] in the idea that children could function as precocious actors, authors, editors, and collaborators," which "reflects their hope that the authority of adults does not obviate the possibility that the child can enjoy a measure of agency and creativity: though not entirely autonomous, they can take a hand in their own self-fashioning" (209). The chapters of *Artful Dodgers* investigate the multiple ways these authors rehearse the possibility of that self-fashioning in their children's literature: through, for example, savvy child narrators, such as the young authors in Dickens's *A Holiday Romance* (1868), or the plucky and often quite capable boy heroes of nineteenth-century adventure fiction, such as Jim Hawkins in *Treasure Island*. Like Gubar, I make clear in my own analyses of Golden Age children's literature how textual children model the ways Victorians imagined the fraught relationship between adult desire and child autonomy.

Gubar's work on children's theater, in *Artful Dodgers* and beyond, is even more in line with my project in its attention to real young people and the scholarly challenges of writing about them. As Gubar notes, because children's theater relied on the participation of children—indeed, she argues it originated in their private play—it has long been neglected in studies of children's literature; "studying its history," Gubar notes, "involves attending to the practices and discourse of young people in schools, at home, on the amateur and professional stage, and in the audience," which is difficult in a critical climate dominated by skepticism about the possibility of writing about real children ("Introduction" viii). However, as Gubar's research makes clear, children's theater—"an inherently collaborative art form" that "set[s] before the public child performers who at once embodied script-following conformity *and* creative self-expression" (*Artful* 34)—has enormous potential in helping scholars think through issues of childhood and agency. While Rose reads child actors as objects of adults' voyeuristic pleasure, Gubar turns to an archive of advertisements, memoirs from young audience members and actors, fan letters, and other material to demonstrate the profound influence real children exerted on the emergence of children's theater.[14] This influence began before child performers took the stage. As Gubar makes clear, children's and adult's dramatic culture were mutually constitutive; the popularity of private theatricals—such as domestic dramas performed by children—inspired public, professional productions, which in turn provided imaginative fodder for young people's dramatic reenactments at home ("*Peter*" 481). Taken as a whole, Gubar's work provides a sustained analysis of children's theater as an intergenerational practice that foregrounds, rather than forecloses, the agency of young people, and she invites future scholarship on forms, both familiar and understudied, that might do the same.

Between Generations takes up Gubar's challenge: that we no longer "limit ourselves entirely to the discussion of adult ideas, practices, and discourse" and that we continue working toward critical accounts of children as creative subjects, even if we "cannot speak in certitudes" (*Artful* 33). In expanding upon Gubar's scholarship, I start from many of the same fundamental assumptions. In particular, as is already clear, I position children as collaborators in the production of literature and culture. My account of intergenerational collaboration, like Gubar's work on children's theater, complicates models of childhood theorized by Rose and Nodelman; I espouse what Gubar coins the kinship model of childhood, "premised on the idea that adults and children are akin to one another," emphasizing "relatedness, connection, and similarity without implying homogeneity, uniformity, and equality." This model reminds us "not to underestimate the capacities of younger people [or] overestimate the powers and abilities of older people" ("Risky" 453, 454). I am also invested in recuperating children as agentic subjects despite what Gubar calls the "thorny epistemological problems about what counts as evidence" (*Artful* 33). The evidence of child collaboration I document in *Between Generations* is certainly inflected by the cultural force of childhood as a construct. However, like Gubar, I contend we should not therefore ignore such evidence but should, instead, approach it with nuance and generosity. "Such a stance," Gubar explains, shifts us away from a hermeneutics of suspicion and "toward what we might call the hermeneutics of recuperation, a rigorous yet generous style of thinking that allows us to appreciate as well as criticize, believe as well as doubt, build and tinker as well as dismantle and deconstruct" ("Hermeneutics" 304). My own recuperation of the tradition of adult-child collaborations that led to many Golden Age texts, then—collaborations that were not merely textual but were, in fact, rooted in real relationships between adults and children—builds upon the work that Gubar and others have begun. I continue to unearth evidence that real children transformed and helped create children's culture, and I not only introduce new archives and objects of study—for example, the participation of children in toy press printing ventures, their role in the work of Child Study scholars, and their work as artists and illustrators—but also propose new methodologies for studying these artifacts, which I outline below.

While I explore some children's theater in *Between Generations*, particularly in Chapter Four, children's plays are not at the center of my project—but children's *play* is. I examine both young people's contributions to children's literature and their play in the larger realm of children's culture, framing both as means through which young people exercised creative agency alongside, or even in resistance to, adult authority. For example, I consider the ways children played with words as they listened to stories and devised secret languages, with images as illustrators and art students, and with toys such as coloring books and toy presses. In this way, my work aligns with that of Robin Bernstein, who has theorized the interdependence among children's literature, material culture, and child agency ("Children's" 162, "Toys" 458–59). Examining toys and other artifacts of childhood as an integral part of children's literature, Bernstein posits, revises passive models of childhood. "When we view children's literature as something adults produce and children consume," Bernstein writes, "of course we see power emanating from the top down.

But if we understand children's literature as persistently integrating with material culture and play... we see adults producing children's literature *and* children's material culture, and we see children playing with and through both." That play is unpredictable; it "is not simplistically resistant; rather, it is creative, symptomatic, anarchic, ritualistic, reiterative, and most of all, culturally productive ("Toys" 460). Notably, hypothesizing about how real young people might use the material and literary scripts we provide them—scripts that often draw on popular constructions of childhood—reconfigures the relationship between real children, whom Bernstein describes as "tangible and fleshly," and figures of childhood, which are "abstract and disembodied" (*Racial* 22). In Bernstein's work, the child-as-construct does not obscure the embodied child or colonize it, as Rose or Nodelman contend. Instead, children are "virtuoso performers of childhood" who "understand with precision the behaviors that children's things script" (*Racial* 29). As children respond to the scripts provided to them, "childhood and children coproduce each other" (22).

Children's play, like any lived experience of childhood, is difficult to document. Bernstein, like Gubar, turns to ideas of performance, introducing the concept of "scriptive things" and a methodology for reading them: "using archival knowledge and historical context to determine the documented, probable, and possible uses of a category of object." The "horizon of known and possible uses" of a particular artifact, like the uses of a dramatic script, can include "resistance, interpretation, and improvisation," and while the scripts of a toy, for example, might limit its uses, that toy still provides opportunities for a child's exercise of individual agency (*Racial* 8, 11). This approach to children's material culture balances the possibility of child agency with attention to the unavoidable social power of adults and, because it does not rely on determining with certainty one individual's particular use of an object, addresses the problem of the ephemerality of children's engagement with material culture. The goal of reading scriptive things, according to Bernstein, is to consider an object's possible uses in historic context in order to make "responsible, limited inferences about the past" (*Racial* 79). Bernstein, whose work focuses on nineteenth-century American childhood, describes this method in *Racial Innocence: Performing Childhood and Race from Slavery to Civil Rights* (2011) and uses it to analyze children's doll play in light of the construction of race; however, approaching children's material culture as scriptive is a flexible methodology. I use this approach, for example, to theorize how children might have used the popular toy presses of the nineteenth century, which sought to socialize boys into systems of commerce and literacy but also provided a means for all children to challenge familiar adult-child relationships through the composition, publication, and circulation of their own texts.

In *Between Generations*, then, I draw upon and expand the work of scholars such as Conrad, Gubar, and Bernstein, as well as many others whose work acknowledges the child as an active participant in cultural production.[15] I reject the critical commonplace that adults alone define the limits of child autonomy through myopic, idealized constructs of childhood while real young people, hobbled by passivity and powerlessness, are incapable of creative agency. Instead, I take seriously the contributions of child collaborators, whose participation in nineteenth-century literature and culture is palpable, profound, and often exercised in creative partnerships with adults. As I explain in more detail below, I contribute to the ongoing critical conversation about child agency by approaching real children's creativity simultaneously as a practice particularly visible in collaborative modes of authorship—rooted in the production of material texts as well as in their content and use—and as an organizing principle of extraliterary approaches to childhood, such as education and Child Study, that impacted the lives of Victorian children beyond books. Each of the chapters of *Between Generations* focuses on an authorial model that accommodates adult-child partnerships both inside and outside of texts: collaborations among storytellers and auditors, between coauthors, among adults and child experts or authorities, and between child illustrators and adult authors and educators. This structure underscores how intergenerational collaborations were volatile and elastic, dependent on personal, historical, and social circumstances. However, it also allows me to provide, for each model of multiple authorship, examples from across the nineteenth and early twentieth centuries, demonstrating the persistence and adaptability of collaboration as a paradigm for reordering adult-child relationships.

LOCATING THE CHILD COLLABORATOR

While Gubar and Bernstein approach the delicate project of writing about real children by turning to performance studies—a critical framework that, through attention to embodied subjects and flexible scripts, recuperates children's play (and plays) while recognizing the limitations of child autonomy—I do so by turning instead to publication history.

Common definitions of professional authorship often exclude children or elide their participation, not only because children, who are often not paid for their contributions to texts, are considered (likely sometimes wrongfully) willing amateurs but also because accepted norms of authorship tend to reinforce existing biases about who is entitled such creative authority and therefore ignore purportedly "passive" subjects, such as children; however, an approach to publication history that is attentive to young people as social actors allows a long view of the Golden Age texts I study—from inspiration and composition to illustration, publication, and reception—laying bare the many moments when and methods through which children might intervene in a text. This approach demands an awareness of the conventions of authorship and publication that can enable but might also limit or otherwise shape child agency.

I recover the collaborative child through publication history by assembling what I call composition narratives: assemblages of documents that detail authors' creative processes. These documents might include, in addition to the completed text, prefaces, introductions, dedications, essays, letters, journals, biographies, and other materials written by authors (young and old) as well as family, friends, critics, and historians.[16] As I hope my brief reading of Browning's "The Pied Piper" at the start of this introduction makes clear, composition narratives are threshold textual spaces, mediating between authors' experiences in crafting a text and the formal publishing conventions—such as title pages, reviews, and advertisements—that usually declare sole authorship. The children's literature I analyze throughout *Between Generations*, when situated in the context of composition narratives, unfolds to reveal varied formations of intergenerational collaboration. For example, in Chapter One, I discuss Thackeray's "prelude" to *The Rose and the Ring* to enumerate the people and social circumstances that made his satire possible, including his M. A. Titmarsh pseudonym, his daughters, the fictional storyteller Miss Bunch, and the pantomime tradition. Joining Thackeray's account of the text's composition are documents that corroborate or complicate his narrative. For example, Thackeray's contemporary, Frederick Locker-Lampson, published a commemorative poem about Thackeray's friendship with the young Edith Story, who listened to early drafts of *The Rose and the Ring*. Each document introduces new contributors and new opportunities to make clear the subtleties of multiple authorship, and examining them together provides the most complete picture of Thackeray's experience writing his "fireside pantomime." Composition narratives such as this one make room for more inclusive accounts of authorship that reveal multiple and sometimes unexpected contributors, and they mandate a circumspect evaluation of the relationship between literature and contextual material, such as biography. In assembling the deep backstories of Golden Age texts, I do not, in the words of Walsh, reframe each text as "a kind of mystery to be unraveled" to reveal a "true" story or "true" child (71); in fact, the often contradictory accounts that frequently comprise a single composition narrative do not allow for such certainty. Instead, I assemble information available about a text's genesis to track evidence of a real collaborative child as well as echoes of how both real and imagined children, in the words of Bernstein, "give body to each other" (*Racial* 22). I therefore use the word "narrative" with intention, to signal this play between real child and construct.

These composition narratives reveal three types of intergenerational collaborations that weave throughout the chapters of *Between Generations*: fictive, real, and hybrid partnerships. I use the phrase *fictive collaborations* to refer to representations of adult-child partnerships within children's literature that do not immediately correspond to adult-child relationships in the real world. For example, in Chapter Two, I examine collections that represent the storytelling circle, such as Mary Cowden Clarke's *Kit Bam's Adventures* (1849), arguing that these imagined scenes stage child listeners as active participants in narrated tales. Fictive collaborations have received more critical attention than other types of adult-child partnerships; Gubar examines such collaborations in *Artful Dodgers*, for example, alongside her work on real children and the theater, and Knoepflmacher's work on the *Just So Stories*, described above, also considers how fictional adults and children forge creative partnerships. While some would argue, in the Jacqueline Rose tradition, that these purely textual collaborations are not evidence of adults' understanding of children as creative collaborators—that instead they are evidence of adults rehearsing desirable constructions of adulthood—I contend that fictive depictions of intergenerational collaboration are not merely adult fantasies of childhood but instead are imaginative experiments, gesturing toward authors' exploration of children as discerning listeners, authors, illustrators, and editors. The fact that such partnerships are fictive rather than real certainly matters, but it does not undermine the imaginative possibility of the trope of adult-child collaboration.

I put these fictive partnerships in conversation with real collaborations, which involve a living adult and child working together, each contributing in a significant manner to create a text or other cultural artifact. I include in this category adult-child partnerships that produced both published and manuscript texts. For example, as I discuss in Chapter Two, Stevenson and his stepson, Osbourne, collaborated to create a series of toy press publications that circulated among family and close friends, and Osbourne subsequently partnered with his nephew Austin Strong to write and illustrate *Treasure Island: A Melodrama in Five Acts*. I also include in this category partnerships in which an adult creates the conditions that enable children to expand upon his or her work. For instance, Kipling's captions to the illustrations for *Just So Stories*, which I discuss in Chapter Four, invite young readers to paint or otherwise alter his images. I focus on interactions between real adults and children recorded by multiple sources, such as letters and prefaces, that both reinforce that a creative partnership indeed took place and provide descriptions of that partnership from different perspectives. Stevenson and Osbourne's work together, for instance, is documented in written accounts by each partner as well as in critical biographies and other extratextual accounts. By marshaling as much information as possible about these creative partnerships, and by maintaining the skepticism I would exercise in any account of authorship by a child or an adult, I arrive at the clearest possible sense of these intergenerational collaborations.[17] Of course, the information I present about real collaborations is mediated; I learn about them through written accounts, which—like all accounts of authors' writing processes—are subject to misrepresentation, idealization, or faulty memories. However, I maintain the idea of real collaborations because I insist that it is important, in the face of a critical tradition that tends to look askance at the possibility of writing about real children, to acknowledge that these partnerships did, according to all available evidence, occur.

While I therefore attempt to recover, as clearly as possible, the circumstances of these real partnerships, most of the adult-child collaborations included throughout *Between Generations* fall somewhere between the categories of real and fictive. These hybrid collaborations—the true center of this project—are grounded in relationships between actual adults and children, but adults fictionalize those relationships, sometimes by representing them in literature meant for children or adults or describing them in accounts of their authorship in terms that, to borrow Bernstein's language, seem to refer not to "tangible and fleshly" children but instead to "abstract and disembodied" childhood. The result is a creative partnership caught in the dynamic relationship between real child and child-as-construct, each both referring to and obscuring the other as an author struggles to account for the living child's contributions to a text and dominant discourses of Victorian childhood. Disentangling such complex representations of intergenerational collaborations—approaching them with the skepticism that children's literature demands but also with open-mindedness to the possibility of a child's creative agency—is a complex but productive practice. I consider at length a canonical example of a hybrid collaboration in Chapter Four: Barrie's relationship with the Llewelyn Davies brothers in the composition of *Peter Pan*, which the author describes in multiple conflicting documents. The boys appear as authors, as masters of play, as exacting collaborators, and as Romantic idealizations of youth—sometimes, it seems, all at once.

The tangled composition narrative of *Peter Pan*, which provides an excess of information about the text but destabilizes its publication history, might seem anomalous, but many authors blurred the lines between living child collaborators and idealized creative childhood; the practice, in other words, extended far beyond canonical texts such as *Peter Pan*. To see a hybrid collaboration in action, consider Samuel Rutherford Crockett's *Sweetheart Travellers: A Child's Book for Children, for Women, and for Men* (1895). Crockett's text is a collection of loosely connected stories fictionalizing his journeys through the countryside with his daughter Maisie, nicknamed Sweetheart, on a wicker-seated tricycle.[18] Critics introduced *Sweetheart Travellers* as an adult-child collaboration. Robert H. Sherard, writing in *The Author*, notes, "I have often thought that for writing a book for children a child would be one's best collaborator. S. R. Crockett seems to share my opinion, for he tells me that he is writing a Christmas book in collaboration with his little daughter Maisie" (9). Sherard's depiction of Maisie as collaborator is substantiated by the published text of *Sweetheart Travellers*, in which Crockett represents his daughter as instrumental both in the events that inspired the tales and in the book's composition and publication. "Truthfully," he writes in the preface, "the book is not mine but Sweetheart's" (x). Crockett is the narrator, but he often calls himself Sweetheart's "working partner," a co-conspirator who helps her craft imaginative stories about their travels through Galloway and Wales (77). Now and then, Crockett includes an editorial note or revision because he is "commanded by Sweetheart" to do so, and he explains that "she will of a certainty look to see if I have kept my promise" (4). Maisie, as Sweetheart, is partner and contributor, editor and owner of the book.[19] Despite Crockett's claims of Maisie's influence, it is difficult to determine precisely what Maisie, who was seven years old when *Sweetheart Travellers* was published, contributed to the book. Maybe she added nothing at all, aside from inspiration and a few clever snippets of dialogue; maybe she sat side by side with her father, recalling their adventures as he recorded them. The composition narrative for this text—which includes, in addition to the text itself, a descriptive preface as well as reviews and interviews with the author—does not describe Crockett's authorial methods in detail, and even if it did, we might not believe it.

However, what is apparent in the text and paratexts of Crockett's book is his desire to recognize Maisie as a contributor, and that desire exists in tension with his awareness of the studied constructedness of his heroine. Crockett, in fact, takes *as his subject* the multiplicity of Maisies, and *Sweetheart Travellers* is, in a sense, a book about the difficulties of representing a real child. "I possess not one but many Sweethearts in the course of a day," Crockett writes (310). Among those Sweethearts is an idealized Romantic child. "To look into her eyes is to break a hole in the clouds and see into heaven" (1). But there are other Sweethearts. For example, there is the Sweetheart who charms older suitors—a girl who is not divorced from the world of adult sexuality but rather profoundly implicated in it; this Sweetheart is a fickle lover who tortures the "grave and reverent seniors [who] have been proud to do obeisance to our Giddy-pate-a-dreams for no brief space," Crockett notes. "She drags them captive at the wheels of her chariot" (138). The final two chapters of *Sweetheart Travellers* are preoccupied with Crockett's inability to locate an essential Sweetheart. He quickly introduces and dismisses a series of girls, each occupying a paragraph or two before being displaced for yet another Sweetheart who, more often than not, contradicts her previous iteration. Fairy tale Sweetheart is displaced by the Sweetheart of riotous play, who must step aside for the Sweetheart poring over dense catechisms, who must make room for the Sweetheart who politely receives guests in her parlor. All these representations of Sweetheart originate from the living Maisie—a child who, according to Crockett's biographer, "spoke her mind when it was necessary" and "had devastating, deflating opinions" (Donaldson 47, 143). Sweetheart, then, is a patchwork of real and imagined girls. At one point, the narrator admits that Sweetheart "has as many names as there are people in the village" (19).

Hybrid collaborations, such as the partnership between Crockett and his daughter, identify a real collaborative child and then, frustratingly, obscure her. However, this difficulty is useful rather than paralyzing in an exploration of child agency; it forces us to consider the ways authors perform a range of ideological acrobatics when confronted with living children. Crockett could be insisting upon the social realities of a living Maisie as daughter and collaborator while displaying pointed self-awareness about the multiple ways writers and readers understand childhood. For example, while the narrator claims that Sweetheart's identity is multiple and shifting, seemingly pure construction, this overdetermined figure is undermined by accounts of *Sweetheart Travellers* that substitute the fictional character for the living girl without comment or self-consciousness; a feature on Crockett in *The Windsor Magazine*, for example, includes a photograph of Maisie among her toys with the caption "'Sweetheart' and Her Dolls," described as the "most characteristic portrait of Miss Crockett" (Cromwell 497). Alternatively, Crockett could be attempting to provide Maisie a venue for her own storytelling but acknowledging the obstacles, including his own idealized perceptions of his daughter, that impede such a radical project. Crockett rehearses this very authorial problem in *Sweetheart Travellers* when Sweetheart, in an encounter with a published author, laments the disappointing limitations of those in the writing profession. Sweetheart asks the writer to provide a complete history of a character from his book, and she is disappointed when he cannot do so. "Sweetheart could not make out," the narrator explains, "how the author of a book . . . could fail to know more about one of his most important characters" (141). Readers of *Sweetheart Travellers* might be left wondering about Crockett's portrait of Maisie herself, a little girl whom he seems to know everything yet nothing about. The confusion generated by hybrid collaborations such as this are productive, bringing to the fore the flashpoints between adult authority and child agency.

PARENTS, TEACHERS, AND GUARDIANS

The creative partnerships I discuss throughout *Between Generations* follow close on the heels of Romantic constructions of childhood and, as Crockett's sometimes-angelic Sweetheart makes clear, authors who entertained the possibility of adult-child collaboration participated in that powerful paradigm of childhood. Certainly Romantic childhood was a complex construct.[20] Even that go-to Romantic poet of childhood, William Wordsworth, offers seemingly contradictory figures in his work. While in *Ode: Intimations of Immortality from Recollections of Early*

Childhood, he famously describes the cherubic child "trailing clouds of glory"—praising the "visionary gleam" of childhood, its "glory and . . . dream," and lamenting that, for adults, those visions are only obliquely glimpsed as "something that is gone" (470)—he describes a much more earthbound childhood in his *Prelude*. That poem, as Robson has argued, "depicts a child whose vivacity is more likely to express itself in legally dubious excitements [such as poaching] than in moments of angelic purity, and an adult whose connection with his former self is still strong" (*Men* 17). Recent work on Romantic childhood, both real and imagined, has demonstrated that the creative child was not only a figure invoked by the poets but also an important part of late eighteenth- and early nineteenth-century literary culture. Laurie Langbauer, for example, makes clear that for the Romantics, young people "were just as much actors as objects," and in her book *The Juvenile Tradition: Young Writers and Prolepsis, 1750–1835* she recuperates young people's writing as a self-conscious tradition in Romantic period, when "youth . . . wrote *as* youth and felt that their identification with other young writers was vital" ("Prolepsis" 891, *Juvenile* 2). Langbauer's exploration of Robert Southey's support and publication of the young Henry Kirke White's poetry suggests that the adult and child writers of the Romantic period in many cases anticipated the intergenerational collaborations that, I argue, arose in full force in the Golden Age.

However, to establish the foundation for the Victorian collaborative child that I explore throughout the following chapters, I would like to turn briefly not to the Romantic juvenile writer but instead to the Enlightenment child. I find that it is in children's literature of the eighteenth century that adult authors, less burdened with the inescapable machinery of the figure of Romantic childhood, offer a clear view of the young person who would become the collaborative child. Writers for children in the eighteenth century were inspired by educational theorists such as John Locke, Jean-Jacques Rousseau, Mary Wollstonecraft, and Maria and Richard Edgeworth and produced books designed for what Lissa Paul calls "thinking and knowing" children—young people "who were encouraged . . . to see themselves as citizens, as participants in the world" (150, 3). Young readers in the 1700s were entertained by a spectrum of texts written for children, adults, and mixed audiences, from moral tales such as John Bunyan's *Pilgrim's Progress* (1678) to folk literature and fairy tales such as "The Children in the Wood" and "Dick Whittington and His Cat," but many prominent and widely read authors introduced in their children's fiction socially engaged child characters who oppose slavery, promote education for the oppressed, speak out against animal cruelty, identify and follow fitting vocations, and join communities of like-minded readers. Taken as a whole, these authors frame children as subjects of great potential social agency. But this agency is indeed potential. The children who appear in these eighteenth-century texts, and the children imagined to be reading them, are constructed as "in transit *to* adult authority" (67). In this section, I will focus briefly on how these eighteenth-century texts explore the possibility of child agency but, for the most part, stop short of fully realized adult-child partnerships.

Many adults writing on childhood at this period recognize the child's capacity for reason and social participation but arrive at that recognition not by collaborating with children in thoughtful discourse but through debate with one another. This debate is registered in children's literature, which often is surrounded by paratexts that directly address a purchasing parent, teacher, or guardian and invite conversation regarding how adults should mold young readers into "socially responsible and acceptable children" (Paul 6). For example, in the preface to *An Easy Introduction to the Knowledge of Nature* (1780), Sarah Trimmer positions herself as a participant in the contemporary conversations about the child's moral and literary education by quoting at length Isaac Watts's *A Treatise on the Education of Children and Youth* (1769) as the inspiration for her text. She also insinuates her own work into the classroom by advising educators about how students should use the book: "When scholars have read these books through," Trimmer advises, "I would recommend that they should not only read them again, but hear a portion of them explained in the school every day, and be questioned in classes to see whether they really understand them or not" (vii). Even eighteenth-century texts associated with the rise of more playful books for children address adults in a manner that engages debates on proper education; for example, Newbery's *Little Pretty Pocket-Book* (1744), known for its publisher's dedication to instruction and delight, addresses children through content replete with illustration and rhyme but begins with an essay on adults' responsibilities toward children's physical and mental well-being, including advice on diet, exercise, and discipline. In many ways, Enlightenment literature for children is a partnership among adults with an eye toward the child as a future collaborator.

Consider Maria Edgeworth, whom scholars often include in critical accounts of collaboration. She published the popular three-volume treatise

Practical Education (1798) in partnership with her father, Richard Lovell Edgeworth, and followed that joint effort with a number of volumes of collected stories for children that demonstrate her pedagogical principles: *Moral Tales for Young People, Early Lessons, Continuation of Early Lessons*, and *Rosamund: A Sequel to Early Lessons*.[21] Edgeworth positions her writing on education and for children as part of ongoing conversation with her father and other contemporaries. For example, in the preface to *The Parent's Assistant* (1796), titled "Addressed to Parents," she provides teaching strategies, explains her goals as an author, and interprets for adult readers the purpose of some of the stories that follow. The "object" of "Lazy Lawrence," for example, "was to incite a spirit of industry," and "care has been taken to proportion the reward to the exertion, and to demonstrate that people feel cheerful and happy when they are employed" (v). Read together with Edgeworth's preface, *The Parent's Assistant* is an educational manual, alerting concerned mothers and fathers to the moral pitfalls that await their children, and a storehouse of texts parents can use to avoid such dangers.[22] Children are framed as future social subjects—future agents in the public sphere.

Anna Laetitia Barbauld, one of Edgeworth's contemporaries, also was aware of the advantages of collaboration; many of her publications were products of creative partnerships with family members and reproduced, in their pages, models of adults working in partnership to foster the intellectual growth of socially engaged children.[23] Between 1792 and 1796, Barbauld and her brother John Aikin collaborated to produce *Evenings at Home, or, The Juvenile Budget Opened*, a six-volume collection of dialogues, short tales, and other texts.[24] According to Daniel E. White and Michelle Levy, Barbauld "conceive[d] of literary production according to a model of familial collaboration," and Barbauld and Aikin "wrote and published extensively with and for their family to such a degree that collaboration with family lay at the root of their literary practices and ideals" (White 511, Levy 22). This domestic collaboration is fictionalized in the frame narrative to *Evenings at Home*, which describes the Fairborne family: a master, a mistress, "a numerous progeny of children of both sexes," and a steady stream of visitors (1.1):

> As some of [the visitors] were accustomed to writing, they would frequently produce a fable, a story, or dialogue, adapted to the age and understanding of the young people. It was always considered as a high favour when they would so employ themselves; and after the

pieces were once read over, they were carefully deposited by Mrs. Fairborne in a box, of which she kept the key. None of these were allowed to be taken out again till all the children were assembled in the holidays. It was then made one of the evening amusements of the family to *rummage the budget*, as their phrase was. One of the least children was sent to the box, who putting in its little hand, drew out the paper that came next, and brought it into the parlour. This was then read distinctly by one of the older ones; and after it had undergone sufficient consideration, another little messenger was despatched for a fresh supply; and so on, till as much time had been spent in this manner as the parents thought proper. (1.3–4)

The text sharing Barbauld describes is, in many ways, a partnership among adults. The collaboration suggests the participation of the Fairborne children but reinforces familiar adult-child power structures. The children read the stories of the budget aloud, but they are not responsible for any of its contents; the stories are inaccessible to them, kept locked away by Mrs. Fairborne. Their parents decide the time, place, and duration of storytelling, and it is the adults who assemble the children, who only speak for as much time "as the parents thought proper." Children give voice to a dialogue between visitors and watchful parents about what is best for their education. The roles the young are allowed to play are ranked by age and experience; younger siblings, the "least" of the children, are messengers, while the "older ones" are readers, a function that signals their approach to adulthood and the accompanying privileges of composition. The budget in *Evenings at Home* is represented as a venue for adults to communicate their concerns about how to help the young navigate their moral and religious duties as well as their new literacy.

This agenda is reiterated in the fables, dialogues, and short dramas included in the volumes of *Evenings at Home*. In other words, Aikin and Barbauld fictionalize their own methods of familial composition through the characters of the Fairborne family, and the fictional Fairbornes and their visitors in turn reproduce, in the stories they contribute to the budget, their roles as interlocutors on early childhood education. For example, "Nature and Education: A Fable" uses the allegorical figures of the title to dramatize the consequences of conflicting pedagogical philosophies. Each figure in the fable cultivates a young tree; Nature leaves the sapling to thrive without intervention, and Education prunes the tree carefully and guides its branches with strong ropes. Education wins the day, transforming a cramped crab tree into a "sightly plant." The story concludes that while it is difficult to curtail the forces of nature, "something may be done by taking pains enough" (3.128). This fable seems to be meant more for parents and educators than their children and students. Choosing to represent a topic that not only concerns adults but also incites debate and disagreement, Aikin and Barbauld engage reading adults to collaborate—to compare their own systems of education to those represented in the text, to join in the discussion.[25] This is only one selection from the miscellany that comprises *Evenings at Home*, and other stories are more explicitly directed to a child reader's sensibilities. However, this example demonstrates how Aikin and Barbauld use the genres and rhetorical strategies common in didactic children's literature, such as the fable, and repurpose them to address the adults tasked with the education of the young.[26]

Evenings at Home does include a tale—appropriately, a dialogue—that foreshadows the possibility of child agency that will animate later intergenerational collaborations. "A Lesson in the Art of Distinguishing" introduces a young boy, Charles, and his father, who initiates a conversation on the importance of accurate definition. Children reading or listening to the dialogue may relate to Charles, but the dialogue casts a sideways glance at the adult reading the volume, presumably a parent or teacher who could learn from Charles's father the proper way to introduce this lesson and its desirable outcomes. Charles, with the assistance of his father, parses the definition of a horse—a moment that, according to Tess Cosslett, may have inspired Bitzer's lecture on the topic in Dickens's *Hard Times*. At the end of the dialogue, Charles's father summarizes the object of their exercise in a statement that could be drawn from an educational treatise by Watts or Locke. "Remember . . . that nothing is more useful than to learn to form ideas with precision, and to express them with accuracy," he remarks. "I have not given you the definition to teach you what a horse is, but to teach you to *think*" (2.136).

However, the story clearly communicates young Charles's objections to the art of definition, and the dialogue suggests the beginning of a new attitude toward the place of children's voices in children's literature. After his father has led him to a clinical definition of a horse—"an animal of the quadruped kind, whole hoofed, with short erect ears, a flowing mane, and a tail covered in every part with long hairs"—Charles remains unsatisfied. "But, papa," he remarks, "if I had never seen a horse, I should not know what kind of animal it was by this definition" (2.132, 134). His father replies with an invitation to participate: "Let us hear, then, how you would give me an idea of a horse" (2.134). Charles provides description rather than definition; a horse, for Charles, is "a fine large prancing creature, with slender legs and an arched neck, and a sleek smooth skin, and a tail that sweeps the ground . . . [that] snorts and neighs very loud, and tosses his head, and runs as swift as the wind" (2.182). This passage, more than any other moment in the dialogue, captures the cadences of child speech: the accumulation of adjectives, quickly strung together with a series of "ands." The reader cannot help but agree with Charles that his definition is more compelling than his father's. Charles not only speaks in a voice that begins to resemble that of a child but also presents a perspective that the teaching adult must acknowledge and accommodate. As Cosslett notes, the dialogue "incorporates its own critique, including both Father's abstract ideas, and Charles's concrete experience and down-to-earth objections. . . . Barbauld's project is not to dichotomise, but to reconcile" (29). That reconciliation is, albeit, brief. "We have a great many beautiful descriptions from ancient authors so loosely worded that we cannot certainly tell what animals are meant by them," Charles's father warns, "whereas if they had given us definitions, three lines would have ascertained their meaning" (2.136). Here, the adult decidedly controls the conversation. However, Barbauld's "A Lesson in the Art of Distinguishing" betrays how that Enlightenment child would transform and adapt into the collaborative child, the young reader or writer who would engage in new forms of adult-child relationships in the Victorian and Edwardian periods.

BETWEEN GENERATIONS

This account of eighteenth-century children's literature is necessarily cursory; however, Trimmer, Edgeworth, and Barbauld exemplify how the outlines of agentic, participatory childhood began to emerge (but were not fully realized) in Enlightenment children's literature. The collaborative child reappears in even stronger forms throughout the nineteenth century and in particular in the Golden Age of children's literature, when changes in cultural discourses of childhood and in the shape of publishing for young people created the circumstances that allowed intergenerational collaboration to thrive as a practice both in books and in life. In each of the chapters in *Between Generations*, which I overview in the remainder of this introduction, I trace how adults imagined and practiced adult-child partnerships in a range of authorial and cultural circumstances. I begin with later—and more collaborative—examples of the type of spoken exchanges that Barbauld's "A Lesson in the Art of Distinguishing" offers. Chapter One, "Active Listeners: Child Auditors as Creative Collaborators," explores one of the most ubiquitous adult-child relationships in nineteenth-century literature and culture: the storytelling adult and the listening child. The scene is familiar—a narrating crone or maiden aunt, a domestic hearth—and it frames children as rapt, silent listeners. However, writers such as Thackeray, Gatty, Clarke, and Mary Molesworth understood the role of child auditors differently. Through their literature for children and in the composition narratives surrounding that literature—including essays, letters, and other materials exploring the task of writing for young readers—these authors underscore the material influence listening children have on the plot, pace, and character of told tales. Texts such as Clarke's *Kit Bam's Adventures*, Thackeray's *The Rose and the Ring*, and Gatty's *Aunt Judy's Tales* reject the notion of a unilateral transmission of narrative and posit instead that storytelling is an act of mutual meaning-making, a collaboration among child auditors and adult narrators. These authors' attention to the ways imaginative children speak back to adult plots draws upon a tradition of folklore scholarship and anthropological discourse that associates children with oral culture—a connection that relies, in part, on familiar associations between children and "primitive" societies. However, I argue that storyteller-auditor collaborations also make room for children's creative agency in a manner that anticipates theories of children's language acquisition developed in the Child Study movement and, in particular, that movement's theorizations of how children can transform the English language through patterns of listening and repetition.

While my first chapter is a broad survey of storyteller-auditor collaborations, my second is a more focused case study of one particularly complex partnership. "Family Dynamics: The Strange Case of Robert Louis Stevenson and Lloyd Osbourne" examines the fourteen-year collaboration between Stevenson and his stepson. Stevenson's relationship with Osbourne was forged over printing technologies and genres that, I contend, foster intergenerational amity: toy printing presses and adventure stories. I provide a brief history of each, demonstrating that both rely on familiar and gendered assumptions about the power inequalities of adult-child relationships. Those marketing the toy press, for example, framed it as a masculine pastime that initiated young men into trade and ambition, while the adventure novel served the dual purpose of entertaining readers and educating them as future leaders of the empire. However, through close readings of the texts Stevenson and Osbourne produced together—in particular their toy press productions, *Treasure Island*, and *Ebb-Tide* (1894), a novel they coauthored when Osbourne was in his midtwenties—and through careful attention to the ways both authors describe their contributions to these endeavors, I find that the pair acknowledged but manipulated the roles usually assigned to adult and child in ways that grant Osbourne creative agency. Their coauthored writings explore the interplay between the adult publishing world and the childlike imagination, between other and self, and among multiple contributors to a text.

Chapter Three, "Collaborating with the Authorities: Children as Authors, Experts, and Critics," explores a spectrum of texts and institutions in which adults consult children as authoritative figures regarding their own literature and culture. I begin with Dickens, William Brighty Rands, and Barrie—all authors who invert the familiar power hierarchies of adult-child relationships. Both Dickens and Barrie create fictions of child authorship—Dickens in *A Holiday Romance* and Barrie in the dedication to *Peter Pan* (1928)—while, in his poetry collection *Lilliput Levee* (1864), Rands joins a tradition of topsy-turvy narratives in which adults are subject to merciless child rulers. The composition narratives attached to these texts reveal that children were implicated in these re-imaginings; for example, the barbarous but creative boys Barrie imagined in his dedication are uneasy hybrids of the living Llewelyn Davies brothers and Barrie's overwrought relationship to his play and to childhood in general. However, these adult-child relationships are largely fictive, spaces in which adult authors imagined a model of collaboration that allows adult-child partnerships based on children's radical narrative authority. The second half of the chapter considers real collaborations in which adults solicited the expertise of living children. I explore two arenas where these collaborations took place: published reviews of children's literature in surveys of reading preferences conducted by Child Study scholars and librarians, and shifting educational policies and school examinations. Drawing on the work of Victorian children's literature essayist Edward Salmon, American librarian Caroline Hewins, and author and school inspector Matthew Arnold, I demonstrate that those tasked with managing, educating, and writing about children recognized the epistemological challenges of accessing children's voices but, in the face of that difficulty, persisted in recognizing children as active agents and authorities on childhood.

I discuss education in Chapter Four as well, but primarily the sort that happens at the easel or drawing table. "Pictures of Partnership: Art Education, Children's Literature, and the Rise of the Child Artist" offers a new perspective on one of the most familiar collaborative models examined in Victorian studies: partnerships between authors and illustrators. I interpret illustrations by and for children through nineteenth-century ideas about children's relationship to art, articulated in debates about art education stretching from Rousseau to Franz Cizek. Particularly at the fin-de-siècle, educators and critics express respect for the imaginative and spontaneous elements of children's drawings and dismiss drawing exercises, popular in the eighteenth century, that require precise imitation of adults' art. While most critics locate an admiration for children's art in the early twentieth century, I locate the beginnings of this movement in the mid-Victorian period. As early as the 1840s, author-illustrators such as Edward Lear devised styles that suggest intergenerational collaboration—fictive creative partnerships that gesture toward young artists even when children did not participate in a text's composition or illustration. Others, such as Browning, Gatty, and David Starr Jordan even sought out child artists for adult-authored texts. Composition narratives for their texts reveal that they engaged in real collaborations that generated illustrated records of both adult authority and child agency. Adult-child partnerships, real and fictive, that call upon the artistic resources of young people in fact offer some of the most nuanced examples of how, throughout the nineteenth century, children were invited into systems of cultural production in both formal and informal, public and private ways.

The first four chapters of *Between Generations* interrogate the borders of child agency in the nineteenth and early twentieth centuries through the framework of multiple authorship. In my conclusion, "Mentors and Muses: Why the Collaborative Child Matters," I argue that the child collaborator has maintained its cultural and critical resonance long past the Victorian and Edwardian period. I provide two case studies of twenty- and twenty-first century intergenerational collaborations: Arthur Ransome's mentorship of young writers Katharine Hull and Pamela Whitlock in the publication of their first novel, *The Far-Distant Oxus* (1937), and photojournalist Timothy Archibald's partnership with his son, Eli, over the photobook *Echolilia* (2010). These studies are evidence that adult authors and artists continue to adopt intergenerational collaboration as a creative process that allows for child agency. These final pages look backward, connecting contemporary collaborations to their origins in the nineteenth century, and project forward, speculating about how the recognition of the collaborative child will continue to change in response to new paradigms of childhood and authorship.

CHAPTER ONE

Active Listeners
Child Auditors as Creative Collaborators

In the winter of 1854, the young Edith Story, staying in Rome with her family, fell ill. It was a tense time—Story was suffering from the same fever that had recently claimed the life of her six-year-old brother—but the long weeks of her convalescence were brightened by visits from William Thackeray. He would sit at Story's bedside and read chapters from his manuscript-in-progress: a comic Christmas book titled *The Rose and the Ring*. Years later, after Thackeray's death, artist Richard Doyle commemorated this storytelling scene in a woodcut. His illustration depicts Story reclined on a sickbed, eyes closed, her rest so complete it suggests death—an interpretation supported by the bunch of flowers she clutches in her hands and the sepulchral domes of Rome outside her window. Thackeray, on the other hand, is alert, leaning eagerly forward in his bedside chair as he pauses to decipher the tiny handwriting on the pages clutched in his hand. Doyle's scene rehearses the adult-child relationships we often assume to be the origins of children's literature: the adult author crafting a tale for a passively listening, even dreaming, child audience. The familiarity of that adult-child pairing is reproduced in later accounts of Thackeray's relationship with Story, which dwell upon the frailty of the young girl and the genius of the author. For example, Henry James, in his 1903 biography of Story's father William Wetmore Story, remembers her as "the little convalescent girl" who listened to the "immortal work" as "the great author sat on the edge her bed" (286). Lilian Whiting, in *The Golden Road* (1918), waxes sentimental about "Edie," the "little maid of six" who possessed such enviable memories of the "great novelist," a man who eventually gifted her the bound manuscript: "a sumptuous volume, bound in rich Venetian red, with roses and rings in gold decorating the cover, and her own name also in golden letters"—a story bequeathed to Story (108–9).

An overdetermined story, perhaps. U. C. Knoepflmacher argues that over time the storytelling scene between Thackeray and Story transformed into a "sentimental myth" that "exaggerated the regressiveness of *The Rose and the Ring* by converting Edith into [its] exclusive recipient." Knoepflmacher contends that situating Thackeray's "Fireside Pantomime for Great and Small Children" completely within the childlike space of Story's sickroom ignores that the Christmas book itself resists such isolation, not only because the tale "never lingers in a childhood Eden" (suggesting instead that "growth is all") but also because Story herself remembers Thackeray as a mediator between the "sequestered space" of her sickroom and the bustling city outside (*Ventures* 85). I agree that the anecdote, and particularly Doyle's illustration of Thackeray and Story, misrepresents *The Rose and the Ring* and its authorship, and like Knoepflmacher I am interested in troubling the purportedly firm boundaries between the worlds of adult and child. However, I dispute not the way this origin story inflects our understanding of Thackeray alone but instead its facile depiction of the storytelling moment shared by the author and the child. Characterizing Thackeray as an engaged teller and Story as a passive listener obscures the child auditor's active role in the moment of narration. This is indeed a "sentimental myth"—a tale told and retold that elides certain details in service to well-worn ideas of adulthood, childhood, and authorship—and we should reinterpret Thackeray's narration to question these powerful paradigms of child listener and adult narrator.

For example, many of the romanticized accounts of Thackeray's visits excerpt Story's own recollections of those evenings, which were published in *Cornhill* in 1911 under her married name, Marchesa Peruzzi de' Medici, as "Thackeray, My Childhood's Friend." However, subsequent writers excerpt selectively, with an eye toward constructing the pleasing vignette of adult listener and child teller. Story's description of Thackeray's bedside readings in fact challenges the picture of meek young girl and the benevolent author presented by Doyle and others. While she concedes that she was "a little fragile child just coming back to life," she also describes herself as a happy and active participant in Thackeray's storytelling. Thackeray, after reading a chapter from his manuscript, would discuss with his young listener "the people in the story" who, Story notes, "were real people to me and to him." Sometimes he would say, "Now you must tell me a little story to amuse me." Story notes, "I tried my best to recall something that he would like, that I had heard, or invent a little tale. At these times he would sit by the table and draw some illustrations of what I was telling him, in pen and ink." All these drawings were lost but one: a sketch entitled "Zackeray Hubs and his foxtree teapot" (178–79). Even this remaining title suggests how Story's nonsensical imagination inspired Thackeray's pen. At these moments, Story was drawing material from the adult world—using existing narratives "that [she] had heard" and even creating a character whose first name, Zackeray, resembles the last name of her visitor—and reinterpreting that material into fodder for a collaboration with Thackeray, their evenings transformed into a creative partnership between adult artist and child storyteller.

We also know that Story was not the only young person who contributed to the origins of *The Rose and the Ring*. Thackeray wrote his pantomime to entertain his daughters Anny and Minny, then sixteen and thirteen, and a group of their friends, who persuaded him to write a story to accompany the Twelfth Night characters he had drawn for their amusement. Such entertainments were not unusual. The "Roman English colony" where Thackeray and his daughters took up lodgings, Gordon Ray notes, was "a center of juvenile amusement" (Introduction v), raucous with games shared by adults and the young people staying there: storytelling by Hans Christian Andersen, for example, and a musical Pied Piper parade of children led by Robert Browning himself (James, *William* 286). The Twelfth Night games and the story that grew from them are fictionalized in the preface to the published *Rose and the Ring*, in which Thackeray's pseudonymous narrator, M. A. Titmarsh, responds to the demands of a large family of "young people" and their governess, Miss Bunch, to compose a history for a set of humorous sketches (2–3). The influence of the young listeners extends beyond their participation in intergenerational play and their demand for a story. Between the party's Twelfth Night celebrations and the text's publication in 1854, Thackeray adapted the Italian manuscript "to fit the story told for Edith Story and his daughters to the Christmas book pattern," and Anny and Minny were tasked with copying out a draft of these revisions in an effort to preserve the original manuscript intact (Ray, Introduction viii). The resulting published text promises that the intergenerational collaborations modeled by Thackeray's partnerships with this series of young people will continue. The narrator ends the preface reflecting on how others, aided by the published book, might reproduce the storytelling scene where the tale originated—"if these children are pleased, thought I, why should not others be amused also?"—and the title page illustration, which Thackeray added during revisions, visualizes one such future telling, depicting a hearth surrounded by a narrating older woman and listeners of all ages, including a contemplative boy who directs his reverie toward smoky silhouettes of characters in the fire (2).

I offer this brief publication history of *The Rose and the Ring* as a case study. This text, like many touchstones in Victorian children's literature, emerged as a collaboration between adults and children, although this reading of its construction and initial reception is often obscured by popular representations of Thackeray's storytelling. The genesis of the text is distributed among a series of real and imagined child and adult storytellers, listeners, illustrators, and editors. Thackeray and subsequent generations of publishers, narrators, and listeners preserve the text's potential to generate intergenerational partnerships. Thackeray's pantomime, then, is a rich example of the hybrid intergenerational collaborations I describe in my introduction: partnerships grounded in relationships between adults and children that are both real and fictionalized, described using language associated with powerful cultural constructions of childhood. The documents that surround *The Rose and the Ring* indeed depict the material, real-life conditions in which Thackeray and others created this story. However, representations of those collaborations are refracted and transformed through Story's recollections, James's biography, the preface to *The Rose and the Ring*, and the other materials that comprise the text's composition narrative. Descriptions of the story's origins recognize, refer to, and sometimes subvert the culturally familiar figures of the storytelling adult and circle of young listeners—stock characters that nineteenth-century authors return to ritualistically and that tap into assumptions that associate children with passivity and orality and adults with narrative authority. Because the text's origin stories recall these familiar figures so explicitly, it seems inevitable that Thackeray's Titmarsh befriends not just any governess in the preface to his story, but Miss Bunch: a figure who, as Knoepflmacher notes, is "named after the traditional Dame Bunch" (*Ventures* 99). This detail records Thackeray's self-conscious indebtedness to prominent cultural narratives about childhood, storytelling, and oral culture. The origins of *The Rose and the Ring* are both a reality and an imagined tableau.

That suggestion of theatricality is signature Thackeray. The "Fire-Side Pantomime" of *The Rose and the Ring*, after all, follows the puppet show of *Vanity Fair* (1847–1848) and the melodrama of *Pendennis* (1848–1850).

The text's multiple composition narratives not only foreground the performed narrative of *The Rose and the Ring* but also privilege it over the final, printed product. The tale loses something in its transformation from holiday entertainment to ink-and-paper commodity—a deterioration that is most evident within the nineteen chapters and accompanying illustrations of the text itself. The book strains to reproduce the dynamic relationship between storyteller and auditor enjoyed by those first, intimate audiences. Joan Stevens identifies several moments in which the text and illustrations "involve collaboration between teller and audience," encouraging listeners to engage in a conversation with both the adult author's text and, assumedly, with the adult reading the tale aloud. She points out a moment where Thackeray provides instructions, directed at the individual narrating, to solicit the participation of listening children. The tale's characters are sitting down for a feast when the narrator notes, "You may be sure they had a very good dinner—let every boy or girl think of what he or she likes best, and fancy it on the table." A footnote suggests that asking children which foods the characters should eat would be "a very pretty game" (73–74). The delicacies that appear rely on what listeners "fancy"; Thackeray does not provide a menu. This collaboration, however, is fragile, as it depends on the insertion of images at precise moments in the text. The first edition of the published book suggests, through the inclusion of a woodcut, that the story's action ceases, "that the actors hold their tableau," while the children make up their minds as to the nature of the feast (Stevens 14). However, editions of *The Rose and the Ring* published after Thackeray's death often dramatically changed the number and placement of illustrations and therefore undermine his crafted interplay between text and image, between reader and audience.

Many recognized the book's struggle to operate as both spoken and read—its protean status as dramatic production, narrated tale, and printed text. For example, Frederick Locker-Lampson, in a memorial to the relationship between Thackeray and Story—the poem "The Rose and the Ring, Christmas, 1854, and Christmas, 1863"—shifts uneasily from references to the oral storytelling moment to the printed tale.[1] During most of the poem, Locker-Lampson refers to the printed text. However, at the end of the second stanza, at the very heart of the poem, he describes a meeting between Thackeray and Story, in which Thackeray "begs (with a spine vastly supple) / She will study *The Rose and the Ring*" (146). The spine here belongs not only to the book but also to Thackeray, an ambiguity that underscores the story as it originated in the physical body of the storyteller. As part of Thackeray, the tale was "vastly supple," but Locker-Lampson's poem commemorates Thackeray's death, and the tale the now-adult Story holds has lost its narrative flexibility. Locker-Lampson not only calls *The Rose and the Ring* the "last and best of his Toys" but also a "shrine of his glory," granite and immovable (147). The poem is rife with such ambiguities and contraries. It is both joyful and mournful—documenting what Locker-Lampson calls Story's "mirth chequer'd grief"—and attempts to narrate the book's composition and its plot simultaneously. When Locker-Lampson concludes with the lines "And you see there's a nice little story / Attached to *The Rose and the Ring*," he gestures both to the exploits of the "droll couple" sketched in the manuscript's pages and the story of Thackeray and Story themselves (147).

Locker-Lampson's poem implies that the creative partnerships enabled by an oral tale erode once the story is reduced to print. The moments of intergenerational collaboration recorded both in the creation and in the content of *The Rose and the Ring* depend on oral performance, when the narrative is unfixed, infinitely variable, and receptive to revisions according to (and proposed by) perhaps widely dissimilar configurations of audience. While Thackeray's story may have been successful in recreating the conditions of oral narrative in its first editions, performed stories necessarily undergo fundamental transformations when translated into a written manuscript and, subsequently, a printed text. As Walter Ong argues, the movement from oral to print culture is a "reduction of dynamic sound to quiescent space, the separation of the word from the living present, where alone spoken words can exist" (82). Even the careful arrangement of Thackeray's text cannot conceal the tension between the finality of the published book and what Ong calls the "context of give-and-take between real persons" that characterizes spoken language (79). Thus, while the *Morning Chronicle* claims that Thackeray "makes his book speak like a man" (Ray, *Thackeray* 98), that speech is necessarily mediated, the transmission of story from teller to listener subject to a series of interferences.[2]

In what follows, I explore how authors for children attempted to overcome these disadvantages of print and embrace the spontaneous nature of the spoken word both by partnering with children in storyteller-auditor collaborations and by representing those partnerships in their fictions. My first section maps shifting understandings of the relationship between children and language from the late eighteenth to early twentieth centuries. I begin with Rousseau's *Émile* (1762), a text that contributed to the association between told tales and children's literature in the Victorian period, and move forward to the fin-de-siècle and the establishment of the field of Child Study. Scholars involved in this field reiterate, in a scientific register, cultural assumptions about children and oral culture but consider collaborative patterns of adult-child collaboration forged over language-learning in which children transform the linguistic world they share with adults. Associations between children and oral culture are a central concern for fairy-tale collectors, such as Jacob and Wilhelm Grimm, the focus of my second section. I explore not only the Grimms' preconceptions about childhood and fairy tales as expressed in the materials surrounding their *Kinder- und Hausmärchen* collections but also English translations of the tales, in particular Edgar Taylor's *German Popular Stories* (1823) and *Gammer Grethel* (1839). These volumes influenced story collections for children published throughout the latter half of the nineteenth century, many of which use a storyteller-auditor format or frame story. In the third and final section of this chapter, I examine collections by Mary Molesworth, Mary Cowden Clarke, and Margaret Gatty, paying attention to how storytelling scenes, both the real gatherings that inspired these authors and fictional moments of narration in their texts, were enriched by and facilitated intergenerational collaboration. Children inside and outside these stories, real and imagined, participate as collaborators, transforming narrative through a creative agency based on active listening and critical response. Throughout this chapter, I attend to how visual culture provides clues to how the way Victorians understand representations of oral culture in children's literature, examining storyteller-auditor relationships in illustrations that highlight the flexibility of the told tale, the collaborations enabled by storytelling, and the connection between narration and the child's imagination.

EAR-MINDED CHILDREN

Locker-Lampson was not alone in privileging the spoken word over the printed text, and he was certainly not the first to do so. In *Émile* (1762), Rousseau argues that parents and educators, if guided by careful observations of their charges, will change the way they teach children to negotiate language, both spoken and printed. He notoriously contends that reading—in fact, the printed word in general—has no place in a child's early curriculum, an unorthodox decision he justifies with his observations of the development and natural learning habits of pre-adolescent children.[3]

Like Locke, Rousseau insists that children learn primarily through sensory experience. The child, before he learns to reason, "only attends to what affects his senses," Rousseau writes, gathering "sense experiences" as "the raw material of thought" (35), and tutors should promote sensory learning exclusively and reject methods that employ books and abstract, cerebral study. "To substitute books for [feet, hands, and eyes] does not teach us to reason, it teaches us to use the reason of others rather than our own," claims Rousseau. "To learn to think we must therefore exercise our limbs, our senses, and our bodily organs, which are the tools of the intellect" (107). Reading the world is much more important than reading books, a claim Rousseau formulates in various ways throughout his treatise. Émile's "whole environment is the book from which he unconsciously enriches his memory" (90). "Let the senses be the only guide for the first workings of reason," he writes. "No book but the world" (56).

Rousseau's attack on reading is part of a larger cultural discourse on the relationship between children and language that, in the words of Jacqueline Rose, "set up childhood as a primitive state where 'nature' is still to be found" (44). According to writers such as Rousseau, Rose contends, children can "take language back to its pure and uncontaminated source in the objects of the material world," bypassing the arbitrariness of the linguistic sign, "what is felt as most problematic and unstable about language itself" (47). The movement from childhood's oral language to adulthood's written language signals what Janie Vanpée calls "the passage from nature to culture" (40) and what Rose calls, more pointedly, a movement from the "purity and immediacy" of the spoken word or even gestural communication to the "obtrusiveness and aridity of written culture" (49). Rousseau articulates this complex set of assumptions early in his treatise:

> All our languages are the result of art. It has long been a subject of inquiry whether there ever was a natural language common to all; no doubt there is, and it is the language of children before they begin to speak. This language is inarticulate, but it has tone, stress, and meaning. The use of our own language has led us to neglect it so far as to forget it altogether. Let us study children and we shall soon learn it afresh from them. (36)

Here, Rousseau conflates the linguistic infancy of the race with the infancy of the individual, foreshadowing the language of recapitulation that would support later theories of language acquisition. His suggestion that by observing children, adults can attempt to understand the pure form of communication, the "natural language common to all" that children speak before they are educated into linguistic norms, fits into a larger constellation of associations between children, oral culture, and innocence and between adults, written culture, and the deterioration of language.

Rose and Vanpée focus on Rousseau's opposition between children and adults in terms of oral and written culture, the innocence of spoken language and the deterioration of that innocence by the printed word. This construction of childhood imagines that young people offer a "natural" stability that opposes and perhaps compensates for the inherent *instability* of systemized language. However, Rousseau's description of "innocent," spoken language capitalizes not on its fixity but instead on its freedom and fluidity. The early babblings of infants, which Rousseau describes in the strange formulation "the language of children before they begin to speak," fascinate him not only because they are echoes of a linguistic infancy but also because the meaning of this early speech is not attached to particular and reproducible orders of letters, sounds, words, or sentences. Children's language can be "inarticulate" yet possess "tone, stress, and meaning."[4] It can signify without structures and norms of usage; it can communicate without using the "art," or more pointedly the artifice, of adults' linguistic codes. While Rousseau entertains the possibility that children such as Émile have "a grammar of their own," he acknowledges that this grammar has "rules and syntax that are more general" than the customs of adults' language (43). By mandating that children learn through the material world and the spoken word, Rousseau attempts to preserve within Émile the fluidity of language before it is compromised by print culture, or at least to restore that fluidity where it has been lost. When we read Rousseau's contention that children have an intimate relationship with the spoken word alongside his demand that adults study children to recapture that first, natural language, the result is a sort of partnership: a collaboration in which adults work alongside children in order to reclaim the advantages of oral culture.

However, Rousseau's Romantic notions of childhood largely preclude this possibility of intergenerational collaboration. Like many writers, he idealizes childhood as necessarily separate from the experiences of adulthood, even if he had to safeguard or retroactively construct that "natural" state by isolating young people from the culture that threatens to corrupt them. Yet the model of childhood that began to emerge in the works of Rousseau—a model that associates children with the infancy of the race and in particular the infancy of language—crystallized but shifted in the late nineteenth century and, as I will show, generated opportunities for adult-child collaboration. Tess Cosslett notes that at the fin-de-siècle the Romantic child was "being reconstituted as the evolutionary child, more primitive and more poetic, literally closer to animals, than adults" ("Child's" 480). This model was formalized in the Child Study movement, a precursor to developmental and educational psychology that marshaled the methods of a range of scholars, amateur and professional—psychologists, anthropologists, linguists, biologists, educators, and parents, among others—to build a portrait of all aspects of child life. As Sally Shuttleworth notes in her detailed examination of Child Study, "Victorians opened up the child mind to literary, scientific, and medical scrutiny. Although Romantic writers had established a cult of the child, it was the Victorians who created the first detailed literary and scientific studies of child development" (*Mind* 1). A number of historical and cultural factors made England in the 1880s and 1890s a particularly fertile environment for this. Adrian Wooldridge suggests "a widespread anxiety among politicians and social commentators about the degeneration of the British population" produced in part by the ill health of new populations of children who appeared in schools as education became increasingly compulsory. He also identifies a "mounting popular interest in the peculiar mental qualities and emotional needs which distinguished children from adults," characterized by "a heady combination of utilitarian calculation and romantic sentiment" (19). By the fin-de-siècle, persistent Romantic sentiments of innocence were complicated by an emerging awareness of how scientific inquiry into childhood could change the way adults manage children in day-to-day life.

Complicated is an accurate word, for while the phrase "Child Study movement" suggests coherence, the field was expansive and multifaceted from its origins—a productive messiness that registers how Child Study accommodated multiple and sometimes contradictory ideas about childhood and the proper methods of studying young people. In England, the Child Study movement began with at least two separate organizations. One, the Childhood Society, was formed in 1896 by the British Medical Association in order to compile a report on "the state of development and brain power of school children" (Wooldridge 30). The Society was led by Francis Warner, who with the help of twenty-three volunteers examined thousands of schoolchildren, paying particular attention to their physiological traits: measurements, movements, and behaviors. The society's work was utilitarian; its members followed what W. B. Drummond calls the "Collective or Mass method," which "consists in the examination of special points in a large number of children for the purpose of gaining knowledge of the typical course of development" (17). The Childhood Society's approach was often at odds with the methods of the Child Study Association, founded after three British schoolteachers returned to England from the 1893 World's Fair in Chicago, inspired by an address delivered by G. Stanley Hall.[5] Unlike the Childhood Society, which consisted primarily of professional scientists, the Child Study Association included a large contingent of educators and parents. The organization is remembered for the work of James Sully, whose *Studies of Childhood* (1895) was, according to Wooldridge, "one of the most widely quoted handbooks on psychology until the 1910s" (47). Members of this association practiced what Drummond calls "the Individual Method," or "the careful recording of the events in the life of an individual child as they occurred" (16). These studies are usually more narrative than the statistics-heavy research of the Childhood Society, but they vary widely in scope and rigor, including, for example, Charles Darwin's "A Biographical Sketch of an Infant" (1877), a short piece on the first behaviors of his son published in *Mind* magazine, as well as more extensive and formal studies, such as William T. Preyer's two-volume *The Mind of the Child*, published in German in 1882 and translated into English in 1894, which traces the development of intellectual faculties in children.[6]

Both organizations had their critics, but the methodologies of the association garnered more public acceptance than the physiological preoccupations of the Childhood Society. In 1907, the Childhood Society was absorbed into the London Branch of the Child Study Association to form the Child Study Society. This new organization continued to pursue the goals of the movement as articulated by Hall, who defined Child Study as

> partly psychology, partly anthropology partly medico-hygiene. It is closely related at every step to the study of instinct in animals, and to the rites and beliefs of primitive people; and it has a distinct ethico-philosophical aspect—partly what a recent writer classed as the higher biology—with a spice of folk-lore and of religious evolution, sometimes with an alloy of gossip and nursery tradition, but possessing a broad, practical side in the pedagogy of all stages. (689)

Six years earlier—in his opening comments in the *Paidologist*, the official journal of the Child Study Association—Hall mentioned a number of other schools of thought influencing Child Study, including "embryology of rudimentary organs" and "the psychology of the deaf, blind, idiotic, insane and criminal classes" (Shuttleworth, "Inventing" 144). The diversity of Child Study ensures that no one ideology dominates its scholarship.[7] Scholars attempted to understand childhood through every available means, and the spectrum of methodologies they employed suggests a rather sophisticated understanding of the challenges of interpreting children's minds and bodies.

Child Study scholars, like Rousseau before them, were attuned to how their research could be undermined by the child's relationship to spoken and written language. Many recognized that the tools they used to access children's voices and inner lives inevitably privileged adult assumptions and conclusions about childhood. "Study of the mind traditionally had employed the method of introspection," notes Holly Blackford, "a method not possible in the less articulate child. . . . Introspection would have to give way to direct observation, but observation required interpretation. And how could those removed from childhood interpret what and how the child sees?" (371).[8] Child Study scholars were aware of these challenges and described them in language that anticipates current scholarship in childhood studies on the problems of accessing children's voices. Blanche Dismore, for example, in her 1902 study of children's vocabularies, laments the necessity of employing direct observation and the even more problematic method of writing exercises to assess children's understanding. "If we could look directly into children's minds without the intervening medium of writing it would be better, but we cannot," writes Dismore. "If children were constructed like magic lanterns, it would be most instructive to seat a dozen of them before a large screen and study the widely different pictures they projected" (43–44).[9] Dismore, craving unmediated information about children's minds, is frustrated by the indirect methods available to her. Unexpectedly, by identifying children as subjects of scientific inquiry—by insisting that, in the words of Hall, "children are not little adults, with all the faculties of maturity on a reduced scale, but unique and very different creatures" (700)—Dismore and her colleagues ensure the young are, to some extent, inaccessible and always slipping just beyond the adult's grasp.

This explains Child Study scholars' preoccupation with speech and the importance of language to adult-child relationships. After all, when children learn language, they acquire a mode of communication that adults share. Problems of interpretation arise, but when children learn language, they are initiated into a sign system that communicates to curious adults the thoughts and impressions of childhood more fully and directly. Many Child Study scholars therefore begin their research with theories of children's language acquisition, including detailed considerations children's speech patterns. An English translation of French scholar Hippolyte Taine's article "On the Acquisition of Language by Children," published in *Mind* in 1877, incited a string of similar studies, including Darwin's meditation on his infant son's early negotiations of language in "A Biographical Sketch of an Infant" and F. Pollock's 1878 "An Infant's Progress in Language."[10] Some of the most influential publications in the field include extensive chapters dedicated to language. For example, Bernard Perez's *The First Three Years of Childhood*, translated from French into English in 1885, features a three-part chapter "On Expression and Language," and Sully includes in his *Studies of Childhood* a chapter titled "The Little Linguist."

Studying children's language acquisition required redefining child listeners as collaborators, active participants in the creation of the linguistic worlds that surround them. Reconceiving adult-child relationships in this manner was not altogether unfamiliar at the fin-de-siècle; remember that Rousseau had imagined children as linguistic collaborators as early as the late eighteenth century, when he recommended that tutors, who usually demonstrated their authority over the child through the force of the printed word, should instead learn from the speech and gestures of their pupils. However, Child Study scholars more explicitly inverted adult-child, speaker-listener dynamics, acknowledging both how children *receive* language—how, in learning to speak, they listen to the mother tongue as spoken by adults—and, as I will make clear, how they *respond* to language through repetition and transformation. It is children, Child Study scholars suggest, who maintain the creativity and fluidity of spoken language. The adult-child partnerships Child Study scholars detect between adult speakers and child listeners are hybrid collaborations, incorporating both scientific modes of looking at real child subjects and romanticized constructions of childhood. In other words, Child Study scholarship about language acquisition is characterized by the "combination of utilitarian calculation and romantic sentiment" that Wooldridge detects in the movement as a whole. Experts' careful analyses of syllables and sentence building are often inflected with humor and sentimentality.

Sully, for example, notes that the first attempts of "the young learner of our tongue" are "half pathetic, half humorous," imperfect imitations of speech full of "quaint errors" that "provide ample amusement" to adult listeners (133, 147)—a description that betrays sentimental or desirable models of childhood. However, Sully and his contemporaries produced exhaustive accounts of the sounds children produce, the stages of physical and cognitive development at which they produce them, and their approximations of or differences from adult speech—accounts that belie more than a casual interest in baby talk and suggest a serious interest in real children. Such scholars dissect what Rousseau had dubbed nearly a century earlier "the language of children before they begin to speak" in order to better understand "the language common to all," although they were motivated by quite a different ideology (36).[11]

For while Child Study experts cast children's language in terms very similar to Rousseau's formulations—contending that children reenact the origins of language and suggesting their speech is pure but fluid, free from the intrusion of the written sign—these associations between children and "savage" races in their theories of childhood speech are an outgrowth of the recapitulation theory, or the contention that the individual repeats the development of the race. As Jessica Straley explains in her study of evolution and Victorian children's literature, "though, in its rigorously scientific formulation, [recapitulation] applies only to embryos, it was quickly extrapolated into a description of children" beyond their development in the womb; as an example of this phenomenon, Straley quotes physician Louis Robinson's claims that "an animal until independent of parental care, and even beyond that point, until the bodily structure and functions are those of an adult, is still, strictly speaking, an embryo" (7). Extending recapitulation into childhood transformed the ways adults interpreted child life, and Child Study scholars assumed that "the child inherits the abilities, memories, and habits of his ancestors and exhibits them in his growth in much the same order as they were first acquired" (Wooldridge 25).[12] A child's speech patterns, then, were read as the race's acquisition of language writ small. Alexander Francis Chamberlain, a contemporary and interlocutor of Sully, based his exploration of children's speech on recapitulation theory and reiterates Rousseau's argument that infants' babblings hold the key to determining the first human language: "The speech of little children has always been a source of wonderment to man," writes Chamberlain, and many scholars, dating from "Psammetichus, King of Egypt," have "turned to childhood for the solution of the problem of language origins" (113–14).[13] G. T. W. Patrick aligns children with ancient, oral cultures—"like the primitive man," the child is "ear-minded," a "talking and hearing animal"—and this leads him to conclude that children should not learn to read or write until they are ten years old, a recommendation that would please Rousseau (390). For Chamberlain and Patrick, as for Rousseau before them, the child is a cultural artifact that can reveal the secrets of the race's linguistic past. If children are at times depicted in Child Study literature as bumbling speakers whose errors are amusing, they are more often described as specimens that provide insight into the race's history.

Recapitulation theory would seem to rob the "little linguist" of all expressive agency. According to Child Study, children are the unwitting bearers of the history of language, and their early speech is fated simply to repeat the sounds and syllables of their ancestors. Evolutionary history was a script all children follow; as Straley argues, the child of recapitulation was "dragging behind him vestiges of our savage and bestial prehistory" (21). For instance, Charles Johnston, in "The World's Baby-Talk" (1896), pictures children following in the exact footsteps of their forebears; he writes that "in the prattle of every baby we have a repetition, in a minor key, of the voice of the earliest man, and by watching the first movements of speech in a baby we can see once more the steps in articulate language which the whole world of man once took in dim ages long ago" (499). Fittingly, studies in children's speech often begin with the various ways children mimic the development of language through repetition itself, outlining strategies of language acquisition such as onomatopoeia, the reproduction in speech of sounds from the natural world, and imitation, the repetition of the sounds produced by a speaker who has mastered the language. A meticulous application of these theories would collapse all child speech into formulaic evidence, categorizing every sound that escapes children's lips as echoes of a previous generation's contribution to the mother tongue.

However, some Child Study scholars resist such formulations and, in fact, focus on moments when children's expressions are creative and unexpected, evidence not of passivity but of agency. Children, they suggest, discover a range of ways—some subtle, others bold—to negotiate and transform the language they hear. Frederick Tracy, for example, suggests in *The Psychology of Childhood* (1894) that while the child "builds up his own vocabulary" from "the intonations of those around him," his practice of imitation is most accurately understood as "active hearing," and "perhaps not wholly involuntary" (128, 132). Tracy records children's critical engagement in the act of listening and suggests that they exercise a degree of selection in the sounds they repeat and add to their vocabularies. Moreover, many Child Study experts contend that the child's sense of hearing is nuanced and finely tuned, much more perceptive than that of adults, and it is this acuity that enables an infant to learn language through listening and imitation.[14] Chamberlain writes that "the skill with which children observe and reproduce accent, intonation, cadence, etc., is wonderful, their ears seizing an infinitude of inflections lost to the adult ear" (140). Taine similarly notes that children's senses are "much less blunted than our own" and "perceive delicate shades that we no longer distinguish" (251). It is the unique ability of children to *listen*, to hear the complexities of the sounds that surround them, that makes them experts in repetition and mimicry. For example, Taine observes a direct correspondence between children's aural acuity and their speech, which is characterized by a "flexibility [that] is surprising," expressing "all the shades of emotion, wonder, joy, willfulness and sadness" and "equals or even surpasses a grown up person" (253).

Others note even more creative ways children respond to the sounds and words they hear. Sully, for example, contends that the child's impulse to imitate adults' language "leads the child beyond the servile adoption of our conventional sounds to the invention of new or onomatopoetic sounds"—that "the working of this impulse may, in a certain number of children at least, strike out original lines of its own independently of the direct example of example and education" (144, 146). According to Sully, the child "in reproducing transforms," and scholars who listen carefully to children will witness "frequent outbursts of originality in bold attempts to enrich our vocabulary and our linguistic forms" (148, 147). While some of these transformations are simplifications or mispronunciations of adult speech, others, he argues, are creative inventions. The terms Sully uses to describe the nature of adults' language and children's imitation and invention are noteworthy. Adults are characterized by a fixity of language; they make "conventional sounds" that "a certain number of children"—whom Sully later identifies "intelligent," of "precocious originality"—reject for "new" and "original" language of their own (162). Sully provides pages of examples of children's speech, noting, for example, a child who "invented the form 'dag' for striking with a dagger" and "the pretty term 'tell-wind' which a boy of four years and eight months hit upon as a name for a weather-vane" (168–69). These clever word forms are for Sully genius in their own way and often are more logical than the corresponding and correct terms used by adults. By using terms like "invented" and "hit upon," Sully suggests that these new words are not endearing mistakes or anomalies but contributions. According to Taine, this inventiveness is both admirable and educational. "Originality and invention are so strong in a child," he writes, "that if it learns our language from us, we learn its from the child" (257).[15]

For Sully, children's linguistic ingenuity is legible not only in individual words and phrases but also in entire strategies of language building. For example, according to Sully, both the child and "primitive man" expand their vocabularies and develop skills of interpretation and classification through generalization and analogy, in which they apply words and phrases they have heard used to signify one object or idea to another with similar properties. Sully notes that

> such extension, moving rather along poetic lines than those of our logical classifications, is apt, as we have seen, to wear a quaint metaphorical aspect. A star, for example, looked at, I suppose, as a small bright spot, was called by one child an eye. The child M. called the opal globe of a lamp a "moon." . . . Taine speaks of a child of one year who after first applying the word "fafer" (from *chemin de fer*) to railway engines went on to transfer it to a steaming coffee-pot and everything that hissed or smoked or made a noise. (163)

Children's language is again more inventive than that of adults. Drawing an unexpected association between a coffee pot and a railway engine, identified by an infantilized version of the term *chemin de fer* provided by the adult world of linguistic signs, is a much more "poetic" move than the "logical classifications" of adults, who are educated into the norms of the language. Sully demonstrates through accounts of children like M., who astutely notes the correspondences between "the opal globe of a lighted lamp" and a moon, that children fulfill active roles as wordsmiths rather than passive roles as mirrors to the language of adults or the linguistic development of their "savage" ancestors.

Embedded in Child Study scholarship, then, is a paradox. Writers in this field assume, like Rousseau before them, that children are linguistic innocents, their speech valuable because it records the origins of language. However, many Child Study scholars simultaneously imply that children are authorities in the nature of language, adept at manipulating the spoken word. Children are vital participants not only in the project of deciphering the earliest language but also in the continued transformation of language that keeps speech vibrant. Adults may expect "servile adoption" of the mother tongue, but children instead delight and surprise by striking out on more inventive pathways to expression. Scholars couch these gestures toward children's creativity in heavy-handed arguments that align children's imitative impulse with the repetitions they claim characterized the first "savage" speakers of the language. Chamberlain, for example, claims that children's "invention" is in fact "the prime trait allying him with his kin of long ago," who similarly transformed language through inexact repetition (127). However, as the above passages demonstrate, these writers are unwilling to deny all inventiveness on children's part, and their careful discussions of imitation become opportunities to record how children do not remain silent and passive in their reenactment of linguistic history. They are active agents in determining the language they use and the language we use around them. These patterns of language acquisition are an intergenerational collaboration—perhaps more accurately a symbiotic relationship between adult scholars who, interested in the origins of language, rely on children to reenact the linguistic past and children who, in the process of learning to speak, listen to and transform the language of their parents and teachers. Hall recognizes the collaborative nature of Child Study when he writes that one advantage of the movement "is that it helps to break down to some extent the partitions between grades of work, so that the kindergartner and university professor can cooperate in the same task" (700).

The creativity children exhibit in transforming spoken language culminates not in precocious transformations of the mother tongue but instead in the abandonment of that language altogether through the development of what Child Study scholars call the "secret languages" of children.[16] Horatio Hale introduced early research on the topic in an 1886 address to the American Association for the Advancement of Science titled *The Origin of Languages, and the Antiquity of Speaking Man*. Hale documents the observations of two lesser-known scholars, Miss E. H. Watson and Dr. E. R. Hun, and uses their data to argue that "when two children who are just beginning to speak are left much together, they sometimes invent a complete language, sufficient for all purposes of mutual intercourse, and yet totally unintelligible to their parents and others about them" (9). Hun describes the secret language of a four-and-a-half-year-old girl, who "never employed the words used by others," using instead "words of her own invention" (525).[17] What Child Study scholars find remarkable about these languages is their independence from the linguistic world of adults; children's secret languages were, as Sully points out, "not susceptible of explanation by imitation" (146). In other words, experts argue that these languages are not generated through patterns of listening and response but instead are generated spontaneously by particularly creative children, who are able to bypass the listening stage of language acquisition and proceed independently to language building.

While Child Study scholars' descriptions of children's language acquisition emphasize interactions between adult speakers and child listeners—even if they illustrate how children can manipulate that relationship—accounts of children's secret languages describe partnerships comprised solely of children. For example, Oscar Chrisman describes the "Berkshire gabble," a language invented by two girls between the ages of ten and fourteen. Grown into adulthood at the time of Chrisman's writing, these women recollect that the "gabble," like many secret languages explored by Child Study scholars, was "unintelligible" to others, devised independently from the influences of adult speech. They recorded more than two hundred words in a personal dictionary—terms that described "any appearance, quality, or feeling they could not express by means of the English language" ("Secret-Language" 57). Their method of generating this vocabulary is an example of how children could direct the collaborative energy of the speaker-listener dynamic to the service of language creation. The sisters, with a friend, agreed upon a sensation to name and then split the task of inventing an appropriate term. "One shouted 'I choose the first syllable'; another, 'I choose the second'; and the remaining child had to take the last one," remembers one of the sisters. "If the word sounded to them like the sensation, they left it as it was; if it did not, they changed it" ("Secret-Language" 57). Chrisman provides a glossary, and the definitions reveal that the girls often used their collaborative language to describe sensations germane to childhood. Some terms are comments on situations that arise in the schoolroom; *fomo*, for example, means "nervousness about squeaking slate pencils," and *rewish* indicates "feeling numberless eyes on you as you are about to recite something." Others suggest a child's distaste for the adult world and its manners: *faxsy* means "stuffy-parlorish" and *hamalet* translates to "the indulgent cheeriness of mothers" ("Secret-Language" 57). The Berkshire gabble records the limitations of adults' language to describe children's experiences.

While Child Study scholars were charmed by young speakers' occasional variations from standard speech, they found in such secret languages even stronger evidence that children can resist or exceed widely accepted evolutionary narratives. Chrisman categorizes language learning into three stages: "acquiring of the mother-tongue," followed by "a language made up by children who, perhaps, find themselves unable to master the mother-tongue," and finally the "secret-language period," which "is a thing of child nature" ("Secret-Language" 54–55). This final stage surpasses the child's successful mastery of language. In crafting new languages, children wander from the paths of their ancestors, no longer slavishly repeating the race's linguistic history. While some argued that the secret-language period fits easily into the evolutionary model of childhood, repeating "a corresponding period in the race of man . . . an instinct for language making," Chamberlain dismisses this as flawed logic: "the utter artificiality in the making of the words of not a few of these secret languages, and their great lack of the real raw material out of which grew primitive grammar, forbid the belief that they have ever played such a *rôle* in the history of the race" (137). In a later series of articles on children's languages published in the *North-western Monthly*, Chrisman recognizes that some types of secret languages might resemble primitive modes of language making, in particular that the design of secret language vocabularies, and the means by which children learn them, capitalize upon "the habit of imitation, which is so strong in children" and in "savage" races ("Secret Languages" 192). However, he concludes that many secret languages, especially those that feature original vocabularies rather than revisions to existing words, "show a side of child-language which is very full of ingenuity and originality" ("Secret Languages" 378).

In some ways, the ingenuity of young language makers alienates adults. The sentiment Rousseau expressed at the beginning of *Émile*, the idea that we "know nothing of childhood" (1), resurfaces as Child Study scholars find that they need glossaries in order to understand what appear to be simple exchanges between children. "We are just beginning to learn," writes Chrisman after describing the Berkshire gabble, "that we do not know our children" ("Secret-Language" 55).[18] While some of the secret languages Chrisman records in his study were shared among adults and children alike in families, schools, or even entire neighborhoods, scholarship on the phenomenon is preoccupied with children's secrecy, claiming that many languages were designed with the intent of excluding adults—to "occasionally mystif[y] . . . elders by using strange words"

("Secret Languages" 192). In some cases, these languages were not merely independent from adult language but aggressively exclusive. Chrisman, for example, notes that these languages "are so jealously guarded that only a very few [children] know them, and they must be so familiar with them as to speak them so rapidly that no one will get the key" ("Secret-Language" 55). And when Chrisman imagines the responses of adults returning to the secret languages of their own childhoods, he emphasizes both the familiarity of one's young self—"many years may have passed, and yet come ringing out, as in joyous childhood, these sacred things"—and the irrevocable gulf between the "old gray-headed fellow nodding over his evening paper" and the "little, teasing, mischievous boy of twelve" who devised secret vocabularies. He suspects that some who read his articles will "at once rummage among their treasures, and out will come the faded brown paper with the hieroglyphics . . . and the key will be hunted up, and the messages of childish days will be read again and again" ("Secret-Language" 54). His description recalls an archaeological dig; he reproduces examples of such childhood code, and they do resemble hieroglyphics. Understanding the languages that came so naturally to children, even to understand those languages that adults invented in their own youth, requires an act of excavation.

Or an act of intergenerational partnership. Chrisman's study relies on samples of children's secret languages submitted by readers, and the responses he receives suggest that the distance between young and old is not impassable. Chrisman's work is made possible by the cooperative efforts of children and adults. Here and there, sentimentality interferes with his scientific project, and in those moments he obscures the vital roles of real children, replacing them with desirable constructions born of adult nostalgia. For example, he notes that "languages of childhood so indelibly stamp themselves upon the growing mind that years and years may pass, yet when a reminder comes . . . at once they begin to flow off the tongue as when a barefoot boy wading in the creek to catch crawfish for bait; and the cipher comes back to one just as when a bashful, blushing boy in school one penned to his blue-eyed neighbor his sweet verses in language which only she and he could comprehend" ("Secret Languages" 193). These barefoot, blue-eyed children evidence the ways Child Study scholars, like all nineteenth-century writers on childhood, at times reiterate persistent notions of ideal and innocent childhood. But alongside these idealizations, Chrisman acknowledges the living young people who make his study possible—and their willingness to work alongside adults.

He collects secret languages "given by children of eight, by youths of fifteen, by young people of twenty, by people of thirty, forty, fifty, and even some in the seventies" ("Secret Languages" 187–88). He praises the law school dean who recorded a secret language his twelve-year-old daughter uses at school, and the college professor who sent a language with the following note: "For the information I am indebted to a little girl friend, who . . . furnished me with the key to the alphabet and examples of the language." While secret languages such as the Berkshire gabble might feel foreign to adults, Chrisman concludes that these linguistic practices ultimately inspire amity and collaboration between generations. "Thus," he notes, "is child life interwoven with our own" ("Secret Languages" 188).

THE LIPS OF THE STORYTELLER

Despite Chrisman's pleasure in childhood languages, the young are destined to be initiated into the regulated vocabularies and grammars of the mother tongue. Even the child who recognized a moon in the globe of a lamp must grow up and learn the "proper" names of things, and Chrisman and other scholars could not resist plotting ways to redirect the creative energies evident in secret languages toward "correct" modes of speaking. For example, G. W. A. Luckey, editor of the *North-western Monthly*, wonders if the secret languages of children can be repurposed as tools in teaching language and literature (243). However, the cultural investment in children's association with spoken language resonated throughout the nineteenth century. In particular, literature for children, while bound to print culture, betrays the influence of constructions of childhood that assumed a troubled relationship between the young and the printed word, and when authors and publishers were tasked with determining what forms of fiction could best serve a child audience, many turned to narrative approximations of told tales—stories that, I argue, accommodate child agency in ways other forms cannot. In the remaining two sections of this chapter, I explore how associations between children and oral culture contributed to the absorption of told tales into children's literature in the nineteenth century and how the figure of the collaborative child that was so important to Child Study surfaces in these materials. Here, as a test case, I examine the history of Jacob and Wilhelm Grimm's collections and their English translations.[19]

The Grimms were interested in the instability of the spoken word and in how that instability enables collaboration between tellers and listeners across generations, geographies, and cultures—how a single told tale can exist in several variants because speech, unlike print, adapts to the context of its narration. In other words, the Grimms worked under a now commonplace assumption: that, in the words of Alan Dundes, "context can influence text" (26–27) and that, as Maria Tatar contends, "the tellers of tales collaborated with audiences to produce new stories based on old ones" (277). For the Grimms, the most powerful stories in their *Kinder- und Hausmärchen* (hereafter *KHM*), which first appeared in two volumes (1812, 1815), were those that revealed traces of multiple storytellers and audiences. "These different versions," writes Wilhelm in the preface to the second volume, "seem more noteworthy to us than they do to those who see in them nothing more than variants or corrupt forms of a once extant archetypal form. For us, they are more likely to be attempts to capture, through numerous approaches, an inexhaustibly rich ideal type" (1.2.410).[20] Each variant sprung from new tellers and listeners, and it was the multiplication of collaborating teller-listener circles that makes these tales "inexhaustibly rich." This preoccupation with how the stories they collect are "refashioned by the lips of the storyteller" (1.1.401) continues into the second edition of 1819, in which Wilhelm attributes the "special nature" of the tales to their longevity; they are not the products of single storytellers but of "traditions" (2.1.415). "No one can dispute the fact that they have been handed down over the centuries," he writes, "transforming themselves continually in their outer manifestations" as those who once listened become the next generation of tellers (ibid.).[21] While the brothers celebrated the fecundity of oral tales, they were aware of the implications of recording unstable stories; they felt the richness of oral culture could not be contained in print. In acknowledging that tension, the Grimms hoped to capture the qualities of narration in the volumes of the *KHM*. In a footnote at the end of their first preface, they call for the compilation of new tales beyond the versions included in the collection. "We ask those who have the opportunity and the desire to help us to improve the details of this book," Wilhelm writes, "to complete its fragments, and especially to collect new and unusual animal fables. We would be most grateful for such information" (1.1.407). Recording oral tales for the Grimms was an ongoing process, a venture that recognized their collections would always be incomplete and open to new collaborators, whose deviations from the "essentials" would prove the vitality and flexibility of spoken language.

This call for contributions gestures toward the ever-changing nature of oral tales, but the Grimms acted as "retellers" and collaborators in larger ways. In particular, over the numerous editions of the *KHM*, the Grimms changed the format, presentation, and content of the tales in response both to cultural assumptions that figured oral culture as childlike and to an audience that, increasingly, consisted of children. While the brothers did not explicitly turn to child collaborators, children nevertheless exerted a powerful influence over the publication history of the *KHM*. First, the figure of the child is essential to how the brothers frame their collection and characterize the oral tale. Like Rousseau, the Grimms understood the relationship between oral and print culture through a framework of youth and age, innocence and deterioration. Working with oral tradition requires them to access elements of storytelling they imagine as naïve and pure, and they represent the communities where the tradition of oral culture remains viable as childlike. Wilhelm notes that "the custom of telling tales is on the wane," suggesting that German culture is somehow growing up, away from the tradition of telling tales, and that "the custom persists only in places where there is a warm openness to poetry or where there are imaginations not yet deformed by the perversities of modern life" (1.1.402). In the second volume of the first edition, Wilhelm makes a similar claim: "Devotion to tradition is far stronger among people who always adhere to the same way of life than we (who tend to want to change) can understand" (1.2.409). Wilhelm's nostalgia suggests that cultures that continue to tell stories are out of time. They need not grow up, instead redirecting the impulse to change onto the stories themselves; the stories transform while the tellers remain static.

The Grimms may not explicitly equate oral cultures with childhood, but they embrace a set of associations that equates childhood with innocence, the purity of the spoken word, and the vulnerability of that innocence. And if storytellers were, according to the Grimms, childlike, then the stories themselves, in a sense, belong to children. The Grimms did not intend their collections for children, at least not at first; however, in the preface to the first edition, Wilhelm suggests that the tales collected in the *KHM* were once the property of the young. While they "have almost always been used as the stuff of longer stories," he notes, they were truly the domain of children; "but what belonged to children was always torn out of their hands, and nothing was given back to them in return" (1.1.406). This sentiment intensifies in the preface to the second edition; there, they describe the stories they have collected as "children's stories" that are "also called household tales" because "their simple poetry can bring joy to everyone just as their wisdom can instruct everyone who hears them, and since they remain at home and are passed down from one generation to the next" (2.1.412). These stories remain simple, rooted in the domestic. They are the youth of the more sophisticated narratives German culture will produce in its "civilized" adulthood.

These prefaces employ the child as shorthand for a set of assumptions about storytelling and oral culture. However, as their project progressed, the Grimms found that real child listeners reinforced the characterization of oral cultures as childlike. Jennifer Schacker explains that while the Grimms attempted to present the tales as artifacts of scholarly interest, they learned that child readers as well as scholars claimed the stories. While friends and colleagues "offered criticisms of the *KHM*," writes Schacker, "there was one audience apparently undaunted by the . . . tomelike appearance of the book: children. Letters from Joseph von Görres indicate that his daughter loved the collection, as apparently did the Savigny children. In fact, the dual appeal of the *KHM* was increasingly to be cast not in terms of scholars and general readers, nor instruction and pleasure, but in terms of adults and children" (24). The Grimms responded to child audiences by transforming the format, presentation, and content of the tales. The scholarly apparatus of numerous variants and annotations included in the first volume of the first edition was, in the second volume, exiled to an appendix. Introducing the second volume, Wilhelm concedes that parents' concerns that the collection "might prove embarrassing and would be unsuitable for children" may be "appropriate in certain cases" (1.2.410). As David Blamires notes, the changes the Grimms made to the second volume "turned the collection increasingly into a work calculated to appeal to a child readership. . . . Through the removal of morally questionable elements from certain stories and their alignment with the values and feelings of the middle class . . . the Grimms created a work of immense appeal" ("Workshop" 81).

The transformation of intent and content between the first two volumes of the *KHM* reveals that the Grimms struggled with two fundamental shifts in assembling the collections. The first was a shift from told tale to printed text. They negotiated the difficulty of what Ong calls the "reduction of dynamic sound to quiescent space" not only by including multiple variants of each tale in their collections but also by calling for the submission of new stories, suggesting that their project, if it is to respect the nature of oral culture, must remain open-ended. The second shift was a movement from a scholarly project to a publishing venture aimed at implied readers or listeners increasingly assumed to be children.

1.1. George Cruikshank, title vignette for volume 1 of *German Popular Stories*, collected by the Brothers Grimm and translated by Edgar Taylor. London: C. Baldwyn, 1823. EC8.C8885.823g v.1. Houghton Library, Harvard University.

This required, conversely, *closing down* narrative possibilities and denying the full spectrum of meaning a told tale can achieve. Privileging the *Kinder* over the *Haus*, the Grimms removed certain stories—often, as Tatar has noted, those that deal with pregnancy or incest—either for ease of reading or in response to the concerns of parents and teachers.[22] The transformation of the *KHM* is both evidence of children's influence over the publication and revision of fairy tales, folklore, or oral narratives and an exercise in negotiating the conflicts inherent in constructions of childhood as akin to oral traditions. For while the Grimms imagined storytelling cultures as childlike, and while they catered to child audiences thought to be particularly delighted by oral tales, the types of narratives oral traditions may generate—sexual, perhaps, or inaccessibly archaic—were not easily absorbed into the genre of children's literature, which demands tales suitable for the young.

1.2. George Cruikshank, title vignette for volume 2 of *German Popular Stories*, collected by the Brothers Grimm and translated by Edgar Taylor. London: James Robins & Co., 1826. EC8.C8885.823g v.2. Houghton Library, Harvard University.

When the Grimms' collection was first translated and published in England in 1823, it was immediately framed as children's literature.[23] This first translation—*German Popular Stories, translated from the Kinder and Haus Märchen, collected by M. M. Grimm, from Oral Tradition*—included thirty-one of the tales translated by Edgar Taylor and illustrated by George Cruikshank. Taylor notes that his translation "makes no literary pretensions; that its immediate design precludes the subjects most attractive to matters of research; and that professedly critical dissertations would therefore be out of place" (xii). He abandons scholarly aims in service to the pleasures, especially for children, of reading and listening to the tales. In his preface, he advocates re-admitting these "loveliest dreams of fairy innocence" into "the libraries of childhood" and the nurseries of England—nurseries that he contends are sadly ruled by reason, producing "lisping chemists and leading-string mathematicians." Fairy tales, according to Taylor, re-educate England's youth back to their natural state—from "rigid and philosophic" rationalists to the fanciful creatures they are meant to be (iv). Accordingly, Taylor, like the Grimms before him, edits the tales with a child audience in mind, minimizing the scholarly apparatus and practicing a "scrupulous fastidiousness" in selecting only stories appropriate for the young (xi). The introduction of the Grimms in England as decidedly children's literature is also recorded in Cruikshank's title vignette illustrations to the volumes (Figures 1.1 and 1.2). These images reiterate on a visual register the redefinition of the tales: their shift from stories meant to entertain entire communities of adults and children to stories meant for the young. In his analysis of Cruikshank's etchings for Taylor's volumes, Robert L. Patten contends that the illustrations "imply that at some level Cruikshank understood the communal and oral nature of these tales." Patten notes a number of elements in the two scenes that construct similar scenes of narration. The leaded windows and the roaring fires, the suggestion of winter without and warmth within, combine to convey "a sense of community sheltered from the cold and the dark and bound together by tales of mirth and magic" (250–51). Yet as Patten notes, the audiences certainly shift. In the first volume, Cruikshank depicts "a man sitting before a huge hearth read[ing] to a laughing audience of old and young adults," while the second features "an old woman" who "holds a circle of children spellbound with her stories" (248).

Yet these illustrations indicate other, subtle differences. The expressions on listeners' faces in the first vignette suggest a raucous, humorous tale; a figure in the forefront is collapsed with laughter, a second seated on a stool clutches his side in paroxysms of mirth, his mouth wide with joy. A few scattered cups on a nearby table and the figure near the fire nursing a drink evoke a kitchen or even a tavern, where the ease of company is aided by spirits. Karen E. Rowe calls this image "a ribald environment of a hearthside scene" (68). The central storytelling figure reads from a printed text. The second title vignette, however, depicts a quieter moment of storytelling. The children listening crowd closely around their storyteller in an intimate circle, one child leaning an elbow on the old woman's knee. In this image, Cruikshank suggests the closer, familial relationships played out in the nursery or drawing room, an atmosphere supported by small details: a family of cats by the fire and an ornately carved chair, perhaps an heirloom. Rowe argues that illustrations such as this vignette "embedded in the popular consciousness images of grandmothers, mothers, nursemaids, and governesses gathered at homely hearths, attended by an audience frequently of children," and that "such illustrations both reflected and fostered an identification of fairy tales with the predominantly female realm of domesticity" (65). I would add that the elderly woman narrates from memory, the absence of a printed text suggesting that her stories are the sort the Grimms truly valued—tales that shift over time under the influence of many tellers and audiences.[24] These stories are out of time and find their counterpart in the spinning wheel on the right side of the image, an object that recalls both the origins of told tales in women's spinning rooms and the continual working and reworking of story. They are fluid, like children's grasp of language, able to accommodate new meanings, new listeners. The first image contains no spinning wheel but does include an hourglass; time there is not standing still, and soon the listeners will have to disperse.

The popularity of Taylor's translation and Cruikshank's illustrations cemented *German Popular Stories* as a collection meant for the young, and further editions in England and throughout Europe were edited and marketed accordingly. Scholars have provided ample evidence that *German Popular Stories* fundamentally changed the dominant perception of fairy tales as Taylor and subsequent translators and editors of the Grimms took into account the needs of a child audience—or, as John Ruskin writes, as they catered to the "majestic independence of the child-public" (60).[25] However, I contend that Taylor, in his own preface, depicts the creative agency of child audiences as a force surpassing the influence they exert as potential readers. According to Taylor, his translation owes its existence to a collaboration between adult narrators and child auditors, a partnership that grants listening children—for this is certainly a text meant to be read aloud—considerable influence over the stories' circumstances of publication. He stages this partnership in the first sentences of this preface:

> The Translators[26] were first induced to compile this little work by the eager relish with which a few of the tales were received by the young friends to whom they were narrated. In this feeling the Translators, however, do not hesitate to avow their own participation. Popular fictions and traditions are somewhat gone out of fashion; yet most will own them to be associated with the brightest recollections of their youth. They are, like the Christmas Pantomime, ostensibly brought forth to tickle the palate of the young, but are often received with as keen an appetite by those of graver years. (iii–iv)

Taylor frames the fairy tales in his collection as narrated stories that not only charm and entertain across generations but also require the active participation of old and young. According to Taylor, his project of translation and publication owes its creative impulse to children, the circle of "young friends" who received the told tales with "relish"; the passive voice of the phrase "the young friends to whom they were narrated," in fact, makes invisible the adults reading these stories aloud. The finished product of *German Popular Stories* is depicted as a product of both the children's enthusiasm and the necessary intervention of the adult translators, who "do not hesitate to avow their own participation," an unusual phrase that represents the feelings of the translators as secondary to the enthusiasm of the young friends. Taylor chooses to represent the translation of the tales in a manner that depicts the roles of adult teller and child listeners as fluid and interchangeable; by the end of the passage, listening children are accompanied in their rapt attention by "those of graver years." Taylor ends this 1823 preface by quoting a passage from Richard Johnson's 1621 chapbook, *The History of Tom Thumbe, the Little*. Johnson writes that the "old and young" have "chimed mattins" with these stories and that "the old shepheard and the young plow-boy" have "carold out the same" (Taylor, *GPS* iii–iv). By describing storytelling as caroling and chiming, Johnson suggests both the auditory nature of the told tale and the collaborative pleasure of narration.

In 1839 a new Taylor translation of the Grimms' tales was published, titled *Gammer Grethel; or German Fairy Tales, and Popular Stories, from the Collection of MM Grimm, and Other Sources*—an edition that illustrates in nuanced ways how editors and writers of fairy tales and other narrated texts began to consider child auditors as collaborators. Some tales were dropped and others, not all drawn from the Grimms' collections, were added. The stories were divided into groups of three or four under the headings "Evening the First," "Evening the Second," and so forth, arranged to be narrated on twelve consecutive nights. Taylor describes this new incarnation of the Grimms' tales as a further concession to his young friends. He notes that the translators, as in previous editions, were "induced to compile this little work by the eager relish with which a few of the tales were received by the young friends to whom they were narrated." His circle of child listeners had grown far larger since his first translation, and it is for this new "race of that class of readers for whose entertainment such stories are more peculiarly adapted" that he has again taken on the task of "re-arranging, revising, and adding to [the] budget" of appropriately entertaining tales (iii). *Gammer Grethel*—which references the narrating old woman, Gammer Grethel, in its title, preface, and frontispiece—prioritizes the oral nature of the stories and the narrating voice in particular. Many claim Taylor did not pay attention to the particular oral nature of the tales, especially in early editions of *German Popular Stories*; Brian Alderson, for example, argues that the "narrative voice" can be found only "at the margins" of the 1823 edition ("Spoken" 61). Yet *Gammer Grethel* reinstates the narrator and uses her to structure the entire text.

Gammer Grethel asserts a very particular narrative voice: she is a teller who embodies, in a single figure, the type of intergenerational collaboration Taylor privileges. He introduces her as "Our Gammer Grethel, the supposed narrator of the stories," noting that she "in fact lived, though under a different name. She was the Frau Viehmännin, the wife of a peasant in the neighbourhood of Hesse-Cassel, and from her mouth a great portion of the stories were written down by MM. Grimm" (vii).[27] Evoking Dorothea Viehmann—for this is how her surname is spelled in the Grimms' descriptions—has unique advantages for Taylor, because she is a teller who mediates between oral and printed culture, between childhood and adulthood. Viehmann, Wilhelm explains,

> narrates carefully, confidently, and in an unusually lively manner, taking great pleasure in it. At first she speaks spontaneously, then, if you ask, she will repeat what she has said very slowly so that, with a little practice, it can be transcribed. In this way, much was taken down *verbatim* and no one will fail to recognize its authenticity. Those who believe that oral narratives are routinely falsified, that they are not carefully preserved, and that long recitations are, as a rule, impossible, should have the chance to hear how precisely she stays with each story and how keen she is to narrate correctly. (1.2.408)

In this passage, Viehmann is the embodiment of all that is attractive about the spoken word. She is "unusually lively," and she "speaks spontaneously," able to adapt her narration easily and seamlessly to the demands of her listeners. She relates stories that are unquestionable in their authenticity. However, she also embodies all the advantages of the printed text. She is careful and precise, she can repeat "very slowly" for the benefit of those transcribing her stories, and she is predictable, able to narrate "correctly" so her tales can be recorded "verbatim." Taylor was perhaps attracted to Viehmann because of her simultaneous representation of both the fluidity of the spoken word, associated with childhood, and the fidelity of the printed word, associated with the adult norms of printed language. She is, in a single figure, adult and child, representing both sides of the collaboration central to Taylor's project.

Yet Taylor chose to fictionalize Viehmann as Gammer Grethel—a choice he made, I argue, to suggest in a manner even more pronounced than the Grimms the simultaneous adult and childlike nature of this narrator. "Gammer" is an archaic designation meaning "mother," and Taylor's narrator therefore joins figures such as Mother Goose or Mother Bunch in the ranks of storytelling women. "Grethel," on the other hand, is a familiar German name that takes on a unique significance in the context of fairy tale culture, for Grethel—sometimes in English translations Grettel or Gretel—is the child who shoves a scheming witch into an oven to save her brother. By invoking "Hansel and Gretel," Taylor recalls a tale type that demonstrates powerfully the child's ability to hear, understand, and overthrow the adult plot—notably by incinerating the crone, often the storytelling figure, in the oven, a fire that echoes the hearth. Gammer Grethel, then, is a name that suggests both a tradition of adult and particularly female narrators and a fictional tradition of children who can overturn the authority of that narrator. If Viehmann is a storyteller who draws upon the advantages of both childlike oral culture and adult written culture, her fictional incarnation as Gammer Grethel intensifies and complicates this dual nature, demonstrating how children and adults can coexist and collaborate as storytellers and how children can become a subversive force in the relationship between storyteller and auditor.

Gammer Grethel's name may have recalled for Taylor the almost violent power the fictional child possesses. However, the variant of "Hansel and Gretel" that features Gretel's violent triumph over the witch was not included in an English translation of the Grimms' tales until 1884, in Margaret Hunt's *Grimms' Household Tales*.[28] However, Taylor did include stories in his collections that fictionalize the creative authority of the child—tales celebrating child characters who, like Taylor's "young friends," can act as collaborators, changing a story through listening and response. As active listeners, these child characters manipulate the circumstances of narration and plot. Perhaps the most striking example is Tom Thumb, a character who appears in a number of storytelling traditions, including French, German, Danish, Scots, and British; this story caught the imaginations of the Grimms, who single him out as a particularly persistent stock character of fairy and folk literature—"a remnant of ancient divine beliefs" who is "full of cunning and skill" (2.1.421, 426). Tom appears at first as an unlikely character to influence in any significant way the story around him. He is an impossibly exaggerated child, born "not much bigger than [a] thumb" and remaining the same size as he ages. In some versions of the story he is even smaller—the size of a grain of rice or a millet seed (Malarte-Feldman 969). However, Wilhelm notes that he "is able to turn every accident for which his small size is responsible into an advantage" (2.1.426). The narrator of the story similarly emphasizes Tom's cleverness despite (or perhaps because) of his size, contending that "he soon showed himself to be a clever little fellow, who always knew well what he was about"—a phrase suggesting Tom's awareness of his own narrative and his ability to manipulate plot ("Tom" 58).

Tom's cunning is due not simply to his small size but more importantly to how the invisibility that results from that size allows him to overhear the plots of the adults around him. Responding to what he hears, Tom transforms those plots to his favor. The definition of an active listener, Tom eavesdrops unobserved and, predicting events to come, literally scrambles into the ears of other characters, contributing his small voice to the story-in-progress. For example, early in the tale, Tom overhears his father talking to two strangers who have seen Tom steering his father's horse and cart by whispering into the animal's ear. The men offer to purchase Tom, hoping to turn a profit by making him the center of a traveling sideshow. The narrator notes that "Tom, hearing of the bargain they wanted to make, crept up his father's coat to his shoulder, and whispered in his ear, 'Take the money, father, and let them have me. I'll soon come back to you'" (60). When Tom's captors fall asleep that evening, Tom escapes and hides, ensuring his own safety and his father's profit. He is free for only a few moments before he repeats the trick. Just as he is falling asleep, he hears two men passing, and Tom becomes privy to their plan to rob a local parson (62). Tom responds by offering to help. Startled, the thieves search for the source of the diminutive voice: "'What noise was that?' said the thief, frightened, 'I am sure I heard some one speak.' They stood still listening, and Tom said, 'Take me with you, and I'll soon show you how to get the parson's money. . . . Look about on the ground,' answered he, 'and listen where the sound comes from'" (62). Tom offers to crawl through the parson's window bars. Once inside, he "call[s] out as loud as he could" questions to the robbers, waking the parson's wife (62). In both scenarios, Tom manages, by listening to the plots of adults and answering with his own narrative, to direct the tale and foil the desires of malevolent adults. Those who are accustomed to determining the course of events become, instead, listeners, hunting for the source of his small voice.

AUNT JUDY AND THE LITTLE ONES

Associations between children, oral culture, and innocence or primitivism appear and resurface throughout children's literature and culture: in Rousseau's prohibition of written material for children, in theories of language acquisition undergirded by recapitulation, in cultural connections between children and early storytelling societies. Jacqueline Rose claims such associations are the symptom of adults' need to conceive of "both the child and the world as knowable in a direct and unmediated way, a conception which places the innocence of the child and a primary state of language and/or culture in a close and mutually dependent relation" (9). Sue Walsh takes up Rose's position, renouncing what she sees as a habit among children's literature scholars themselves to associate childhood with orality and, in turn, orality with "direct or near direct access to an ostensible reality" (96).[29] However, I argue that Golden Age authors did not deploy the figure of the child as a creature of oral culture merely to preserve the imagined bonds between childhood, innocence, and the spoken word on the one hand and adulthood, deterioration, and the written word on the other. Instead, many authors recognized but self-consciously manipulated this set of associations in order to extend to the listening child an invitation to participate in literary culture, both spoken and written. Just as Child Study scholars recognized the possibility of children's creative agency despite the developmental narratives of language and expression fated by recapitulation, and just as those collecting and publishing fairy tales recognized young people's roles in the print culture of fairy tales while maintaining the link between childhood and romanticized oral culture, authors of texts for young people used the dynamics of storytelling in life and in books to create opportunities for children's creative agency. In other words, the fact that many Victorians were invested in cultural ties between childhood and oral culture—ties often rooted in adult desire—need not, and in fact did not, prevent them from simultaneously forwarding more agentic paradigms of child life.

The listening child as collaborator appears perhaps most clearly in the many successful story collections published throughout the nineteenth century. These included collections of familiar stories, such as John Harris's *Mother Bunch's Fairy Tales* (1802), as well as literary fairy tales, such as Hans Christian Andersen's stories, which were translated into English beginning in the 1830s. Publishers, perhaps inspired by the success of these collections, released other children's books that, like *Gammer Grethel*, were framed as narrated stories—collections that included not only fairy tales and folklore but also adventure stories, sea yarns, and domestic tales. In these collections, the storyteller-auditor relationships that are implied at the margins of the Grimms' *KHM* or Taylor's translation in prefaces and frontispieces are absorbed into the book, often fully introduced into the text as frame stories. The narrator-listener groups depicted in these frame stories are an organizing device and, at times, an entirely separate narrative, depicting the relationships between the characters telling the tales and those listening. In this section, I examine an array of these story collections published from the mid- to late nineteenth century, paying particular attention to how authors for children worked in collaboration with their young auditors as they composed their texts and how they reproduce those storyteller-auditor partnerships in the stories they include in their collections.

For example, in *Kit Bam's Adventures; Or, The Yarns of an Old Mariner* (1849), author Mary Cowden Clarke and Cruikshank suggest through illustration and story a complicated and collaborative relationship among storyteller, auditor, and text. Clarke organizes her collection with a frame story: Kit Bam narrates his fantastic adventures to the adolescent children of the Swallow family, who despite their approach to adulthood, are "never . . . too old to enjoy a good story" and who particularly relish the entertainments of their father's seafaring friend (15). However, in his frontispiece for the volume, Cruikshank illustrates not the storytelling depicted in the frame narrative, which is common in collections of domestic tales, but instead a scene from one of Kit's sea tales: a moment when the adventurer finds himself surrounded by the grateful family of a young mermaid he has rescued (Figure 1.3). Cruikshank's frontispiece includes all of the cues indicating a storytelling scene: a central, seated adult monopolizes the attention of a group of children, who sit on his knees or rest on the floor. But these listeners are not children but young mermaids; Cruikshank replaces the drawing room with a stone cavern and the hearth with a view of the open ocean. The frontispiece's composition, by reproducing but fantastically transforming a traditional storytelling scene, simultaneously suggests Kit Bam's narration to the Swallows and one of the narrated tales the young listeners imagine in partnership with their storyteller. The Swallow children so resemble the characters of the story as to be mistaken for them, and this near interchangeability is significant as part of a collection that relies so completely on those children for its creative energy. Kit's young listeners dictate his storytelling through persuasion and pointed questions. "For another yarn!" exclaims Fanny, bursting into Kit's cabin. "But, in the first place, I want you to tell me about the very first adventure you ever had. What was the first strange event that ever happened to you? And how old were you?" (37).[30] Cruikshank's image captures the influence of the Swallow children, implying that the boundaries between teller, listener, and tale are permeable and therefore that, if the teller is part of the tale (in this case quite literally, as Kit Bam is the hero of his stories), then the children are, as well. The Swallow children, in fact, suggest a threshold existence between generations; they "were childlike, but not childish, in taste and feeling" and "still loved a long twilight tale, and listened to it with all their old-young delight" (4).

The slippage between the domestic setting and a fantastic landscape represented in Cruikshank's frontispiece to *Kit Bam* is perhaps attributable to assumptions about the child's imagination, which many thought pictured a story vividly and even tactilely as it is narrated, making it alive and material. Many writers, illustrators, educators, and scholars throughout the nineteenth century frequently articulate the collaborative potential of storytelling in terms of the visual and suggest that listening to a narrated tale, especially when those listeners are children, is the same as "picturing," building images in the mind. Sully, for example, argues that words "have a powerful suggestive effect on children's imagination[s], calling up particularly vivid images of the objects named" and that to speak aloud the name of an object or a description of a scene may be to call forth in the mind of a child an image "which is in itself an approach to a complete sensuous realization of the thing" (55). However, it is also possible that the blurred boundary between home and away is a function of a masculine model of the child imagination. *Kit Bam* is a somewhat unusual in that, while written by a female author, its frame story features a male storyteller. Frances Browne wrote a similar collection of stories told by a fictional male adventurer—*Our Uncle the Traveller's Stories*,

1.3. George Cruikshank, frontispiece for *Kit Bam's Adventures; or, The Yarns of an Old Mariner*, by Mary Cowden Clarke. London: Grant and Griffith, 1849. Watkinson Library, Trinity College, Hartford, Connecticut.

published ten years after Clarke's, in 1859—and in 1902 Rudyard Kipling would publish his *Just So Stories*, a collection of tales narrated by an autobiographical paternal figure that transport the "Best Beloved" child listener to the landscapes of India and beyond. Collections such as *Kit Bam* suggest that the imaginative transportations made available to child listeners in male-narrated stories might function differently than their counterparts featuring female frame narrators. Despite the presence of both male and female listeners in Clarke's collection, one could argue

Kit's stories are designed to appeal to a boyish fancy, which possesses "a desire for travel, and ambition for honourable adventure," as Maltus Questell Holyoake writes (408). These tales invite child listeners to leave the "homely hearth" and explore the world beyond the drawing room.

However, Clarke's frame narrative resists a reading of Kit Bam's stories as a rehearsal of a purely masculine adventure narrative. The simultaneously domestic and fantastic scene of Kit surrounded by mermaid children depicted in Cruikshank's frontispiece suggests a narrative that references the adventure story but persistently gestures back toward the domestic scenes that dominate the genre of the narrated tale. Kit indeed was once the quintessential hero of an adventure tale; he "has seen a vast deal and passed through a great many adventures in his time," and in his youth he "had been faithfully employed in a course of active exertion, uncomplaining hardship, many perils, and ceaseless wandering" (11). However, in his later years, he has been invited to stay with the Swallow family, where he lives in a "snug cottage, with [a] cosey sitting-room and comfortable bedroom," which Kit claims is "as warm a berth as heart could desire" (14). While Kit's language here recalls his seafaring years, the proximity of "berth" and "heart" suggests "hearth," and indeed Kit's storytelling is described in language that incorporates both the maternal tradition of domestic storytelling and the masculine mode of adventure stories. Mr. Swallow notes Kit "will spin you a yarn as long as a ship's cable" (15). Knoepflmacher argues that many literary fairy tales by Victorian men instead betray an impulse to "recover a lost 'femininity,'" a desire to reclaim a childhood space that is gendered female and suggests a sense of arrested development (*Ventures* 11).[31] While Knoepflmacher does not discuss Clarke's collection, the sea tales narrated by Kit Bam are reabsorbed into the female tradition of nursery storytelling according to the pattern he describes. Clarke's collection, then, blurs the line between adult tellers, child listeners, and the stories they share, appropriating tropes of both masculine and feminine traditions of oral culture.

Feminine storytelling traditions in fact accommodate collaboration particularly well, and many authors and illustrators feature creative partnerships forged over domestic storytelling not only in paratexts, such as frontispieces and introductions, but also through the tales included in their collections. Rowe argues that female storytellers are often considered adept at gauging audience needs and transforming their tales accordingly. She offers the example of Scheherazade, who "told and remolded [her stories] in such a way as to meet the special needs of the listener"—in her case, the entertainment and appeasement of King Shahryar (60). Female storytellers usually inhabit spaces less exalted than the king's bedchamber, but as Knoepflmacher argues, everyday spaces such as the family home or kitchen also can foster collaboration. He points to the Gatty household, which generated numerous collaborative works for children, and he presents in particular *Six to Sixteen* (1876), written by Gatty's daughter Juliana—a young woman who would later gain renown as a children's author under her married name, Juliana Horatia Ewing—as an example of fictionalized domestic collaboration. Characters Margaret and Margery embark on a creative partnership to write their autobiographies, choosing to retreat to what Knoepflmacher calls an "exclusively feminine space" ("*Aunt*" 150). Margaret explains, "It is by this well-scrubbed table, in this kitchen, that our biographies are to be written. They cannot be penned under the noses of the boys" (8). Victorian collections of stories for children are often introduced by frame stories such as this: scenes that reference familiar props or spaces such as the kitchen table, the drawing-room fire, the small stool at the perfect height for a young listener. These cues signal to readers that the relationships represented in the volume will both operate according to intimate, familial relationships and provide the possibility for collaboration.

That collaboration was often intergenerational, relying on the input of child listeners. Molesworth, for instance, valued the sharp critique of a child audience. In "Story-Reading and Story-Writing" (1898), she insists that in writing for children "it is necessary to become, in some sense, a child again . . . to see through child-eyes; to hear with child-ears—above all, to feel with child-heart" while still retaining "one's own older experience, wider grasp, and greater wisdom" (774). Her somewhat sentimental contention that authors for children should reinhabit childhood, a practice that in an earlier essay she calls "clothing your own personality with theirs," has led many to contend that Molesworth's success results from clear recollections of her own girlhood, what Roger Lancelyn Green calls "the extremely vivid memory of her own child-mind" ("On the Art" 584, Green 53). However, Molesworth complicated the assumption that she could relive her childhood, noting in "On the Art of Writing Fiction for Children" (1893) that "remembrances of one's own childhood . . . it is well to recall and dwell much upon," but "as time goes on . . . we grow away from our child selves," which "cannot but to some extent be lost" (345–46). Living children, not recollections of lost childhood, were much more powerful influences on Molesworth's work, providing critique of her stories and models for her child characters. Helen Delves Walthall, Molesworth's niece and goddaughter, noted that "we, her own children, and her other nephews and nieces, appear in several" of Molesworth's tales (Green 44), and the author tested her stories by reading them aloud, first to her own children and later to her grandchildren. She nestled the manuscripts in a newspaper or between the covers of a book to hide the fact that the stories were her own, hoping her young listeners would provide candid critique. She recommended this practice in many interviews and essays, noting that "in writing for children the criticism, which you may be pretty sure will not be too flattering, of a group of intelligent boys and girls is *in*valuable" ("On the Art" 585). One of Molesworth's grandchildren remembers that "sometimes she was still in process of writing and would ask our advice, and quite often took our suggestions ... we felt quite proud to have our opinions asked and used" (Green 49). Molesworth indeed considered her young listeners' responses a vital part of her process; in a letter to Macmillan submitting *Tell Me a Story* for publication, she reassures the publisher that "*all* of [the stories] have in the first place been 'criticised' by my own children at home" (Cooper 183). In her storytelling practices, then, Molesworth encourages the collaboration that storytelling to a circle of children can inspire but, in fact, attempts to bypass the emotional biases familial relationships might introduce. Her partnership with the children listening to her stories is both professional practice and domestic ritual; in her biography of Molesworth, Jane Cooper calls it an amusement that also served a "utilitarian purpose" (182).

Molesworth fictionalizes her child partners in *Tell Me a Story*, published in 1875 under the pseudonym Ennis Graham. This text is a hybrid collaboration; in its very title, it pays tribute to the child listener as the incentive to narrative, and it represents as characters the real child auditors who contributed to its creation. Like many Victorian story collections for children, Molesworth's book first represents the collaborative nature of narration in its frontispiece, in this case an illustration by Walter Crane (Figure 1.4). Crane's image, which depicts a storytelling circle, complicates the assumedly passive role of listener. The child listeners surrounding a central storytelling figure—some sitting on the floor, some standing, a younger child clambering onto the storyteller's lap—recall the close circles of children around Cruikshank's elderly storyteller in his *German Popular Stories* frontispiece. Crane emphasizes the intimacy of this family group by enclosing them within a close border, framing them like a portrait. Viewing this picture before reading the stories, it would seem

'Naughty, *naughty* aunty,' he said ; 'Ted will shake you, and shake you, to make you good.'—P. 4.

1.4. Walter Crane, frontispiece for *Tell Me a Story*, by Ennis Graham (pseudonym for Mary Molesworth). London: Macmillan, 1886.

that the teller, like Cruikshank's, narrates from memory. She is only different in her youth and dress, both of which suggest that this woman is an example of images of the storytelling aunt, a younger incarnation of the elderly storytelling figure.[32]

However, Crane has chosen to illustrate a moment from the book's introduction when the child, not the storyteller, is the center of attention. This is not a circle of spellbound children but an active group of siblings. Young Ted, in this image, is angry with his aunt, who laments, "O children! dear children! . . . truly, truly, I don't know what stories to tell. You are such dreadfully wise people now-a-days—you have long ago left behind you what *I* used to think wonderful stories—'Cinderella,' and 'Beauty and the Beast,' and all the rest of them; and you have such piles of story books written for you by the cleverest men and women living! What could I tell you that you would care to hear?" (3). Yet the siblings are dissatisfied with their collection of children's books—they privilege the narrated tale over the printed book and, apparently, reject transcriptions of traditionally told tales—and Ted threatens to "shake" a story out of his aunt. Her expression in Crane's illustration reads as distress, but the narrative makes clear that this is a playful moment that reveals just how much the adult narrator depends on the creative contributions of her young charges. After Ted's tantrum, the aunt will only agree to an evening of storytelling if one of her listeners, Madge, will partner with her. "If I try to rub up some old stories for you," inquires the aunt, "don't you think you might help? You, Madge, dear, for instance . . . couldn't you tell them something of your own childish life even?" Madge responds with a reciprocal offer of collaboration, agreeing to contribute her own story if her aunt "wouldn't mind writing it down" (4–5). In this household, the roles of adult narrator and child auditor are not fixed—in fact, for a moment the aunt considers a carnivalesque future when "it will be the children telling stories to amuse the papas and mammas, and aunties . . . like the 'glorious revolution' in 'Lilliput Levée!'" (3)—and the storytelling moment is characterized as creative partnership, a collaboration requiring the participation of both storyteller and auditor to generate story.[33] Moreover, by presenting to readers a familiar domestic scene, this frontispiece models for readers of *Tell Me a Story* how they can replicate the dynamic intergenerational relationships represented inside the text.

While both Clarke's and Molesworth's collections, and in particular the frontispieces to their texts, represent creative play between adult teller, child listener, and narrated story, Gatty is an author who famously relied on children to inspire her storytelling both outside the text, in her habits of composition, and inside the text, in the narrative frames of her collections. Gatty was motivated by the presence of children, claiming that her "power of writing for children" depended on "being surrounded" by them (Maxwell 52). For example, Gatty composed *The Fairy Godmothers, and Other Tales* (1851), a series of literary fairy tales, as an entertainment for her then eight sons and daughters.[34] The first story, which gives the collection its title, obviously draws on fairy tale structures and plots. Christabel Maxwell notes that the tale follows "the well-known device of a godparent being invited to a child's christening and bestowing a gift which seemed highly incongruous to the other guests, but which later proved to be of inestimable value" (105). Perhaps it is the nature of this gift in Gatty's story, "the love of employment," that leads children's literature scholar F. J. Harvey Darton to lament Gatty's first collection as cloyingly didactic, claiming that the title characters "were not merely like the godmothers of traditional fairy-tales in being the vehicle of definite morals; they invented the morals beforehand, and stressed them, with a good deal of verbiage" (284). Gatty's fiction certainly bears some resemblance to earlier edifying literature for children; the dedication to *The Fairy Godmothers* indeed promises to illustrate for Gatty's children "some favourite and long cherished convictions." However, it was not the moral possibilities of the fairy tale that appealed to Gatty. As I will show, Gatty seemed to delight instead in the flexibility of the told tale—the way narrated stories can accommodate not only a lesson but also the opportunity for a young student to answer back and revise the story.[35]

Gatty's collections therefore often reconstruct the scene of storytelling. In her *Domestic Pictures and Tales* (1865)—a text that in its title both recalls the Grimms' *Kinder- und Hausmärchen* and registers the narrative possibilities of the verbal, textual, and visual—Gatty frequently stages scenes of narration, illustrating how such gatherings facilitate both the transmission and the transformation of story from one generation to the next. The most striking example is in the second chapter, which recounts "Robin the Conjurer," a story that the narrator—most likely Gatty herself, as the collection is largely autobiographical—remembers her father telling her when she was a girl. Gatty introduces the story both by describing the circumstances and habits of storytelling in Gatty's household and by suggesting in more abstract terms how the story exists, separate from her individual biography, as an oral tale across time and space and between generations of parents and children. It is a passage worth quoting at length. Gatty remembers

> a "dear darling story" of my own childhood, which I have never seen in print exactly as I heard it, although it is, no doubt, one of those old nursery traditions which have found their way into many countries from some unknown original source.
>
> Owing, I suppose, to frequent repetition, I remember the incidents of the tale quite clearly. . . . And so strongly does everything connected with a "dear darling story" fix itself on the childish mind,

that I can recall even the when and where of the relation of this favourite tale.

A low-roofed parlour in a parsonage house, in a lonely, flat, agricultural county, near an estuary of the sea. Its walls covered with books to the ceiling, wherever there was space; except where a grand pianoforte stretched along one side to the door. Time—evening. Persons present—a father, almost approaching middle-age, and two very little girls: no one else. And the father telling them, not for the first time, but as a specially-called-for repeated treat, a story,—*this* story—the story of "Robin the Conjurer," which I am now, in return, going to tell for the use of kind papas in time of need, as well as for the amusement of listening children. . . .

But I must tell it my own way. Everybody has a way of their own in story-telling, and it is only the incidents and a few points of description I profess to remember exactly. This is of no consequence, however. The story can be told in many ways, as grown-up tellers will discover. It can be made very short for very young listeners, as it is easily concentrated; or it can be left at length for those old enough to enjoy details. (15–17)

This description highlights the flexibility of told tales. This is a story passed down through many generations, nearly untraceable (although Gatty, perhaps inspired by the Grimms' detailed annotations, provides a footnote explaining that the story can be traced to "Grimm's 'Professor Know-All'" as well as to an older German ballad and an Italian variant). The story is stable and predictable, intertwined in the narrator's mind, through repetition, with particular scenes and circumstances; she can "recall even the when and where of the relation of this favourite tale." However, it is simultaneously amenable to infinite variation based on its narrator—for "everyone has a way of their own in story-telling"—and its audience—"very young listeners" or "those old enough to enjoy details." Although the narrator is committing the story to print, she has faith that the story will maintain this unique status as fixed and fluid, familiar and changeable, because, like the *German Popular Stories*, it will continue to be shared between generations. (It seems notable, then, that the room the narrator associates with the story is filled with books, stand-ins for the stability of print, except along one wall, which is home to the piano, a suggesting the flexibility of sound.) In Gatty's text, as in Taylor's translation of the *Kinder- und Hausmärchen*, it is a circle of children that demands the moment of narration, "a specially-called-for repeated treat," and ensures the continued life of the narrated story—its ability to nimbly respond to the needs of the audience.

Domestic Pictures and Tales stages the *potential* for collaboration in the storytelling moment; however, the listening children still appear as passive auditors, subject to the creative authority of an adult teller. The framed tales progress largely uninterrupted, and the image of the circle of listeners fades as the plot gains momentum. However, as Marah Gubar has argued, Golden Age texts frequently "explore strategies for facilitating noncoercive cooperation between adults and children, between storytellers and story receivers." Children's literature that depicts storytelling scenes, Gubar argues, often makes clear that "the prescriptive power that adult scripts wield over children is mitigated by the force of revision, a mode of active appropriation that . . . is available to adults and children alike" ("Revising" 43). As they rehearse scenes of narration and, more often than not, moral instruction, these texts also lay bare the ways that young people can resist the seduction of the adult storyteller and, in fact, take over as storytellers themselves. Taking as a case study Juliana Ewing's *The Brownies* (1865), Gubar reviews a number of ways storytelling scenes introduce the possibility of joint meaning-making, pointing out in particular the possibilities of interruption, repetition, revision, and wordplay. Importantly, Gubar makes clear that revising our idea of storytelling—emphasizing its collaborative potential of narrated tales over their prescriptive influence on young listeners—also revises potent models of adult-child relationships. While, after Rose's *The Case of Peter Pan*, the adult storyteller is often assumed to be a suspicious figure, attempting to seduce child listeners with potentially malicious intent, collaborative storytelling scenarios emphasize not only the child's ability to take in the adult but also the potential pleasure of flirtation for both adult and child.

In this way, Ewing takes after her mother, because in her famous collection *Aunt Judy's Tales* (1859) Gatty herself provides a portrait of how the potential for collaboration suggested by the circle gathered around the fire, represented in her earlier tales, can be realized in the telling of narrated tales—a genre that, because it is spoken, can be spontaneously transformed in collaboration with the young listeners, who are particularly adept at editing a story-in-progress through interruption and response. The stories in *Aunt Judy's Tales* depict a group of children, a crew of brothers and sisters identified as Numbers 1 through 9, who, as Maxwell notes, were "endlessly busy and had within call a number of adults highly talented and willing to co-operate" (112). In *Aunt Judy's Tales*, the "highly talented" adult is Aunt Judy herself, a character based in fact on Gatty's daughter Juliana, who concocts a series of stories to keep the children busy. While Gatty certainly sentimentalizes the playful relationships between adults and children, and while she capitalizes on cultural connections between children and oral culture, she goes to great lengths to represent how storytelling enables "co-operation" between adults and children in big and small ways. Gatty's *Aunt Judy's Tales*, then, is a hybrid collaboration, recognizing the intergenerational collaborations so important to the real children in her household through fictionalized children and storytellers.

For example, the story of "The Little Victims," the first included in *Aunt Judy's Tales*, represents how an adult storyteller interacts with her young audience during narration, revising the tale in response to her auditors' creative contributions. Aunt Judy tailors the characters, setting, and events of the story to reflect the experiences and opinions of her young listeners. The children gathered to listen are "restive," having endured "one of those unlucky days which now and then will occur in families, in which everything seemed to be perverse and go askew" (3). Trapped indoors by "a dark, cold, rainy day in November," the children pester their parents and the servants and "had, as they call it, nothing to do" (4). Judy accordingly tells the story of "eight little Victims, who were shut up in a large stone-building, where they were watched night and day by a set of huge grown-up keepers, who made them do whatever they chose" (5). This exaggeration of the children's circumstances immediately suggests that this is a tale meant to teach Nos. 1 through 9 a lesson about patience or useful employment; such a reading supports the suggestion that Gatty is part of the didactic school of children's literature and the statement, within the fictive world of the story, that Aunt Judy is always ready with a "curious" tale that tempers "drollery and amusement" with "some off scraps of information, or bits of good advice" (1–2).

However, Gatty tempers the didacticism of the tale by documenting the reactions of the "little ones" to Judy's narration; the listening children never completely disappear but, rather, are always present, responding to the story in a manner that may or may not align with the teller's intentions. The children transform the tale into a series of scenes they can picture in their minds and, notably, into a narrative sympathetic to their point of view. They begin this transformation with a seemingly innocent request, on the part of No. 7, for a definition:

"Was the large stone building [where the Little Victims were kept] a prison, Aunt Judy?" inquired No. 7.

"That depends on your idea of a prison," answered Aunt Judy. "What do you suppose a prison is?"

"Oh, a great big place with walls all around, where people are locked up, and can't go in and out as they choose."

"Very well. Then I think you may be allowed to call the place in which the little Victims were kept a prison, for it certainly was a great big place with walls all around, and they were locked up at night, and not allowed to go in and out as they chose."

"Poor things," murmured No. 8. (5–6)

Confronted with a potential teaching moment—an opportunity to suggest a more accurate word or to provide her own, "correct" definition of a prison—Judy instead considers how her story "depends" on the responses of her listeners and, in particular, on the answer to the question she poses to No. 7: "What do *you* suppose a prison is?" No. 7 not only suggests this very particular word, prison, to describe the circumstances of the characters that so closely resemble himself and his siblings; he also provides his own definition for that term, which is comprised of concrete details about the image of a prison that No. 7 has formed in his mind—"a great big place with walls all around, where people are locked up, and can't go in and out as they choose." His definition rejects any suggestion of punishment or culpability. Those inside this prison did not behave, and are not behaving, in any way that calls for discipline; in fact, the inmates are pitiable, "Poor things." Gatty stages this moment in a manner that demonstrates how child listeners can challenge and, eventually, achieve a compromise with the storyteller, even on the level of the individual word. This story recalls the active listeners described by Child Study scholars such as Sully and Tracy, powerful agents that can transform the language they use and the words adults use around them. If Aunt Judy began her story to teach the children a lesson—to reprimand them, for example, for idleness on a dreary day, or for ingratitude—the listening children exert their own agency as listeners to ensure that their fictional counterparts remain blameless.

No. 7's brief interruption at the start of the tale is the first of a series of similar moments throughout "The Little Victims" when the listening children disrupt the narrative, in an increasingly bold manner, with questions, comments, and protests that alter both the story and the storyteller's purpose and strategy. For example, when Aunt Judy has described the Little Victims' ingratitude for their soft beds and wholesome meals, and as she prepares to describe their dreadful reluctance to wash their hands, No. 6 forcibly interrupts. "'Oh, Aunt Judy! . . . you need not tell any more! I know you mean *us* by the Little Victims! But you don't think we really *mean* to be ungrateful?'" (20). No. 6 has discerned Judy's strategy and demands that she reconsider the fundamental premise of her tale. Judy judiciously reflects and responds to No. 6's protest. First, she mitigates the harsh lesson that had, initially, inspired her story; she insists to No. 6, "you—oh! I beg pardon, I mean the *little Victims*—were not really ungrateful, but only thoughtless" (22). No. 6's intrusion into the narrative reminds her that "it [is] not well to magnify childish faults into too great importance," and she therefore reassures her listeners that the lesson she is trying to impart in fact "never ends, even for grown-up people" (21). As the first story in *Aunt Judy's Tales*, "The Little Victims" sets a precedent regarding the nature of storyteller-auditor relationships. In story collections such as Gatty's, listeners initially appear powerless as receivers, rather than crafters, of story; however, Judy's reactions to her audience demonstrate how listeners should, in fact, be framed as collaborators, creating a tale in partnership with the narrator. Judy's listeners call attention to the individual elements of the story—such as setting, word choice, and theme—and, through active listening and interruption, encourage her to revise spontaneously, assuring that the story remains responsive to the needs of this particular audience.

This new collaborative dynamic is particularly significant in the storytelling scenarios represented in children's literature because it complicates the assumed roles of authority between adult storyteller and child listener. Judy's deferral to her listeners transforms the hierarchy of storytelling. In fact, there are many moments in *Aunt Judy's Tales* when the children's influence cannot be accommodated by response and interruption, the creative tools available to listeners, and is expressed instead through moments when Nos. 1 through 9 imagine themselves as storytellers, equal or even superior to Judy herself. At the end of "The Little Victims," for example, No. 7 tells his mother, "When I am old enough . . . I think I shall put Aunt Judy in a story. Don't you think she would make a capital Ogre's wife, like the one in 'Jack and the Bean-Stalk,' who told Jack how to behave, and gave him good advice?" (25). No. 7, the first to protest Judy's decision to discipline her young charges by fictionalizing them as the Little Victims, ends the tale by transcribing Judy into a fairy tale, picturing her as a classic character who assists the young Jack in defeating the enormous giant. Judy's advice is equated with that of a fairy tale character whose counsel enables the small's triumph over the great.

Aunt Judy's Tales presents a similar reversal, both textually and graphically, in "Cook Stories," the third story in the collection, which depicts the children at play in their nursery, adorned in "bits of rubbishy finery on their heads and round their shoulders, to imitate caps and scarfs"—garments that, while meant to imitate snobbish ladies, could easily be mistaken for the costume of an elderly storyteller (47). They have put on these disguises, in fact, to become storytellers of a different sort; they are pretending to be elite women swapping rumors and complaints about their kitchen staff while Judy, busy in the nursery wardrobe, eavesdrops, unexpectedly finding herself to be a listener instead of a narrator.[36] The children's newfound authority as narrators and Judy's displacement to listener is registered graphically in Clara S. Lane's illustration for the story. Lane portrays one of the older girls as narrator; she is the center of attention, seated in the foreground, while Judy lurks, listening, in the background. The exchange of roles becomes even clearer when this image is placed alongside Lane's frontispiece for the collection (Figures 1.5 and 1.6). Lane has chosen, for both the frontispiece to *Aunt Judy's Tales* and for the illustration of "Cook Stories," to represent the storytelling circle, and the arrangement of the figures is nearly identical in the two images. Both include a group of listening children clustered on the left side of the image. The listeners are, in both images, focused on narrating figure on the right, who sits in a slope-backed chair. Both illustrations feature a solitary figure in the background, standing apart from the scene but, as suggested by the slight tilt of the gaze, listening to the story. The fundamental difference between the images is the identity of the storyteller. In the illustration for "Cook Stories," a child narrates, while in the frontispiece it is Judy who has captured the attention of her listeners. These images, in their near perfect correspondence, suggest the interchangeability of adult storyteller and child auditor; both can narrate with authority, and both can, instead, contribute as listeners. Like Cruikshank's frontispiece for *Kit Bam's Adventures*—in which the listening children blend subtly into the characters of Kit's tale, suggesting their contribution to the details of the story being told to them—Lane's images for *Aunt Judy's Tales* suggest the intimate relationship between adult and child, storyteller and auditor, that is central to Gatty's representation of narration.

1.5. Clara S. Lane, frontispiece for *Aunt Judy's Tales* by Margaret Gatty. New York: Robert Carter and Brothers, 1859. Courtesy, American Antiquarian Society.

Storyteller-auditor collaboration has interesting consequences: all present at the moment of narration in Gatty's works—tellers and listeners, adults and children—are potential contributors. Gatty's perspective is, perhaps, not unusual in the nineteenth century. As I argue above, Rousseau, in *Émile*, presents a model in which children, whom Rousseau imagined as particularly adept at manipulating the nontextual world, collaborate with adults to reveal the origins of language, and the Grimms, in the paratextual materials that introduce the *KHM*, represent a symbiotic relationship between tellers and listeners, mediated by the

1.6. Clara S. Lane, illustration for "Cook Stories" in *Aunt Judy's Tales* by Margaret Gatty. New York: Robert Carter and Brothers, 1859. Courtesy, American Antiquarian Society.

always-changeable oral tale. Moreover, Gatty was likely invested in the idea of intergenerational collaboration for more personal reasons. She was part of a family skilled in collaborating—as storytellers and listeners, as writers and readers, as journalists and editors—to produce literature for both children and adults. As a young woman in 1828, Gatty and her sister, Horatia Scott, initiated the Black Bag Society, a small group of literary and social notables who, throughout the year, composed short works of domestic fiction and contributed them in a black velvet bag, which was opened over the Christmas holidays for a celebratory reading.[37] While the society accommodated "Honorary members," who were permitted to listen without contributing—real life equivalents of the eavesdropping figure in Lane's illustrations to *Aunt Judy's Tales*—most of those gathered around the Black Bag during the annual reading were "Efficient Members," who enjoyed the literary entertainment only if they had contributed to its contents (Maxwell 48–49). The methods of collective composition and narration practiced by the Black Bag Society were important to Gatty, who fictionalized the society in the story "The Black Bag" in *Aunt Judy's Letters* (1862), the sequel to *Aunt Judy's Tales*. This story depicts a community of storytelling in which all listeners are truly contributors, and the story includes, at the center of that community, an object that represents multiple contributors across generations: the bag itself. The narrator of "The Black Bag" notes that "there was an attraction in the very fact of [the bag's] having survived to serve, under the same name, and for the same purpose, children's children. . . . It served to make the old bag venerable, and perhaps rather mysterious, in their eyes" (140).[38]

Gatty represents the collaborative relationship between storyteller and auditor and maintains the dynamic nature of the oral tale in *Aunt Judy's Letters* even though, as the title indicates, the collection purports to be a record of the *written* correspondence between Judy and the children. Judy gathers, from notes the children send her, the problems they face and responds with stories that address their particular circumstances. Although mediated through the post, Judy's stories adapt to her audience, as she managed to do spontaneously in *Aunt Judy's Tales*. Moreover, each story is sent in a sealed envelope, and the opener is provided with guidelines for narration. The first story that arrives is so sealed and labeled with a note: "For No. 8," it reads, "But not to be opened till the evening, and then to be read by No. 1" (8). The readings that ensue each time a letter from Aunt Judy arrives allow the children to interrupt and debate the story, just as they did when Judy was present and narrating. Judy's letters, then, are not only written stories meant to be enacted orally but also models for how a printed text, when read to children, can reinhabit the character of a narrated tale: its flexibility, for example, and its affective possibility.

The most significant work of intergenerational collaboration in Gatty's biography, however, is surely *Aunt Judy's Magazine* (1866–1885), which Knoepflmacher dubs "a journal that openly proclaimed its identity as a Gatty family enterprise" ("*Aunt*" 152). Susan Drain has written on the familial collaboration that produced this magazine, which included the collective efforts of not only Gatty and her children but also, among others, Gatty's husband, Alfred Gatty, and Juliana's eventual spouse, Alexander Ewing. In recording the various contributors to the magazine, and in tracing its development through the generations of Gatty's family, Drain mentions many elements of the publication that draw upon the connection between the Aunt Judy figure and the oral tradition. These regular features attempt to recreate, in the homes of its readers, the intergenerational relationships that can be built through the interactivity of storytelling. Drain writes that the "example of family collaboration, described in *Aunt Judy's Tales* and *Letters*, was reinforced by the editor in such pieces as 'Nights at the Round-table,'—an occasional feature which presented stories within a family network of teller and listeners.... The allusion to King Arthur and the equality accorded his knights at their round table underlines the idea that all children were equally welcome to participate, according to their abilities, in the family activities" (14). *Aunt Judy's Magazine* also regularly featured "Nursery Nonsense," detailed descriptions of fictional scenes meant "to be read to the *very* little ones ... and also to give the young artists of a family an opening for the exercise of their talent" (Drain 11).[39]

This feature continued to build upon the collaborative circle of storyteller-auditors and encouraged *Aunt Judy*'s readers to collaborate as artists and performers. Others function in similar ways; Gatty included yearly Christmas pantomimes and plays, which called for actors, set designers, and costumers, and Caroline Sumpter has demonstrated that the magazine's correspondence columns offered a forum for both readers' words of praise and their criticisms, revealing "a persistent interest among readers in the power relationships within the periodical," as well as encouragement for correspondents "who were interested in developing their writing skills" (62–63). For Gatty, the tradition of storytelling and the intergenerational partnerships it engenders were writ large in the figure of Aunt Judy, a name that began as a playful title for her daughter but circulated among wider and wider audiences through Gatty's stories and her magazines, eventually representing an "honorary aunt" for all of her readers.

CONCLUSION

The careful calculations of Child Study scholars, the storytelling impulse of Edgar Taylor, Gatty's representations of storytelling scenes: they all seek, in different ways, to reconnect with a moment when intimate and face-to-face discourse between generations, between adults and children, was possible. They evoke nostalgia for a moment when language was spontaneous, adaptable, and rooted in the intimate relationship between speaker and listener. The desire to create an active (or even interactive) conversation between generations—to somehow reinhabit the "living present" of the spoken word, even if that experience is mediated by the printed text of fairy tales or story collections or the catalogued vocabularies of children's secret languages—is at the heart of texts as disparate as Chrisman's research and Gatty's and Taylor's translation.

That desire is fraught and complicated, resting on a series of conflicts and tensions. First, these writers and artists struggle to communicate the intergenerational possibilities of the *spoken* word through *printed* text, and it is perhaps for this reason that so many authors for children not only stage scenes of storytelling but also feel compelled to justify the value of narrated tales—a genre that, perhaps, seems quaint or old-fashioned—in an era that witnessed such as explosion of printed texts for children. The narrating grandmother in "Grandmamma's Throat," included in Gatty's *Aunt Judy's Letters*, responds to a group of children clamoring for a story by musing, "I almost wonder why you want me to tell you a story, when you have such a number of nice books to read" (115)—an image that echoes the "piles of story books written for you by the cleverest men and women living" that the auntie in Molesworth's *Tell me a Story* references. And Molesworth includes a similar moment in her later collection, *An Enchanted Garden* (1892). The two child protagonists in the collection's frame story, brother and sister Rafe and Alix, find that they "could not get any one to tell them any more stories!" Molesworth's text tries to articulate why these children are led on a search for a storyteller, in particular "someone old enough to remember the beginnings" of all told tales, despite their extensive library of children's books. "They had read all their books through," the narrator explains, "over and over again, and besides, books aren't *quite* as nice as 'told' stories. At least not when they have to be shared by two." The separate readers "never managed to keep quite together" (10, 3). Printed texts generate a sort of literary disharmony that the spoken word, a medium of partnership, holds the promise to remedy. Rafe and Alix—like Thackeray's young friend Edith Story—prefer the told tale.

Most importantly, however, the collaborative possibilities of spoken tales requires these storytellers—and, in fact, contemporary scholars—to adopt a complex and perhaps contradictory position on the relationships among language, children, the stories we tell the young, and the ways children participate in their own literary culture. The literary and extraliterary collaborations I describe in this chapter are founded in conceptions of childhood as innocent of language, rooted in Romantic models of child-as-origin. However, the theories and stories that these intergenerational partnerships generate understand children instead as savvy storytellers, creative wordsmiths, and powerful forces in the stories told and written for them. Scholars such as Sully and Taine, and authors such as Molesworth and Gatty, recognized that Romantic models of childhood, while seductive, could not accommodate the imaginative agency of children they found both inside and outside children's literature. In response, they transformed those accepted paradigms into constructs of childhood that make room for the child who sees a tell-wind rather than a weathervane, or the young listener who imagines himself as David slaying Goliath, that giant of stories.

CHAPTER TWO

Family Dynamics
The Strange Case of Robert Louis Stevenson and Lloyd Osbourne

"Were you never taught your catechism? . . . Don't you know there's such a thing as an author?" Captain Smollett, commander of the *Hispaniola* in *Treasure Island*, asks this of Long John Silver in Robert Louis Stevenson's "The Persons of the Tale" (1887).[1] This short essay, published in a collection called *Fables*, stages a conversation between the two characters "in an open place not far from the story" (183). The two "puppets," as Stevenson calls them, have a pipe and debate which character the author esteems most and the nature of fiction until Smollett shouts, "There's the ink-bottle opening. To quarters!" and the two hurry back into the narrative (187). As the captain's reference to the catechism suggests, Smollett and Silver assume their author is a divine figure. He is a creator—Silver explains to Smollett that "the Author made you, he made Long John, and he made Hands, and Pew, and George Merry"—and his favor or disfavor decides the fates of the pirates and sailors of *Treasure Island* (184). However, Stevenson does not see himself this way. In another fable titled "The Reader," Stevenson seems skeptical about a writer's influence over his text. The story opens as a disgruntled reader throws a volume to the floor in disgust. The spurned book addresses the man, advising him that he "need not buy" the author's message; the book then narrates a fable of its own (213). In "The Reader," the author certainly does not possess the godlike power Smollett and Silver describe; instead, a text's meaning is the product of literal conversation between reader and book.

Stevenson habitually reflects on the complex nature of authorship, addressing style, plot, character, and literary history as well as the professional side of the book trade, including the relationships among authors, publishers, and readers and how those ties influence the writer's profession.[2] In "Authors and Publishers" (1890), for example, he outlines the tangled and often predatory interconnections among the many actors in the literary marketplace, from writer to bookseller. "A Chapter on Dreams" (1887) and "My First Book" (1893) describe the genesis of two of Stevenson's most important works, *Strange Case of Dr. Jekyll and Mr. Hyde* and *Treasure Island*, and situate those texts amid a number of forces—familial, literary, financial, and even fantastic—that materially affected their content and publication. These essays do not always represent the social network of authorship in a positive light; his perspective on the author's role in the negotiations among publishers, printers, suppliers, booksellers, and readers is often cynical. However, he is deeply interested in and even hopeful about the relationships among authors: collaborators working on the same text. Biographer Claire Harman writes of "Stevenson's readiness, almost compulsion, to meld creatively with his closest friends," and in his lifetime he began (but did not always complete) collaborations with many writers and acquaintances, including W. E. Henley and Edmund Gosse, as well as with family members, including his cousin and wife. Stevenson's most sustained collaborative project was with his stepson, Samuel Lloyd Osbourne.[3] The pair coauthored three novels as adults, but when Osbourne was a young man the two collaborated on a number of projects, from the ephemeral—poetry collections printed on Osbourne's toy press—to the canonical—Stevenson's memorable adventure novel, *Treasure Island*.

What follows is a thorough exploration of Stevenson's collaborations with Osbourne and, briefly, a consideration of the afterlife of that partnership in Osbourne's later literary career. As discussed in the previous chapter, authors such as Mary Cowden Clarke and Margaret Gatty appropriated the form of narrated tales to represent and consider critically children as collaborative listeners—intergenerational partnerships influenced by paradigms of the child and language formulated in fields from folklore to Child Study. A different constellation of personal and cultural values underpins the Stevenson-Osbourne creative partnership; theirs is an extensive collaboration that reveals not only Stevenson's nuanced understanding of authorship but also how didactic technologies and genres designed to enforce adult authority over child consumers—here, the toy press and the adventure story—can encourage instead intergenerational amity and partnership. Through both privately printed and publicly circulated texts, Stevenson and Osbourne explored the web of relationships that surround and in fact comprise the figure of the writer:

between adult and child, between author and businessman, and among multiple contributors to a text. Authorship emerges in these documents as a social act among multiple generations and personae, familial, literary, and psychological. Stevenson and Osbourne's partnership provides a rich and sustained example of hybrid collaboration; it is at once real, played out in moments of face-to-face creativity and composition, and fictive, infused with popular discourses of childhood and authorship. Moreover, tracing this collaboration from Osbourne's childhood ventures with his stepfather, through the pair's coauthorship as adults, and into Osbourne's maturity, this chapter illuminates how the child's growth and eventual entrance into adulthood transforms—sometimes limits, sometimes nuances, always changes—the practice of multiple authorship.

THE SMALLNESS OF THE PAGE AND OF THE PRINTER

The collaboration between Stevenson and Osbourne began over small press printing, a fad among boys in the nineteenth century and particularly in the United States, where Osbourne was born and spent much of his childhood. Scaled-down models of professional printing presses were produced as early as the beginning of the sixteenth century, and amateur printing on small presses was a hobby among the fashionable and wealthy by the mid-1700s.[4] However, it was not until the nineteenth century that small presses were mass-produced and marketed to a wider public (Moran 228). In 1834, the well-known London-based engineering company, Holtzappfel & Co., was one of the first firms to release a small press that was portable, affordable, and easy to use, and other firms in England and the United States soon followed. Samuel Lowe of Philadelphia introduced portable presses in the 1850s, and Boston's Woods and Company brought out the Novelty, a small press used largely among tradesmen, in the late 1860s. Across the Atlantic, Jabez Francis of Essex produced a press called the Everybody's, and a scaled-down iron hand press called the Albion was displayed at the International Exhibition of 1862 in London (Moran 233–38, Harris 15–16).

These presses were designed for a number of uses, from publishing family periodicals to printing labels for medicine bottles. All of these practices, however, allowed press owners to opt out of the social networks that surround publication. As Will Ransom notes, private presses promise "complete personal freedom in thought and expression and exemption from exterior influence or compulsion" and are used by "craftsmen, authors and artists, prophets and dilettantes," who, breaking free from the demands or even censorship of the publisher, can determine not only what to print (anything from private poetry to subversive propaganda) but also how it appears on the page (175, 177). This artistic freedom was matched by a degree of financial liberty, because small presses—which could fit unobtrusively on a tabletop, in a parlor, or behind the counter at a small business or workshop—were advertised as a means to avoid the delay and expense of sending small jobs, such as labels and advertisements, to the printing office.[5] Retailers of small presses capitalized upon the sense of artistic and financial independence fostered by the small press with slogans emphasizing autonomy. "Every man his own printer!" exclaims an advertisement for the Lowe's conical press (Hart 4).

The small size of the machines and their potential for intellectual entertainment during leisure hours were a natural fit for a younger audience, and soon many of the small presses used by adults in offices and for private publication were also marketed to boys.[6] While throughout the nineteenth century, children were increasingly considered specialized consumers, the small press was a product that united adults and children as a dual customer base that manufacturers often addressed within a single advertisement. For example, the Kelsey company, one of the most successful US marketers of small presses, promised in one advertisement, "Business men save expense and increase business by doing their own printing and advertising. For Boys delightful *money-making amusement*'" (Mosley 9). These presses assumed a particular mode of masculinity, reinforcing constructions of boyhood as adventurous and ambitious, ready to explore the world outside the home. In the latter half of the nineteenth century, as Claudia Nelson notes, boys' literature and culture begins to present a secular mode of masculinity that "suggests that worldly success, not heavenly rest, is true happiness," stressing "such values as physical strength and courage, industry, common sense, and even good luck" (*Boys* 106). This new model of boyhood, Nelson argues, turns the imaginations of young men toward material rather than spiritual gain. Claims like Kelsey's illustrate how the press was marketed across generations as a printing technology through which adult and child could pursue financial independence—in their own ways, of course, as "amusement" for boys and "business" for men. The Boston firm Golding & Company represented this synthesis of the interests of adults and children graphically in a small card advertisement published in 1880. The card, produced on the press itself, was both an advertisement and a demonstration of how purchasers could use these presses for simple projects, such as small-scale advertising. On the left-hand side of the advertisement, which features an image of the press at its center, is an appeal to adults: *"EVERY MAN should have one to do his own printing and advertising."* On the right-hand side, an appeal to boys: *"EVERY BOY should have one for amusement, instruction, and to make money, by doing Society and Business Printing"* (Harris 18). Printed on the same surface, typographically parallel, the activities and social spheres of men and boys are addressed simultaneously. The small printing press, quite literally in this Golding advertisement and more generally in the culture of small press printing, existed *between* two generations.

The appeal of small presses among children grew rapidly and transformed how manufacturers marketed the machines. As Elizabeth Harris notes, by the mid-1870s boys' printing shops were flourishing, and younger press owners comprised the majority of the market in the small press (3, 8). Engineering companies, led by Kelsey, began to produce presses designed exclusively for boys, advertising them in popular periodicals such as *St. Nicholas Magazine* and *Youth's Companion* (Spencer 14). In 1874, for example, B. O. Woods & Company produced the Novelette—a children's press to complement their earlier model, the Novelty—that included a packing case that could become a stand for the press, "putting it at the right height for a very small printer" (Harris 17). An emphasis on the child-appropriate scale of the small press became common practice, and advertisers frequently featured children in marketing materials and instruction manuals demonstrating the ease of operating these machines. The lucrative potential of presses for boys remained one of their key selling points—Kelsey, for example, assured that a boy *"will never want for amusement or pocket money"* after securing a printing press and outfit (Harris 4)—but the moneymaking ventures the presses enabled were presented in a new light: as one of many educational benefits of small press printing. For instance, A. Neely Hall writes in *The Boy Craftsman* (1905), his handbook of "Practical and Profitable Ideas for a Boy's Leisure Hours," that activities such as printing for profit are important for young men. Through such pursuits, "the average boy learns to so appreciate the value of hard-earned money that it is pretty certain he will spend it only for something with which he can earn more or which will prove useful to him in his work and play" (iii). The money boys earn printing cards, programs, and other projects commissioned by friends, family, and neighbors teaches boys how to manage their finances and reinvest their earnings in new sets of type, type cases, and supplies.[7] Toy press printing, then, was a self-sustaining enterprise; its profits maintained its practice, and fathers and other authority figures reproduced its ideologies by giving presses to the next generation of amateurs.

These lessons in responsible spending, in fact, were part of a larger scheme of education in neatness, attention to detail, grammar, spelling, professionalism, and citizenship. For example, the small press prints of C. H. O. Daniel, later the provost of Worcester College in Oxford, included educational tasks; his first publications were exercises such as "an alphabetical index of the first words of each of the twenty-five verses of the General Epistle of Jude," a task Daniel "had been set [to] by [his] parents" (Madan 59). Such publications were submitted to a parent for inspection, a task that was probably difficult for the many boys, including Daniel, who struggled to attain the clean, straight lines of professional prints.[8] Perhaps it was the challenge of overcoming these difficulties that made the press appear useful for developing the enterprising character of a younger generation. A label on the box of the Baltimorean press manufactured by J. F. W. Dorman epitomizes these ambitions: "The moral mental and physical development of the boys, should be the study of all who love this country, and desire to perpetuate its institutions. In no way can this be more effectually aided than by the use of one of our presses" (Harris 5). The small press, like some nineteenth-century literature for children, is sold as a learning tool that unites education and entertainment, a fitting choice for young men because it familiarizes them with the behaviors that will be expected of them when they reach adulthood.

However, while scholars such as Harris document the growing trend in small press printing among boys, they do not note how radically the assumptions behind the marketing of the presses change when the customer base is primarily children. If the small press was marketed to adults as a means to resist the collaborative nature of printing, to sever social relationships and gain artistic or financial independence, it was imagined to do the opposite for young people. Small press ventures for boys were supposed to acculturate boys by *building* relationships, many between adults and children that followed familiar intergenerational models. For example, Harris notes that boys were usually given presses by their fathers (8), and therefore a boy's printing press was, from its purchase, part of a parent-child relationship, an object that could strengthen familial bonds or reinforce a father's authority. In more general terms, small press manufacturers assume a teacher-pupil or professional-apprentice relationship.

Boys learned, under a mentor's guidance, the negotiations that comprise a trade, and they were prepared to enter the adult social sphere as savvy businessmen. These adult-child relationships were at times collaborative. Some boys, for example, maintained friendly relationships with local printers and even received printing stock from their offices (Harris 9). Such partnerships, however, were perhaps rare—professional printers, Harris notes, were at times hostile to boy amateur printers—and more often relationships formed over the press presumed adult authority.[9] Children's presses were not objects that released young printers from the constraints and expectations of the social world but instead toys through which adults could exert influence and discipline.

Boys may have remained junior partners, if partners at all, in the relationships they formed through their press ventures with fathers, professional printers, and other adults, but the partnerships they formed with other children—relationships that the companies selling the presses may not have anticipated—were much more collaborative. The portable, low-cost press, as Truman J. Spencer notes, "gave amateur journalism the greatest impulse it has ever received," and soon communities of boys were using small presses to write, edit, and print household, schoolroom, and community periodicals (14). Amateur journalism among children existed before the small press became popular, but these efforts were often single, handwritten copies passed hand-to-hand or imperfect work produced on makeshift, homemade presses.[10] Machines like the Novelette and Albion enabled young journalists to generate multiple copies for circulation among family, friends, schoolmates, and other amateur printers, and this increased distribution generated a collaborative network of child editors, especially in the United States. "The exchanging of papers naturally led to correspondence and occasional visits between editors," writes Spencer. "From this grew an increasing desire for a more concrete medium for cooperation, interchange of ideas, forming friendships, and gaining experience in the conduct of organized bodies" (14). As early as 1857, American boys formed societies of amateur journalists and editors that encouraged competition, both friendly and vicious, as well as constructive criticism and a trade in ideas and practices; through the collaboration of small press owners, amateur periodicals grew increasingly sophisticated and well-produced.[11]

Amateur journalists not only forged collaborative relationships with one another but also worked to exclude adults from their juvenile enterprise. Youth, "unaided, undirected," Spencer writes, is the "essence" of amateur journalism (6). Boy printers were not entirely independent; amateur journalism, after all, was often called the "mimic press," a phrase that suggests its project is a reaction to adult forms, and many writers (including Thomas G. Harrison) extoll the practice as an "Educational Institution and School for Professional Journalism" (9). Amateur periodicals often include contributions from adult friends and family alongside pieces by school friends and siblings, and Charles Scribner Jr. advertised, organized, and hosted the first recorded assembly of child journalists in Boston—an adult publisher providing the resources and perhaps guidance for the boys' meeting. However, the collaborations that presses enabled between boys did change the landscape of small press printing, encouraging young men to revise and expand their press productions. Moreover, amateur journalism was one use of the small press in which boys were encouraged, even by adults, to seize authority. Warren J. Brodie, who was elected to the post of official editor of the National Amateur Press Association in 1899, published an influential editorial in that organization's newsletter calling for the reinstatement of young people as the leaders of the amateur journalism movement. "The place for the old-timer at conventions is 'way up on the back shelf," writes Brodie. "It is time that the 'old guard' took a back seat and remained in it" (Spencer 59). The replacement of the old guard with the new as the popularity of amateur journalism continued into the late nineteenth century was not without contention. Younger printers called first-generation amateur journalists "the fossils," and "the few remaining amateurs . . . of the first generation, fought hard against the ambition of the more youthful aspirants." However, Harrison claims that by 1878 older printers "were almost entirely driven to the wall" (56–57).

Osbourne received a small press when he was about twelve years old and living in California, sometime in late 1879 or early 1880. It was most likely a gift Stevenson purchased for his soon-to-be stepson to continue the boy's education while he traveled with his parents on their honeymoon (Hart 4).[12] Osbourne's press resembled the English-made Model, the press of choice among the boy printers registered in *The California Amateur Directory* at the end of the nineteenth century (Hart 5).[13] In the words of W. Dods Hogg, Osbourne's press was small enough to be "placed in an old-fashioned band-box and . . . lifted without great effort by one person." It could print a "sheet or card of only modest dimensions" by pulling a lever that lowered an inking plate (Hart 6). Osbourne's first print productions—composed near Sonoma, where he was studying at the Locust Grove School—were three editions of a periodical by S. L.

Osbourne and Co. called *The Surprise*. Osbourne calls *The Surprise* "a great National Newspaper" (Hart 7), and these first prints consist of a few pages of family and classroom news, written with the audacity of a schoolboy. Osbourne includes tidbits about a boy's social life—"Marble time has come," he reports authoritatively in his first edition. He also serializes a piece of fiction called "A Pirate Story," a sample of the "stories of wild adventure, Indian fights, and tales of the underworld" and what Spencer calls the "prevailing trend of writings for youth" that boys replicated in their own productions (Osbourne *Surprise*, Spencer 107). However, while *The Surprise* seems typical of amateur journalism, there is little evidence that Osbourne was collaborating with other young printers in the manner Spencer describes as so prevalent in late nineteenth-century America. In the first issue of his periodical, Osbourne reprints "a letter that the Editor has received from a little boy," Harry McGrew—whether with or without McGrew's permission or participation is unclear—but for the most part it appears that S. L. Osbourne and Company, at this early stage in Osbourne's ventures, was in fact S. L. Osbourne alone.

Despite this, early on Osbourne demonstrated an interest in using his press to form collaborative relationships. His isolation from the networks of amateur journalism is not surprising; organized boys' journalism largely did not reach the Pacific Coast until the mid-1880s, and Osbourne spent much of his youth out of school, traveling with his mother and new stepfather, primarily to Davos-Platz in Switzerland, to cure Stevenson's persistent lung ailments. Therefore, the boy initially tried to form creative partnerships with nearby adults, with limited success. His first issue of the *Surprise* proclaims, "We are happy to say that we have secured the services of J. D. Strong as our espeshial artist and agent in San Francisco," but it seems that Strong, Osbourne's brother-in-law, never followed through. Once established at the Belvedere Hotel in Davos with his family, Osbourne began a new periodical, the *Davos News*, including on the first page of the first issue, "I sincerely hope when any news has come please send it up to the office." However, submissions must not have been forthcoming, or else Osbourne lost interest, because the *Davos News* published only three issues. Osbourne later recalled that, while at the Belvedere, he took on a number of small printing jobs for pay, mostly programs and tickets for plays and concerts staged by the guests, the profits of which he hoped would help compensate for the expensive tutors required for his education. His initial patron, a "gentleman with a black beard," was a "formidable" man, "exacting about spelling" and likely to send Osbourne back to the small, frigid upper room that served as his printing office if the programs included any mistakes (Osbourne, Preface vii–viii). Osbourne's relationship with this gentleman was far from collaborative, demonstrating instead the authority an adult could exert over a child. When the black-bearded gentleman passed away, Osbourne worked briefly with his successor, a "frolicsome" lady who "had a disheartening way of saying 'Oh, bother' when the little boy appeared" (Osbourne, Preface xv). This lady had no respect, according to Osbourne, for his printing efforts and committed the cardinal sin of correcting the freshly printed copies with a pen before distributing them to guests.

While Osbourne formed a number of partnerships through the operations of his small press, then, most were either brief and relatively unsuccessful or not collaborations at all but instead relationships following familiar adult-child power dynamics. However, Osbourne found a dedicated collaborator in Stevenson. The emerging author followed his stepson's publishing venture "with absorbing interest," notes Osbourne in a preface to a later reprint of some of his press productions. "Then [Stevenson's] own ambitions awakened, and one day, with an affected humility that was most embarrassing, he called at the office, and submitted a manuscript called, 'Not I, and Other Poems,' which the firm of Osbourne and Co. gladly accepted on the spot" (Osbourne, Preface ix). Stevenson's contribution to his stepson's printing venture was accompanied by a letter:

> Mr. Sam, Dear Sir, if the enclosed should be found suitable for the pages of your esteemed periodical, you will oblige me by giving it an early insertion. My usual charges are at the rate of the price of half a doughnut per column; but to a gentleman of your singular penetration, and for the pleasure of appearing in a magazine which is, if I may so express myself, the cynosure of literary circles, I am content to offer you an abatement of 68:005 percent upon the terms above stated. (*Letters* 3.67)

Stevenson's tone, of course, is teasing. His exaggerated humility in addressing his stepson as "Mr. Sam, Dear Sir," his praise for Osbourne's schoolboy publication as "the cynosure of literary circles," and his request of pay by doughnuts demonstrate that the collaboration between the author and his stepson was, from its outset, playful. One of the press's primary functions was to encourage a loving familial relationship between

Osbourne and his new stepfather, and in addition to using the press to publish their literary efforts, Stevenson and Osbourne used it, in unconventional ways, as a toy. They staged toy theater productions—shows such as *Robin Hood* and *The Miller and His Men* that kindled Stevenson's memories of afternoons coloring puppets for his Skelt's toy theater—and Osbourne printed tickets of admission for their performances. They used the m-square pieces from the press as stand-ins for food and munitions in elaborate war games (Hart 23).[14] Henry James notes that Stevenson prized not only the imaginative side of boyhood but also the boy's "capacity for successful make-believe" (Hart 23), and Stevenson's participation in Osbourne's ventures illustrates that he understood play as he understood the act of reading a compelling story: as an activity that requires him to "take an active part in fancy" and to "join in it with all his heart" (Stevenson, "Gossip" 179, 180).

Stevenson's contribution also suggests the unique nature of the Osbourne-Stevenson collaboration. This partnership does not conform to the typical relationships associated with the small press, such as parent and child or professional and apprentice, and yet it is not entirely a game. Stevenson's letter demonstrates his willingness to be an earnest contributor to Osbourne's efforts, and, notably, the title poem "Not I" suggests his refusal of the singular "I" for the plural "we." The author possesses both the commitment to play and the experience in the publishing world to collaborate with Osbourne in building a proper press operation, and as a result the pair imagines together a nuanced author-publisher relationship. Stevenson provides copy while Osbourne provides the press, sets the prices for their productions, and coordinates circulation and sales. Their interactions replicate, in miniature, the fraught relationship between the author's creativity and the printer's practical and financial interests. At times, their partnership was mutually profitable. *Not I and Other Poems* "was an instantaneous hit, selling out an entire edition of fifty copies," remembers Osbourne. "The publisher was thrilled, and the author was equally jubilant . . . jingling his three francs of royalties with an air that made the little boy burst out laughing with delighted pride" (Preface ix–x). This success emboldened Osbourne, who "got the idea of becoming a publisher of more booklets by Stevenson, for from each new title he might net something like two or three dollars after giving the author just one free copy, and a suitable royalty of, say, seventy-five cents" (Hart 31). Osbourne's growing confidence hinted at the more contentious aspects of the author-printer relationship, which found expression in Stevenson's letters to friends. To Edmund Gosse, Stevenson writes: "I would send you the book, but I declare I'm ruined. I got a penny a cut and a halfpenny a set of verses from the flint-hearted publisher, and only one specimen copy, as I'm a sinner" (*Letters* 3.306).

While this tongue-in-cheek letter betrays the great fun Stevenson is having with his stepson, the mock-serious language he uses—his lament that he is "ruined," his reference to Osbourne as "the flint-hearted publisher"—epitomizes the significance of Stevenson's toy press collaborations with Osbourne. Stevenson's concerns, while trivialized through play, are real obstacles he encountered in the literary marketplace. In the early 1880s, Stevenson was both assisting Osbourne in his printing ventures and beginning his career as a writer, confronting the creative and financial obstacles of authorship, including the tensions between his craft and the social processes that communicate it. Stevenson may have been attracted to the toy press as a means to explore these issues lightheartedly. The toy press compresses, physically and temporally, the otherwise large and lengthy process of publication, creating a miniature model of the book trade. It allowed Stevenson to test varying levels of collaboration between author and publisher. His ventures with Osbourne reveal both Stevenson's conviction that these two agents must act in tandem and his doubts that an ideal partnership is possible, a complex position articulated in "Authors and Publishers." There, Stevenson recognizes the associations among author and publisher and a number of other social actors as collaborative, necessary, and mutually transformative. "The publishing trade does not stand alone," writes Stevenson. "It is one of three or four interdependent trades: the author, the publisher, the printer, the bookseller, the paper-maker, all hang together, they are fleas upon each other's backs" (261). This characterization of publishing as parasitic and unsympathetic is part of a bitter tone throughout the essay, which describes how one partner can determine the fate of the other; "the author comes first," notes Stevenson, but "is kept outside the ring," and "the bookseller comes last" and "has the heavy end of the stick" (261). These relationships are not mutually beneficial, writes Stevenson, due to the conflicting interests of those invested in the printing process. "The author will always continue to regard his venture by itself, the publisher must always continue to think of it as one of many; and the two points of view are hard to bring in focus" (263). The ideal relationship between publisher and printer, papermaker and bookseller, can only take place, Stevenson implies, if the interests of all coincide.

The poems Stevenson wrote for Osbourne, and in particular the poems in *Not I*, anticipate Stevenson's theories about what the relationship between author and printer could be if such agreement were possible. Some verses put the printer and author in conversation to demonstrate their seemingly inevitable conflict. In the second poem of *Not I*, for example, Stevenson writes:

> I own in disarray;
> As to the flowers of May
>   The frosts of Winter,
> To my poetic rage,
> The smallness of the page
>   And of the printer. (5)

Here, Stevenson playfully blames the restrictions of the materials of publication and the printer himself—"the smallness of the page / And of the printer"—as forces substantially inhibiting his creativity. They are naturally at odds, seasonal opposites. The final poem, however, is more optimistic:

> The pamphlet here presented
> Was planned and printed by
> A printer unindent-ed,[15]
> A bard whom all decry.
> The author and the printer,
> With various kinds of skill,
> Concocted it in Winter
> At Davos on the Hill.
> They burned the nightly ta-
> But now the work is ripe (per
> Observe the costly paper,
> Remark the perfect type! (7–8)

In this poem, the printer is a co-creator and conspirator. Stevenson acknowledges the materials of the printer's trade that often go unmentioned in a poem's text, the "costly paper" and "perfect type," as equipment necessary to transfer the imagination of the author to print. As Stevenson writes, it required "various kinds of skill," the artistic talent of the author and the dexterity of the printer, to produce *Not I*. This poem is one of four in the collection, three of which describe the author and printer as collaborators, symbiotic creative forces. Osbourne decorates the pamphlet's final page with an image of a pair of clasping hands, illustrating the collaboration described in the preceding verses. These poems are Stevenson's suggestions for perfecting the act of publication by integrating the interests of the author and the publisher. He makes evident the necessity of both by printing them on the same page, and the poems in *Not I* are evocative examples of dialogic collaboration—a mode of multiple authorship in which, as Andrea A. Lunsford and Lisa Ede explain, collaborators "generally value the creative tension inherent in multivoiced and multivalent ventures" (133). In rehearsing both the conflict among the actors who contribute to a text's publication and the merits of those partnerships, Stevenson allows the contradictions of authorship to exist within a completed text; moreover, he allows for Osbourne—a boy whose role in the creation of these poems is liable to be overlooked—to remain discernable in the text as printer and partner. In the verses included in *Not I and Other Poems*, then, Stevenson is careful to record the real conditions of this adult-child partnership.

The two relationships Stevenson and Osbourne formed during their press ventures, their bond as playfellows and their author-publisher partnership, were not discrete but intertwined, and the poetry collections they produced, due to this dynamic of the playful and the practical, are valuable to Stevenson studies. These ephemera, products of what Stevenson scholars have dubbed "the Davos Press," are usually read as witty but insignificant early work of a writer who, just a few years later, would gain renown as the author of *Treasure Island*.[16] By 1921, Osbourne notes, a product of the Davos Press could "occasionally be picked up at one of Sotheby's auctions," as they had "risen to the dignity of 'Davos booklets; Stevensonia; Excessively rare'" (Preface ix). Yet their significance exceeds their status as seeds of Stevenson's later work. They illustrate how Stevenson, with Osbourne, tried to unite the commercial and creative worlds—a project that would preoccupy him throughout his career—and anticipate how in the future he would portray the negotiations of authorship through a collaborative discourse of youth and age, of childlike imagination and adult professionalism.

MAPPING TREASURE ISLAND

Stevenson and Osbourne's printing ventures continued after *Not I* with two collections of *Moral Emblems,* short poems by Stevenson accompanied by his own woodcut illustrations, as well as a pamphlet for Margaret Stevenson's birthday, a collection of verses titled *The Graver and the Pen,* and an unfinished poem entitled *Robin and Ben.* When Osbourne printed *The Graver and the Pen* in 1882, he was fourteen years old, and the poems in the collection suggest the pressure his adolescence exerted on the pair's playful collaboration.[17] "The Disputatious Pines," for instance, seems to speak directly to the Stevenson-Osbourne partnership:

> The first pine to the second said:
> "My leaves are black, my branches red;
> I stand upon this moor of mine,
> A hoar, unconquerable pine."
>
> The second sniffed and answered: "Pooh,"
> "I am as good a pine as you."
>
> "Discourteous tree" the first replied,
> The tempest in my boughs had cried,
> The hunter slumbered in my shade,
> A hundred years ere you were made.
>
> The second smiled as he returned:
> "I shall be here when you are burned."
>
> So far dissention ruled the pair,
> Each turned on each a frowning air,
> When flickering from the bank anigh,
> A flight of martens met their eye.
> Sometimes their course they watched; and then
> They nodded off to sleep again. (lines 1–18)

It seems natural to read these lines as a portrait of the contentious elements of Stevenson and Osbourne's partnership. Stevenson appears as the "hoar, unconquerable pine," claiming ownership of the moor through age and experience. Osbourne, the younger specimen, responds with adolescent arrogance and bravado: "Pooh, / I am as good a pine as you." Its retort to the elder pine's claim of seniority—the smirking yet threatening remark, "I shall be here when you are burned"—resonates even after the trees' conflict is interrupted by a flock of birds and, moments later, slumber. If *Not I and Other Poems* represents the tensions of collaboration only to resolve them, this poem introduces an enmity between generations that is more fundamental and perhaps more difficult to overcome.

"The Disputatious Pines" illustrates how the Stevenson-Osbourne partnership became increasingly complex and how the pair used their joint productions to communicate those changes. "New standards were imperceptibly forming," writes Osbourne (Preface xvii). Reimagining Stevenson and Osbourne as trees acknowledges, at a slant, the younger partner's continual growth, the older partner's march toward death, and the reconfiguration of power dynamics embedded in these shifts in maturity. Osbourne was, inescapably, older. Their partnership remained a negotiation among experience, imagination, business, and play, but their later work reveals an awareness of how intergenerational rivalry that resulted from Osbourne's age and the demands of the professional world could infringe upon the game. In this section, I discuss the first widely published text generated by the Osbourne-Stevenson partnership, *Treasure Island*. I begin with an account of how the adventure story was constructed as a genre that elides strict categorizations of adult and child before turning to the creative partnership between Stevenson and Osbourne, examining how their collaboration continued through *Treasure Island*'s publication, expanding to include multiple familial and literary generations. Stevenson represents *Treasure Island* as a narrative both inspired by collaboration between stepfather and stepson and indebted to new partnerships with family and friends and previous generations of adult authors and child readers. This partnership is best understood, like all of Stevenson and Osbourne's creative ventures, as a hybrid collaboration—both a true partnership between living contributors and a fictive account of intergenerational collaboration. The composition narrative of *Treasure Island* both records Stevenson and Osbourne's cooperation and obscures the true nature of that partnership through familiar tropes and culturally freighted language of the childlike imagination and the professional author. In other words, the novel and the documents surrounding its composition—letters, essays, and reviews—reveal new and sometimes difficult dynamics of collaboration and the way this authorial practice intersected with pervasive assumptions about childhood.

Publishers and authors marketed the adventure story to both adults and children from its origins, and the genre emerged from literary traditions for both audiences. J. S. Bratton notes that writers of boys' stories turned to "a handful of adult novels which by the 1860s had come to be regarded as good books for boys" as fictional models for their own stories: Sir Walter Scott's Waverley novels, James Fenimore Cooper's *Last of the Mohicans*, and Daniel Defoe's *Robinson Crusoe*, for example (104). However, while scholars often cite these romances as the primary tradition shaping the adventure story, Nelson argues that the working-class penny dreadful, which "provided sex, violence, sensation, and escapism to an audience that by the 1860s was increasingly youthful," also influenced the genre (126).[18] Authors catered to the interests boys and men purportedly shared: new and exciting landscapes, daring characters, and plots that required plucky heroes to exhibit physical prowess. It is not surprising that many authors of boys' adventure stories—including Captain Frederick Marryat, Captain Mayne Reid, Charles Kingsley, and G. A. Henty—began their careers writing for adults. For example, R. M. Ballantyne, author of *The Coral Island*, began writing for children only when his publisher noticed the author's *Hudson Bay*, a text for adults about his adventures at remote Canadian trading posts, and suggested that the Ballantyne write a story for children (Sutherland 39).

Authors of children's adventure tales tempered the influence of the adult romance and sensation traditions with moral or didactic elements that recall the devices of early nineteenth-century children's literature. Bratton notes that authors transformed the plots and conventions of the romance into children's adventure stories by "narrowing [their] scope and interests" and by stating in a clear manner "the lessons to be learnt from the action of the tale" (110). Some of the most influential adventure stories are informed by the evangelical, pious tone of early children's literature or the encyclopedic, factual prose thought appropriate for young readers. Marryat, for example, incorporated frequent moral lessons into *The Settlers in Canada* (1844), the first tale he wrote explicitly for young readers. At the start of the tale, character Mrs. Campbell greets her family's sudden rise in fortune with just such a lesson, saying to her husband, "I have often felt that we could bear up against any adversity. I trust in God, that we may be as well able to support prosperity, by far the hardest task . . . of the two" (4). When, in the very next chapter, her husband laments the reversal of this good fortune, she replies with pious resignation. "It is hard, my dear husband, if we may use that term," she admits, "but, at the same time, it is the will of Heaven" (8). Ballantyne's *Coral Island* intersperses the adventures of three boys wrecked on a deserted island with instruction in natural history. When Jack, the oldest, spies "a tree of remarkably beautiful appearance," he swiftly declares it "the celebrated breadfruit tree" and lectures the younger boys, Ralph and Peterkin, on its merits. The breadfruit tree "affords capital gum," Jack notes, "which serves the natives for pitching their canoes; the bark of the young branches is made by them into cloth; and of the wood, which is durable and of a good colour, they build their houses" (52).[19] Uniting adventure and instruction, *Coral Island*, like many adventure stories, self-consciously addresses audiences of old and young, taking part in literary traditions for both adults and children. In fact, many nineteenth-century readers and reviewers (and critics today) categorize adventure stories written explicitly for children with those composed for an adult audience, such as *Last of the Mohicans* or H. Rider Haggard's *King Solomon's Mines*.[20]

Scholars of boys' adventure stories suggest a spectrum of historical, cultural, and ideological motives for the emergence and popularity of the genre. Most understand its success as an example of how, in the words of F. J. Harvey Darton, the "spatial expansion of the mind" and the "prosperous geographical destiny" that accompanied the sprawl of the British Empire influenced the shifting paradigms of children's literature (298–99). As Jeffrey Richards argues, adventure stories for boys were "steeped in every aspect of imperialism" and acted "not just as a mirror of the age but an active agency constructing and perpetuating a view of the world in which British imperialism was an integral part of the cultural and psychological formation of each new generation of readers" (3). Bradley Deane joins Richards in connecting adventure fiction to the shifting imperial project—a project that transformed, Richards notes, from "evangelicalism [and] the commercial and cultural imperialism" of midcentury to "the aggressive militarism" of the end of the century (5). Deane, in fact, argues that late century adventure fiction exhibits through its immature and often amoral adult male characters an "imperial play ethic," revealing that "imperialists found in enduring boyishness a natural and suitably anti-developmental model of identity"—a model that perfectly suited an "empire that had ceased to strive towards idealistic ends [and] no longer required its heroes to grow up" (690). Others locate the adventure story in broader Victorian conceptualizations of manhood important but not limited to imperialism. Guy Davidson, for example, characterizes the adventure story as part of the "response to the diversification and expansion of the literary marketplace in the 1880s" that resulted in "the revival of the romance." The romance, according to Davidson, was "a means of reinvigorating and re-masculinising a national literary culture regarded as having been rendered effete and effeminate by the excessive influence of realism" (60). Nelson makes a similar argument for the rise of the genre to popularity or even to a status of "high culture," noting that the trials of Oscar Wilde encouraged Victorians to restate their culture's masculinity at the fin-de-siècle (146). Adventure stories, these critics contend, mediate between a boy readership and the men that authors, publishers, parents, and teachers hope those boys will someday become: men who can rejuvenate a deteriorating society and rule an empire. The genre, then, demonstrates not only the united interests of man and boy in desert island tales but also the man's interest in the boy—the desire to use these tales to introduce boys into a code of mannered masculinity that unites generations as robust citizens of the empire.

The participation of young and old dominates not only the public perception of adventure tales but also their content and generic conventions. As Marah Gubar explains, the sea or pirate story "encourages boy readers to believe that a juvenile crewmate—however young and inexperienced he may be—can function as an invaluable collaborator in the important work of taming the unruly world outside England" (*Artful* 69). Moreover, the prefaces, dedications, and other paratextual materials that construct a dual readership for the genre reiterate these intergenerational relationships. Darton calls this the "deliberate fusion of father and son into one reader," the making of boys and men into "one class," an integration that he argues still has not dissolved (296, 294). Ballantyne prefaces *Coral Island* with a note from the fictional Ralph Rover, who insists that he presents his book "especially for boys" but concludes the preface by addressing "any boy or man" who may be holding the volume (5). In a similar manner, the narrator of *King Solomon's Mines*, Alan Quatermain, dedicates the tale to "all the big and little boys who read it" (Haggard 37). W. H. G. Kingston, promoting *Kingston's Magazine for Boys*, explains that he writes for all ages and classes, urging his readers "to get it into naval and military libraries, both for officers and men, at home and abroad—into institutes and village libraries" (Bratton 129). *Young Folks*, the periodical that published Stevenson's *Treasure Island* from October 1881 until January 1882, was published as *Old and Young* between July 1891 and September 1896, when it was rechristened as the still age-ambiguous *Folks at Home*. While the generations' investment in adventure tales and periodicals would differ—grown men may read with a nostalgia their younger counterparts do not—the adventure story persistently addressed an intergenerational readership.

The success of *Treasure Island* among child readers is debatable, but reviews of the novel's 1883 one-volume publication praise its cross-generational appeal.[21] *The Academy* notes that it "is calculated to fascinate the old boy as well as the young" (362), and the *Pall Mall Gazette*, in a review likely written by Andrew Lang, remarks that it is "a book for boys which can keep the hardened and elderly reviewers in a state of pleasing excitement and attention" (4). Henley praises *Treasure Island* in *The Saturday Review* as "a book for boys which will be delightful to all grown men who have the sentiment of treasure-hunting and are touched with the true spirit of the Spanish Main" (737–38). Stevenson encouraged this intergenerational reading of his novel; in the one-volume edition of the *Treasure Island*, he added two paratexts that were not part of the serialized novel, and both speak to the cross-generational appeal common in the adventure story. The first is a prefatory poem titled "To the Hesitating Purchaser":

> If sailor tales to sailor tunes,
> Storm and adventure, heat and cold,
> If schooners, islands, and maroons
> And Buccaneers and buried Gold,
> And all the old romance, retold
> Exactly in the ancient way,
> Can please, as me they pleased of old,
> The wiser youngsters of to-day:
>
> —So be it, and fall on! If not,
> If studious youth no longer crave,
> His ancient appetites forgot,
> Kingston, or Ballantyne the brave,
> Or Cooper of the wood and wave:
> So be it, also! And may I
> And all my pirates share the grave
> Where these and their creations lie! (2)

This poem appears to isolate rather than unite generations of readers, setting the adult author and his generation apart from the purportedly "wiser youngsters" and "studious youth" who may not delight in an ancient sea tale. However, the poem deploys a common argument for the cross-generational appeal of the adventure story. Stevenson represents a love of "Kingston, or Ballantyne the brave, / Or Cooper of the wood and wave" as a natural state of boyhood, their inherited "ancient appetites" an almost genetic desire. Uniting an appeal to young readers with an appeal to primitive literary tastes, Stevenson adopts the discourse of the romantic revival of the 1880s, a movement that valued the adventure story for its ability to fulfill man's primal needs, those elements of his nature connected with both his ancestry and his childlike spirit. Stevenson uses similar language in "A Gossip on Romance," published in 1882 between *Treasure Island*'s serialization and its book publication, in which he argues that the adventure tale or romance meets the most basic needs of the reader's humanity, satisfying his mind "like things to eat," and that it "is to the grown man what play is to the child," delighting both "the schoolboy and the sage" (179, 180, 175). As Davidson argues, the value of romances such as *Treasure Island*, according to Stevenson, "depends upon, and is articulated through, a construction of the male child as a locus of natural, spontaneous experience," and their success is achieved through the meeting of a reader and his impulses, both primitive and childlike, in the pages of fiction (63). If boys do not enjoy *Treasure Island*, they have forfeited their gendered inheritance, denying those appetites that connect them to their ancestors. "If this don't fetch the kids," Stevenson writes of *Treasure Island*, "why, they have gone rotten since my day" (*Letters* 3.224).

Stevenson is interested not only in the nature of this inherited tradition, shared between men and boys, but also in its reproduction. In the last lines of his prefatory poem, he describes one means of continuing the tradition. Even if the current generation rejects *Treasure Island*, the tale will "share the grave" of adventures past. It is just such hidden treasures, like hidden maps and documents in sensation fiction or gothic tales that turn up "in the secret drawer of an old ebony secretary," that act as the germ of further adventures, to be unearthed by future generations less effete in their literary tastes ("Chapter" 216). *Treasure Island* itself begins with a similar act of recovery, when Jim Hawkins and his adult companions, Doctor Livesey and Squire Trelawney, salvage Captain Flint's treasure map from the deceased Billy Bones's sea chest. Moreover, the title of this prefatory poem, "To the Hesitating Purchaser," suggests another, more concrete means to reproduce the intergenerational appeal of the adventure story: through the professional world of authorship, publication, and circulation. Familiar tropes and narratives of the adventure story are transmitted from author to author—from Kingston, Ballantyne, and Cooper to Stevenson—while, through the commodity culture of the marketplace, the appetite for them is passed along from reader to reader, from the adults who once enjoyed those authors to the boys of today. Stevenson unites the imaginative impulses of the adventure story, which join generations through a creative inheritance, with the genre's dependence on the commodification of the literary market: two distinct and, perhaps, incongruous understandings of the adventure tale.

The second paratext Stevenson added to the one-volume edition of *Treasure Island* is a dedication to Osbourne:

> To
> LLOYD OSBOURNE
> An American Gentleman
> in accordance with whose classic taste
> the following narrative has been designed
> it is now, in return for numerous delightful hours
> and with kindest wishes, dedicated
> by his affectionate friend
> THE AUTHOR

This dedication resituates the relationship between adult and child, author and reader, imagination and marketplace addressed in "To the Hesitating Purchaser" within the familial model of stepfather and stepson. Osbourne, fifteen years old at the 1883 publication of *Treasure Island*, is characterized here, with affection, not as a boy but as an adult, an "American gentleman" with "classic taste," and the time he spent with Stevenson is transformed into "numerous delightful hours," a phrase suggesting leisure time between equals. Stevenson and Osbourne's collaborative relationship, since their small press ventures, was both a friendship based on imaginative play and a partnership founded on the professional practices of authorship, and here it is represented in a manner that again complicates distinctions of age and generation. More importantly, however, this dedication is the first suggestion of how Stevenson expands upon the cross-generational potential of the adventure tale. While the genre, since its origins, was directed toward an intergenerational readership—adventure fiction, perhaps, was uniquely dedicated to the simultaneous address of old and young that U. C. Knoepflmacher and Mitzi Myers theorize as cross-writing—Stevenson's story is staged a *product* of an intergenerational collaboration. It is a narrative composed through the joint efforts of an adult and a real child. While the final line of the dedication announces Stevenson as author, that line mirrors Lloyd's name, also in capitals, seven lines above. Stevenson used the adventure tale to unite the creative strengths of adults and children both by creating a final text that holds intergenerational appeal and by incorporating multiple generations in the act of composition. In other words, Stevenson used the genre of the adventure story, already replete with potential for intergenerational relationships, to explore how adults and children can comprise not only one reader but also one author.

I will explore Stevenson's collaboration with his stepson over *Treasure Island* in more detail in a moment, but it is important first to note that Osbourne was not the author's sole interlocutor. While many reviewers praised the novel as evidence of Stevenson's original genius—a review in the *Graphic*, for example, insists that "there is no resemblance between Mr. Stevenson and any other boys' writer" (599)—Stevenson, in "My First Book," confesses the great debt he feels toward a series of other writers who, like Osbourne, influenced *Treasure Island*.[22] In a frequently quoted passage of the essay, Stevenson catalogues the ways his mapping of *Treasure Island* is indebted to the tradition of adventure fiction: "No doubt the parrot once belonged to Robinson Crusoe. No doubt the skeleton is conveyed from Poe.... The stockade, I am told, is from *Masterman Ready*. ... It is my debt to Washington Irving that exercises my conscience, and justly so, for I believe plagiarism was rarely carried farther" (280). Many read this passage as evidence of Stevenson's struggles with the norms of popular literature and his aspiration for high art. Glenda Norquay, for example, interprets this admission as Stevenson's recognition of "the commercial and intertextual context in which he operates"; he names his sources, "but at the same time lays claim to the uniqueness and originality necessary for the 'artist'" (67). Yet it is important to note the particular method of intertextuality Stevenson describes. He suggests that his novel is a pastiche, an accumulation of the landscapes, characters, and plots of his literary predecessors, and that his role as author, whether he fulfills it consciously or unconsciously, is to integrate his own tale into a narrative already articulated. A successful adventure story requires originality, but it also requires its author to encounter and manage previous literary generations in a process of composition that is, at its core, collaborative. Stevenson emphasizes that this is an act of creative negotiation, not merely allusion or imitation, by taking pains to stage in "My First Book" an encounter between himself and the authors who shape his work—a meeting expressed in tropes and metaphors drawn from the adventure story. "These useful authors had fulfilled the poet's saying," he writes, because "departing, they had left behind them 'Footprints in the sands of time; Footprints that perhaps another—' and I was the other!" (280). These lines are quoted from yet another source text: "A Psalm of Life" by Henry Wadsworth Longfellow, which employs themes of shipwrecks and footprints. Stevenson imagines himself occupying the same landscape as Defoe, Poe, Irving, and Marryat and encountering their footprints like Crusoe encounters Friday's. He discovers that he is not alone in this literary endeavor.[23]

Stevenson's figuration of his relationship to his literary ancestors through images of footprints and discovery recalls an earlier moment in "My First Book": a rhapsodic digression on the suggestive power of maps. Maps fire Stevenson's imagination:

> The names, the shapes of the woodlands, the courses of the roads and rivers, the prehistoric footsteps of man still distinctly traceable up hill and down dale ... here is an inexhaustible fund of interest for any man with eyes to see, or tuppenceworth of imagination to understand with. No child but must remember laying his head in the grass, staring into the infinitesimal forest, and seeing it grow populous with fairy armies. Somewhat in this way, as I pored upon my map of *Treasure Island*, the future characters of the book began to appear there visibly among imaginary woods; and their brown faces and bright weapons peeped out upon me from unexpected quarters ... on these few square inches of a flat projection. ("First" 279)

If the footprints of past authors represent Stevenson's negotiations with the literary tradition of the adventure story, the figures and footsteps on these maps document a different source of inspiration: a return to the active, adventurous imagination of childhood. This passage illustrates and expands on Stevenson's theories on the imagination forwarded in "Child's Play." In that essay, Stevenson identifies the physical play of children and their attachment to toys and "props" as evidence of a flaw in the young's powers of fancy, but he admires the child who, in possession of a more embodied imagination, "acts his parts." "That stage-wardrobe and scene-room that we call memory is so ill-provided" with firsthand experiences that the child cannot contain his imagination within the mind. Instead, he must "body out" his play, moving his limbs to imitate the characters of his fancy and using everyday objects to aid his make-believe; "he leaps, he runs, and sets the blood agog over all his body. And so his play breathes him; and he no sooner assumes a passion than he gives it vent" (177). The adult, on the other hand—whose fancies are "transformed and seen through theories and association as through coloured windows"—instead participates in an "intellectual form of play" that does not require physical activity (171, 177). Stevenson's love of maps, however, demonstrates how the child imagination is enabled and enriched by the influence of the adult's social world; the markings on the map are the raw materials for a childlike fancy, which can perceive the narratives these materials inspire. Fairy armies arise out of the map for the watching child like the soldiers and fleets of ships that populate the Land of Counterpane in Stevenson's *A Child's Garden of Verses* (1185). The two-dimensional map, its flat names and shapes, become three-dimensional when the author approaches it as a child would, "laying his head in the grass, staring into the infinitesimal forest."

Stevenson's model of collaboration, colored by the tradition of adventure fiction and figured through the images of maps and footprints, suffuses every stage of *Treasure Island*'s production, including its composition, publication, and plot. It is possible to trace the power of this model through the series of maps that appear outside and inside the text, each written on by more than one hand. The first, and perhaps most famous, is a watercolor map Stevenson and Osbourne created together in Braemar, Scotland, in the summer of 1881. In separate accounts, Osbourne and Stevenson contest the artist responsible for the map, and the differences between their stories demonstrate how a real collaboration—the creation of the map by both Stevenson and Osbourne—can adopt elements of fictive collaborations—story-like elements that narrativize the collaborative process and introduce cultural assumptions about childhood and authorship. Examining these accounts side by side reveals that this map incorporates both the sense of professional negotiation and the intersection of adult and child imaginations that maps and their markings signify for Stevenson. Osbourne's account, published in a preface to *Treasure Island* in the mid-twentieth-century Vailima edition of Stevenson's works, reads,

> I happened to be tinting the map of an island I had drawn. Stevenson came in as I was finishing it, and . . . leaned over my shoulder, and

was soon elaborating the map, and naming it. I shall never forget the thrill of Skeleton Island, Spy Glass Hill, nor the heart-stirring climax of the three red crosses! And the great climax still when we wrote down the words "Treasure Island" at the top right-hand corner! . . . "Oh, for a story about it," I exclaimed . . . somehow conscious of his own enthusiasm in the idea. ("Note" x–xi)

A moment later, Osbourne registers his annoyance at his stepfather's piracy of his own childish work: "After writing in a few more names he put the map in his pocket, and I can recall the little feeling of disappointment I had at losing it. After all, it was my map" (xi). The difficulties of adult-child collaboration, always an uneven power relationship, are evident here, exacerbated by Osbourne's adult entrance into professional authorship; he was, at this point, a man remembering his childhood. By insisting that the map originated in his own creative endeavors and that Stevenson, recognizing its potential, appropriated it for the purposes of his story, Osbourne assigns himself a pivotal role in a novel that, by the time Osbourne was writing his preface, was a cultural touchstone. "Had it not been for me, and my childish box of paints," writes Osbourne, "there would have been no such book as *Treasure Island*" ("Note" xi).[24]

Recounting the map's origin, Osbourne acknowledges but manipulates the larger-than-life reputation of his most immediate literary ancestor, just as Stevenson negotiated with the weight of past fictions such as *Robinson Crusoe* and *Masterman Ready*. Osbourne's description of his relationship with Stevenson suggests intergenerational rivalry rather than collaboration. As a child, Osbourne may have been aware of the importance of the map to Stevenson's career—at least, the grown Osbourne projects this awareness onto his youth—and with the arrogance of the young pine in *The Graver and the Pen*, he takes the last word, claiming a substantial contribution to his stepfather's legacy. Stevenson's account of the map in "My First Book," however, is decidedly different:

There was a school-boy . . . much in want of "something craggy to break his mind upon." He had no thought of literature; it was the art of Raphael that received his fleeting suffrages, and with the aid of pen and ink and a shilling box of water-colours, he had soon turned one of the rooms into a picture-gallery. . . . I would sometimes unbend a little, join the artist (so to speak) at the easel, and pass the afternoon with him in a generous emulation, making coloured drawings. On one of these occasions I made a map of an island . . . and with the unconsciousness of the predestined, I ticketed my performance *Treasure Island*. ("First" 278–79)

Here, Stevenson claims both the map and the creative energy it inspires, and Osbourne is relegated to an anonymous "school-boy." The map's suggestive landscape belongs to the author alone, who "ticketed" his own performance. The assumption that Osbourne "had no thought of literature" further alienates the boy from the adventure story the watercolor map would inspire.

These two accounts betray a degree of competition, especially on Osbourne's part. However, the individual ambition evident in these paired accounts is tempered by the implicit suggestion in both that the map and the adventure tale born out of it could not be created without the contribution of both author and schoolboy. While Osbourne self-confidently claims ownership of the painting, he does not discern its narrative qualities until Stevenson enters the scene, "elaborating the map." At this moment, the map is endowed with the "thrill" of adventure. Under Stevenson's hand, the map becomes inseparable from the map in the story; it is "very precious owing to its associations with pirates, and the fact that it had been found in an old sea chest" (Osbourne, "Note" xi). While Stevenson also claims the map as his own, his artistic endeavors are described as an imitation of his stepson's and, notably, a willingness to physically imitate the child's position. Stevenson would "unbend" and "join the artist (so to speak) at the easel," a phrase that seems to describe the two as painting on the same surface. Stevenson authors the manuscript that emerges from the map, but the map, and therefore the manuscript, is impossible to imagine without Osbourne. In Stevenson's account, Osbourne embodies the very subject of the adventure story, emerging as the sort of doomed vessel that often appears at the beginning of sea stories, looking for "something craggy to break his mind upon."

This collaboration between Stevenson and Osbourne itself becomes a map: a guide for a further series of real and fictive adult-child collaborations inside and outside the text of *Treasure Island* that are often established over that exceptionally suggestive object, the map, and that integrate generations in an act of joint authorship. For example, Stevenson composed the first chapters of *Treasure Island* quickly and followed his individual efforts with a daily ritual of cooperative reading, response, and revision: "Day after day . . . I read aloud my morning's work to the family,"

Stevenson writes, noting that his son, wife, and parents were sometimes joined by a series of visitors, including Gosse, Sidney Colvin, and Alexander Japp, who passed the manuscript along to James Henderson, editor of *Young Folks*, for publication ("First" 280). While several family members and friends participated in these readings, it was Osbourne and Thomas Stevenson, the author's father, who proved the most enthusiastic contributors. As Stevenson's wife Fanny writes, Thomas "would sit entranced during our daily chapter, his noble head bent forward, his great, glowing eyes fixed on his son's face. Every incident of the story could be read in his changing countenance. At any slip in style, or taste, or judgment he would perceptibly wince" (F. Stevenson xiii–xiv). This interest transformed into participation, and as Stevenson notes, his father "set himself actively to collaborate" ("First" 280). Thomas Stevenson contributed a number of details, including the name of Captain Flint's old ship, the *Walrus*, some specifics regarding the marooned man, Ben Gunn, and the inventory of Bones's chest, which he "must have passed the better part of a day preparing, on the back of a legal envelope" ("First" 281). Stevenson expanded the possibilities of intergenerational collaboration, including not only literary ancestors but also previous and subsequent familial generations, building a multigenerational partnership.[25]

Thomas Stevenson includes, at the bottom of Bones's chest, Flint's treasure map, the fictional counterpart to the Braemar watercolor map and a document that will send Jim, Trelawney, and Livesey on their adventure. In his description of this map, Stevenson again underscores the map's potential for intergenerational collaboration through the act of writing:

> The doctor opened the seals with great care, and there fell out the map of an island, with latitude and longitude, soundings, names of hills, and bays and inlets, and every particular that would be needed to bring a ship to a safe anchorage upon its shores. . . . There were several additions of a later date; but, above all, three crosses of red ink—two on the north part of the island, one in the south-west, and, beside this last, in the same red ink, and in a small, neat hand, very different from the captain's tottery characters, these words: "Bulk of the treasure here." (62)

This map records a legacy of explorers, chronicling their discoveries not through footprints but instead through layers of handwriting. This map is a composite of two or more hands—the original instructions printed on the map, supplemented by "additions of a later date," "three crosses of red ink," and notes "in a small, neat hand, very different from the Captain's tottery characters"—and yet these various hands work together to create, like the Braemar map, a tale that not only transforms Jim, the squire, and the doctor into actors embarking on a new adventure but also constantly offers new narrative possibilities. The map has been spread on the table only for a moment when the squire, inspired by its notes and information, casts his companions as stock characters in an adventure story. "You'll make a famous cabin-boy, Hawkins," decides Trelawney. "You, Livesey, are ship's doctor; I am admiral" (44). The squire's bold proclamations and careful arrangements for the journey cannot contain the narrative potential of the map. Jim pores over it before boarding their ship, the *Hispaniola*, imagining a number of possible journeys. "I approached that island in my fancy, from every possible direction," he muses. "I explored every acre of its surface; I climbed a thousand times to that tall hill they call the Spy-glass, and from the top enjoyed the most wonderful and changing prospects. Sometimes the isle was thick with savages, with whom we fought; sometimes full of dangerous animals that hunted us" (47). Jim examines this map as Stevenson studies its counterpart in "My First Book," detecting the "brown faces and bright weapons" that promise adventure. Both documents illustrate a number of possible stories—the prospect of savages or wild beasts, of danger or daring victory. The map is a palimpsest, representing through layers of ink or footprints the integration of collaborators' contributions, of past authors and original fictions, and the narrative possibility such intersections produce.[26]

Yet for Stevenson, intergenerational collaborations pose unique challenges—namely, the difficulty of overcoming what are considered to be fundamental differences between adult's and children's imaginations. In "Child's Play," Stevenson represents children's and adults' imaginations not only in terms of the embodied and the intellectual, respectively—a distinction between the child whose blood is "agog over all his body" and the adult, who carries out his fantasies "while sitting quietly by the fire or lying prone in bed" (177)—but also in terms of landscape and footprints. "Although the ways of children cross with those of their elders in a hundred places daily, they never go in the same direction nor so much as lie in the same element," he writes. "So may the telegraph-wires intersect with the line of the high road, or so might a landscape-painter and a bagman visit the same country, and yet move in different worlds" (174).

Children and adults are not isolated due to the content of their fancies—"children," Stevenson notes, "think very much the same thoughts and dream the same dreams, as bearded men and marriageable women"—but instead due to the way they express the movements of the imagination. The imaginations of the adult and child may "cross in a hundred places daily," may "visit the same country," and yet never find a mutual "element" in which to enact and narrate their similar fancies. The old and young, like the bagman and the landscape painter, see the same horizon but experience the view in widely different ways.

For Stevenson, then, collaborating with a child involves overcoming both the difficulties commonly associated with multiple authorship—assigning authorial roles, crafting a cohesive voice, or resolving differences of style, for example—and the widely different ways adults and children engage the physical world and their very bodies while exercising their imaginations. True collaboration with a child, for Stevenson, requires not only a creative consideration of the same landscape but also, on the part of the adult, a physical exertion, a consideration of the embodied, youthful imagination. In the world outside *Treasure Island*, Stevenson practices this approach to adult-child collaboration by exhibiting the liveliness of a boy when engaged in imaginative play with the young Osbourne. For example, the complex war games Stevenson staged with Osbourne in Switzerland, while not necessarily physically rigorous, allowed Stevenson to engage both the filtered and organized imagination of the adult and the passion and imaginative commitment of the childlike imagination the author describes in "Child's Play." The pair bent over a map of mountains, towns, rivers, and bridges sprawled on the floor of the attic of Chalet am Stein. Stevenson took the movements of his toy soldiers so seriously that "he studied [Edward Bruce] Hamley's *Operations of War* and other military documents, planned extensive campaigns, wrote reports by war correspondents for fictitious rival journals, and in general played the game more fully and intensely than even the boy did" (Hart 23–24). Osbourne notes that he and Stevenson "used to play . . . with unfailing zest, until [their] knees would ache and [their] backs get sore with the stopping and kneeling," but the very physical engagement with their game was balanced with an intellectual commitment to its accuracy: predictions of the ways weather impacts combat, for example, and estimations of how far troops with heavy artillery could travel in a day (Stevenson, *Letters to Young Friends* 306–7).[27] In these games, Stevenson integrates the spontaneous boyhood game of toy soldiers, which he plays with an intensity and even a bodily commitment that matches Osbourne's, with the informed adult imagination, filtered through war manuals and the features of military correspondence.

In the fictive world of *Treasure Island*, Stevenson imagines a more complete intersection of the vigorous, active child imagination and the limited imagination of the adult. Some of the most important pivots in the plot—moments when the story could move in a number of directions—are marked by a momentary physical contact and sometimes confusion of adult and child bodies. In other words, within the world of the novel, adults do not simply re-embody the childlike imagination to create narrative but instead act in cooperation with the child's body, physically appropriating it to move the plot forward. Early in the tale, for example, the blind pirate Pew and the young, able-bodied Jim work together as one, whole body in order to deliver the ominous black spot, the pirate equivalent of a death sentence, to Billy Bones. When Pew finds Hawkins outside the Admiral Benbow Inn, he grips the boy's arm "like a vice" and leads him into the parlor, where the sick Billy Bones rests. Pew tells Bones to remain seated and hold out his left hand while ordering Jim to "take [Bones's] left hand by the wrist, and bring it near to my right." "We both obeyed him to the letter," Jim notes, "and I saw him pass something from the hollow of the hand that held his stick into the palm of the captain's, which closed upon it instantly" (26–27). Pew's insistence that Jim help him deliver the black spot is unnecessary; though blind, Pew is self-sufficient and even agile, exiting the parlor directly after handing over the black spot and hurrying down the road "with incredible accuracy and nimbleness" (27). However, Stevenson deliberately stages the collective action of disabled adult and able child, the simultaneous and complicit movement of the arms of both adult and child, during this key moment in the plot. The delivery of the black spot leads to Jim's discovery of the treasure map. Bones, unnerved by this news of his impending death, dies of "thundering apoplexy," leaving behind his treasure and documents (28).

More central to the plot of *Treasure Island*, however, is the relationship between Jim and the sea cook, Long John Silver. Silver is surprisingly swift on one strong leg; when Jim first encounters Silver at the Spy Glass tavern, he notes that the one-legged Silver "carried a crutch, which he managed with wonderful dexterity, hopping about upon it like a bird" (52), and that his movements were not impeded on board the *Hispaniola*, where he "had a line or two rigged up to help him across the widest spaces—Long

John's earrings, they were called; and he would hand himself from one place to another ... as quickly as another man could walk" (64). However, despite his agility, Silver appears throughout the novel as the disabled adult counterpart to the youthful Jim. Silver calls Jim "the picter of my own self when I was young and handsome" and, once on the island, he tells Livesey that he and Jim sleep "stem to stem" in the stockade (168, 180). When the wounded body of the cunning Silver is imagined next to the strong body of the naïve Jim—when the two characters collaborate in conversation or in action—the result is the sort of narrative possibility inherent in the treasure map. For example, as the *Hispaniola* lies moored offshore Treasure Island, Silver lays his hand upon Jim's arm and muses: "This here is ... a sweet spot for a lad to get ashore on. You'll bathe, and you'll climb trees, and you'll hunt goats, you will; and you'll get aloft on them hills like a goat yourself. Why, it makes me young again. I was going to forget my timber leg, I was. It's a pleasant thing to be young, and have ten toes, and you may lay to that" (74). Here, Silver's consciousness of his "timber leg" leads him to superimpose his own youth onto the young body of Jim, and Silver's past experiences on the island intersect with Jim's potential, generating a list of possibilities that recalls the "sea-dreams" and "charming anticipations of strange islands and adventures" Jim imagined before his journey (47). Even when the narrative is nearly complete, when the battle for treasure between Silver and his mutinous crew and the band of men led by the squire and doctor is at an end, the collaboration between Silver and Jim remains a site for imaginative and narrative possibility. "Ah, you that's young—you and me might have done a power of good together!" exclaims Silver (173).[28]

Jim's encounters with Pew and Silver may momentarily align the adult and child imaginations, generating narrative possibility through a confusion or collusion of youthful and older bodies; however, these relationships also offer a portrait of the potentially volatile nature of collaborative relationships. As Gubar argues, *Treasure Island* can be read as a "cautionary tale of a boy who is seduced and betrayed" by the adults who appear to respect and flatter him (91), and Jim learns throughout his sea adventures that collaboration can disguise treachery, brutally or artfully. The "pleasing vision of juvenile power and potency is constantly punctured," Gubar writes, for "each time Jim gets established as a heroic figure, his agency is quickly shown to be chimerical; his collaboration compelled; his actions circumscribed" (82). Pew and Silver resort to deceit, intimidation, and even violence, feigning helplessness—in Pew's case, literally twisting Jim's arm—in order to take advantage of the boy's youth and assumed naïveté. These collaborations quickly deteriorate into exploitation or dissolve into enmity. Once Pew has taken advantage of Jim's keen eyes to deliver the black spot to Billy Bones, their partnership ends abruptly, and Silver's hand on Jim's shoulder, his lamentations about the burden of his wooden leg, are staged—a malicious act meant to lull his shipmates into a false sense of security before he makes his violent bid for the wealth hidden on Treasure Island.

Notably, Stevenson, a self-professed admirer of the unbridled youthful imagination, does not allow the underhanded manipulations of the adult world to undermine Jim's efforts at every turn. At times, Jim's youthful activity ultimately ends an intergenerational partnership. In particular, Stevenson stages an exhilarating victory for Jim over the coxswain Israel Hands. The two find themselves alone aboard the *Hispaniola*, unwilling collaborators in steering the schooner into the sheltered northern inlet of the island. "Our interests jumped together," concedes Jim. Hands "issued his commands," which Jim "breathlessly obeyed," and the two navigate the schooner through the narrow Northern Inlet "with a certainty and neatness" (154–55). However, once this joint interest is gone, once the boat is safely run aground, their collaboration ends, and the very forces that made their partnership successful threaten to destroy it. Jim's youthful, healthy body, which moments earlier deftly executed Hands's orders, enables him to dodge the coxswain's attacks and best him in a fast-paced battle of wits and daring. Jim remembers their duel as "such a game as I had often played at home about the rocks of Black Hill Cove, but never before, you may be sure, with such a wildly beating heart as now. Still, as I say, it was a boy's game, and I thought I could hold my own at it, against an elderly seaman with a wounded thigh" (157). Violence and adventure is, here, a game—an evocation of the playfully delinquent children in the romance tradition. Jim's agility, sharpened through the games of childhood, gets the better of Hands, who at the close of the scene falls into the shallow water of the inlet, shot by Jim's dual pistols. The contest this scene stages—between adult and child plots, adult and child bodies—recurs throughout the Stevenson-Osbourne partnership and resurfaces, in fact, in many Golden Age intergenerational collaborations, as adult authors wrestle with the task of acknowledging child agency alongside the very real disparities of power, physical and social, between young and old.

THE IMPOSSIBILITIES OF COLLABORATION

The collaborations I have examined thus far are intergenerational; they call upon generations past and present, professional and familial, and extend from father to son and from literary predecessor to novice. However, the dyad at the center of these creative partnerships, Stevenson and Osbourne, engaged in what I define more precisely as adult-child collaboration. Osbourne was a young adolescent during the pair's early literary ventures: thirteen years old when he printed *Not I and Other Poems* and fifteen when *Treasure Island* appeared in one volume in 1884. As I note above, Stevenson and Osbourne's work together was also what I call a hybrid collaboration, revealing both a recognition of the advantages of actual adult-child partnerships and an idealization of those relationships. Osbourne's status as a child was important to the very real conditions of his collaboration with Stevenson; it is unlikely, for example, that Stevenson would have experimented with toy press printing without the participation of Osbourne, and therefore the boy's identity as a schoolboy enabled a particular type of collaborative, literary play. However, Osbourne's youth was also vital to *representations* of their partnership that were perhaps fictionalized or romanticized. Stevenson's accounts of his collaborations with Osbourne are steeped in admiration for the child imagination, and critical accounts of their work together sometimes strike a tone of sentimentality. James D. Hart, for instance, ends *The Private Press Ventures of Samuel Lloyd Osbourne and R.L.S.* by recalling their first creative partnerships with a nostalgic finality; "if they went on to further, more mature collaboration in still another land, across the Pacific," Hart writes, "it was the period of youth and playthings of youth that both enjoyed most in their associations together" (46).

Stevenson and Osbourne did move on to "more mature collaboration . . . across the Pacific." The two began coauthoring novels in the late 1880s, publishing three before Stevenson's death in December 1894: *The Wrong Box* (1889), a dark comedy; *The Wrecker* (1891, 1892), a nautical mystery; and *The Ebb-Tide* (1893, 1894), an adventure tale. The few years that passed between the pair's *Treasure Island* days and their later collaborations brought significant changes. Stevenson had established himself with *A Child's Garden of Verses*, *Strange Case of Dr. Jekyll and Mr. Hyde*, and *Kidnapped*, among other titles. Osbourne had become a young man in his twenties with literary aspirations of his own that exceeded the circulation of a toy press venture. While the two still approached their partnership with good humor and a sense of play, their work was no longer a lighthearted experiment between a relatively unknown writer and a precocious young printer or a lark between a schoolboy home for the holidays and a man with a taste for adventure stories. Instead, the three novels Osbourne and Stevenson coauthored represent a partnership between two professional authors. Both had a stake in the venture—and a name on the title page. Their renewed collaboration brought both creative and more practical, economic benefits; for example, Osbourne's coauthorship secured American copyright for their early novels until the passage of the International Copyright Act in July 1891 (Smith 263). While Osbourne had yet to embark on a solo career, he was pleased that Stevenson "regarded [him] seriously as a fellow-craftsman; sought [his] judgment and often took it" (*Intimate* 99).

The transformation of the pair from collaborative playmates to professional coauthors and its consequences are discernable in two of Stevenson's descriptions of his work with Osbourne. The first occurs in "My First Book," referenced above, in which Stevenson describes the genesis of *Treasure Island*. In that essay, Stevenson boasts that the creative energy generated by the first collaborative watercolor map of Treasure Island inspired him to dash off the first half of the novel. "The next thing I knew, I had some paper before me and was writing out a list of chapters," he rejoices. "How often have I done so, and the thing gone no farther! But there seemed elements of success about this enterprise. It was to be a story for boys . . . and I had a boy at hand to be a touchstone" (279). While "My First Book" records the composition of *Treasure Island* in 1881, that essay was not published in *The Idler* until August 1894, when Stevenson was completing his final collaboration with Osbourne, *The Ebb-Tide*. Judging from Osbourne's and Stevenson's accounts of their process, Stevenson found coauthoring with the adult Osbourne arduous and sometimes frustrating. Osbourne notes that, for the most part, he provided an initial plot outline—"I always wrote the first draft, to break the ground"—and the two passed the draft back and forth as it was "written and rewritten by Louis and then myself in turn," the draft "worked over and over again by each of us as often as was necessary" (Balfour 40–41). In a letter from Stevenson to his cousin Bob—written in September 1894, a month after the publication of "My First Book"—Stevenson remembers the toil of collaborating with Osbourne over *The Wrecker*:

The great difficulty of collaboration is that you can't *tell* what you mean. I know what kind of effect I mean a character to give—what kind of *tache* he is to make; but how am I to tell my collaborator in words? . . . I, as a personal artist, can begin a character with only a haze in my head, but how if I have to translate the haze into words before I begin? . . . These are the times that illustrate to a man the inadequacy of spoken language. Now—to be just to written language—I can (or could) find a language for my every mood, but how could I *tell* anyone before-hand what this effect was to be, which it would take every art that I possessed, and hours and hours of deliberate labour and selection and rejection, to produce? There are the impossibilities of collaboration. Its immediate advantage is to focus two minds together on the stuff, and to produce in consequence an extraordinarily greater richness of purview, consideration, and invention. (*Letters* 8.364)

There is no serendipitous coming together of author and printer here, no enthusiastic pounce from treasure map to manuscript page. This partnership is characterized by a breakdown of communication, a disjunction between the practices of one "personal artist" and another. Working with the older Osbourne, Stevenson finds that collaboration is a disordered, backwards process—that he must communicate to his stepson his needs as a professional author, but this "deliberate labour" impedes rather than encourages creativity. While collaboration certainly enhances the creative process—providing "extraordinarily greater richness of purview, consideration, and invention"—the task of committing that material to the page is stymied by coauthorship. Describing the pains of collaboration at nearly the same moment that he was publishing an essay on how easy his earlier collaborations with Osbourne had been, Stevenson perhaps was feeling nostalgic for the ease of partnering with a child.

All three novels coauthored by Stevenson and Osbourne evidence this new mode of collaboration and its "impossibilities"; however, I will focus on *The Ebb-Tide*, the last of their joint works. The novel is subtitled *A Trio & Quartette*, gesturing toward the possibility of harmony and, perhaps, dissonance. As this subtitle suggests, the novel explores the dynamic between first three and then four collaborators, exceeding the dyad of coauthorship as well as the themes of duality that, in the wake of *Strange Case of Dr. Jekyll and Mr. Hyde*, often characterize Stevenson studies. The novel recounts the adventures of three men living in an abandoned prison on an island in the South Seas: Robert Herrick, an Oxford-educated man who has failed spectacularly through a string of careers; Huish, a "vulgar and bad-hearted cockney clerk"; and the American master-mariner Davis, who disgraced himself by crashing his boat while drunk (7). Davis is commissioned to captain a schooner with a freight of champagne and convinces his friends to board with him, steal the boat, and head for Peru. Davis and Huish drink much of the cargo before realizing that the remaining bottles are full of water, and when the schooner is then blown off course by foul weather, they redirect to the nearest land. There, they meet an Englishman named Attwater—a missionary with a streak of Long John Silver malignancy who controls the island with "silken brutality," overseeing a troop of natives in an offshore pearl expedition and preaching his own brand of fervent Christianity (72–73). Attwater separates Herrick from his companions, and Herrick finds his loyalties caught between the domineering pearl fisher and Davis and Huish, who are plotting to rob Attwater, kill him if necessary, and flee.

In the first half of the novel, Herrick, Davis, and Huish form a stable community. While their temperaments and histories threaten to alienate them, they have learned to empathize with one another over their shared fate. They keep each other warm at night, lying in "one wet mass" in their makeshift home, and while the drunken behavior of Huish and Davis bothers Herrick, he admits that they "were become brothers; there was an implied bond of loyalty in their cohabitation of the ship and their past miseries" (88). The disagreements that do occur arise when they attempt to narrate their adventures or their hopes for escape in language all three find accurate. For example, the novel opens with the men on the beach, bored, ill, and hungry. Davis asks for a story to ease their distress, and Herrick obliges with an escapist tale resembling the *Arabian Nights*, in which he is rewarded for a random act of kindness with a magic carpet journey to London. Initially, his companions speak up to elaborate upon Herrick's tale, imagining in unison their own escape from the island. Their cumulative tale demonstrates what Stevenson calls the "advantage" of collaboration—the "greater richness of purview, consideration, and invention." Davis, for example, speculates about how long the journey would take and the type of currency commonly found aboard a flying carpet—which, apparently, is double-eagles (10). However, the chapter ends with the others explaining that they fundamentally disagree with the manner in which Herrick composes a story. Their dispute is one of genre. Huish raves that Herrick's tale is "like the rot there is in tracts" (9). "I think you are about the poorest 'and at a yarn," he gripes. "Crikey, it's like *Ministering Children*! I can tell you there would be more beer and skittles about my little jaunt" (11).[29] Davis thinks something autobiographical rather than fantastic would be more suitable and suggests getting rid of Herrick's "fancy rigs" and opting instead for the tale of a holiday feast among family (12). Herrick's story degenerates into a draft to be reconsidered, amended, and eventually rewritten completely, and the exchange of edits and revisions is cut short only when a storm forces the three men to quit the tale and take shelter.[30]

The minor disagreements among Huish, Davis, and Herrick are resolved at the close of "The Trio," the first half of the novel. That section ends with a chapter titled "Partners," an account of how the three agree upon the best course of action after discovering their sham cargo and limited supplies. Their semantic squabbles, however, are amplified in "The Quartette," the novel's second half, where the delicate balance of their partnership is destabilized by the addition of a fourth person. Tensions mount when Attwater blatantly favors the cultured Herrick over his coarse companions, whom he calls "vulgar wolves" (85), and the partnership among Huish, Davis, and Herrick is undermined fatally when Huish and Davis conspire to exploit Herrick's intimacy with Attwater to determine the location of Attwater's cache of pearls. Herrick is torn between his obligation to his partners and his own ethical impulses, which encourage him to take a different, if lonely, course of action and warn Attwater of the impending attack:

> The three lives went up and down before [Herrick] like buckets in a well or like the scales of balances. It had come to a choice, one that must be speedy.... Horror of sudden death for horror of sudden death, there was here no hesitation possible.... And no sooner was the thought formed (which was a sentence) than the whole mind of the man ran in a panic to the other side; and when he looked within himself, he was aware only of turbulence and inarticulate outcry. (87–88)

It becomes clear in this passage that the uneasy collaboration Herrick formed with Huish and Davis cannot survive his allegiance to Attwater. Notably, his conflict, like the many tensions experienced between Stevenson and Osbourne as they drafted the novel, finds expression through references to language and communication. Herrick must commit to a sentence: a word that refers to a verdict or condemnation—a decision regarding who is to die and who is to live—but which also recalls the difficulties of written language. He must write a single line that will either confirm his companions' plot or allow Herrick to take possession of his own narrative, abandoning his partners and demonstrating an ambition similar to that of the ruggedly independent Attwater. But he feels paralyzed, helpless to move the plot forward, turbulent and inarticulate.

The Ebb-Tide ends with the collapse of collaboration: an acknowledgment of its impossibility, to use Stevenson's word. Herrick abandons his friends and informs Attwater of their treachery and soon is brandishing a Winchester alongside the pearl fisher. The trio is reduced to a duet, but Huish and Davis remain partners. Together, they write an apologetic letter designed to gain them access to Attwater's compound. The letter represents, through its language, both men; while the note is dictated by Davis and uses his refined vocabulary, Huish transcribes it in his own coarser dialect: "It is with feelin's of shyme and 'artfelt contrition that I approach you," records Huish. "Our Mr. 'Errick 'as left the ship, and will have doubtless communicated to you the nature of our 'opes. Needless to s'y, these are no longer possible" (120). Huish and Davis land on the beach to deliver the letter to Attwater, and for a brief moment the novel stages a confrontation between the steadfast collaborators and Herrick, armed with his gun. Attwater murders Huish, and Davis is forced to give up his designs on the pearl treasure. Herrick lives with Davis under the unspoken but ironclad rule of the pearl fisher, and his sentence—his one-line emendation of his friends' plan—has collapsed their collaborative narrative into a single story: what Vanessa Smith calls Attwater's "poetics of absolute authority" (278).

Stevenson himself interpreted the plot of *The Ebb-Tide* and its composition as a commentary on the challenges of collaboration. In letters, he charts the halting progress of the book—which changed forms and titles many times, from *The Schooner Farallone* to *The Pearl Fisher* and finally to *The Ebb-Tide*. When Colvin described the novel as the "working out of an artistic problem of a kind," Stevenson heartily agreed: "Well, I should just bet it was!" (*Letters* 8.160). The composition of the book was a fragmented process; Osbourne wrote the first four chapters in 1889–1890, and Stevenson lightly revised that portion of the novel but did not finish the manuscript with the final "Quartette" section until 1893. Stevenson's account of writing *The Ebb-Tide* sometimes celebrates, sometimes briefly mentions, and often completely ignores his stepson's contributions. Osbourne's name goes unmentioned, for example, when Stevenson refers to "the ever-to-be-execrated *Ebb Tide*, or Stevenson's Blooming Error," and Stevenson spares Osbourne when he dubs the book a "rancid yarn" that has put him in a "state of over-exhaustion and fiction-phobia" (*Letters* 8.94, 8.90). Osbourne appears with more frequency when Stevenson's spirits are buoyant. For example, he marks the beginning of their endeavor and Lloyd's ambition as a collaborator in a letter to Colvin in March 1892, listing the text as "quite planned and part written ... The Pearl Fisher (To-day.) (With Lloyd a Machine)" (*Letters* 7.251). Stevenson is particularly concerned with Osbourne's participation, and any official recognition of his coauthorship, as the novel approaches publication. When Colvin read the incomplete manuscript and, disgusted with its criminal heroes, expressed reservations, Stevenson responded with concerns about the book's impact on Osbourne's career. "I propose, if it not be too late, to delete Lloyd's name," Stevenson writes. "He has nothing to do with the last half. The first we wrote together, as the beginning of a long yarn. The second is entirely mine; and I think it rather unfair on the young man to couple his name with so infamous a work" (*Letters* 8.155–56). Once Colvin read the narrative's final pages and reconsidered his initial reaction, Stevenson changed his mind. "Since you rather revise your views of *The Ebb-Tide*, I think Lloyd's name might stick, but I'll leave it to you. I'll tell you just how it stands. Up to the discovery of the champagne the tale was all planned between us and drafted by Lloyd; from that moment he has nothing to do with it except talking it over" (*Letters* 8.158). Stevenson is at times optimistic, at times cynical about his collaboration with Osbourne—but ultimately protective of the more fragile reputation of his young coauthor.

If Stevenson found his later collaborations with his stepson difficult, Osbourne likely did as well—although for different reasons. Partnering with a literary celebrity is an expedient but difficult means to launch a solo career. Reviews of novels written collaboratively by the two reveal that many considered Osbourne an impediment to enjoying a new novel by Stevenson. A critic reviewing *The Ebb-Tide* for *The Saturday Review*, for example, assures readers that the book is "intensely Stevensonian," concluding "it is better to have Mr. Stevenson and another than not have Mr. Stevenson at all" (330).[31] A review of the same novel in the *Speaker* concedes that "Mr. Stevenson and partner faithfully copy Mr. Stevenson alone" (362). When Osbourne began publishing his own work in the early twentieth century, embarking on a literary career that would produce over a dozen novels and short story collections, reviewers measured his talent against the work of his more famous stepfather. A critic in the *Nation* writes that Osbourne's *The Adventurer* "bids fair to take its place among a not too numerous company of . . . Stevensonian kindred" (518), and a *National Magazine* review of Osbourne's *A Person of Some Importance* notes that "the influence of Stevenson seems to permeate many of the [book's] situations" (241).[32] Stevenson haunts his protégé, a past collaborator who demands acknowledgment. Many scholars and critics, both contemporary to Osbourne and today, still contend that Osbourne's best work is about his stepfather, and Osbourne is largely remembered for his introductions to Stevenson's works; his memoir *An Intimate Portrait of R.L.S.*; and *Memories of Vailima*, meditations on living with Stevenson in the South Seas that Osbourne composed and edited with his sister, Isobel Strong.

Osbourne is figured not only as the lesser author but also as an eternal boy. In this way, Stevenson and Osbourne's later collaborations remain adult-child partnerships—although in this case Osbourne is ridiculed rather than idealized. Stevenson himself at times referred to Osbourne as a child; in an 1893 letter to J. M. Barrie, he calls the then-six-foot-tall Osbourne "The Boy," noting good-naturedly that his stepson "keeps nothing of youth but some of its intolerance" and that "when he is good he is very, very good, but when he is cross he is horrid" (*Letters* 8.46–47).[33] This was affectionate teasing, of course; in the same letter, Stevenson notes that he himself has the "general appearance of a blasted boy—or blighted youth" (*Letters* 8.44). However, some critics infantilize Osbourne is less affectionate ways. A reviewer writing under the name "THE BARON DE B.-W" in *Punch*, for example, narrates his experiences reading *The Wrecker* and, like many before and after him, assumes that the ill-conceived or poorly written elements of the novel belong to the younger partner. "Had OSBOURNE interfered with STEVENSON, or was STEVENSON allowing OSBOURNE to have his say, reserving himself for a grand *coup* at half-price?" the Baron bemoans. "Would OSBOURNE chuck STEVENSON overboard, or was it to be t'other way off?" (48). The reviewer interprets the novel as a purely profit-driven venture and resents the authors' greed because it undermines a good story.

That position is reflected in Edward J. Wheeler's accompanying cartoon—an image that purposefully plays with ideas of play and youth in order to frame Stevenson as childlike and Osbourne as childish (Figure

2.1. Edward J. Wheeler, cartoon for "Our Booking-Office" by Baron De-B.W in *Punch* 103 (July 30, 1892): 48. Image courtesy of Hugh Thomas.

2.1). Stevenson and Osbourne are pictured playing on the shore, both dressed in youthful sailor suits. Stevenson is shown in profile, his moustache and mature face belying his age. He is concerned with the story; he is pictured with a quill behind his ear, manipulating the sails of a model ship and surrounded by the puppets that represent his characters. Childhood looks good on Stevenson, who is inspired by the sort of youthful adventures that readers such as *Punch*'s Baron love. But Osbourne, who faces away from the viewer—for, the cartoonist implies, who would recognize the unknown Osbourne's face?—is small and childlike, the back of his head obscured by a wide-brimmed hat. He is a greedy and grasping, surrounded by money: one bag labeled pence, shillings, and pounds, another boldly proclaiming "TREASURE." When *The Wrecker* was published, Osbourne was twenty-four years old, but here is figured as a child—not because he is imaginative and playful but instead because he is the amateur, the grasping young writer desperate to ride along on Stevenson's coattails. Wheeler's cartoon, then, simultaneously registers Osbourne's growth into adulthood and exiles him to childhood. As a grown man and professional author, Osbourne is now a visible collaborator. However, what he gains in recognition he loses in respect; he is now subject to the critical barbs of reviewers and readers. He might be older in years, but he is once again a child—not in growth but in public opinion. The *Punch* reviewer's nautical language—"Would OSBOURNE chuck STEVENSON overboard, or was it to be t'other way off?"—transports both men back to the *Hispaniola*. Osbourne is Jim Hawkins wrestling with Israel Hands on the deck, but the outcome here does not favor the younger combatant. And Wheeler's cartoon seems to resolve the dispute between the older and younger tree in "The Disputatious Pines." No matter how the younger tree grows, and despite his confidence and bravado, he will never surpass the "hoar, unconquerable" tree Stevenson. Osbourne's status as an adult, for many reviewers, only makes the impudent boy's imposture all the more laughable.

But it seems that Osbourne understood, as Stevenson did, the social process of composition and publication and the advantages of creative partnerships. Osbourne's career reveals a continuing commitment to such partnerships—particularly collaborations with Austin Strong, Osbourne's nephew and Stevenson's step-grandson. Osbourne and Strong first collaborated in May and June 1902, when Osbourne was thirty-four years old years old and Strong was twenty-one; they produced a typescript play titled *Treasure Island: A Melodrama in Five Acts*. Their work—which, according to the manuscript's title page, was composed "under the authorization of Mrs. Robert Louis Stevenson"—was likely never staged. However, the typescript includes a complete adaptation of Stevenson's novel and elaborate set designs drawn and colored by Strong. Each of Strong's designs is accompanied by a trace outline of the set with a corresponding key explaining elements of the drawings, some descriptive—labels identifying, for instance, the Admiral Benbow Inn and the half-set table before it—and others relating to the practicalities of stage management—for example, a note advising that the coastal highway leading away from the Benbow "must be made practicable and allow for the weight of galloping horses."[34]

Even before the plot of *Treasure Island: A Melodrama in Five Acts* unfolds, the material text of the typescript recalls past collaborations between Stevenson and Osbourne. This manuscript, like Stevenson and Osbourne's toy press collaborations, is enabled by both the free impulsive play of amateurism and the possibilities of the miniature. In 1902, when Osbourne and Strong composed the script and designed its sets, neither had significant experience in the theater; Osbourne was a novelist, and Strong was beginning a career as a landscape architect. This might explain, in part, why the typescript appears less like the plans for a workable stage adaptation of the novel and more like a game dreamed up by two boys at play. The exaggerated plot (which I will discuss in a moment) and Strong's brightly colored set designs, each framed in a page-width proscenium arch, could double as material for the toy theater shows Osbourne staged with Stevenson in Davos. Osbourne remembers those productions in *An Intimate Portrait of R.L.S.*, recalling how Stevenson "painted scenery for my toy theatre—a superb affair, costing upward of twenty pounds and far beyond our purse—[and] helped me give performances and slide the actors in and out of their tin stands, as well as imitating galloping horses, or screaming screams for the heroine in distress" (36). The miniature stage created the perfect venue for family entertainments. Strong also appreciated the creative potential of the toy theater. Years after collaborating with Osbourne over their *Treasure Island* melodrama, Strong left landscape architecture for a career in the theater and, like Stevenson and Osbourne, was inspired by the sense of play and possibility provided by the miniature.[35] "In planning my plays I have a little theatre of my own," he explains in a 1907 interview, "just large enough to fit on the top of an ordinary dining table. This miniature playhouse is fitted up with scenery, electric lights, and stage properties of all sorts" ("Chat" X1). The typescript of *Treasure Island: A Melodrama in Five Acts*, like the small poetry collections Stevenson created with his stepson, is unpublished and largely uncirculated, the trace of a creative partnership that would develop into more formal publications in subsequent years.

While Osbourne and Strong's script recalls these early collaborations over small presses and toy theaters, the manuscript of course shares a closer kinship with *Treasure Island*, and it expands and complicates that novel's already collaborative composition narrative. As I argue above, Stevenson acknowledges the many creative partners who contributed to his novel, including authors from Defoe to Kingsley who established the adventure tradition and Stevenson's own family members, especially his stepson and father. He reproduced that pattern of intergenerational partnerships in the adventures of Jim Hawkins, Squire Trelawney, Doctor Livesey, and Long John Silver. Osbourne and Strong maintain the collaborative possibilities of the novel. If Osbourne's role in the novel's origins remains unrecorded on the novel's title page—his instrumentality to the book's composition legible only through Stevenson's wry dedication, family letters, or footnotes to scholarly editions—in this script Osbourne claims his authorship alongside Strong on a cover page that announces its collaborative production and, in its reference to Fanny Stevenson, its connection to the family line. The typescript reveals itself as the product of many hands and therefore serendipitously resembles the map of Treasure Island that Stevenson describes in the novel—that document crossed

2.2. Austin Strong, original set design for Act I of *Treasure Island: A Melodrama in Five Acts* (1902), by Strong and Lloyd Osbourne. Robert Louis Stevenson Museum, St. Helena, California.

over with longitude and latitude, notations from a later explorer, and red ink leading adventurers to treasure. The majority of the script is written in black, typed ink, but it bears traces of other hands that contributed at later moments: small pen notations in Strong's handwriting, frequent underlines in red ink highlighting stage directions, and Osbourne's bold pencil signature.[36]

At times elements of the typescript are readily identifiable as the contribution of one collaborator or another. Strong, for example, signed and dated his set designs, and Osbourne's signature appears on the title page of the script as a whole and on the title page of Act II in particular, perhaps in a bid to claim the text. However, parsing out each man's role in the collaboration is, in the end, impossible. The multiple authors of the text are absorbed into and even obscured by the manuscript, and references to creative partnership, between Strong and Osbourne or among that pair and earlier adaptations of the novel, emerge only here and there. For example, Osbourne and Strong's stage directions and blocking suggest, like Stevenson's prefatory poem to *Treasure Island*, that the visual vocabulary of their adaptation relies on previous tellings of the pirate story. At the beginning of the typescript, they note that Billy Bones "sweeps the horizon with his telescope and then takes the attitude, smoking his pipe, that Mr. [William Brassey] Hole depicts in his drawing. Vide Treasure Island, Cassell and Co's illustrated edition, page 2" (3).[37] This pose is reproduced in Strong's set design for Act I, a painting that includes not only the Admiral Benbow Inn, situated on a quiet cove, but also Bones's contemplative figure, his back to the viewer and one arm akimbo as he stares across the water (Figure 2.2).

Yet this story, while based on the novel *Treasure Island*, is quite a different narrative than Stevenson's. In this adaptation, Jim—like Osbourne and Strong—has grown into manhood. His mother has died, and he is responsible for the upkeep of the family's unprofitable inn. The curtain rises upon Ruth Trelawney—the squire's daughter and Jim's love interest, a character created by Osbourne and Strong—who comforts Jim as he explains to her that he has sold the inn and plans to sail abroad to reclaim his fortune:

> My father, a captain in the Royal Navy, was in birth the peer of yours. He sank with his ship under the weight of Spanish guns, and his widow—with the pittance she was left—condemned herself and me—(indicating the inn) to this, Ruth, to this![38] It rests with me, now that I am a grown man and with the blood of gallant gentlemen coursing through my veins—to win back the position it was once ours to hold, so that in time I may look your father in the face and say: "Squire Trelawney, I have the honour to ask your daughter's hand." (2)

The arrival and prompt death of pirate Billy Bones at the Benbow derail Jim's plans. However, his adventure is not abandoned but reimagined, transformed when Bones uses his final breath to give Jim Captain Flint's treasure map and suggest its promise of wealth and romance. While in Stevenson's novel, Silver elaborates on the possibilities of the treasure map, here Bones describes them, translating the youthful dreams of adventure described by Silver into the desires of a marriageable young man. While Silver promises the young Jim the types of island adventure a boy audience might covet—"you'll bathe, and you'll climb trees, and you'll hunt goats, you will; and you'll get aloft on them hills like a goat yourself" (64)—Bones promises this older Jim property, power, and sex. "You have there the key to unlock the world," Bones gasps, handing over the map: "palaces and rent-rolls, a seat in Parliament, great parks and houses, beautiful women on their knees afore you" (12).

The nature of Jim's adventure, then, is changed. His maturity and his motives to recover his family's wealth and social stature transform the book's central relationships. The adventure plot of Stevenson's *Treasure Island* accommodates intergenerational collaboration both inside and outside the text; the narrative is designed to appeal to audiences of men and boys, and his plot, like the plots of many adventure tales, invites a young explorer to fight and sail alongside grown men and share in the spoils. Osbourne and Strong, however, rearrange Jim's narrative into an adventure tale complicated by and sometimes subsumed into an inheritance and romance plot that promises not intergenerational collaboration but instead heterosexual marriage. As the crew of the *Hispaniola* prepares for their voyage, Ruth's relationship with Jim remains a focal point, and Jim's pursuit of the squire's daughter overwrites his quest for treasure. Ruth notes that, in a love note, Jim calls her "the biggest treasure he knows of—and if he only had a map of my heart with red crosses—!" (22). Moreover, the collaborative relationships Stevenson suggests among Jim and the many father figures of the story are foreclosed. The squire is now a potential father-in-law rather than a fellow swashbuckler. Most importantly, Silver—who in the novel often imagines himself in a sly partnership with the young Jim—is killed off quite suddenly in the final act, buried alive in a treasure cave by Ben Gunn. Silver is captured off-stage, and Ben's actions remain undescribed, documented only in his maniacal explanation: "Never you mind how I did it—you'd better be careful, or I'll put you in too! (Then he giggles again as though at the recollection)—it done me good to 'ear 'im screaming, 'e caught like a rat in a trap and a-firing of his pistol!" (68). Jim, the doctor, and the squire have barely completed an inventory of the treasure when Jim selects from his newfound riches an engagement ring for Ruth. While Stevenson's novel concludes with Silver's parrot screeching the haunting "pieces of eight!"—a refrain that echoes through Jim's nightmares and leaves his island adventure largely unresolved—Osbourne and Strong end their adaptation with the happy announcement that the crew is heading home and an official record of Ruth's betrothal in the ship's log: "Miss Trelawney betrothed to James Hawkins—all hands extend heartiest good wishes—!" (74). Osbourne and Strong's script, by privileging Jim and Ruth's romance plot over the adventure plot of Jim and his fellow treasure hunters, undermines the promise of intergenerational collaboration. The partnerships that invite collaboration in Stevenson's source text—among Jim, Squire Trelawney, and Doctor Livesey and between Jim and Long John Silver—are, after all, largely homosocial.

However, that possibility is not gone but instead reframed. At the moment of their engagement, Jim and Ruth imagine their union as part of a series of relationships, stretching backward for generations and epitomized in the ring Jim selects for Ruth's finger:

> JIM: (Turning over the rings and holding up several in turn to the light. Both he and she exclaiming at their magnificence.) This hoop of diamonds—this shall be the pledge of our plighted troth. (They both regard it tenderly). How many bright eyes have sparkled—now sightless in the tomb—how many, rheumy with the weight of years, have recalled with these flashing stones the time when their lovers sought and found them. Ah, Ruth, if each could tell it's [sic] story, I doubt if we could regard them without tears.
> RUTH: Think of them torn from womens' [sic] hands on the bloodstained decks of ships!
> JIM: Surviving guilt and blood, surviving agonies endured and now forgotten, surviving scenes of crime and wickedness and horror! (Holding up the ring) To come at last to bind two honest hearts together. I invoke all true souls who have ever worn this ring, all those women now dead and gone, to whom these bits of chyristal [sic] were once charged with love—to guard, to cherish, to protect my sweet maid from harm! (Puts ring on Ruth's finger; she looks at it in silence and then presses it to her lips). (n.p.)

The stories that adhere to Ruth's ring are unnarrated; Jim and Ruth only speculate about the bright eyes and broken hearts of the women who have worn Ruth's ring. However, the ring and its history of *marital* romance recalls the opening poem of *Treasure Island*, where Stevenson rhapsodizes about the *genre* of the romance, which features "all the old romance, retold / Exactly in the ancient way." The repetition that punctuates Ruth and Jim's description of the rings' past—how many and how many, surviving and surviving—suggests that the stories crystallized in the hoop of diamonds accrue and collect, overlap and weave together.

Ruth and Jim imagine their engagement and the ring that signifies their union as a sort of palimpsest. Like the text of *Treasure Island*, a tale that borrows and rewrites a tradition of adventure stories, and like the treasure map that leads to Flint's trove, this marriage is described as the next tale in an overlapping series of narratives, each borrowing from the previous telling. Moreover, in uniting Jim and Ruth, Osbourne and Strong join two characters invested in retelling old romances. Jim's quest for treasure is an attempt to rewrite himself into his own bloodline of "gallant gentleman." Ruth is even more adept at appropriating adventure narratives. She first appears on stage "dressed in a dark-green riding costume . . . high boots, [and] a three-cornered hat," carrying a silver-mounted riding whip, and she negotiates the adventure tale by inhabiting the role of female buccaneer: "Kitty Morgan, the female buccaneer" who "was shipwrecked and swam ashore with a rope in her mouth!" (1, 21–22).

CONCLUSION

Osbourne and Strong, in adopting and reshaping familiar narratives, joined a network of collaborations inherited from Stevenson—an almost self-perpetuating tradition of creative partnerships. They continued collaborating after the amateur efforts of *Treasure Island: A Melodrama in Five Acts*, extending their collaboration well into adulthood just as Stevenson and Osbourne had continued their own collaboration. Together, they wrote at least two more plays.[39] Their next effort, *The Exile*, was written while the two vacationed in California and depicts Napoleon marooned on Elba. It was performed in London in 1903 but was not precisely a success; in *The Saturday Review*, Max Beerbohm sniffed that he had "never saw a worse specimen of historical drama" (615), and Strong noted that he "didn't make enough money out of it to buy [himself] a sandwich" ("Chat" X1). Yet the two were not deterred, and wrote another play: *Little Father of the Wilderness* in 1905, a one-act Strong describes as his "start toward a possible success" ("Chat" X1). Stevenson still haunts their partnership, and certainly Osbourne in particular struggled with his stepfather's legacy. And yet the family dynamics of Stevenson, Osbourne, and Strong seem to celebrate the potential of multigenerational collaboration, despite its challenges and failures. Stevenson, in fact, anticipated this tradition of familial collaboration in his dedication to *Catriona*, addressed to Charles Baxter and written in Samoa in 1893:

You are still . . . in the venerable city which I must always think of as my home. And I have come so far; and the sights and thoughts of my youth pursue me; and I see like a vision the youth of my father, and of his father, and the whole stream of lives flowing down there far in the north, with the sound of laughter and tears, to cast me out in the end, as by a sudden freshet, on these ultimate islands. And I admire and bow my head before the romance of destiny. (vi)

Stevenson imagines this "romance of destiny" extending into his past, backward through his bloodline and northward to Edinburgh. Osbourne and Strong assured that it continued into the future, as well—into Samoa, back to London, across the ocean to California, and beyond.

CHAPTER THREE

Collaborating with the Authorities
Children as Authors, Experts, and Critics

In the early 1980s, Peter Hunt argued that children's literature scholars should read like children (or at least try to). Doing so, he acknowledged, requires disposing with entrenched beliefs and practices that prevent adults from accurately assessing children's responses to texts, such as persistent ideas about young readers' literacy and their relationships to language, character, and image. How do we "cross the gap," he asks, "to see what is really happening on the child's terms rather than dealing in the ingrained assumptions about children's perceptions and competences?" (47). Hunt recommends "a total rereading of texts from what we might call a childist point of view" (45). Scholars can generate childist readings, Hunt explains, both "through the book"—by applying poststructuralist theory to children's texts, reading radically and as a child, and challenging preconceptions we bring to texts as adults—or "through the child"—by observing and recording in detail children's interactions with books. It is a method that delights in a kind of critical mimicry. "We already have our resisting readers," he writes, and "to understand what [children] mean, we will have to emulate them. And that, I am glad to say, might mean anarchy, or something like it" (58). As his prediction of chaos indicates, Hunt anticipates that childist readings will misalign with adult interpretations of children's texts in productive ways. Children are a subculture and a counterculture, Hunt argues, and he hopes a "radical rereading" from a childist point of view "may mean redrawing the maps of children's books" (57)—revising the canon by taking into account children's authority and experiences with books instead of adult ideas about what is suitable for child readers. Scholars continue to contemplate the possibilities and pitfalls of childist criticism; Hunt's attention to children's interpretive capacities have troubled scholars convinced of the unavoidable sway of adult constructions of childhood but found a tentative foothold in some discussions of child agency and childhood studies.[1]

When he first published his ideas about reading like a child, Hunt was joining a conversation that was at least a century old.[2] Victorians also struggled to reconcile their assumptions about childhood with what might anachronistically be identified as a childist approach to children's literature and culture; in popular periodicals, in political debates about education, and in children's literature itself, some speculated that the child's perspective—intellectually and physically—was not only different from but also equally important to that of adults. For example, Dinah Maria Mulock Craik addresses adults' assumptions about children and the impact of those assumptions on children's books in her 1860 essay, "The Age of Gold," published in *Macmillan's*. "Much poetic nonsense is talked about concerning the 'innocence' of children," Craik writes. "Taking a sober, candid revision of our own childhood . . . few of us can remember being very good or very happy in those early days. Most of us, we confess—or rather, we hope—were a great deal naughtier then than now. Otherwise . . . we should have assumed our wings, and mounted direct to paradise" (293). Craik seems determined to remain earthbound, and her project is, in part, to dismantle adult-centered assumptions about the nature of childhood. Such clearheadedness is particularly important, Craik implies, for those who write for young readers, and she proposes to those authors a perhaps impossible task that anticipates Hunt: "The first necessity to secure the attention of little people, is to make yourself a child," she explains, "not in a condescending, carefully-acted fashion, but by coming down, literally and entirely, to their level, and trying to see everything from their point of view. Their interests must be your interests, their reality your reality" (303). Craik's insistence on "literally and entirely" reinhabiting childhood emphasizes her respect not only for the intellectual habits of real children but also for their very physical being in the world. Her reader might imagine her crouched on the floor, among the shoes and shins of adults, attempting to assess how children get to know the world around them, physically and emotionally. Craik suggests that children see the world differently, that they read and appreciate books in ways that challenge adults' preconceptions. Writers are "too apt to forget how uncommonly 'sharp' is the little public they have to deal with," she writes ("Want" 291). Certainly now and then Craik offers portraits of childhood that betray nostalgia or sentimentality, but she is interested in understanding as fully as possible who children are as embodied subjects, what they enjoy reading, and how adults can adapt to those desires.[3]

Hunt and Craik propose, more than a century apart, similarly collaborative projects. Faced with the challenges of understanding children and child readers in particular, both encourage adults to partner with young people; adults should either imagine a child reader as a guide or work alongside real children, paying attention to both their worldview and their experiences as physical, growing beings. Such partnerships introduce anxieties about how to access children's responses in the most pristine form, for neither Hunt nor Craik can escape their status as adults, and they do not claim to. However, their work is part of a larger impulse to invite children into roles of authority regarding children's literature and culture—roles typically occupied by adults—through creative collaboration. In this chapter, I examine nineteenth- and early twentieth-century texts for and about young people in which adults extend such invitations. I argue that many adults represent children as experts who can speak in support of, in critique of, and at times against the expectations of adults. Some of these child authorities are purely fictional or largely fictionalized. For example, in the first section of this chapter, I examine the work of Charles Dickens, William Brighty Rands, and J. M. Barrie, who upend traditional adult-child relationships to entertain the possibility of child authority—especially in representations of child authorship and topsy-turvy plots. However, by the end of the nineteenth century, many adults were exploring ways to collaborate with real child authorities, and in the final two sections of this chapter I trace the influence of children as cultural critics and as students. While the upside-down logic of the child in charge was a popular (and sometimes quaint) notion for many Victorians, a survey of real and imagined child authorities reveals, understandably, that adults considered complete child autonomy undesirable or impossible. In the examples that follow, adults do not cede power completely to children but ultimately negotiate, instead, shared authority—a collaborative partnership between generations in which adults recognize that children are the experts on childhood and adapt to their perspectives.

TURNING THE TABLES

Framing children as authorities requires some acrobatics—or at the very least a few funhouse mirrors. Children, after all, are often assumed passive or powerless, in literature and in life. In her 2010 study *Power, Voice, and Subjectivity in Literature for Young Readers*, Maria Nikolajeva proposes as one of the organizing principles of children's literature aetonormativity: "adult normativity that governs the way children's literature has been patterned from its emergence until the present day." Nikolajeva argues that "nowhere else are power structures as visible as in children's literature, the refined instrument used for centuries to educate, socialize and oppress a particular social group" (8). But children's literature itself, according to Nikolajeva, can "subvert its own oppressive function," and she theorizes moments in literature for young readers that depart from patterns of the powerful adult and powerless child: instances when children "are allowed, in fiction written *by adults* . . . to become strong, brave, rich, powerful, and independent—*on certain conditions and for a limited time*" (9, 10). These rebellious children enjoy a version of the Bakhtinian carnival; they appear in fictions that, rather than substituting fools for kings, swap the social status of powerless children and powerful adults. While children usually (but not always) return to their nurseries and schoolrooms at the end of the adventure, their temporary authority resonates beyond the text. In Nikolajeva's words, "even though the protagonist is most frequently brought back to the security of home and parental supervision, the narratives have a subversive effect, showing that the rules imposed on the child by the adults are in fact arbitrary" (10). Once children have occupied the throne, their status as jesters no longer seems so natural.

Many Victorian and Edwardian children's writers were preoccupied with the potential of children's literature to empower, if only temporarily, child characters through reversals of authority.[4] Age reversal plots in particular, which hinge on the inversion of naturalized power relationships, proffer (and then, often, take away) unprecedented child agency. For instance, in one of the most prominent examples of a Victorian topsy-turvy plot, F. Anstey's *Vice Versâ; or, A Lesson to Fathers* (1882), father Paul Bultitude and his son swap bodies when the young Dick discovers the wish-granting power of a magical stone from India; the book follows the hard-hearted father as he negotiates the indignities of school, an experience that (as the book's title suggests) teaches the paterfamilias sympathy for his son.[5] While, at the end of the narrative, grown man and schoolboy once more occupy their correct bodies, the concluding sentences of Anstey's novel, addressed to the reader, hold out the possibility of further reversals: the stone is missing, perhaps "dashed to pieces" but perhaps "still in existence, with all its dangerous power as ready for use as it ever was" (348). Other boys—maybe even the boys reading the book—may find the stone and wish their fathers into their schoolhouse days while they enjoy the luxuries and respect of maturity. However, while Anstey's novel promotes empathy between father and son, its plot requires an assumed difference, even enmity, between generations. I am interested, instead, in texts that consider how the powerful child can be a partner rather than a foe. The texts I explore in this section, like *Vice Versâ*, are topsy-turvy narratives, but they offer fictional laboratories in which adults speculate on how a child's authority could facilitate adult-child collaboration. In other words, the trope of the powerful and even subversive child reflects and exaggerates the ways real children might participate in the production of their own literature and culture.

Of course, the subversive child is not always a viable creative partner and, in fact, representations of such rebels are often at the child's expense. Before turning to successful intergenerational collaborations between adults and authoritative children, it is useful to identify how topsy-turvy plots can, in fact, make such partnerships difficult, if not impossible. The authoritative children at the center of Dickens's *A Holiday Romance, in Four Parts* (1868), which appeared simultaneously in the American periodical *Our Young Folks* and in Dickens's *All the Year Round*, offer one such example. The four-story sequence—one of the few texts Dickens wrote for a child audience—is narrated by William Tinkling, aged eight, and Robin Redforth, aged nine, along with their "brides" Nettie Ashford, aged "half-past six," and Alice Rainbird, aged seven (428).[6] The first tale is a frame story in the voice of Tinkling, who recounts his failed attempt, alongside Redforth, to free their brides from Miss Grimmer's school and the children's decision—upon realizing, in the words of Rainbird, that "grown-up people WON'T do what they ought to do, and WILL put us out"—to "educate the grown-up people" in the merits of imagination (404, 406). "Let us, in these next Holidays now going to begin, throw our thoughts into something educational for the grown-up people," Rainbird suggests, "hinting to them how things ought to be. Let us veil our reading under a mask of romance" (406). The result is a fictive collaboration among the child authors; between those children and the adult characters who persistently attempt to foil their adventures; and between the writing children and Dickens, the true author of *Holiday Romance*.

Dickens grants his child characters not only the privilege of narration but also fictional authorship, and in the frame story, the children experience the mental and physical realities of the writing life. Beginning on the first page of the story, they struggle with decisions regarding setting, character, plot, and other story elements and with the conflicts and compromises that surround the writing process before, during, and after composition. "I am Editor," avows Tinkling on page one. "Bob Redforth ... wanted to be the Editor of it, but I said he shouldn't because he couldn't. *He* has no idea of being an editor." To spite the self-proclaimed editor, Redforth "shak[es] the table on purpose" (399), causing Tinkling to scrawl unevenly across the page. Dickens draws attention to how the children adopt the language, roles, and behaviors associated with authorship, inflects these behaviors with childlike arrogance and naïveté, and in the process creates a multilayered, comic illusion that they are indeed in charge and that he is merely lending his name to their creation.[7] Taking such authorial posturing into account, Tinkling's first sentence—"This beginning-part is not made out of anybody's head you know"—reads both as a differentiation of his introductory materials from the stories that follow and as a proclamation that these children are not creations of Dickens's imagination, not "made of out anybody's head" (399). Instead, they exist separately as authors with whom Dickens must contend and to whom he must, sometimes, submit.

However, Dickens does not empower his young collaborators; instead, he suggests that his child authors, and perhaps the children reading them, have limited influence on the world around them (and the books created for them). As Marah Gubar argues, *Holiday Romance*, "far from denying the authoritative clout of adults . . . chronicles the children's efforts to usurp, deflect, or reverse that power." While Tinkling, Redforth, Rainbird, and Ashford are decidedly rebellious writers, they must piece together scraps of adult culture—from the imperial adventure to the domestic romance—in an attempt to seize authorship (*Artful* 31). Moreover, while Dickens's child authors are adept and imaginative subjects whose creativity reveals adults as foolish and dim-witted, their attempts to assert authority remain for the most part unrecognized by the adults around them. When Princess Alicia, in Rainbird's story, manages to keep the royal household financially afloat through her own ingenuity and creative housekeeping, the adults in the story remain unimpressed. "They think we children never have a reason or a meaning!" she laments (411). When Nettie Ashford, in her story, describes a school run by the child-teacher Miss Lemon that is meant to educate the grown-ups, the project is a failure, and when the story ends, the misbehaving adults remain at school without the hope of a holiday. If Craik imagined that adults, and in particular children's authors, could (and should) turn to children as the authorities of child-life and attempt to embody that child perspective, then Dickens's *Holiday Romance* seems to make a mockery of that hope; the rift between child and adult remains as wide, if not wider, at the end of the story sequence as it was at the beginning of the children's authorial project.

Dickens himself pokes fun at his characters, and many twentieth-century critics deem his attempt to stage child authorship a decided failure, in part because his attitude toward his child narrators is patronizing. F. J. Harvey Darton, for example, finds that "the alleged narrators ... speak too often with a voice and mind like those of Charles Dickens being playful in his fifty-sixth year," noting that Dickens "pretends to take seriously, but laughs a little superciliously at, the tremendous trivialities of make-believe which are so real in childhood" (293). Anita Moss agrees, arguing that "most readers detect a condescending tone in Dickens's treatment of the childish cuteness of his narrators; his attempts to render the child voice strike many readers as affected and strained. . . . Ironically, he succeeds in making his child characters ridiculous" (91, 88).[8] Indeed, Dickens's attempts to represent the children as viable authors are at odds with those moments when he undermines their seriousness. For example, while Tinkling describes his expedition with Redforth to rescue their child brides with a serious spirit of adventure—"A vow was entered into between the Colonel and myself that we would cut them out on the following Wednesday" (399)—the mission is also inflected by the perspective of an adult chuckling over Tinkling's shoulder. Redforth is "lightly armed with a paper-knife buttoned up under his jacket" and waves "the dreaded black flag at the end of a cane" (400). Their plan of attack, "rolled up around a hoop-stick," is a rough drawing that leads Tinkling to concede that his "real ears don't stick out so horizontally" (400). Tinkling's introduction both represents a childlike commitment to the adventure and undermines that transformation, reminding readers that the boys' plot is surrounded by an adult world that does not participate in the game.

One tale in *Holiday Romance* approaches the possibility of intergenerational collaboration founded on child authority: Redforth's pirate story.[9] Redforth is the child most opposed to the rational adult world. Called "the Pirate" even in the frame story, he refuses to concede that his attack on Miss Grimmer's school is an act of make-believe and belligerently refers to "the grown-up people" as "tyrants" (404, 405). He channels this violent energy into an adventure story in which Captain Boldheart (Redforth himself) chases adventure aboard his schooner, harpoons a whale, stifles an impending mutiny, and encounters a tribe of savage cannibals. Of the three stories in *Holiday Romance*, the pirate adventure is the most successful in its commitment to the child's imagination, and Redforth's account of Boldheart is not undercut as frequently by an adult's perspective. When Redforth explains the pirate captain's circumstances, there is no suggestion we should doubt his earnestness. "It seems that our hero, considering himself spited by a Latin-Grammar-Master, demanded the satisfaction due from one man of honour to another," Redforth explains. "Not getting it, he privately withdrew his haughty spirit from such low company, bought a second-hand pocket-pistol, folded up some sandwiches in a paper bag, made a bottle of Spanish liquorice-water, and entered on a career of valour" (418). While Boldheart's melodramatic manner suggests the exaggerated, broad strokes of play, the reality of this landscape is never put into question. Boldheart's ship remains a noble vessel and never reverts to a packing case; his pocket-pistol remains a deadly weapon and does not reveal itself to be a walking stick or pointed finger; the China Seas do not dissolve into an everyday drawing room. There are moments when Redforth's childish ignorance is apparent. For example, he notes a tense moment aboard his ship when "some murmuring, in which the expressions, 'Aye, aye, sir,' 'Union Jack,' 'Avast,' 'Starboard,' 'Port,' 'Bowsprit,' and similar indications of a mutinous undercurrent, though subdued, were audible" (419). Redforth displays the extent of his nautical vocabulary; unfortunately, none of the crew's "mumbled atrocities" are mutinous in the least. However, this moment is rare in a tale that immerses the reader in the child imagination, a tale that belongs to Redforth and his pirate double, Boldheart. We take Boldheart at his word when he shouts, "'This adventure belongs to me. . . . Let no *man* follow'" (419, emphasis added).

Boldheart rules over the adult world without mercy, cutting down any adult who questions his authority and tolerating only those grown-ups who support his mission. The most heated conflict in the story is between Boldheart and the Latin-Grammar-Master, whose pedagogical tyranny over young boys makes him Boldheart's natural enemy. When Boldheart finds his former instructor "in a hamper with his head shaved," ready to be cooked alive by a tribe of cannibals, Boldheart convinces the savages to allow the man to "remain raw" only on two conditions: "that he should never under any circumstances presume to teach any boy anything any more," and "that, if taken back to England, he should pass his life in traveling to find out boys who wanted their exercises done, and should do their exercises for those boys for nothing, and never say a word about it" (424–25). Boldheart subverts the pedagogue's rule over the child by making him a slave to the student and forces the professor to admit that adults have nothing to teach children (and that to pretend otherwise is presumptuous). He attempts to maintain the decorum of a respectable captain, giving the Grammar-Master a chance to redeem his ways, but unfortunately the professor is, in the end, incorrigible. When Boldheart's parents, aboard a ship called the *Family*, visit the ship to reclaim their son, the Grammar-Master negotiates with them to end Boldheart's adventures and send him back to the world of adult authority. "It was in the course of the night that the ... thankless traitor was found out," records Redforth. "He was hanged at the yard-arm the first thing in the morning" (426). Adults only figure in Redforth's imagination to reinforce the strength of his fantasy. The *Family* flies the flag from the Redforth garden as their standard, reminding Boldheart of the domestic order of home—in which child submits to adult, son to father, pupil to professor—and yet his parents do not insist upon reclaiming Boldheart and instead sustain the game, bringing him greens and fresh meat, touring his ship, expressing proper amazement at the might of its cannons, and obediently following his orders to sail away. Adults in Redforth's tale must abide by the child's rules, collaborating (or colluding) with the young to shore up the powers of the imagination in order to shut out the "real" world. Adults who fail to submit to the powerful child suffer the fate of the Grammar-Master. Dickens's pirate story stands alone in *A Holiday Romance* as an example of the carnivalesque possibilities of children's literature identified by Nikolajeva—the ability of children's literature to "subvert its own oppressive function" and allow young people "to become strong, brave, rich, powerful, and independent—*on certain conditions and for a limited time.*"

By the time Dickens published *Holiday Romance*, William Brighty Rands had been exploring for years such subversions of adult authority, both in his literature for children and in his essays on child life and children's books—and in a manner that promises amity rather than enmity, collaboration rather than alienation. The titular poem in his collection *Lilliput Levee: Poems of Childhood, Child-Fancy, and Childlike Moods* (1864), a volume that was popular in the nineteenth century but is largely forgotten today, epitomizes such subversions:

> Oh, the Glorious Revolution!
> Oh, the Provisional Constitution!
> Now that the Children, clever bold folks,
> Have turn'd the tables upon the Old Folks!
>
> Easily the thing was done,
> For the Children were more than two to one. (7)

The children of Lilliput have made it their task to destroy all signs of adult authority and indulge in those pleasures parents and teachers deny them. They raided the chemist's and "kick'd the physic all down the street," and they stormed the schoolhouse and "burnt the books" (8). They dined on nuts and negus and "munched the puffs at the pastrycook's," and they disciplined and catechized parents and teachers. In the poem's final lines, after cataloguing an impressive array of misbehaviors, the narrator discovers that the King and Queen of Lilliput are searching for a Poet Laureate:

> Said I to myself, here's a chance for me,
> The Lilliput Laureate for to be!
> And these are the Specimens I sent in
> To Pinafore Palace. Shall I win? (13)

This final question, directed at both the child holding the book with the children who live in Lilliput, is crucial to the book's reversals of authority. As Gubar argues, "this moment alerts young readers to their own power of discrimination, of weighing rather than simply absorbing the literary offerings of adults. Since this poem prefaces the rest of the collection, it invites child readers to view the rest of Rands's work with an evaluative eye" (*Artful* 151). Rands assumes that child readers are intelligent and discerning, Gubar argues, and as such he is one of many Golden Age writers who understood the child not as "an innocent Other" or "a less evolved breed of being" but instead as a clever and precocious young person (151). In this way, Rands adopts what Gubar has dubbed the "kinship" model of childhood, which is "premised on the idea that children and adults are akin to one another, which means they are neither exactly the same nor radically dissimilar." This idea of childhood "indicates relatedness, connection, and similarity without implying homogeneity, uniformity, and equality" ("Risky" 451).

Understanding children in terms of kinship does not grant them complete authority—they may not be king and queen, as they are in *Lilliput Levee*—but it does encourage adults to abandon the assumption that children are inherently inferior or passive, and it allows parents, teachers, and writers for children to acknowledge the ways children participate in their own literature and culture. In fact, I argue that Gubar's account of Rands and his approach to childhood suggests not only the clever child but also the collaborative child, fictive and real—a figure that becomes even more apparent if we read *Lilliput Levee* through Nikolajeva's theories of children's literature as carnivalesque. In order to emphasize "how uncommonly 'sharp'" children are (to borrow Craik's phrase), Rands uses the subversions of the carnival to disrupt adult power and suggest the arbitrariness of adult authority. Why shouldn't children critique poetry intended for them? Is this any more ridiculous than allowing adults to do so? Rands's work disrupts the aetonormative assumption that *adults* are the arbiters of children's literature—and then lets that challenge stand. While Nikolajeva argues that such topsy-turvy fictions rarely sustain the raucous reign of child rebels, usually resolving in the return of the status quo, *Lilliput Levee* is an exception. Rands suspends the moment of child supremacy in the concluding "L'envoi," where he once again offers "ye dear Lilliputians"—and his child readers—his "versifications," supposedly for their enjoyment and their judgment (112). Rands's respect for children as interlocutors and authorities, then, extends beyond the boundaries of his text. While he does not advocate for complete child rule—the young people there tend toward destruction, nailing doors shut and cutting the legs off parlor-chairs, and their world is fantastical, populated by giants and rocs (10, 9)—the exaggerated reversals of Lilliput denaturalize adult authority, and the consequences reverberate throughout Rands's writing for and about children.

Lilliput Levee, in fact, anticipates arguments Rands makes elsewhere for a reconceptualization of adult-child relationships as collaborative partnerships based on respect for the child as an embodied subject and a constant questioning of adults' authority. For example, Rands might agree with the Lilliputian children who "kick'd the physic all down the street" and "munched the puffs at the pastrycook's." In his essay "The Nurture of Children" (1869), he argues for "less medication and more hygiene" and notes that "the taste of children for sweets is one to which there need be no check, except the ordinary rule which applies to all kinds of excess"—recommendations that he acknowledges do not align with common ideas of how to raise healthy and disciplined children (122, 128). Even more striking parallels exist, however, between *Lilliput Levee* and Rands's "Children and Children's Books" (1866), where the children of Lilliput—who were "more than two to one"—reappear, this time in a milder guise. Despite the fact that children are "more than two to one," Rands laments, "how little some of us reflect upon the space they occupy, the place they fill, in the great picture of existence!" He argues that children "'influence' us just as much as we 'influence' them" (464), his quotation marks putting into question not only the direction but also the nature of "influence" in general. Adults, therefore, should approach their relationship with young people in terms of mutuality rather than complete authority, and doing so requires a recognition of the very bodies of children—"the space they occupy, the place they fill." Throughout this essay, Rands develops a theory of intergenerational partnership based on sympathy—a position that places adults and children on more equal footing with one another than many adults are accustomed to. "The child contains, in little, all that the adult contains," Rands writes, "and should be dealt with upon that hypothesis" (464). For Rands, this means looking to children's preferences and experiences, rather than assuming adults' expertise, to determine best practices for nurturing and educating children. He advocates "living strenuously for [children], and with them"—to consider children through the "sympathies" they share with adults ("Nurture" 123). Living "for" children and living "with" them seem to be two different propositions, the former suggesting the superiority of young people and the latter suggesting a more democratic relationship, but both revise familiar patterns of adult-child relationships.

Rands's promotion of sympathy between adults and children is central to his understanding of children's literature as a collaborative project between adults and children. Adults, Rands notes, "meddle with children a great deal too much, and wait upon them a great deal too little. By waiting upon them, I mean, of course, laying ourselves out to them, in willing sympathy, treating them as we do our equals in noble friendship" ("Children" 465). "Meddling," for Rands, is epitomized in "books which inculcate particular views of life, and specific lessons," texts that presume children are "crude, shapeless lumps, that had to be 'turned' into figure on the lathe" (465). In order to pursue a "noble friendship" with children, adults must abandon their assumptions about the child's innate inferiority or passivity; this is not common practice, as "the majority of parents, instead of buying, for presents, books that will please the children, buy such as please themselves" (465). While Rands is surprised at "the inaptitude of the old folk in finding out what the young like," he is confident that by allowing children to select the literature that pleases them—which, he contends, will include everything from Hans Christian Andersen to William Wordsworth—and by sharing that literature with them, adults will forge just the sort of sympathetic relationship with children that will breed amity between generations. For Rands, then, the topsy-turvy plot of *Lilliput Levee*'s title poem is a fictional exaggeration, but it exaggerates an important reconsideration of authority between real adults and children, particularly when it comes to children's books. Adults *should*, according to Rands, revise their interactions with children, understanding the young not as subjects of adult authority but instead as partners and collaborators.

Rands elaborates upon this model of intergenerational partnership in later publications for children that recall but moderate the unchecked child sovereignty of Lilliput. For example, his *Lilliput Lectures* (1871) are, in effect, a case study in how the sympathetic model of adult-child relationships might transform children's literature into a collaborative enterprise. In the introduction to the volume, Rands frames the essays that follow, which tackle everything from art to God to government, as the product of adult-child collaboration—and as opportunities to reproduce such partnerships among his readers. He describes the volume as "an avowed attempt by a grown person to mediate, in the light of his recollection of what used to puzzle him, between the mature mind and the young mind in certain matters in which the attempt is not often made. They are, in fact, confidential and personal:—'You are young, and I am grown-up,—let us talk these matters over, with a clear understanding that it is so'" (4). Rands does not seek to ignore the differences between adults and children; in fact, he wants to maintain a "clear understanding" of such differences. However, those differences enrich rather than thwart meaningful discourse. To find middle ground between children's and "grown-up" perspectives, Rands uses as guidance both his memories of childhood and "[his] intercourse, in teaching capacities, with children" (6). Recognizing that memory is not enough to support substantial and respectful relationships with young people, Rands turns to embodied children, supplementing recollections of his own childhood with experiences with real children. While those adult-child interactions took place in the classroom—an environment that often assumes adult authority—Rands characterizes teaching as dialogue. Learning is reciprocal, according to Rands; "one single hour of frank *life* with children," he writes, "life in which they give as much as they receive—is worth a whole quarter's 'schooling'" ("Children's" 465).

Notably, to explain some of the book's challenging subjects, he turns to metaphor, a rhetorical device that, in his understanding, helps bridge the "young mind" and "mature mind." "In these Lectures," he writes, "I am going to give little boys and girls . . . a piece of string or strap to tie things together with. This, you must know, is what is called a metaphor, or figure of speech . . . for what I am going to do is to give you thoughts put into words which will help you to tie separate bits of knowledge together in your own heads, making it much easier for you to carry them" (16–17). This is the first metaphor of many Rands deploys throughout the *Lectures*, and as a whole the collection often introduces complex topics through ideas child readers are presumably accustomed to: a chapter on science begins with familiar lessons in music and geography, for example, and the chapter on art and artists starts with a story about a boy pretending to be Robinson Crusoe. While the pedagogical influence of Rousseau and others might dictate that adults adhere to concrete language in teaching children, Rands finds abstractions useful. Rather than consider the limits children's ignorance might place on adult-child dialogue, he places his faith in children's competencies, assuming that adults can offer the young not simply new knowledge but also, perhaps more importantly, ideas and language to help young people make sense of their existing expertise.

Rands assumes children bring a lot to their literature: knowledge of their world, intellectual curiosity, and a willingness to work with adults to consider complex questions. Decades later, J. M. Barrie would posit that children brought nearly everything to his play *Peter Pan*—and that he brought very little. Barrie was anxious about the authorship of *Peter Pan* even in its early drafts, which he titled "Anon." The program to the first production of *Peter* in 1904 lists as author Ela Q. May, the actress who played Liza, the housemaid (Rose, *Case* 76), and in a now-famous example of imagined child authorship, Barrie claims in his 1928 "To the Five: A Dedication" that some "disquieting confessions must be made in printing at last the play of *Peter Pan*, among them this, that I have no recollection of having written it" (75).[10] Barrie proposes a number of possible authors, including a "depressed man in overalls" who wanders the theater where the play is rehearsed holding "a mug of tea or a paint-pot" and expressing a "hopelessness [that] is what all dramatists are said to feel at such times." He also considers "a large number of children" he has seen "playing Peter in their homes with careless mastership, constantly putting in better words," who could have "thrown [the play] off with ease." These children are "careless" masters and superior wordsmiths, adept young writers who seem to run (or fly) circles around Barrie, who only faintly recalls the "long job" of writing *Peter*. Barrie notes how the children mimicking Peter's adventures at home have the power to influence the very content of the play. "It was for such as they," writes Barrie, "that after the first production I had to add something to the play at the request of parents . . . about no one being able to fly until the fairy dust had been blown on him; so many children having gone home and tried it from their beds and needed surgical attention" (77).

Theater, of course, is collaborative, and Barrie was a successful playwright before the premiere of *Peter*, experienced in the partnerships among actors, theater managers, set and costume designers, and any number of creative figures who participate in bringing a script to the stage.[11] However, it is the child collaborator, and in particular the child author, who troubles Barrie. After all, as Barrie notes in the dedication, he does not struggle with the authorship of his other plays as he does with *Peter*. In his dedication, he notes that the composition of his first piece, *Ibsen's Ghost*, and "that noble mouthful, *Bandelero the Bandit*" are vivid in his memory. "I can haul back to mind the writing of almost every other assay of mine, however forgotten by the pretty public," notes Barrie, "but this play of Peter, no. . . . How odd, too, that these trifles should adhere to the mind that cannot remember the long job of writing Peter" (76). It seems Barrie felt *Peter* demanded a more circumspect consideration of the relationship between inspiration, composition, and production that other works do not require. This play is steeped in the codes and behaviors of play and, as many scholars have noted, Barrie's work exhibits both an intimate connection to that childlike perspective and a deeply felt alienation from it.[12] Understandably (and usefully), many scholars read Barrie's renouncement of authorship as a rhetorical gesture that registers a complex psychological relationship to childhood—not as a serious commentary on the role of young people in the composition of the play.[13]

It is important to consider, as these scholars do, how Barrie's authorial amnesia might indicate the psychological shell game children's authors perform to conceal a complex and sometimes sinister construction of ideal childhood. However, I argue that it is equally important to read this dedication as Barrie's attempt to recognize the influence of child authors, both real and imagined, on his most famous play. In other words, I would like to do something Barrie scholars only rarely do: take seriously his difficulty of accepting ownership of *Peter* and explore the topsy-turvy logic that children are responsible for the play, rather than the adult author.[14] In the dedication and in the play itself, Barrie rehearses his discomfort with claiming a text indebted to the make-believe adventures of the Llewelyn Davies brothers and to his own young self. He does deploy the language of lost youth and nostalgia, but he also provides a compelling account of the process of collaborating with children as well as the challenges of participating in, and representing, such intergenerational creative partnerships. In other words, Barrie wrestles with both the real contributions children, as authorities of make-believe, made to *Peter Pan* and their symbolic freight as figures of childhood, and his dedication therefore provides an account of *Peter* as a hybrid collaboration. Approached in this way, Barrie's dedication suggests that *Peter* is a case study in the boundaries of child authority. How much power can an author cede to the child?

For Barrie, the act of writing not only makes clear his isolation from childhood but also offers an opportunity for true intergenerational collaboration. Take, for example, his thoughts on his penmanship: "In my schooldays I wrote the most beautiful copperplate," he notes. "Sometimes of an evening I still gaze at it with proud bewilderment. It went, I think, not gradually with over-writing, but suddenly like my smile" (*Letters* vi). Barrie includes this anecdote in a letter to a friend; he is poking fun at his nearly illegible adult scrawl.[15] However, the defamiliarization Barrie experiences contemplating his childhood writing is an apt description of the troubles he faces as an author for children. In *Peter*, Barrie takes on a genre that asks him to write, essentially, as a child—in a manner that pleases a child, that demonstrates his understanding of child life, on topics that capture a child's imagination—and yet he is a man who finds his own child writing more foreign than familiar. Focusing on his childhood "hand," Barrie emphasizes that youth is both an intellectual and a physical state, and that maturation of both mind and body interrupt the possible connection between adult and child. To overcome the obstacle of his age, Barrie collaborates with children who, in a sense, can write for him. At times, these collaborations are purely fictional. For example, Barrie represents the child as a collaborator in *The Little White Bird*, a novel for adults that includes one of the earliest versions of the Peter Pan story. The narrator, an aging man lonely for child companionship, pieces together the story of Peter with the assistance of the young David:

> The following is our way with a story: First, I tell it to [David], and then he tells it to me, the understanding being that it is quite a different story; and then I retell it to him with his additions, and so we go on until no one could say whether it is more his story or mine. In this story of Peter Pan, for instance, the bald narrative and most of the moral reflections are mine, though not all, for this boy can be a stern moralist, but the interesting bits about the ways of babies in the bird-stage are mostly reminisces of David's, recalled by pressing his hands to his temples and thinking hard. (132–33)

This collaboration muddles the borders of authorship: his story or mine? However, it becomes increasingly clear that the adult's role in telling the tale is subordinate to the child's. The narrator's contributions provide an outline: the "bald narrative" and "moral reflections" to be filled in by the child. The contributions of David are not only more imaginative (the "interesting bits") but also drawn from personal memories of a phase of youth the adult can no longer access ("the bird-stage" of babyhood). Adult and child meet through a collaboration that recognizes adult and child expertise as well as adult and child bodies; the young David "press[es] his hands to his temples" to recall his life in the "bird-stage." While this is a fictive account of intergenerational partnership, there is also evidence that Barrie engaged in collaborations with children less elaborate than the "long job" of *Peter Pan*. In some cases, he required the presence of a close child-friend as an aid to composition. For instance, Barrie's novel *Sentimental Tommy* (1896) relies extensively on his boyhood memories, and he found that "the companionship with a real boy"—in this case friend Arthur Quiller-Couch's son Bevil—"helped to bring the memories swinging back" (Birkin 32). Later, in 1903, Barrie drew up a contract with Jack Llewelyn Davies, recognizing the boy's contribution of a one-line joke in the play *Little Mary* and granting him a halfpenny share in each night's earnings.[16]

The dedication to *Peter Pan* offers a more extensive account of how Barrie's work was, in his view, a joint production between himself and the Llewelyn Davies brothers. Throughout the first paragraph, he uses the possessive pronoun "we" to indicate the collective action of adult and children: "We first brought Peter down, didn't we, with a blunt-headed arrow in Kensington Gardens," he reminisces shortly before noting, "we had good sport of him before we clipped him small to make him fit the boards" (75). Nonetheless, the more persistent note throughout the dedication, and the more striking stance Barrie takes, is his insistence that his role in imagining Peter is ultimately negligible. "You had played [Peter] until you tired of it," confesses Barrie, "and tossed it in the air and gored it and left it derelict in the mud and went on your way singing other songs; and then I stole back and sewed some of the gory fragments together with a pen-nib" (76). The play is pilfered moments from the boys' adventure play, and these moments are unaltered by Barrie aside from his ability to sew them together with his pen. Here, Barrie is drawing a pointed contrast between boys' contributions—their ability to put on and take off roles like costumes, changing directions and "songs" intuitively and without forethought or consequence—with the adult world of professional authorship—which operates according to certain rules and is mired in the marketplace. The latter works in service to the former. At one point, Barrie characterizes his transcription of the Llewelyn Davies's boyhood adventures as "merely a cold decision to turn you into bread and butter," a phrase that appropriates the transformations of childhood make-believe for adult, financial ends. The alienation Barrie feels from his own creation, an outgrowth of his alienation from boyhood itself, becomes particularly troubling when Barrie considers the "cold rights" of the play, trying to determine who *owns* Peter. "I talk of dedicating the play to you, but how can I prove it is mine?" asks Barrie. "Any one of you five brothers has a better claim to the authorship than most, and I would not fight you for it" (77).[17]

Of course, Barrie contributed more to *Peter* than he admits here, and early on in the dedication he does claim authorship to some degree. "I think I wrote Peter," he surrenders, "and if so it must have been in the usual inky way" (77). Having forfeited the point, he sets to proving himself author—a reckoning that makes clear his desire to distribute ownership of the play among his child self and his child companions. Regarding the former, he offers a range of evidence: memories of the washhouse where he staged his first dramas, for example, which was the original for the Wendy house, and his early proclivity for "wrecked island" stories (78). But this is complicated logic for Barrie. It requires reconciling his alienation from childhood with the intimate relationship he senses between his childhood exploits and adult character. In service to his claims of authorship, he attempts to resolve this tension, offering the image of a house with many rooms:

> Some say that we are different people at different periods of our lives, changing not through effort of will, which is a brave affair, but in the easy course of nature every ten years or so. I suppose this theory might explain my present struggle, but I don't hold with it; I think one remains the same person throughout, merely passing, as it were, in these lapses of time from one room to another, but all in the same house. If we unlock the rooms of the far past we can peer in and see ourselves, busily occupied in beginning to become you and me. (78)

Barrie registers detachment from childhood but rejects the notion that he is *completely* alienated from his young self, transformed into a new person entirely. He may be cut off from his childhood by a series of doors, but he can travel imaginatively through these rooms to observe himself. It is impossible for Barrie to reinhabit youth; he will always see his child self as a double, bodily separate and perpetually absorbed in his own concerns and activities. Eventually, Barrie's discomfort with claiming such an intimate connection between adult and child selves folds in upon itself. "Of course this is over-charged. Perhaps we do change," he concedes. But even in this moment, he clings to childhood tenaciously, claiming that there survives in the adult "a little something in us which is no larger than a mote in the eye, and that, like it, dances in front of us beguiling us all our days. I cannot cut the hair by which it hangs" (79). The image of the "mote in the eye," the "little something in us" that remains as our essential being, resonates with a description of Peter found in the stage directions of *Peter*, during the final battle with Hook. Hook, befuddled by Peter's swordsmanship and even more so by his seeming immateriality, muses that Peter is "less like a boy than a mote of dust dancing in the sun" (145).[18]

According to Barrie, however, it is not his own childhood memories that act as "the strongest evidence that [he is] the author" of *Peter* but instead the privately printed photo-essay, *The Boy Castaways of Black Lake Island, Being a Record of the Terrible Adventures of Three Brothers in the Summer of 1901, Faithfully Set Forth by No. 3* (79).[19] The volume, comprising a preface and a series of photographs accompanied by explanatory chapter titles and captions, chronicles the make-believe adventures of

George, Jack, and Peter Llewelyn Davies when they set out in the *Anna Pink* "to be wrecked" on the shores of Black Lake. *Boy Castaways* is a vital ur-text for *Peter* and registers how Barrie understands the brothers both as real children who contribute to the story that would eventually transform into *Peter* and as imagined child authors. On the one hand, the boys contribute to the text in believable, logical ways. For example, Barrie claims the photographs are all "taken by myself," but the content of those images was not under his control; "some of them [were] indeed of phenomena that had to be invented afterwards," he admits, "for [the boys] were always off doing the wrong things when I pressed the button" (81). It seems likely the boys would not follow the photographer's instructions, and their misbehavior transforms the narrative in material ways. However, Barrie also claims that the book is "edited by the youngest" of the boys, who also provides "a long preface" (80). The youngest participant is Peter, aged four at the time. This is an obvious falsehood—a trope of child authorship that communicates Barrie's feelings about the boys' central role in *Boy Castaways* through the *figure* of the child author. In describing his relationship to the brothers, and their relationship to his play, Barrie imagines the authoritative child as both living boy (who runs from the camera and does not follow directions) and fictional child author (who possesses a purely imaginative literacy), and the various manifestations of the brothers work together to suggest both their vital role in the project and the challenges of describing that role without falling into fictionalization. It is telling that, to assert their authority, the boys imaginatively kill off Barrie, who acts the part of Captain Swarthy, the precursor to Hook, in a few comically violent photographs. "The pirate captain's end was not in the mouth of a crocodile," notes Barrie, "though we had crocodiles on the spot. I think our captain had diverse deaths owing to unseemly competition among you, each wanting to slay him single-handed" (82).

If, in his first argument for authorship, in which he calls on his own childhood adventures as precursors to *Peter*, Barrie represents his essential self as Peter, then in this second piece of evidence, Barrie becomes Hook, the pirate captain whose presence in Neverland both enables the make-believe adventures of Peter and the Lost Boys and whose death is always demanded by that crew of orphan boys. Barrie's place in his play is multiple, a relationship of great identification with the imaginative element of the play and unavoidably separate from it. In negotiating his role in *Peter*, Barrie has become both the essence of childhood and its nemesis. His renouncement of authorship is itself a form of play, imaginative and theatrical, a series of make-believe scenes and poses he adopts in order to tease out the unique adult-child relationships that comprise the collaborative authorship of *Peter*. The evidence he supplies speaks to his understanding of children's literature as a genre in which the adult observes and records in as genuine a mode as possible the imaginative play of the child, the intended audience. While readers or audiences of *Peter* may assume that Barrie is the "responsible person"—a role he owns, although hesitantly—he is more comfortable understanding himself as only the transcriber, an adult amanuensis for the boys, who are the primary movers of the tale (77). Barrie can claim to be the author of *Peter* only because he can prove either that he *is* a child, a young boy feverishly reading pirate stories, or that he is decidedly *not* a child but an adult who is powerless, strung up by a ragtag crew of boys dressed as castaways. By offering these alternatives simultaneously, Barrie characterizes the relationship between creative child and writing adult as ambivalent—a relationship of both great intimacy and great violence, of love and hatred.[20]

THAT MAJESTIC CHILD PUBLIC

The Llewelyn Davies boys who appear in Barrie's dedication to *Peter Pan* are hybrids and changelings, a curious mixture of the real brothers and Barrie's fictionalizations of them. However, real children attended performances of *Peter Pan* and read *Peter and Wendy*, and reviews about the play published in popular periodicals recognize or even quote these young people as authorities on the success of Barrie's story for children. Gubar has identified some of these child reviewers in her reading of *Peter Pan* as children's theater. She cites, for example, a 1906 review of the play published in the *New York Times* that documents the enthusiasm of "several hundred children" who, after the performance, "waited at the stage door and threw confetti and flowers at [Peter]. They decorated the carriage with daisies. The driver with difficulty frustrated a plan of the children to take out the horses and pull the carriage home themselves" ("Children Admirers" 9). Years later, when *Peter Pan* was an established yearly holiday performance, *The Bookman* hosted a competition titled "What the Audience Thinks," asking children under fourteen to review the play. The magazine published the winning entry, written by Charlie Assheton, who described *Peter Pan* as "very nice indeed, but when Peter was flying I could see the wires that were attached to his shoulders" ("What" 119).

The periodical *Quiver* also hosted a competition for children on the topic of *Peter Pan*, asking its young readers to choose a scene from the play to illustrate ("Special").[21] Such reviews and competitions evidence that adults not only turned to fictive child collaborators in writing children's literature, as Dickens and Barrie did, but also solicited the perspectives of living children outside the text. The child-as-authority acted, in a sense, as a collaborative child, engaging with adults to comment upon children's literature and culture.

The child reviewer was not universally loved. Eveline C. Godley, in the 1906 essay "A Century of Children's Books," warns readers of the trend in trusting the assessments of child reviewers. While Godley admits that "scarcely one adult reader in a hundred can speak with certainty of how a story, or any given piece of writing, will impress a child" (437), she is wary of the practice of consulting young people instead:

> The modern critic, wishing for a reliable judgment, turns naturally to the children themselves. Interviews and letters are published, all quoting the opinion of authorities between the ages of eight and fourteen, as though their verdict were beyond appeal. Nothing could be more reasonable; that is, from a strictly modern point of view. A child of ten *is* a better judge of what is attractive to children than the most accomplished man of letters. The critic, if he has moved with the times, will make it his business to find out what is attractive, and will ask no further. But a more complete departure from the original intent of children's stories it would be impossible to imagine. Time was when the story was merely a cloak, at best a thin one, for the moral; its engaging qualities served as a means to an end, not as the reason for its existence. The standard, principle, or ideal was always unflinching, and everything else must be moulded to it. Now the ideal must be moulded to suit the child. Everything has to give way before the infallible instincts of childhood; it is the unfortunate outside influence which is looked on with suspicion. (437)

Godley does not recommend a return to thinly disguised didacticism; in fact, she lambastes the heavy-handed moralizing of earlier children's literature. She describes Rosamund's mother from Maria Edgeworth's notorious "The Purple Jar" as "a most repellent person, hard-hearted, priggish, and unreasonable," and she notes of Martha Finley's Elsie Dinsmore that it would be "difficult to say at what moment of her career the eight-year-old . . . is most obnoxious" (441, 443). Yet Godley is equally, if not more, skeptical of what she considers an uncritical acceptance of the "modern theory that children's instincts are a sure guide to what is best, in literature and in everything else," which ends in "an unconcealed effort to please that can only be described as slavish" (449). This "complete departure from the original intent of children's stories" troubles Godley not simply because modern children's books abandon a moral project. Godley also seems to suspect that catering to the desires of child readers threatens familiar patterns of adult authority and child obedience. In the eyes of the "modern critic," Godley frets, "if any one is to be in the position of a pupil it is the author, not the child. This plan might be simple enough, if an author had only to say that he did not wish to instruct a child in order to prevent it from learning. The fact, however, remains that most children do learn something, consciously or unconsciously, from everything that they read" (438–39). What children desire, and what Godley suspects adults desperately provide to them, is not, Godley suggests, what we want children to learn. Perhaps children are learning the threatening fact that their influence is powerful, and that they can transform the literature adults write for them.

Two models of child readers' relationships to adult authors emerge in Godley's essay. On the one hand, children are students of adult author's values; on the other, they are slave-driving critics demanding adults' compliance. Perhaps Godley recognized the rhetorical impact of putting such disparate ideas side by side. However, these extremes obscure the more complex problem of determining how influential child readers' responses *should* be in shaping the nature of books written for them. Writers and reviewers throughout the nineteenth century considered carefully how (or whether) to acknowledge and adapt to young readers' evaluations of children's literature—a task complicated by the hierarchies inherent in adult-child relationships. In contemporary criticism, it is common to recognize the potential adult-centeredness of children's literature, but Charles Lamb had recognized the influence adults exert over the market in children's books as early as 1808, writing to William Godwin, "It is children that read children's books, when they are read, but it is parents that choose them. The critical thought of the tradesman put itself therefore into the place of the parent, and what the parent will condemn" (387). Despite adults' undeniable sway over children's literature, the child reviewer appears in various guises and disguises throughout the Victorian period—as a naïf, as an exacting judge, or as an informed critic, for example—decades before Godley's essay appeared at the beginning of the twentieth century. The "interviews and letters ... all quoting the opinion of authorities between the ages of eight and fourteen" Godley cites, some of which I will explore below, betray a willingness to introduce children into the systems of production and evaluation that ultimately determine the nature of children's literature. In the final decades of the nineteenth century, some adults began to see children not as passive pupils awaiting instruction or demanding readers greedy for pleasure but instead as useful collaborators who could be instrumental in shaping children's literature. Unlike the child characters and fictionalized child authors explored above, who are evidence of adults' *imagined* partnership with child authorities, these child readers—and the documents that attempt to capture their perspectives—reveal that adults consulted children as experts in children's literature, negotiating a sometimes unstable partnership with them as arbiters of literature for young people.

Some of the most common manifestations of the child critic are likely not true children at all but stock figures deployed for comic relief or sentimentality. These young reviewers frequently pass judgment on books and performances intended for adults, and the joke rests in part on the unsophisticated child's inability to comprehend the material before him or her. For example, a frequent contributor to *Punch* who writes under the pseudonym Squibbler explains that "having become, after a good many years of play-seeing and circus-viewing, rather *blasé* of these favourite amusements, I now frequently take with me, to help me in forming an opinion anent the merits of a performance, a young gentleman I call 'Tommy the Tester.' ... This year he has greatly grown both in body and mind, and combines with the keen enjoyment of extreme youth the critical acumen of considerable experience" ("Hengler's" 73). Tommy may indeed be based on one of the Squibbler's young acquaintances, but his alliterative name suggests more character than living person, and his commentary serves a decided purpose in *Punch*: he both recovers the wonder of the theater the Squibbler has lost to age and evades accusations of rudeness when he offers sharp-edged or common sense evaluations, exhibiting a directness his adult counterpart cannot enjoy due to social conventions. He is also, however, the unwitting butt of the author's jokes. When Tommy returns to the pages of *Punch* just a week after his introduction to review the play *The Galley Slave*, his summary of the plot is convoluted and comic, and the editor notes that the review "would, no doubt, have been clearer had [Tommy] been a little older"

("Something" 93). Child respondents such as Tommy are often dupes or darlings, and while they enjoy the immunity of, say, a court jester—the ability to criticize the world of adults without punishment, winning instead laughing appreciation—that privilege is enjoyed at the price of foolishness. While *Punch*'s Squibbler suggests that he is working in collaboration with Tommy, this figure of the child, like the child authors in Dickens's *Holiday Romance*, instead reinscribes and reinforces the distance between generations.

Yet children were not called upon solely to comment naïvely on literature and performances assumed to be beyond their comprehension. By the mid-nineteenth century, turning to young readers or audience members for opinions on children's literature and culture was commonplace—a familiar practice to adults who write and review children's books. A critic in an 1869 issue of the *Examiner and London Review* acknowledges, albeit with some disdain, that "it is customary to say that the children must decide" the value of books published for them ("Among" 307), and indeed many nineteenth-century critics propose that adults abdicate the position of reviewer to children. Mrs. Alaric Watts, for instance, writes in the preface to *The New Year's Gift; and Juvenile Souvenir* (1831) that "an intelligent child is often the best judge of what will most interest other children; and this test, simple as it is, will frequently be found of more use to the writers of books for children, than the sagest counsels of more experienced critics" (vi). Watts's recommendation was excerpted in reviews of her own book and other children's literature; a critic in the *Eclectic Review*, for instance, quotes Watts before noting, "so entirely do we agree with the Writer, that we should feel disposed to print the comments of this shrewd little class of critics . . . in preference to our own, had we had sufficient time to collect their verdicts" (*Ackermann's* 561). Richard Rowe addresses his "young readers" in the first pages of *A Child's Corner Book* (1876), noting that children are "the best judges of books for children; and, therefore, when I write for them, I am very glad if I can get a child's criticism on what I have written before I print it" (4). And a reviewer in the *Outlook*, fawning over E. Nesbit's *The Story of the Treasure-Seekers*, concedes that the novel will appeal to "that majestic child-public which is never in the least uncertain as to what it likes, and why" ("Delightful" 626). This appeal to the "child-public" recalls Rands's comical application for the position of poet laureate in *Lilliput Levee*, but here adult authors are advised explicitly to please real young readers, not just the demanding young King and Queen of Lilliput.

Recognizing the value of children's responses to literature for young people is, of course, not the same thing as granting a young reader the privileges of the reviewer's pen. A survey of young people's reactions to children's literature published in popular periodicals reveals that these reviewers are complex characters. Their presence often implies an editor's interest in accurate accounts of child voices, but such editors do not entirely escape the temptations of the *figure* of the child, and these child reviewers are therefore subject to some fictionalization, condescension, and sentimentality. For example, reviewers in the *Leader* note in 1853 that their assessments of the year's children's books "are, for the most part, guided by juvenile critics who have read them, and pronounced very unbiased, if not very discerning, verdicts." While these editors are snide toward young readers' tastes and toward children's literature as a whole—"we have had much more pressing calls upon our time," they write, "than the reading of a pile of children's books"—they do include the supposed reactions of child readers. *The Ice King and the Sweet South Wind*, by Caroline Butler, for instance, was "pronounced 'so stunning' by a fascinated critic, from whom it was with difficulty secured, for the purpose of notice" ("Children's" 1245). Editors at the *London Review* use a similar strategy. Faced with the holiday selections for 1866, they turned to child readers. "Acting on the Bishop of London's description of the way in which a Privy Council judgment is drawn up," the review begins, "we submitted these books to a committee of young people." The editors may have hoped that the incongruity of a "committee-man" of "five years old . . . his judgment conveyed in the shape of laughter" would draw a smile from their readers, but they also seem to consider the responses of their young collaborators with a degree of seriousness, paying as much attention to the children's emotional responses as to their spoken preferences. The young boy's laughter, the adult reviewer assures, "seemed spontaneous; but there were parts of the book on which the eye did not rest, other parts which the mind rejected, others which were too willfully funny to be fun in reality" ("Children's" 665–66). These reviewers imply that adults can determine the success of children's literature by reading child readers' faces, a strategy picked up by a reviewer signed E.C. in *The Speaker*, who notes in 1902 that the only way of knowing if a young reader truly enjoys a book is to "watch the child narrowly but secretly at the same time. Some children, if they think you expect them to enjoy it, will affect to do so, though they cannot counterfeit the rapt expression of the really absorbed child" (231). Taken together, reviews such as these suggest that evaluating children's books is an intergenerational, collaborative enterprise: adults provide material for review, then observe the responses of child readers (the true authorities) before delivering accounts of young readers' reactions to those adults who will be purchasing gift books for the holiday season.

However, the performing, ready to please children in E.C.'s comment—those who "affect" to enjoy a book if they suspect they should—register the central, sticky problem of the child critic: adults. Children's reviews are collected and published by adults, who may influence a young person's immediate response to a text and edit that response before publication.[22] This at first appears to undermine any attempt to locate the "real" voices of child reviewers. However, it instead points our inquiry in a different direction: toward those writers, like E.C., who recognize the epistemological obstacles of collecting children's perspectives and struggle to find ways to rebalance the power relationships that skew young readers' responses in the first place. The most compelling examples of child critics published in the nineteenth century, in fact, are those whose contributions are framed by adult writers as contested or imperfect but, nevertheless, as close to genuine as possible. Recall Mary Molesworth's practice, cited in Chapter One, of testing her stories by reading them aloud, first to her own children and later to her grandchildren—but ensuring that the manuscripts were nestled in a newspaper or between the covers of a book to hide the fact that the stories were her own. Through such measures, she hoped her young listeners would provide candid feedback. "In writing for children the criticism, which you may be pretty sure will not be too flattering, of a group of intelligent boys and girls is *in*valuable," she writes ("On Writing" 585). Adult writers and critics, like Molesworth, deploy a range of strategies to achieve or at least approach a frank response. They use direct quotation, publish children's comments at length and sometimes without comment or interruption, search for situations in which children are "overheard" rather than directly questioned, and offer examples of child responses that are unexpected and perhaps contrary to adults' expectations. For example, a writer for *The Saturday Review*, sorting through the children's titles published for the 1898 Christmas season, notes that he likes Stella Austin's *Our Next-door Neighbour* because "the pictures are pretty." However, "a child-critic complained in our hearing that 'hardly any of them [the illustrations] are what the book says,' which has a good deal of truth in it. Children are very quick to notice any discrepancies of this sort, and, one would think, a very little care on the artist's part would do away with them" ("Books for Babes" 762). By documenting their methods, these adult reviewers implicitly reassure readers that they are attempting to address the possibility that children's perspectives are biased or even fabricated wholesale by adults. A successful partnership relies on honestly reported opinions of child readers.

At times, adult reviewers and writers comment directly on the ethics and difficulties of consulting child critics. Edward Salmon was one such writer. His 1888 study, *Juvenile Literature As It Is*, offers a book-length commentary on the state of children's literature at the end of the nineteenth century, preceded by an introductory chapter that analyzes young readers' literary tastes.[23] He uses as data survey responses collected by his colleague Charles Welsh, who asked schoolchildren and adolescents between the ages of eleven and nineteen (nearly eight hundred boys and more than one thousand girls) questions such as "What is your favourite book, and why do you like it best?" and "Who is your favourite author?" (13). Salmon reports the results in separate sections on "What Boys Read" and "What Girls Read." Boys love Dickens and W. H. G. Kingston, Daniel Defoe's *Robinson Crusoe*, and Johann David Wyss's *Swiss Family Robinson*. Girls name Dickens, Sir Walter Scott, and Charles Kingsley; favored books include Kingsley's *Westward Ho!* and Elizabeth Wetherell's *The Wide, Wide World*. After providing tabulated results, Salmon includes quoted commentary from the children's responses. At times, he attempts to guide his reader's interpretation of the children's comments. For example, he quotes two boys who enjoy *Swiss Family Robinson* because "it informs you what to do when shipwrecked" but notes that such a response "proves that boys place immense faith in what they read" (18). However, Salmon often allows children's critiques to stand alone; he ends the "What Boys Read" section, in fact, with nearly two pages of uninterrupted commentary "from the pen of a lad of fifteen" whose opinions sometimes seem to cater to adults' preferences—"I hail the monthly numbers of [*The Boy's Own Paper*] with pleasure knowing that, as well as simply reading, I shall also be instructed"—and sometimes seem to strike off in more personal directions. He writes that "although Mr. Louis Stevenson's 'Kidnapped' in *Young Folks' Paper* was very highly praised, for myself, 'Treasure Island' was the more attractive" (20).

Salmon describes his account of children's reading practices as a joint effort between children and the adults who administered the survey. "The interest taken in these questions by boys and girls, as well as by masters and mistresses," he writes, "is proved by the ready replies given on one hand, and the assistance rendered in securing them on the other" (13). Adults here are intermediaries; while teachers are, by title, "masters and mistresses," their role is to "secure" the perspectives of their students and deliver them for compilation, evaluation, and consideration. Reviews of *Juvenile Literature As It Is* remark on this collaborative project, marveling at the novelty of compiling so many responses from young people. In a comment that anticipates Godley's description of the "modern critic," a writer in *The Saturday Review* notes that "Mr. Welsh's novel enterprise must not be a little startling to old-fashioned folk. It emphasizes . . . the changed order of things. In old days boys and girls were not consulted at all in the matter. They took what there was, and little enough there was of it" ("Books for the Young" 575). But Salmon does consider young readers as essential consultants; his assessment of the state of children's literature not only includes the opinions of child readers but also begins with them, the words of young people acting as the foundation of the subsequent chapters.

However, what is even more striking about Salmon's account of child readers is his commentary on the difficulty of obtaining honest and unbiased answers from schoolchildren. Salmon is particularly skeptical of and interested in the girls' responses, which "prove generally more surprising, and on that account more instructive, than in the case of the boys" (21). "Hardly one of the recognized writers for girls is in high favour," Salmon frets; rather than domestic tales and school stories, the female respondents preferred adventure books often considered the territory of boy readers. *The Girl's Own Paper* is their favorite magazine, but *The Boy's Own Paper* comes in second place. "Without attributing any want of frankness to the young ladies who have voted so emphatically for Dickens and Scott," Salmon writes,

> The question may fairly be asked, do their replies really represent what girls like best in literature? Three things, at least, I should say, contributed to make them vote as they have done. In the first place, doubtless they considered it proper to vote for such names as Scott and Dickens, although, perhaps, they had not read two of the works of either; in the second, Dickens' or Scott's works are probably in the school or home library, and hence easily get-at-able; in the third, personal inquiries induce me to believe that young ladies do not take particular notice of authors' names, and such household words as Scott and Dickens would occur to their minds more readily than

the patronymics of the authors who devote their energy solely to writing for girls (30).

Some of Salmon's thoughts regarding the factors that influenced the girls' voting—including his contention that "young ladies do not take particular notice of authors' names"—read as sexist and condescending. However, in this passage he also recognizes that adults' expectations might have skewed the results. These readers, Salmon suggests, may be parroting "acceptable" responses, and the books they can access, those that are "easily get-at-able," are determined by what titles teachers and parents choose to make available. A handful of Salmon's contemporaries were even more distrustful than he was of the surveys. For example, a reviewer in the *Journal of Education* calls the children's perspectives "fallacious guides"; citing unexpected results and inconsistencies, such as the popularity among female respondents of Dickens over a girls' writer such as Juliana Ewing, this reviewer concludes that "lists which produce such absurd results are valueless" (597). A writer in *The Saturday Review* notes that Salmon's account of children's preferences do little more than "illustrate the cruel obstacles to candid confession which are involved." The pressure to perform acceptable literary tastes is too much for these children, the writer argues, and the influence of adults in authority is too great. "All that can be deduced from these tables of favourite authors is, that boys and girls are loyal to the favourites of their fathers" ("Books" 575, 576). Children may be the authorities on children's literature, such critiques imply, but how can adults take advantage of that expertise if children are not reliable collaborators?

However, Salmon's doubts do not undermine his faith in the survey's utility. While he admits that the children's answers "may not be in every case reliable," he insists that "the consensus of feeling, gathered as it is from widely differing sources, is sufficiently consistent to be of immense value" (12–13). Rather than discounting the survey wholesale, he tempers his faith in children's perspectives with attention to the pressures that work upon child respondents.[24] For Salmon, the result is an account of children's literature that offers young readers a mediated but nevertheless real influence on the shape of the genre. For instance, while Salmon has misgivings about the girls' purported love of Scott and Shakespeare, he takes seriously their interest in "*The Boy's Own Paper* and several purely boys' books" (28), arguing that "the explanation of [the survey results], as we will be shown, is that [girls] can get in boys' books what they seldom get in their own—a stirring plot and lively movement" (28). These elements are missing from girls' fiction, Salmon contends, because adults misunderstand girls' needs. "Mr. Welsh is doubtless correct when he surmises that much of the popularity, from the publishers' point of view, of books for girls, is due to the fact that they are bought by parents and friends for the purpose of presentation," he concludes. "If girls were to select their own books, in other words, they would make a choice very different from that which their elders make for them" (31). To support his point, he quotes at length the opinion of one respondent. She notes that "girls as a rule don't care for Sunday-school twaddle; they like a good stirring story, with a plot and some incident and adventures—not a collection of texts and sermons and hymns strung together. . . . People try to make boys' books as exciting and amusing as possible, while we girls, who are much quicker and more imaginative, are very often supposed to read milk-and-watery sorts of stories that we could generally write better ourselves" (28–29).[25] Salmon does not comment on the tantalizing possibility of child authorship—the girl's bold assertion that she would be a better author of girls' stories than adults. Instead, the statement stands uncontested. However, such comments, taken together with the tabulated results of the survey, lead Salmon to suggest that "those who aspire to write especially for girls [should] think twice before giving to the world another story on the usual lines" (31).[26]

Just a few years after Salmon published *Juvenile Literature As It Is*, librarian Caroline Hewins began publishing her own recommendations regarding books for young readers. Hewins was a pioneering figure in children's library services in the United States, where she transformed the subscription-only Young Men's Institute Library in Hartford, Connecticut, into the free Hartford Public Library and established a robust children's department.[27] She published extensively on children's books in trade periodicals but is perhaps best known for her bibliographies of recommended titles: *Books for the Young: A Guide for Parents and Children* (1882), which ran to two editions, and *Books for Boys and Girls: A Selected List* (1897), which ran to three. Unlike Salmon, Hewins at first seems to exclude the input of child readers in favor of an appeal to adults; she begins her preface to *Books for Boys and Girls* by noting that "this list has been prepared as a help in buying books for the smaller public libraries, and also for the home use of fathers, mothers, and teachers, but not for children themselves, who do not like explanatory notes" (5). In revised editions of the same list, she includes some quoted child voices, but these appear as evidence of the sorry state of children's literacy and engagement with books. "'I have never thought about making a friend in a book,' is one of the commonest answers to the question, 'Who is there in a book whom you would like to have for a friend?,'" Hewins writes. "'I have no favorites, for I never read a book twice,' is what many boys and girls say in answer to questions asked by teachers or librarians about their reading" (8). Reflecting on her career in "How Library Work with Children Has Grown in Hartford and Connecticut" (1914), Hewins focuses on authoritative rather than collaborative relationships with children (despite the title's emphasis on working *with* children), describing herself as a sure-handed influence on misguided young readers. She notes that in 1878, in the first bulletin she circulated regarding children's books, she announced her intentions to collaborate with parents—"We shall gladly cooperate with fathers and mothers," she assured her readers, "in the choice of children's books"—and she recounts her efforts to uproot children's tastes in sensational and unsophisticated literature, replacing them with a healthy appetite for "good" books. As the years went on, she writes, "Both boys and girls were beginning to apologize for taking poor stories" ("How" 92, 93).

But this portrait of Hewins's relationships to young readers is misleading. Despite her appeal to parents and teachers as the arbiters of children's reading, Hewins solicited the input of child reviewers and in fact worked in collaboration with young library patrons and local students. "In buying books for children," she writes in *Books for Boys and Girls*, there are many things to be taken into consideration—a child's own likings most of all" (9). Like Salmon, Hewins set about determining those preferences methodically. Librarians, according to Katie McDowell, "often used young people's own words in documenting children's reading choices and library activities," and Hewins was instrumental in establishing the practice of situating survey results in "narrative, qualitative frameworks" that include quoted child responses (73, 79). While Hewins's accounts of child readers are not supported by the clout of statistics or data tables, she does offer a spectrum of young voices. For example, Hewins presented a paper at the Second International Library Conference held in London in 1897, later published in its proceedings, titled "Books That Children Like." She opened her address by explaining that for "eight or ten years I have been in the habit of reading book-lists with comments made by boys and girls from twelve to fifteen years old, and afterwards talking over the lists with their young critics."[28] This is a collaborative process—a back-and-forth carried out through annotations and discussion between the librarian, a recognized authority, and students, who as "young critics" possess an informal power of selection and rejection. Hewins hoped to contribute these comments, along with material drawn from letters she requested from Hartford schoolchildren, to a published list of children's books "with annotations by children themselves," a project proposed by Richard Rogers Bowker, one of the founders of *Library Journal* (111).

At the conference, Hewins presented the children's responses she had gathered thus far, and the transcript of her presentation reveals that, in doing so, she inverted the educational relationships implied by her more formal bibliographies of children's books. While in her preface to *Books for Boys and Girls*, Hewins assumes that children are uninterested in explanatory notes, here children themselves provide annotations to guide and inform librarians, and their quoted voices—what Hewins calls "fair specimens of letters from children whose reading is miscellaneous and not beyond their age" (111)—comprise the bulk of her presentation. She interrupts their commentary here and there with an observation of her patrons' reading habits; for example, she suggests that "Hawthorne's *Wonder Tales* and *Tanglewood Tales* are delightful for children whose vocabulary is large, but the style is too mature for nine-tenths of the children in public schools" (112). However, for the most part she allows the young readers to speak for themselves. "I do not like *Gulliver's Travels*," one reader explains, "because I think they are silly" (112). "I think Henty's books are good," another notes, "but they are too much alike" (115). While Hewins selects which comments merit inclusion, it is noteworthy that she chooses quite a few passages in which children pan favored writers, and the public read those judgments as genuine. A writer in the *Speaker*, describing the conference, includes some of these child voices, noting that they are "unbought verdicts no wise man will despise" ("Librarians" 486).

Years later, Hewins remained intent on continuing her project of published collection of child commentary; however, like Salmon, Hewins uses her account of young readers' responses to a survey to explore the ethics of representing children's voices. In the 1902 volume of the *Library Journal*, she published a "Report on [the] List of Children's Books with Children's Annotations," a survey compiled in collaboration with children's librarian Anne Carroll Moore and "largely based on a consideration of about twelve hundred papers, written by boys and girls in the sixth, seventh, eighth, and ninth grades of grammar schools. A part of them are in the form of familiar letters to a librarian, and the rest in answer to questions prepared in a public library and presented to the same grades" (79). Hewins and Moore include quotations from child readers—both those that demonstrate "lack of thought, lack of imagination, and lack of proportion" (81) and those that reveal valuable insights or "something of an individual flavor" (79)—but they discount a great number of responses for showing "the influence of the schoolroom in the selection of books mentioned . . . in the evident desire to please the teacher in expressing a preference and in a stereotyped form of expression" (80). They pause frequently to consider the workings of adult authority on children's responses. "Do such exercises tend to make children self-conscious, and can we depend upon the spontaneity of written replies?" they ask (81). While "the most valuable kind of comment undoubtedly is to be gathered from the off-hand statements of the boys and girls as they exchange their books or meet for informal book-talks at the library," there are "great difficulties in the way of gathering a body of available material of this kind. . . . If a child should see her writing down what he had said, or suspect that she meant to do so, she would lose his confidence forever. According to his nature he would either never volunteer another expression of pleasure or distaste, or he would make a sensational statement if possible in order to gain prominence in her eyes" (82). Hewins would prefer, in other words, casual responses delivered without the pressures and expectations that accompany the scrutiny of adult authority figures; children will provide such candid responses only if they see librarians as trusted partners rather than spying authorities. That goal is lofty for even the most painstaking librarian-researcher, and—even more distressingly—it is not a goal that all adults administering the survey share. "Teachers often ask for lists in a perfunctory way," Hewins admits, "and care more about neat writing and correct spelling than about what impression a book has made on a child" (82).

But Hewins, like Salmon, does not abandon the project altogether due to the difficulties of capturing children's voices. "At times I have thought that it would be impossible to get honest opinions enough for an annotated list," she concedes, "but in looking over my collection I find that I have more than I supposed" (82). Significantly, compiling a reliable collection of children's comments depends on adults modifying their behavior and expectations—they must take measures to mitigate the anxieties and pressures children feel when subject to the expectations of teachers, parents, and librarians—and Hewins is hopeful that they can, indeed, transform adult-child relationships in this way. She ends her 1902 report by requesting that children's librarians send "from five to ten of the best and most natural expressions of opinion received from children. ... It is to be desired that we have the opinions of more than one child to a book, the point of view of a boy and a girl if possible" (82). Hewins's call for child voices does not resolve the problem that these children's opinions will be mediated and selected by adults, and her request for "the best and most natural expressions" is anything but transparent. What are the "best" responses, and what does a "natural" child voice sound like? However, Hewins recognizes the stultifying influence of the watchful adult eye and attempts to mitigate it in the hopes of collaborating with the expertise of her "young critics" to build a children's library collection that responds to child patrons.

While the child critic of the nineteenth and early twentieth centuries is a complicated and contested figure, behind such figures are real children who collaborated with adults—critics, researchers, librarians, even authors—to shape texts written for young readers. Book historians and cultural theorists have expounded upon the influence of readers on literary production. For example, building on Pierre Bourdieu's account of the field of cultural production and, in particular, the role of audience in granting certain writers and texts legitimacy, Robert Darnton's model of the book's communication circuit posits that the reader "influences the author both before and after the act of composition," as that writer responds to transmitted "notions of genre and style," to previous criticisms and anticipated responses, and to the published reviews of a text (67). Young readers are certainly part of this circuit, and while the means of production and circulation are often wholly in the hands of adults, children's sway over texts written for them in the longer trajectory of the field is not negligible. Adults are not dictators of taste; they engage in an ongoing collaboration with their audience—and this is something the Victorians acknowledged. One critic, reviewing E. M. Field's *The Child and His Book* in *The Edinburgh Review*, describes how the tastes of child critics and adult reviewers work together to transform the genre gradually, and those books that delight both audiences fare best:

> The re-read story which stamped itself upon the [adult's] imagination in his own youth, or the story which he takes as resembling the probably extinct favourite, is selected as the gift-book for the new generation, and it in its turn, and generations to come in theirs, will select according to no other rule. In this manner a classic, or clas-

sical school, of child fiction arises, a product of past recollections blent with upgrowing tastes, and by such processes books which fifty, a hundred years ago ... took their place in the first rank, retain it to this day. (415)

This description of the historical shifts in the taste and tenor in children's literature accounts for the undeniable power relationships that inform the production of children's literature, especially the great force that is the "past recollections" of adults who purchase books for the young. However, the reviewer also recognizes the emergent figure of the child reader, whose "upgrowing tastes" also play a role in shaping "a classical school" of children's fiction. The two figures here, the purchaser and the reader, the adult and the child, are united by a common interest in the genre, which arises as an intermingling of adults' nostalgia and children's tastes.

Yet Salmon, Hewins, and others are granting children greater influence than this model suggests. By positioning them not simply as readers but as critics, as authorities in surveys and questionnaires, as reviewers and arbiters of taste, these adults imply that young readers could occupy a truly influential place in the field of cultural production, even if that role is at odds with traditional understandings of adult-child power relationships, and even if it is consistently threatened by the at times inescapable influence of adult authority. While contemporary children's literature criticism might dismiss child critics and reviewers—reading them as another manifestation of adult desire, nostalgia, or sentimentality—Victorian writers were not so quick to disregard their perspectives, no matter how mediated. Salmon certainly celebrated the opinions of young readers outlined in the first chapter of *Juvenile Literature As It Is* when, in the ensuing chapters, he offered his recommendations of suitable children's books. In his chapter on "Books for Girls," he reflects what he has learned from the young woman who despises "milk-and-watery sorts of stories," noting that "girls' literature would be very much more successful if it were less goody-goody. . . . Girls' literature, properly so called, contained much that is excellent, much that is beautiful and ennobling. It appeals in the main to the highest instincts of honour and truth of which humanity is capable. But with all its merits, it frequently lacks the peculiar qualities which can alone make girls' books as palatable to girls as boys' books are to boys" (123). Other writers betray an anxiety about the power of the child reader who is provided a platform to express his literary tastes. Reviewing Salmon's survey, a critic in *The Saturday Review* cautions that many contemporary writers of boys' literature, left out of the lucky list of favorites, "would have a bad time if book-buyers were to scrupulously follow the indications of Mr. Welsh's plebiscite" ("Books" 576). The child critic, like the fictional child author discussed above, can be a friendly or hostile collaborator, one who affirms, undermines, or transforms adults' ideas of the child reader and children's literature.

COLLABORATIVE CLASSROOMS

In their surveys of child readers, both Salmon and Hewins try to account for the inevitable influence of the classroom on young people's stated reading preferences. It is unsurprising that those interested in unbiased child opinions would worry over the sway of teachers and schoolbooks, just as it is natural that those authors speculating about an unprecedented degree of child authority, such as the writers discussed in the first section of this chapter, would turn the classroom on its head. In the final tale of Dickens's *A Holiday Romance,* young writer Nettie Ashford exults that "the children kept [the adults] at school as long as ever they lived, and made them do whatever they were told" (437). Rands's Lilliputian children "made the Old Folks come to school" and "made them learn all sorts of things / That nobody liked" (10). Barrie's Lost Boys, after returning to London with Wendy, are unhappy students; as they learn their three Rs, they forget how to fly, and "before they had attended school a week they saw what goats they had been not to remain on the island" (*Peter and Wendy* 218). Peter certainly does not value education; he can't read or write—he is "above all that sort of thing"—while Hook, a public school graduate, barely has time to cry "Floreat Etona!" before his humiliating surrender to the crocodile (*Peter and Wendy* 137, *Peter Pan* 146). It seems that only through such exaggerated reversals of authority can the young student gain any purchase in the classroom, where adult-child relationships are strictly codified and policed. For the most part, the education system proceeds under the assumption of child ignorance and adult authority.

However, in this final section, I consider the classroom as a space where adult-child hierarchies were examined and contested. In particular, I look to British education under the Revised Code of 1862 and its aftermath, paying attention to how pedagogical practices in England's schools—and criticisms of those practices—not only reveal shifting ideas about children, power, and authority but also transform adult-child relationships.

Using reports on elementary schools submitted by Matthew Arnold and other Her Majesty's Inspectors (HMIs) as a guide, I demonstrate that while established methods of instruction often frame students as passive, wholly subject to the authority of adults, those arguing against the Code and similar policies describe the advantages of granting children active roles in their instruction. They acknowledge that the young possess physical needs and mental abilities outside of those mandated by inspectors and sometimes admit that educators must rely upon children, experts on their own minds and bodies, to design effective and inspiring classroom management.[29] Critics of the Code stage their resistance to its implementation by calling upon both real children, whose bodily needs are often ignored or assaulted by the Code, as well as the familiar figure of the imaginative child, the expert in make-believe. While certainly this latter paradigm of childhood is overdetermined and idealized—a fictional child collaborator—I find that by calling for curricula that accommodates the imaginative child, inspectors, teachers, and others are in fact calling for recognition of real child agency in the classroom. Education emerges as a hybrid collaborative exercise among teacher, inspector, and pupil—all of whom are experts through their own knowledge and experience—and, at times, inverts the relationship between child and adult.

The Revised Code of 1862 set the stage for a reconsideration of adult-child relationships, as its policies brought to the fore the vexed nature of adult-child relationships in the classroom. The Code was introduced by Robert Lowe, the vice president of the Committee of the Council of Education, in order to standardize inspectors' assessments of school buildings and facilities, teacher performance and training, and student attendance and achievement. While HMIs were responsible for assessing schools before the Code was implemented, their methods varied, subject to individual inspectors' judgment, and the government grants awarded upon completion of inspections depended upon the success of a school as a whole. The new Code established a payment-by-results system in which grants corresponded to individual students' performances in highly regulated examinations of reading, writing, and arithmetic. Each student's attendance was assigned a monetary value; for example, school managers could claim the "sum of 4s. per scholar according to the average number in attendance throughout the year at *the morning and afternoon* meetings of their school"—a system that accounts for the individual student while erasing his or her identity as a learning subject (Arnold 339).[30] Those students who attended regularly as dictated by the Code's criteria were examined according to Standards, or cohorts of students determined not by level of achievement but by age. The expectations for these examinations were spelled out in a rubric; seven-year-old Standard I scholars, for example, must read a "narrative in monosyllables," while twelve-year-old Standard VI students must read "a short ordinary paragraph in a newspaper, or other modern narrative" (Arnold 340, 341). Failure to attain these requisites meant a forfeiture of a portion of the school's funding. Students, in other words, were expected to "earn their grant."

Lowe devised the Code in response to the concerns of a Parliament anxious to ensure the efficient use of funds allotted to education. In this respect, the Code was partially a success; it did, in the words of W. B. Stephens, "end a system under which government was faced with an open-ended, ever-expanding obligation to fund schools over whose standards of instruction it had limited control" (7).[31] In establishing the Code, Lowe represented a Parliament "seeking evidence of good use of their money" with hopes that new standards would encourage teachers and school managers to pay more attention to unsatisfactory attendance and failing students (Pratt 27). However, as educational historians such as Lionel Rose and Pamela Horn demonstrate, the Code's consequences in the classroom were disastrous. Many teachers ignored those students falling behind, instead investing time in those likely to pass the examinations. Instructors neglected subjects excluded from the examination, such as history and geography, while many inspectors critiqued the narrow field of the exam. Inspector W. H. Brookfield, for example, laments the loss of attention to such subjects, which "may quicken and enlarge the intelligence and impart additional interest to the reading of a child." He argues that limiting examinations to more "mechanical" subjects "would seem not unlikely, by cramping and limiting the intelligence of the learner, to retard that progress in mere mechanical acquirement which it was intended to promote" (*Report* 41).[32]

Inspectors who were critical of the Code often contend, as Brookfield does here, that England's classrooms crush students' "intelligence" and "interest," and they suggest, more broadly, that the system of examinations and the culture of memorization and cramming it inspires disempowers the already vulnerable population of children by devaluing creativity and imagination, considered the purview of children.[33] Even before the Code was instituted, many were critical of the ways England's education system stifled students' imaginations. In the 1840s and 1850s, for instance—when education for the working class and the poor was carried out primarily by church and charitable schools and only loosely regulated by the Privy Council Committee on Education—rote learning was the typical method of instruction. This was largely because, according to Lionel Rose, "the monitorial system in the British and National schools had long necessitated this method as a way of teaching large numbers on the cheap" (129). Dickens satirizes the forced memorization of useless information in *Hard Times* (1855), a novel that, through the characters of Thomas Gradgrind and his fancy-deprived daughter Louisa, and through Mr. McChoakumchild and his harried but imaginative student Sissy Jupe, emphasizes what was considered to be the far-reaching consequences of an education that does not recognize the critical role of imagination in the mental development of children.

Learn-and-repeat methods were framed as the enemy of the imaginative child—a figure who was both helpless, because she was at the mercy of unceasingly rational and fact-driven adults, and powerful, because the child's imagination was the best tool to resist such disciplinarians. Proponents of the Code understand the dynamic of the classroom as adult authority exerted over the child, who is a passive recipient of information—children who are, in the language of Dickens's Gradgrindian classroom in *Hard Times*, "little vessels . . . arranged in order, ready to have imperial gallons of facts poured into them until they were full to the brim" (6). Education in this model is a univocal lecture, a one-way transmission of information from instructor to students. Children's voices are merely echoes; they speak to repeat. However, some despaired when the new Code institutionalized rather than replaced rote methods, arguing that students were burdened with the annual visit of the inspector and that teachers scrambled to ensure their students were well versed in the test's requirements. Under this system, the child as an assumed authority in make-believe and the imagination finds no place in the classroom. Just as authors such as Dickens, Rands, and Barrie, as noted above, use the figure of the imaginative child to insist that adults grant children creative agency, those resisting the Code called upon the imaginative child in an attempt to reform what they considered oppressive classroom conditions for England's students. Hence Sissy Jupe's admirable belief that a horse is not a graminivorous quadruped with forty teeth, as Gradgrind would have her believe, but instead a living, breathing creature at the circus.

Opposition to rote memorization and repetition and to the Code in particular, therefore, implies that the payment-by-results system suppresses the young student's instinct for and authority in imagination in favor of rational and "mechanical" thinking. For example, Hartley Coleridge, in "A Nursery Lecture by an Old Bachelor" (1851), ventriloquizes the voice of a witty old man to protest the "unquiet innovations of your all-in-all educationists who would make your little ones read before they can well speak, spoiling their dear lisp with abominable words; which, poor things, they can pronounce so right, it is heart-breaking to hear them." He expresses contempt for methods of "cramming" children with "the theory of animal mechanics, when they should be feeling their life in every limb" (305).[34] Objections, like Coleridge's, to "cramming" emphasize the dangerous misalignment between the Code's expectations and the very physical bodies of children, and the violence of rote methods threatened to break both body and mind. The year the Code was instituted, inspector C. H. Alderson notes that his schools are "marked by a constant tendency to fall into a groove," and that both teachers and students "are apt to fall into a dull, mechanical, and unintelligent way of doing their work" (*Report* 99). Arnold, an inspector from 1851 to 1886, witnessed the inception of the Code and its consequences and used his reports to take a firm stand against it. In his 1863 report, he argues that the old inspection methods were imperfect but nevertheless provided inspectors with the flexibility "to test and quicken the intellectual life of the school."[35] The Code's standardized test procedure, on the other hand, "does not make a call ... upon [the inspector's] spirit and inventiveness" and ensures that "scholars and teachers have their thoughts directed straight upon the new examination" (95, 94). Five years later, in 1867, Arnold describes the "mode of teaching in the primary schools" as "prone to rely too much on mechanical processes, and too little on intelligence, a change in the Education Department's regulations, which by making two-thirds of the government grant depend upon a mechanical examination, inevitably gives a mechanical turn to the school teaching, a mechanical turn to the inspection, is and must be trying to the intellectual life of a school" (113). Arnold, in opposing the Code, understands and appreciates children's (and inspectors') imaginations in very particular terms, encouraging models of creativity that accommodate rather than quash partnerships between fancy and reason and, in turn, between adults and children. He wishes for "inventiveness" and "intelligence"—faculties that require an understanding of the rational world and the ability to think beyond it.

In *The Water-Babies: A Fairy Tale for a Land-Baby* (1862–1863), Charles Kingsley parodies the payment-by-results system and its tendency to distort and poison relationships among students, teachers, and inspectors. It was serialized in *Macmillan's* when the Code was implemented and began to take effect. While *The Water-Babies* is remembered primarily for its representation of the plight of the chimney sweep, the book also addresses the ill effects of overburdening children with facts and figures when the protagonist Tom visits the Isle of Tomtoddies, "all heads and no bodies," inhabited by students transformed to turnips, radishes, and other vegetables (279). The Tomtoddies exaggerate what happens to children under the system formalized by the Code and its blindness to the emotional and physical health of students. The very real power of the adult inspector is here transformed into a tyranny of adult over child; the Tomtoddies live in constant fear of the Examiner-of-all-Examiners and sing a song day and night to "their great idol Examination," a repeated refrain of *"I can't learn my lessons: the examiner's coming!"* (280). They beg Tom to supply them with useless information that they immediately forget: "Can you tell me the name of a place nobody ever heard of," begs one, "where nothing ever happened, in a country which has not been discovered yet?" (281). Hassled by parents who beat them for stupidity and paralyzed by the fear of failing their examinations, these turnip children eventually self-destruct, having "crammed themselves so fast to be ready for the Examiner that they burst and popped by the dozens" (285).[36] According to Kingsley, England's education system proceeded as if children had "no bodies," and under the pressures of examinations, children's real bodies suffered acutely.

Those adults in charge of nurturing the Tomtoddies practice teaching methods that foster conflict rather than cooperation between adults and children; neglect the child's natural instincts for play; and in the end, destroy the child. The Isle of Tomtoddies is overshadowed by a sign that reads "Playthings not allowed here," and when Tom, horrified by the plight of the turnip children, suggests that they be provided with "tops, and balls, and marbles, and ninepins," an authoritative wooden rod replies, "They can't play now, if they tried," because while they were once "pretty little children," their parents "kept them at lessons" instead of allowing them to exercise their bodies and imaginations by picking flowers, making dirt-pies, and dancing around the gooseberry bush, "as little children should" (280, 283–84). The violence on the Isle of Tomtoddies stems from a fundamental misunderstanding between youth and age very similar to the isolation between the children in Dickens's *Holiday Romance* and the adults who "understand [them] so badly." In *The Water-Babies*, the misalignment between adults' expectations and children's needs is epitomized in a "wretched little radish" whose parents beat it for "sullenness and obstinacy and wilful stupidity" because it "couldn't learn or hardly even speak." These parents are unaware that the radish suffers from "a great worm inside it eating out all its brains" (302). These parents are, quite literally, ignorant of the way of their child's mind works (or fails to). As Jessica Straley argues in *Evolution and Imagination in Victorian Children's Literature* (2016), Kingsley's portrait of the Tomtoddies crystallizes the author's critique that the Victorian school "was ignoring the student body and, more pointedly, the students' literal bodies to the detriment of the nation" (57).

Opposition to the Code from Kingsley, Arnold, and others suggests that many adults—including children's authors, inspectors, and teachers—found that the formalization of payment-by-results fundamentally disordered and distorted the power relationships within the classroom. While, according to HMI Scott Nasmyth Stokes, "schools are founded and maintained . . . not primarily in the interests of teachers or managers, but for the advantage of the children themselves" (*Report* 121), reports from Arnold and others argue instead that adults often managed the classroom to the detriment of their students.[37] Teachers saddled pupils with information they could repeat, texts they could read, and sums they could solve without comprehension. Arnold, in fact, called the payment-by-results system "a game of mechanical contrivance in which the teachers will and must more and more learn how to beat us" (125). Inspectors, many of whom before the Code devised ways to ease student anxiety, felt tied to the formalities of a test that they did not fully support—and some were openly hostile toward their young examinees.[38] Arnold does note that students, in a sense, possess the *most* power in the classroom due to "the pernicious notion fostered among parents . . . that a child confers a favour on the school managers by earning money for them," and the resulting "inversion of the proper relations between [students] and their teachers, which has no parallel anywhere else" (119). However, this particular instance of topsy-turvy adult-child relationships does not empower students because the children's authority is compromised by the anxieties of a testing system that threatens to obliterate them. In fact, reports by Arnold and other HMIs critical of the Code betray a desire to make audible those children's voices that, under the pressure of exams, cannot be heard—and to put child voices in tension with a system that often drowns them out. For example, inspector H. W. Bellairs writes in 1862 that many children "are too frightened to exhibit fairly what they know from the extreme nervousness with which they approach a stranger," noting that "there is a great deal in this objection worthy of consideration," recommending "patience and gentleness in the examiner, [which] will enable him to arrive at an accurate estimate of attainments" (33).[39] Arnold also writes of "the difficulty of getting children to speak out—sometimes getting them to speak at all" in the context of exams that play upon the natural timidity of children (96), and he at times quotes the exam responses of students and teachers-in-training.

Arnold, like other critics of the Code, wanted to restore more equitable power relationships, those that existed before the strict standards of the Code—and notably he describes the pre-Code relationships among teachers, students, and inspectors as collaborative. "The whole school felt, under the old system, that the prime aim and object of the Inspector's visit was . . . to test and quicken the intellectual life of the school," Arnold writes. "The scholars' thoughts were directed to this object, the teacher's thoughts were directed to it, the Inspector's thoughts were directed to it. The scholars and teachers co-operated therefore with the Inspector in doing their best to reach it" (94). Arnold underscores his call for cooperation, for the conjoined effort of adults and children in service to academic success, by granting each actor equal weight in his statement; each appears "directing [their] thoughts" to the task at hand. He notes that even if it were possible to append the old examination to the new, "it would no longer be the same inspection, for he would no longer have the children's spirit in it, and without this he could no longer make the same test of their intellectual life" (94–95). What is missing is the child's participation, her "spirit," and the spirit of childhood was, for many Victorians, imagination—what Craik calls "a child's natural birthright, its strongest tendency, its keenest enjoyment" ("Age" 144). Through imagination, children can reclaim the classroom. In his last report—written in 1882, when he had been battling the "mechanical turn" of the Code for twenty years—Arnold considers one strategy teachers use to achieve the "mental engagement" that a true education should encourage:

> Of course a great deal of the work in elementary schools must necessarily be of a mechanical kind. But whatever introduces any sort of creative activity to relieve the passive reception of knowledge is valuable. . . . People talk contemptuously of 'learning lines by heart'; but if a child is brought, as he easily can be brought, to *throw himself*

into a piece of poetry, an exercise of creative activity has been set up in him quite different from learning a list of words to spell, or a list of flesh-making and heat-giving foods, or a list of capes and bays, or a list of reigns and battles, and capable of greatly relieving the strain from learning these and affording a lively pleasure. (228–29)

Here, Arnold concedes that education does consist, in part, of the communication of certain information, and that at times the most efficient method is "mechanical," requiring a teacher's authority rather than cooperation, repetition rather than invention. However, he is uncomfortable with a system in which the children are perpetually in a state of "passive reception," a state that suggests the stagnation of the Tomtoddies in Kingsley's fable, and contends that this passivity should be balanced with activities in which the child is an active, creative agent. If the child is engaged in his or her education, participating in the process, even memorization and repetition—and in particular Arnold's pet project of learning poetry by heart—can be valuable.[40] These exercises must engage the child completely and encourage him to "*throw himself into*" his learning, and Arnold encourages teachers to turn to children in deciding which materials and methods successfully promote the "creative activity." He notes that "it is well to remember that the recipient for this instruction, the child, remains as to age, capacity, and school time, what he was before, and that his age, capacity, and school time, must in the end govern our proceedings" (226). While the curriculum is in the hands of the instructor and the evaluation of those elements of education in the hands of the inspectorate, children and their needs and desires should guide adults or, to use Arnold's even stronger language, "govern" their teachers.

A teacher's assumed control over the classroom is unavoidable—the child's "government" over teachers and inspectors reflects an approach to education, not its practical realities—but it is noteworthy that directly after the passage of the Revised Code in 1862 many HMIs, like Arnold, single out for recognition in their reports methods that require teachers both to turn to their students for guidance and to form closer and more collaborative relationships with them. Some of these suggestions are not revolutionary at all. HMI John Gordon, for example, praises schools where "much of the instruction is connected with matters of some personal interest to the pupils" (*Report* 149), encouraging others to let students' interests guide the lesson plan. Other recommendations touch on the materials made available to students; HMI Charles E. Wilson, for example, is nearly as attentive to students' tastes in readings as Salmon and Hewins would be later in the century. He suggests providing not only books that serve the "purely mechanical part of reading" but also "a story, such as *Robinson Crusoe*, &c., calculated to interest their minds and enlist their sympathies" (*Report* 173). This call for sympathy also appears in HMI Rev. D. J. Stewart's report; he finds most effective smaller institutions in which "it is possible for the teacher to gain individual knowledge of each child under her care" and notes that "what children need most is the sympathy of an earnest and cultivated mind" (*Report* 63, 65).[41] Recalling Rands's collaborative model of adult-child relationships based on sympathy—a bond that eschews adult authority and child obedience in favor of connection and, to use Gubar's term, kinship—this emphasis on a meeting of minds transforms the classroom and its lessons from an authoritative transmission of adult-centered information to a collaborative, intergenerational space.

CONCLUSION

The Revised Code of 1862 was only one of a series of shifts in educational policy in the Victorian period. Later reforms were, perhaps, more attentive to how "the child ... must in the end govern our proceedings," in the words of Arnold. For example, the Elementary Education Act of 1870, better known as the Forster Act, sought to provide "for every school district a sufficient amount of accommodation in public elementary schools available for all children resident in such district" (Rich 89)—a necessary change, as this Act ushered in the beginnings of compulsory education.[42] The official reforms made by the Act were accompanied by other emendations to the school system that focused on the well-being of students. As Gretchen Galbraith explains, the Act launched a number of projects initiated by local school boards, including the introduction of a wider range of subjects (such as history, geography, and grammar) in school curricula and the transformation of classrooms for younger students to include "reading sheets, alphabet boxes, and kindergarten toys" (97). Room for reform remained, but the mandates of the Act and school boards' reforms contributed to an education system guided by children's physical, mental, and emotional needs. Most scholars understand the Forster Act and later policies as a negotiation among government interests, religious societies, charitable and child labor organizations, and parents. However, few accounts of these policies take into account the role of children in transforming the school system. In the mid- to late nineteenth century, teachers, inspectors, and other adults worked to make room for the child voice and considered how children can (or cannot) speak in the classroom. It would be an overstatement to suggest that adults ceded authority to students, but the child as imaginative authority did serve as a guide to those who were in power. In this way, children were potential collaborators in these policies.

These tentative examples of intergenerational collaboration, however, did not prevent adults from continuing to imagine more extreme reversals of power. While, in the policies and debates that transformed British education in the nineteenth century, the child was a sort of authority—but one ultimately under the care of adults—the raucous energy of the child, the expert in play and potential resident of Rands's Lilliput, still haunts the margins of writing for and about children. For example, in the introductory comments of his *Lazy Lessons*, Rands—who was an opponent of compulsory attendance policies—tells the story of two children who shirked school, favoring instead their own methods of education; young Eliza, aged eleven, teaches her six-year-old brother to add and subtract, and in time the two "got to be so clever at different sorts of learning without going to school that the school-board officer, when he called one day, was quite astonished by the baby" (25).[43] Essays on the child's imagination and educators' relationship to it entertain even more subversive possibilities. In "Age of Gold," cited at the beginning of this chapter, Craik notes that nurturing an imaginative child is an "awful" responsibility. "You cannot help feeling," she writes, "though you may be the mother who bore it, that there is something in the creature which you cannot understand," she worries, "something above you and beyond you" (144). Craik doubts adults possess any real authority when it comes to educating a creative child; "as to those who are given to our charge," she writes, "those helpless little ones who, so far as we see, still owe it *to us* whether they grow up to be, unto themselves and society, a blessing or a curse—we can but attempt wisely to guide that which we have no power either to annihilate or to repress" (143). Less than a decade later, in the years immediately following the implementation of the Revised Code and its "mechanical" methods, George MacDonald published his essay "The Imagination: Its Function and Its Culture" (1867), devoting much of the piece to the proper cultivation of the child's creative faculty. He describes the "apparently lawless tossing of the spirit, called the youthful imagination," which is a "young monster" threatening the "real in the world," and emphasizes the responsibility, of parents and teachers to attempt to guide this reckless force toward "true visions" and "noble dreams" (26, 30). Often, then, in Victorian considerations of the child's imagination, this faculty is represented as potentially dangerous, inspiring vague anxieties among those who teach, manage, and write for young people.

This subversive model of the child's imagination suggests that the impulse throughout the nineteenth century to consider how children resist the roles adults assign them could generate a rhetoric of childhood that emphasizes not children's isolation from adults but instead their power in the "grown-up" world. I have explored in this chapter how authors, researchers, librarians, and educators in the late nineteenth and early twentieth centuries negotiate an uneasy collaboration with young people, attempting to cede authority to the powerful, creative child, both fictive and real. These collaborations lead adults to consider the place, and possibilities, of the child's voice—how that voice can determine which stories are told, how they are told, and who tells them. The adult's recognition of children as an influential force in the production of their own literature and culture challenges traditional ideas about children as a passive, obedient to adult authority and desires. Children emerge instead as figures with great imaginative agency. In my next chapter, I'll explore how that agency is evident in not only literary but also visual texts by tracing the emergence of the child as an illustrator-collaborator.

CHAPTER FOUR

Pictures of Partnership
Art Education, Children's Literature, and the Rise of the Child Artist

In *The Life and Letters of Charles Darwin* (1887), Darwin's son Francis writes that his father "was naturally awkward with his hands, and was unable to draw at all well. This he always regretted much, and he frequently urged the paramount necessity of a young naturalist making himself a good draughtsman" (109–10). The Darwin children took their father's advice to heart, making good use of a stack of stray papers he kept in a cabinet under the stairs. Watercolors and pencil drawings by Francis and his brothers and sisters can be found throughout Darwin's archive: an entire series of cavalry soldiers, illustrated fairy stories, brightly colored birds, caricatures, and doodles (Keynes and Kohn).[1] Francis's drawings in particular decorate the reverse sides of the surviving *Origin of Species* (1859) manuscript pages, and some archivists believe that many of the sheets survive only because Darwin saved his son's artwork ("Sheet").[2] Turning over Darwin's "Variation under Domestication," for example, reveals a watercolor by Francis featuring two soldiers on vegetable steeds, created when the artist was around ten years old.[3] One turbaned man sits astride an eggplant while another, wearing a plumed hat and riding a carrot, draws his sword.

The *Origin* manuscript is an unusual document, part scientific study and part family art album; the trained scientist's observations and Francis's amateur artwork create one, continuous document. The text intermingles an evolutionary narrative with the ephemera of quotidian family life, and it records the influence of adult modes of inquiry—here, Darwin's theories and the conventions of natural history—on his son's imagination. Flipping from Darwin's inky notes to Francis's brightly colored paintings and back again, one wonders if Francis's creativity had a similar impact on a father who was re-imagining the natural world in a manner that, at the time, was fantastic in its own way. Indeed, biographers have suggested that Darwin's affectionate relationships with his ten children intersected with his professional practices, and archivist David Kohn explains that Darwin's methods were playfully intergenerational. "The kids were used as volunteers to collect butterflies, insects, and moths," Kohn notes, "and to make observations on plants in the fields around town" (Stayner).[4] The famous Sandwalk where Darwin would stroll and think was not a sacred space but a landscape of both profound reflection and family life; Francis calls the walk "our play-ground as children," where "we continually saw my father as he walked round. He liked to see what we were doing, and was ever ready to sympathize, in any fun that was going on" (93). The Darwin children's art records their participation in their father's mental life. Francis's drawing of the Darwin family home, for instance, offers a glimpse of the Sandwalk through the front door—the young artist's idiosyncratic perspective suggestively depicting the path leading into, rather away from, the house—and a picture of birds, bees, and butterflies recalls his father's theories of natural selection. This painting is a miniature ecosystem; colorful birds hunt insects that in turn feast on flowers. While the imagined barrier between the nursery and the world beyond was never firm, the child art preserved in the *Origin* manuscript records just how permeable that boundary could be.[5]

The *Origin* manuscript is not a collaboration between Darwin and his son—at least not a creative partnership such as those examined in my previous chapters. The threads that connect the *Origin* and Francis's drawings are those of influence, and there is not substantial evidence that either Charles or Francis Darwin considered their work a joint effort.[6] However, Francis's artwork does record a larger turning point in the ways adults valued child artists: a moment, to put it in Darwinian terms, of evolution. Consider, for example, Francis's "fanciful animals," which include birds with fuchsia wings, bright blue tails, and crimson or purple beaks. We can interpret these paintings as an aspiring young naturalist's reproduction of his father's careful scientific drawings; Francis, then, is a charming but imperfect copyist. However, Francis does not simply fail to follow the conventions of scientific study; he flouts those conventions. His birds are spectacular re-imaginings—creative exaggerations, perhaps, of Darwin's more sedate Galapagos finches. Interpreted from this perspective, Francis is, like his father, not simply reproducing what he sees around him but instead using the observable world to forge new narratives: here, new species.

Francis's drawings, in fact, pictorialize two possibilities that structured the ways Victorians theorized child art that I will explore throughout this chapter. On the one hand, child artists were understood as imitators. They were trained to copy the models of adult art that surrounded them and to strive for artistic realism. In this vein, they also were described in theories of recapitulation as human evolution in miniature, fated to reproduce, to mimic human evolution; this perspective colored accounts of child art, as the young were imagined to move through stages of "primitive" artistic development toward refined, "civilized" aesthetics. On the other hand, scholars suspected young artists could be understood instead as inventors. Child art could exceed the practices of adult art and could wander from the well-trod path of evolution through the young artist's imaginative agency. Francis's drawings suggest both paradigms at once: his fantastic birds are in a sense imitations, referring to the accepted forms of scientific illustration, but Francis is also an inventor, calling upon the play of child art to subvert those models. And his work, like his father's, was a little ahead of its time. Throughout the Victorian period, these paradigms of child artists coexisted, sometimes in tension with one another and sometimes simply side by side; however, by the 1880s and 1890s—those years leading up to modernism's embrace of the child's "innocent eye"—child artists who invent rather than imitate became more appealing figures.

This evolution created the ideological and cultural circumstances that accommodated the recognition of child artists as creative collaborators. Young artists, when valued not for their progress toward an aesthetic standard mandated by adults but instead for their perspectives *as children*, were invited into systems of cultural production in both formal and informal, public and private ways. They were creative partners in real and hybrid collaborations—often small-scale, domestic collaborations. They were also imaginative inspirations for a childlike aesthetic that began to appear throughout the art world—because the burgeoning respect for child art at the end of the Victorian period began to transform children's book illustration, as well. The mid-nineteenth century witnessed the rise of some of the most influential children's book illustrators, new printing technologies and new styles of art for children, and the invention of the modern picture book. These developments ushered in a new era of quality and sophistication in children's books, but they also jump-started the careers of artists such as Edward Lear, whose work takes inspiration from child art. In fact, while Francis Darwin was doodling fanciful animals on his father's scrap paper, Lear (a fellow naturalist) was painting his own brightly colored creatures, creating watercolors of nonsense birds for the children of friends and acquaintances.

Recognizing the value of child art and child*like* art created by adults requires a celebration of subversive play and a reconfiguration of the power structures that underpin traditional adult-child relationships—and ultimately leads to the possibility of intergenerational collaboration. Writers, illustrators, teachers, Child Study scholars, and others who expressed appreciation for child art were, in a sense, re-evaluating the position of children in the hierarchical social systems, such as schools and publishing houses, that support the production of art and its circulation. Some adults partnered with child artists, questioning or even rejecting adult standards of artistic quality and achievement and rejoicing instead in child art's carnivalesque transformations and its challenges to "proper" means of representation. Not all examples of adult-child author-illustrator collaborations do in fact subvert those hierarchies—some offer a possibility of rebellion that is, ultimately, unrealized—but these examples gesture toward a broader, more radical reconsideration of child art that would truly take root with the onset of literary and artistic modernism in the twentieth century.

In what follows, I examine adult-child collaborations that draw upon the resources of the child artists, taking into account the role of real children (such as those who populated Victorian classrooms or those who corresponded with adult writers) as well as fictional or imagined child artists. In doing so, I put side by side changing perspectives on art *by* children and new modes in illustrations *for* children to chart the changing perception of children as both producers and consumers of art. I begin by examining writing about children as artists, tracing theories of art education from Jean-Jacques Rousseau to Friedrich Froebel to Franz Cizek, including extensive studies of children's drawings that emerged at the fin-de-siècle through the Child Study movement. This writing proposes the two distinct but intersecting models of children's art production mentioned above: the young artist as imitator of adults' art and the young artist as an inventive, creative subject. In the chapter's second section, I consider published and unpublished texts in which adult authors partner with young illustrators—for example, Robert Browning's "The Pied Piper of Hamelin; A Child's Story," which he wrote for the young artist Willie Macready, and David Starr Jordan's *The Book of Knight and Barbara*, illustrated and edited by young people. I end with an account of the illustrations and creative legacy of Lear, whose work exhibits the influence of child art and child artists. The result is a partial history of the "discovery" of the child artist in the nineteenth and early twentieth century in light of intergenerational collaboration and a reflection on the consequences of that discovery in children's literature and culture.

SCRIBBLE-MINDEDNESS: THE CREATIVE CHILD IN ART EDUCATION AND CHILD STUDY

Both imitative and inventive approaches to child art exhibit respect for young artists, albeit to different degrees. The latter, however—in its celebration of children as creative subjects—holds greater potential to challenge widely accepted adult-child power relationships and grant children imaginative agency. Adults recognize that agency in a variety of ways: through, for example, pedagogical strategies that sympathetically adapt to the child or through their appreciation for child art according to its own methods and standards. Children are imagined as students and muses, as amateurs and unwitting professionals. They are at times valued for their futures as engineers, designers, or draftsmen and elsewhere envied for their innocent eye, a perspective defined by their youth and naïveté. The writers I explore below suggest a progression throughout the Victorian period toward more substantial recognition of child art and therefore more engaged partnerships between adults and young artists. However, it is important to note that this progression is uneven, troubled by the always-complex interplay between constructions of childhood, its lived realities, and the spectrum of child life. For example, while it is possible to locate patterns in the way classroom practices understand young artists, art education varied widely depending on class, gender, geography, and a myriad of other factors. Nevertheless, reflecting on some of the most popular ways adults wrote about child art provides a useful context for the creative partnerships I explore later in this chapter.

Some of the most influential theory of elementary art education appears in Rousseau's *Émile* (1762), in which the author outlines his fictional pupil's education, including his art education, under the direction of tutor Jean-Jacques. There are elements of Émile's art education that, like many of Rousseau's recommendations in his treatise, are progressive in their accommodation of children's developmental needs. For example,

Rousseau detests the instructional methods prevalent in the eighteenth and nineteenth centuries that set students to copy plates, producing only imitations of the work of established artists. "I shall take good care not to provide [Émile] with a drawing master," writes Rousseau, "who would only set him to copy copies and draw from designs. Nature should be his only teacher, and things his only models" (128). Émile, Rousseau concedes, "will make any number of daubs before he proceeds to anything recognizable," and "it will be long before he attains to the graceful outline and light touch of the draughtsman" (129). This approach to the early attempts of child artists was unusual; as art education historian Gordon Sutton writes, "[to] go to the real world of experience for stimulus; to be concerned about the original plant from which some ornamental form had been developed; to accept children's spontaneous drawings as a legitimate stage in child development . . . this was all merely prophetic, and near 150 years ahead of comparable thought in England" (27).[7]

Yet those early daubs are not nearly as valuable as the more accomplished compositions that Émile produces after years of practice. Émile's tutor praises his early attempts as a means to the desirable end of "a truer eye, a surer hand, a knowledge of the real relations of form and size between animals, plants, and natural objects, together with a quicker sense of the effects of perspective" (129). As this passage suggests, Rousseau understood his fictional pupil's art education as a path to mastery, a curriculum leading from imperfection to expertise. While throughout his treatise Rousseau emphasizes the importance of recognizing child nature as markedly different from that of adults, his outline for Émile's art education implies that children's first drawings are not artistically valuable but stepping-stones toward more mature habits of observation and draftsmanship. It is apparent that Rousseau "did not appreciate the beauty of child art," as Donna Darling Kelly contends, and instead "saw the importance of representational drawing" as answering a student's "need for visual sensory enhancement" (17). Werner Hofmann agrees, noting that Rousseau did not recognize "any intrinsic value to the child's first attempts at drawing" (5). While Émile's artistic education eschews imitation and embraces what Rousseau considers to be the child's impulses for spontaneous drawing based in nature, the longer purview of that education leads to the "recognizable," the professional, and perhaps even the vocational, as Rousseau's reference to "the graceful outline and light touch of the draughtsman" suggests. This progression is literalized in the display of Émile's drawings and paintings, which are used to ornament his rooms, arranged in a narrative from awkward, early attempts, displayed in large gilt frames, to his most sophisticated work, which requires only a simple black frame because "it needs no other ornament than itself" (130). Émile moves developmentally and spatially farther and farther from his first attempt, which was "a man such as lads draw on walls, a line for each arm, another for each leg, with the fingers longer than the arm" (129). That first drawing is untaught, unprofessional, and uncivilized, described as scrawled on a wall like a cave painting and therefore almost primitive; in fact, it exhibits many of the qualities of child art that modernists would find appealing. Yet Rousseau interprets those unpolished elements as flaws Émile must overcome.

There is no question that the relationship between tutor and student outlined in *Émile* conforms to common assumptions of adult expertise and child ignorance—and yet Émile's tutor Jean-Jacques creates the illusion of collaboration. He often works alongside his pupil—noting, for example, that he "shall follow [Émile's] example and take up a pencil . . . as unskillfully as he" (129). He often uses the pronoun "we" to imply that he and Émile are two artists working together toward mastery: "We shall colour prints," he exalts, "we shall paint, we shall daub; but in all our daubing we shall be searching out the secrets of nature, and whatever we do shall be done under the eye of that master" (129). But this is a ploy. Nature is not the master, of course; Jean-Jacques is—or, at the very least, Jean-Jacques mediates between nature and Émile. And while Jean-Jacques fosters a creative partnership with his pupil, he confesses to his reader that he is not a collaborator but a rival, challenging his young charge and pushing him toward a critical artistic eye. "In this [artistic] improvement I shall either go side by side with my pupil," he explains, "or so little in advance that he will always overtake me easily and sometimes get ahead of me" (129). This near deceit is part of a pedagogical plan designed to reinforce adult artistic values. Together, Jean-Jacques notes, he and Émile will discover their early drawings' "lack of proportion" and other childish mistakes (129). Rooted in an approach to art education that devalues the child's means of representation in favor of the adult's, Rousseau cannot, or will not, conceive of a true intergenerational creative partnership.

Émile was extraordinarily influential, shaping British ideas of both childhood and education after its first English translation in 1763; nearly every critical account of childhood and child art today discusses the reach of Rousseau's treatise. However, his scheme of art education did not transform immediately how most young people were taught the visual arts in

England; in British classrooms, the imagined child artist of Rousseau's text disappeared, forced out by the very real cultural and economic climate of nineteenth-century England. "Industrial pressures were to dominate the thinking of school authorities," writes Sutton, "rather than philosophic ideals" (28). In particular, government officials and educators tasked with designing and evaluating school curricula began to champion drawing instruction as a means to achieve the nation's leadership in manufacture and design. British manufacturers had for some time bought or copied designs from France, and growing anxiety about England's industrial belatedness led to a desire, according to the 1835 Select Committee of the House of Commons, to "consider the Best Means of Extending a Knowledge of the Arts and of the Principles of Design among the People (especially the manufacturing population of the country)" (Sutton 46). In the words of educationist James Kay-Shuttleworth, "in all manufactures of which taste is a principal element, our neighbours the French, are greatly our superiors, solely, we believe, because the eye and the hands of all classes are practiced from a very early age in the arts of design.... The interests of commerce are so intimately connected with the results to be obtained by this branch of elementary education, that there is little chance that it will much longer suffer the grievous neglect which it has hitherto experienced [in England]" (Sutton 48–49). In the mid-1800s, schools of art and design for adults and children opened throughout England, and educators and artists designed a variety of classroom methods for young artisans-in-training. While these methods differed by region and by institution—they flourished more, for example, in urban areas, and the numbers of pupils varied by class and by gender—drawing, when taught, more often than not was informed by industrial goals.[8]

These methods privilege accuracy and imitation over creativity and invention and demonstrate how closely tied elementary art education became to manufacture and design. Art education in this context consisted almost entirely of exercises in pattern and form. For example, the exercises included in C. E. Butler Williams' widely used 1843 *Manual for Drawing from Models,* which was intended for teachers instructing elementary school students, task students with copying geometrical forms of increasing complexity displayed on a wooden stand: angles in various positions, squares and hexagons, even toothed and beveled wheels (Sutton 51). Other schools and teacher training programs adapted the theories of instrumental Swiss educator Johann Pestalozzi. Edward Biber translated Pestalozzi's treatise *How Gertrude Teaches Her Children* into

English in 1831, and Pestalozzian methods were the bedrock of the Home and Colonial School Society, founded by Elizabeth and Charles Mayo, J. P. Greaves, and Joshua Reynolds in 1836. Pestalozzi was influenced by Rousseau's attention to child nature and promoted learning through *Anschauung*, or sense-impressions. However, British educators likely appreciated how amenable Pestalozzi's approach was to the economic goals of England's elementary schools. His students worked from what Biber translates as an "alphabet of forms"; in the words of Pestalozzi, "lines, angles, and curves were the basis of drawing" (Biber 203). Pestalozzi's exercises, notes art education historian Arthur D. Efland, "were not designed to elicit individual expression or to develop a sense of the beautiful, but to stimulate the rational powers of the mind." The Pestalozzian method promoted "mastery of a linear alphabet" and accuracy in observation and measurement (113). Williams' and Pestalozzi's curricula are just two examples of a widespread practice of art education that began with, and focused on, drafting lines, angles, and other shapes with precision. While some students certainly learned drawing by working from nature, from prints, or from memory, these linear exercises were widely accepted methods of art education.

This design-oriented tradition of drawing pedagogy—in its emphasis on reproduction of predetermined forms, its primary focus on a child's futurity rather than his or her current talents, and its elision of spontaneous drawing and child perspectives—largely excludes the possibility of creative partnerships between adults and children. While Rousseau provided at least the illusion of collaboration, these curricula instead assume unidirectional learning environments, in which the student is beholden not only to the expertise of adults concerned with the nation's economic health but also to their future adult selves, which are imagined as artisans and designers, draftsmen and manufacturers. However, as the nineteenth century progressed, art educators and other scholars of childhood began to articulate new approaches to child art, and the imperfect landscapes and disproportionate human figures Rousseau considered inept attempts by unskilled young artists were valued differently. New art education curricula and the burgeoning field of Child Study began to suggest that children's drawings and paintings could instruct adults, revealing both important information about child nature and psychology and new and imaginative ways of representing the world.[9] Geometric drawing exercises did not disappear from England's classrooms, and a preoccupation with accuracy and "correct" modes of representation remained the foundation of many drawing manuals and exercises; these two approaches to children's artwork—understanding it as imitative of adult art and therefore imperfect, on the one hand, and as admirable and inventive on the other—were not mutually exclusive. In fact, some of the most influential discussions of child art in the nineteenth and early twentieth centuries negotiate complex attachments to both imitative and inventive paradigms, simultaneously recognizing adult authority over child artists and making room for childhood's playful subversions in a manner that accommodates creative adult-child partnerships.

For example, Froebel's kindergarten movement, established in the late 1830s and early 1840s, espouses both imitative and inventive models in child art, and here the two contradict one another, manifesting in some internal tensions in Froebel's ideologies. In *Education by Development, the Second Part of the Pedagogics of the Kindergarten,* Froebel expresses great respect for children's creativity and particularly for their drawing, which he describes as "the starting point, and the spring, as well as . . . the point to which all true, satisfying education refers. Just in this cultivation of the child for creative drawing consists the nature of the kindergarten" (88). Froebel insists that children be left to their own instincts while drawing, asserting teachers "must not disturb the child" (65). Richard Carline, in his history of art education, underscores Froebel's intentions that children's drawing "must be spontaneous," that the teacher's role "should be passive and protective, not prescriptive or categorical" (132). However, in practice, Froebel's methods are more rigid than these theories suggest. He cautions that children's "power of creating by drawing should not exactly be freely used to produce indefinite images, but should be developed according to the laws of cultivation inherent in its nature" (85). His system of gifts stratify the toys and tools meant to aid the creative impulses of kindergartners into specific patterns and developmental stages—from four worsted balls meant to help a child differentiate color, for example, to a series of wooden solids designed for more complex comparisons—and the artistic activities Froebel designs for his students are not an exception. While he encourages "painting, drawing, clay modeling, sand modeling," and other unstructured activities, he particularly promotes occupations such as "stick laying" and "pea work," which limit the materials children use to express themselves to pre-formed straight lines and curves, much like Pestalozzi's "alphabet of forms."[10] Froebel's writings on education, then, celebrate children's sense of play and imagination, but when his theories are read alongside his methods, he seems both to respect the unique qualities of children's art and to caution teachers to control children's creative impulses.

Despite these contradictions, Froebel's legacy in the nineteenth century was, in the words of Kelly, "the installation of 'creativity' into the early education of children" (28)—and his kindergarten also recognizes the child as a creative agent. In 1855, Charles Dickens wrote in *Household Words* that kindergarten methods are successful because the "frolic of childhood is not pure exuberance and waste. 'There is often a high meaning in childish play,' said Froebel. Let us study it, and act upon hints—or more than hints—that nature gives. They fall into a fatal error who despise all that a child does, as frivolous. Nothing is trifling that forms part of a child's life" ("Infant" 578). Dickens admires Froebel's acceptance of "all that a child does," free from judgment by adults who may find their pastimes "trifling." He recognizes that Froebel harbors a genuine respect for children's modes of expression, and that respect is at the center of Froebel's ideas about children's art. According to Dickens's interpretation of Froebel, the creative play of children, including their scribbles and five-legged cats, is valuable not because it suggests the beginnings of a future artist but because it develops the creative energies of children, their ability to invent rather than to imitate. And while Froebel's series of gifts might limit a child's creative expression, the subsequent occupations, as described in Froebel's landmark *Education of Man*, are meant to provide older children access to more flexible modes of representation. "The gift leads to discovery; the occupation, to invention," writes W. N. Hailmann, Froebel's translator. "The gift gives insight; the occupation power" (287). Froebel's kindergarten, as it proliferated throughout England, takes up the intentions of Rousseau and Pestalozzi to educate children according to child-nature and uses those intentions to shape what we might identify as a child-centered pedagogy. Froebel encourages kindergarten teachers to foster "sympathy with childhood, adaptability to children, and knowledge and appreciation of child-nature . . . seeing ourselves with the eyes of a child" (90). The notion that art educators should adapt to children's needs and adopt their perspectives (rather than vice versa), and the notion of the "power" of the child artist, took root in England in part through the popularity of the kindergarten movement and would inform later, more radical approaches to child art.

John Ruskin, while not particularly interested in children's art education, does address the topic in a few paragraphs of the preface to his manual *Elements of Drawing* (1856–1857), and as with Froebel, his approach to child art is contradictory. Ruskin endorses the practice of drawing from models—both from natural subjects such as flowers and from a "limited number of good and amusing prints"—as a practice that perfects young artists' placement of line and color (viii). Parents and teachers should guide children in "economical and neat habits with his colours and paper ... pointing out where a line is too short or too long, or too crooked, when compared with the copy; *accuracy* being the first and last thing they look for" (viii). Children's art, Ruskin implies, is imitative of the processes and norms of adult art, and early drawings are judged as flawed, necessary awkward scrawls preceding later mastery. However, there are suggestions that Ruskin appreciates a childlike aesthetic. For example, he recommends that, aside from advising on certain aspects of proportion and accuracy, parents should "give themselves no trouble in instructing" the child. He acknowledges that some children have a "talent for inventing or grouping figures" and advises parents to let their children scribble on every available scrap of paper (viii). And famously, in a long footnote later in Ruskin's manual, he implicitly appreciates children's imaginations when he characterizes the creative impulse of successful adult artists as childlike. "The whole technical power of painting depends on our recovery of what may be called the *innocence of the eye*," writes Ruskin, "that is to say, a sort of childish perception of ... flat stains of colour, merely as such, without consciousness of what they signify.... A highly accomplished artist has always reduced himself as nearly as possible to this condition of infantine sight" (22–23).[11] Here, Ruskin employs the figure of the child, or the childlike, to describe a certain mode of observation free from the restraints of experience and education that he feels often obstruct an artist's true vision. While Ruskin does not explicitly recommend that his students paint like children, his description of the innocent eye participates in an emerging respect for the imaginative, as opposed to the imitative, elements of children's artwork and, here in particular, a respect for childlike modes of observation.

However, by the end of the century, it was not only Ruskin's figure of the child and its innocent eye, and not only the imagined needs of students, influencing art education but also living children—the subjects of Child Study. As that movement gained momentum, some educators turned to its insights on child nature and development to challenge methods of art education that relied primarily upon imitative exercises. One such educator was Ebenezer Cooke, a student of Ruskin influenced by the methods of Froebel and Pestalozzi and the psychological work on childhood published by scholars such as Herbert Spencer and James Sully. In "The Basis and Beginnings of Brushwork," for example, Cooke frequently calls upon "science"—here, Child Study and other scholarship on child development—to recommend that educators abandon exercises in geometry and imitation in favor of methods that capitalize on children's impulses toward self-expression. Cooke suggests that Child Study, "founded on observation of the child," works "in opposition to the traditions and prejudices of ancient authority, [and] maintained that drawing was a means of expression based on manual movement and design . . . and that all that was needed was that the brush should be put into the child's hand" (92). He outlines a series of exercises that adopt familiar classroom practices but revise them, creating exercises in which imitative and inventive models coexist alongside rather than contradict one another. These methods tend toward artistic freedom, challenge the importance of accuracy, and reference throughout the child's body and movements, emphasizing the living child as artist alongside the work she creates. For example, Cooke adopts a checkered grid for drawing shapes recommended by Froebel but loosens its hold on the young artist's work. If graphed pages are used, Cooke argues, "they should be made by the children freehand, thus exercising straight lines, measurement, and invention. The net-like basis should be varied, and invention should begin at the foundation" (105). The straight line and arc, central to methods such as Pestalozzi's, should be replaced with forms based on the child's natural movements. "Scribble," writes Cooke, "the free movement of the arm, and the muscular sense, are the sources of the child's ideas of form" (99).

And the child's ideas are paramount. Cooke is concerned not with imitation but self-expression, and self-expression arises from *within* the child; it cannot be imposed from without through exercises that rely on copying. Cooke's methods therefore require the art teacher to reconsider adult-child relationships in the classroom and to follow rather than lead the young artist. "We must learn what [the child] can do and knows," he writes. "All that is possible should be drawn out. What it gives, use: accept its elements and methods" (102). Those methods, Cooke recognizes, include not only free-swinging motions of the arm but also the introduction of color, often excluded from elementary art education, as well as subjects that interest young people: birds and animals, children at play, and nursery rhymes and fairy tales. Cooke builds upon Froebel's call for "sympathy with childhood, adaptability to children, and knowledge and appreciation of child-nature." However, in the case of Cooke, this leads to quite fundamental questions about child agency—questions that threaten to undermine the authority of teacher over pupil. "Children themselves form knowledge and means of expression," reflects Cooke. They "express themselves without teaching; and they can continue their own education. The school, with its antiquated and unnatural methods and traditions, often arrests their progress. Are we then to let them alone? If we are to follow the child, of what use are the teacher and school? Should there be any systematic or elementary teaching?" (97). These questions lead to the edge of an autodidactic system that entirely dispenses with adults or the topsy-turvy narratives I explore in Chapter Three.

In response to these questions, Cooke instead proposes in the pages of "The Basis and Beginnings of Brushwork" a collaborative methodology that takes into account both the child's autonomy and the adult's expertise, capitalizing on what the generations share and what one can learn from the other. "We should use both the child's method and the man's," he writes. While geometric and linear methods may not immediately appeal to the child, "to separate measurement and form [from a child's art education] may be questionable," Cooke admits—so he suggests a compromise: for example, "children, and men too, enjoy rhythm, regular beats, repeated patterns, and measured time and space" (104). Cooke had explored this intergenerational approach earlier, in his influential *Alternative Illustrated Syllabus of Instruction in Drawing in Elementary Schools* (1895).[12] This syllabus eliminated geometric exercises in favor of freehand brushwork, natural forms, and curved lines, and its publication allowed elementary schools that adopted its curriculum to diversify their art instruction and foster children's spontaneous activity (Efland 139). Reports issued from schools that used the syllabus demonstrate how new approaches to art could drastically reimagine adult-child relationships in the classroom and lead to teacher-pupil interactions based on creative partnership. For example, the headmaster at a London school serving primarily working-class children in Bermondsey reported in 1897 that under Cooke's system "the teacher recognises to the full that his chief function is to guide the spontaneous activity of the child; to stimulate and direct the creative faculty; to foster the belief in each boy that he possesses power, and to encourage him to put it forth freely. The child is allowed the utmost play for his inventive faculty'" (Coward 103). This report is remarkable in its description of teachers' and students' roles; adult and child here work in tandem, the former supporting the latter. The child artist is celebrated for spontaneity, for play, for his "creative faculty," while the teacher is a guide, supporting the child's artistic practice. The child possesses creative "power." Here, the art classroom accommodates, even mandates, intergenerational, creative partnerships.

In 1884, Cooke argued for his methods, and for the creative child, at London's International Conference on Education and in particular in a session titled Teaching of Drawing and Colouring. Cooke summarizes and comments upon the session in an article titled "Our Art Teaching and Child Nature," where he explains that the panelists were tasked with discussing art education "as a preparation for Designing and Decorative Work," focusing on older students preparing for the manufacturing industry (65). However, all the contributors—J. Sparkes from the School of Art at South Kensington; A. F. Brophy from Finsbury Technical College; and T. R. Ablett, the superintendent of drawing of the School Board for London—address early art education.[13] Their disagreements underscore the clash between curricula based on imitative exercises and those that acknowledged a more inventive child artist. Cooke praises Ablett, who insists that children "not copy merely, but originate, invent" (67) and attacks Sparkes, who contends that the ideal art education follows a "geometrical plan" in which students "analyse and dissect" ornamental figures (Sparkes 201). These exercises, Cooke claims, teach only "accuracy absolute" and "drag the child through all the interminable routine, copying lines only, and exercising only its fingers . . . with no gleam of joyful invention, no stimulating discovery" (75). Throughout his commentary, Cooke calls upon the practices of Froebel, using kindergarten methods to justify his insistence on imagination's precedence over accuracy and form. "Imagination some teachers consider their enemy. Accuracy is ever opposed to it," writes Cooke. "This wide-reaching faculty, which enters into various mental operations, Froebel desires to exercise; and design or inventive drawing is the means, not the end; and though incomplete, his is probably the only system existing of teaching elementary design founded both on the elements of the subject, and the nature of the child" (73–74).

Cooke's attention to the "nature of the child" signals his indebtedness to the contemporaneous Child Study movement. While Cooke argued for spontaneous child art, Child Study scholars examined thousands of drawings, analyzing the style of children's markings, the materials they use, and the subjects they represent. By the 1890s, most major works in the field include discussions of art. Child Study scholars see children's drawings as evidence of children's psychologies and as indicative of universal patterns in human development, physical and mental, usually in the context of recapitulation. Their accounts of child art therefore almost invariably draw explicit connections between "primitive" drawings and those of contemporary children. For example, Corrado Ricci's landmark *L'arte dei Bambini* (1887), one of the first serious studies of child art, opens with Ricci's account of discovering cave drawings in Bologna before moving onto drawings by Italian schoolchildren.[14] Sully's influential *Studies of Childhood* (1895) includes two chapters on child art—"The Child as Artist" and "The Little Draughtsman"—and both display primitive art alongside the work of Victorian children. Alexander Chamberlain's *The Child: A Study in the Evolution of Man* (1900) includes a chapter-long discussion on "The Art of Childhood," featuring a subsection on "Children's Drawings and Those of Primitive Peoples" (192). For these scholars, children's art was vital to a larger quest for knowledge about both the development of the individual child and the human race.

Working within an intellectual framework that demands striking parallels between child art and primitive art, Child Study scholars seem committed to an imitative paradigm that grants the young artist limited, if any, artistic agency. For example, Sully writes of the "art-impulse of children," a phrase that roots creativity in instinct and therefore robs the child of artistic initiative, and he traces a similar impulse in "the drawings of modern savages and those of early art" (298, 332). Earl Barnes, in *Studies in Education* (1896–1897), includes a series of six drawings that trace a child's depiction of a human figure from a chaotic scribble to a fully articulated figure (Figure 4.1). He names this chart "Pictorial Evolution of a Man," a title that collapses the child's art practice and the evolution of the species (22).[15] Children, in these studies, are destined to reenact a predetermined aesthetic development. Moreover, many scholars contend that young artists begin drawing by mimicking the adults around them, moving a pencil across paper without intention. Elmer Brown, in *Notes on Children's Drawings* (1897), suggests that child artists choose their subjects and methods "in imitation of similar figures which they had seen others draw" (59), and Sully argues that a child "may set himself to draw, and make believe that he is drawing something when he is scribbling"; however, these movements are "largely an imitative play-action following the direction of the movements of another's hand" (333). In many Child Study accounts of young people's early attempts at drawing, then,

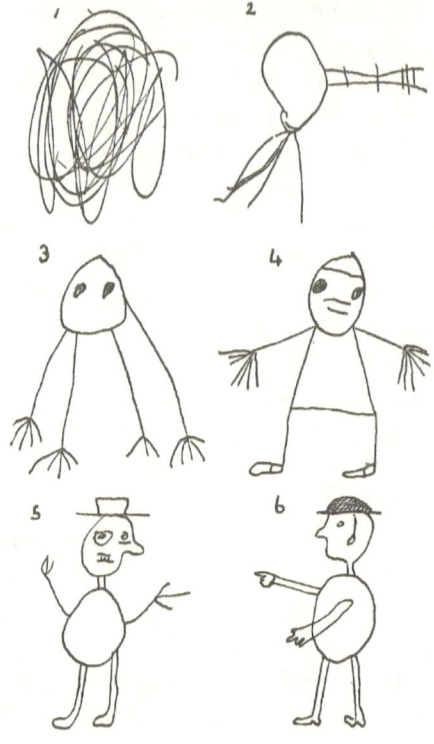

4.1. "The Pictorial Evolution of a Man," included in Earl Barnes, *Studies in Education: A Series of Ten Numbers Devoted to Child-Study and the History of Education*, 2nd ed. Philadelphia: [Stanford University], 1903, 22.

children's art is not their own. It is evidence of the inescapable history of the human race or a mindless (and crude) reproduction of adults' actions.

Yet many Child Study scholars detect something in children's artwork that transcends mimicry. Children, they argue, can transcend the imitative impulse to exhibit judgment and creativity.[16] For example, while Sully insists that "at no stage of this child-art can we find what we should regard as elements of artistic value," at the end of his chapter on "the young draughtsman" he reflects generously on the sometimes-pleasing aesthetics of child art (382). Even in "untutored performances" he finds "faint indications of a freer individual initiative," variances in style that betray "a certain individuality of feeling and aim, that like true artists . . . convey a personal impression" (397). When Child Study scholars stray from their project of identifying universal patterns of child development and focus, instead, on the work on individual, observed children, they discover the child as a creative subject. Brown makes similar concessions; he finds that "imitation of others' drawings as . . . children present is not a copying line for line. It is imitation of the freest sort" and "cannot be regarded as a limiting of individuality, but only as a discovering to the child of new possibilities of self-expression" (68). Others comment on the young artist's movements and lines, again focusing on the embodied child artist. "The [child's] hand moves rapidly," Cooke writes in "Our Art Teaching and Child Nature," and it produces "beautiful curves over the smooth surface, like a skater" (83). While Cooke sees these curving lines as a consequence of children's natural movements, others propose that this style is a matter of choice. For instance, Herman T. Lukens, in "A Study of Children's Drawings in the Early Years" (1896), argues that child artists use "a few, bold, *well-chosen* lines . . . with telling effect to suggest action and indicate expression" (89, emphasis added).

While Child Study scholars' studies of children's drawings are steeped in the language of imitation, then, they often trouble that assumed trajectory—and in those interruptions, the inventive child appears: the child as a creative subject and, potentially, creative collaborator. For example, while Henry T. Bailey's *A First Year of Drawing* (1894) recalls narratives of artistic maturation, a landmark of the imitation paradigm—he notes that a child's art "is a kind of drawing just as an acorn shoot is a kind of oak, or a restless boy a kind of man"—he also admires the stylistic ease of children's art. "The sketch may be crude, but it may embody *ideas*, and these will be forcibly expressed. Children . . . seize the spirit of things as well as their essential forms" (6–7). Along similar lines, Gelett Burgess, in a short essay on children's drawings titled "Some Phases of Primitive Art" (1895), contends that if "the ideal of art is the perfect expression of a thought, is not here [in children's drawing] a perfect art?—for, crude as are the drawings, they are undoubtedly abreast the child-thought" (6). These passages exemplify Child Study scholars' delicate negotiation of imitative and inventive paradigms of child art. They isolate the typical dismissive reception of children's art in uneasy clauses (such as Bailey's "the sketch may be crude") only to undermine that opinion with an account of the child's artistry. Many historians argue that appreciation for child art would not occur in earnest until the twentieth century; John French, for instance, argues that "in spite of training, first-hand observation and sympathy, most pioneer investigators of children's art were unable to see it as an art expression" (331), and Jo Alice Leeds finds that "not until the early twentieth century did radical changes in aesthetic standards allow child art to be appreciated on its own aesthetic terms" (93). However, many adults did see expertise in child art. To quote Chamberlain, children are "scribble-minded and naively artistic in the highest sense" (198).

As the previous paragraphs suggest, new approaches to child art emerging at the end of the nineteenth century and beginning of the twentieth at times evoke a purely fictional child, appropriating the language of Romantic childhood and betraying an investment in the naïve child of nature, for example, or in the child who remains a tabula rasa before adult influence spoils its innocence. This attachment to Romantic childhood was shared by one of the most influential writers and teachers in art education in the early twentieth century: Viennese artist and educator Franz Cizek. His lectures and lesson plans, published in London by devotee Francesca Wilson, appear, at first, Rousseauian in their emphasis on natural childhood and their hand-wringing about preserving the young artist's artlessness. "A child, like a flower, must grow out of its own roots if it is to come to fruition," argues Cizek. "Children live nowadays altogether too sophisticated a life—they see and hear too much—they are taken to cinemas and theatres, and all sorts of alien influences play upon them." Cizek often daydreamed of "that island of his in the middle of the sea—'Far away, where no ship could touch it.' There he would have his garden of God, with children growing in it like flowers" (Wilson, *Lecture* 4).

However, while Cizek's reference to the child-as-flower is idealistic, metaphors that align children with the natural world and plants in particular (which abound in the nineteenth century) draw the reader's attention to the child as a living, growing being—a subject who "must grow *out of its own roots*," whose body is subject not only to the influence of environment but also to its own growth and maturation. Cizek, after all, transformed his idealizations into classroom practices that capitalize on child autonomy and curtail adult authority. In his Juvenile Art Classes, which began in 1897 and were open to children as young as two and as old as fourteen, Cizek focused on "letting children teach themselves" (Wilson, *Lecture* 1). He sometimes encouraged young artists to depict a particular subject through storytelling or conversation and sometimes left them to their own devices. "The teacher ought to learn to 'hover like an invisible spirit' over his pupil," Cizek advised, "always ready to encourage, but never to press or force" (Wilson, *Lecture* 2). Some scholars, noting the sophistication and uniformity of the art young people produced in

Cizek's classrooms, suspect that he was more directive than his theories imply.[17] "He knew what child art was supposed to look like," smirks Efland, "and he knew how to get children to produce it!" (198). However, Cizek was aware of the inevitability of a teacher's influence over his pupils. "I influence only through my presence . . . If I look at a pupil, I influence," he admits. "This kind of influence I cannot exclude" (Viola 44). And, in any case, his methods were far more liberating than others popular in the 1890s. Art historian S. B. Malvern, for example, insists that Cizek's directions "should not lead us to overstating the case for the extent to which he gave direction to children. What he rejected was the conventional and academic notion of the teacher as possessor of some wisdom to be transmitted to the child whose mind was, as it were, a 'tabula rasa' awaiting the inscription of prior and predetermined knowledge" (267).

Cizek, like many art educators and Child Study scholars at the fin-de-siècle, was reimagining adult-child relationships in a manner that lends the child creative agency, and he does so in part by removing child artists from a narrative of artistic development; he did not imagine children as subjects on a trajectory toward more sophisticated representation. "Child Art is an art which only the child can produce," he asserts. "There is something that the child can also perform, but that we do not call art. It is imitation, it is artificial" (Viola 34). Because Cizek's lessons valued spontaneous, inventive child art and vehemently rejected classroom practices that required children to mimic adult modes of representation, the adults in Cizek's classrooms are not teachers but guides, qualified not because they can exhibit artistic expertise but instead because they embody particularly respectful attitudes toward children. Such a teacher "takes his children very seriously, as seriously as they take themselves" and "is gifted with a rare understanding and sympathy with the child mind" (Wilson, *Class* 6, 15). That demand for seriousness and sympathy suggests not adult authority and child passivity but a much more equitable intergenerational relationship—so much so that Wilhelm Viola, a disciple of Cizek's, framed his mentor's classroom work as collaborative. "The teacher and pupils," Viola explains, "are co-workers" (70).

Cizek's methods were popular in England—perhaps more popular than they were in his native Vienna. For example, they significantly impacted the work of Marion Richardson, the full-time art mistress at the Dudley Girls High School outside Wolverhampton from 1912 to 1923 and a teacher whose methods took after Cizek's. Richardson understood and described her responsibilities toward child artists in cooperative terms. In her posthumously published book *Art and the Child* (1948), Richardson claims little influence over her students' "humble intimations." Of the child's artistic capability, she notes, "I could free it, but I could not teach it; and my whole purpose was now directed to this end, as I set out to learn with and from the children" (13). However, that final phrase—"to learn *with and from* the children"—is the cornerstone to her classroom practices. Richardson would describe a scene or story to her students, who, with eyes closed, would imagine it themselves. Once the scene was fully formed in their minds, they would take up the materials Richardson provided and realize the image on paper. What Richardson offered her students was "an extension of their own experience," she writes, including descriptions of landscapes that they had not encountered or that they did not recognize as potential subjects. The children, in turn, provided what Richardson calls "an original and inner quality" that could give "colour and point to [her] words," reducing them "to what was artistically significant" (13). The resulting images were, for Richardson, a record of partnership. "The freedom and happiness of the atmosphere there had made it possible for the children to develop an art which was essentially their own, but which was none the less the result of their partnership with me," she writes (40). Richardson contends that even the smallest details of their classroom dynamic—the shapes and sizes of paper she provided, for example—could transform dramatically the art students produced. "We were, then, interdependent," Richardson writes, "and although I was as self-effacing as I could be, I knew that the children relied upon me rather as an orchestra relies upon its conductor" (41).

VIGNETTES: PUBLIC AND PRIVATE PORTRAITS OF ARTISTIC COLLABORATION

Victorian and Edwardian art educators and Child Study scholars negotiated multiple and sometimes contradictory theories of child artists. However, as the nineteenth century progressed—and as modernism's celebration and appropriation of child art loomed on the horizon—classroom practices tended toward a recognition of children as artists whose work, many argued, could instruct the observing adult in child psychology and artistic representation. The development of new forms of art education that valued young people's art according to its own merits was slow and uneven, but by the time Richardson accepted her position as full-time art mistress at Dudley, she felt empowered to approach the child less as a pupil and more as a partner—and she was not the first to do so. In this section, I survey a series of intergenerational partnerships that ran parallel to the gradual recognition of the inventive child artist in the classroom, a collection of collaborations that took place in familial and literary venues and that recognized, in diverse ways, the imaginative agency of the child artist. Evidence of these partnerships is anecdotal, and when they are referenced in letters, memoirs, or biographies, the illustrated text in question is sometimes unpublished and sometimes lost. However, it is useful to look carefully at those partnerships that have been recorded, for these examples demonstrate that the child artist, both real and imagined, becomes a figure through which adults began to imagine the place of children in cultural production and the playful and sometimes subversive potential of the child artist.

I begin by returning to Browning's collaboration with ten-year-old artist Willie Macready—a partnership that I examine in the opening of this book and that generated one of Browning's most famous poems, "The Pied Piper of Hamelin; A Child's Story." Macready, the son of famous tragedian William Charles Macready, was ten years old and bedridden with a respiratory illness in 1842 when Browning granted his request for, in Browning's words, "some little thing to illustrate" (Peterson 27). The poet first sent Willie the unpublished poem "The Cardinal and the Dog," "which he made such clever drawings for," Browning wrote to his friend Frederick James Furnivall, "that I tried a more picturesque subject, the Piper" (Peterson 27). Willie responded with four pencil illustrations and closed their correspondence with a letter that is simultaneously professional and childlike: his lament that the drawings did not quite live up to his expectations but his hopes that they "will be as great a success as the others" (Macready 350). As I argue in my introduction, the archive attached to the Browning-Macready collaboration—which includes Willie's letters and illustrations, preserved by Browning's sister Sarianna, as well as Browning's own description of their partnership—communicates the seriousness with which Browning and Willie approached their enterprise, despite its private and playful nature. While at first Browning seems to see his partnership with Willie as quite trivial (he sent the young artist a "bit of a poem"), the drawings Willie designed in response to "The Cardinal and the Dog" transformed the project for Browning into a serious partnership between poet and young artist that complicates the assumption that adults create the literature that children merely consume. Here, Browning and Willie are working partners who together produce a poem that would become a staple of Victorian children's literature and a standard text for Golden Age illustrators from Kate Greenaway to Arthur Rackham. Browning recognizes the vital role Willie played in the composition of the poem both in its subtitle, "A Child's Story," and in a dedication appended to its first publication in *Dramatic Lyrics*: "written for, and inscribed to, W. M. the Younger" (209).

"The Pied Piper," when examined as an intergenerational partnership, shows how the growing cultural capital of child art and of children as creative subjects enabled adult-child collaboration. The poem's publishing history and its plot are based on partnerships that privilege the child's contributions in ways that anticipate the shifts in art education and Child Study, outlined above, toward valuing the inventive child artist. For example, Browning's compliance with Willie's request for material—a request that the poet provide not examples of art for him to imitate but instead inspirational material in verse—may signal his respect for the child artist or his understanding of Willie's style as valuable in its own right. In addition to acknowledging Willie in the poem's dedication, Browning records the boy's vital role as illustrator in the poem itself, where he gestures to Willie's influence. For instance, he creates an avatar for the young artist in Hamelin: a young man who, like Willie, is ill and isolated. This boy survives the piper's machinations because he "was lame / And could not dance the whole of the way," and therefore "found [himself] outside the Hill, / Left alone against [his] will" (217). Like Willie, this child transforms sickness and loneliness into creative purpose, and Browning uses the voice of this child—not the voice of the piper, the seductive adult artist—to describe the wonders of the land inside the hill:

> For [the Piper] led us, he said, to a joyous land,
> Joining the town and just at hand,
> Where waters gushed and fruit-trees grew,
> And flowers put forth a fairer hue,
> And every thing was strange and new;
> The sparrows were brighter than peacocks here,
> And their dogs outran our fallow deer,
> And honey-bees had lost their stings,
> And horses were born with eagles' wings. (217)

The boy imagines the piper's promised land in almost painterly terms, focused on image and color: the "fairer hue" of the flowers, the sparrows "brighter than peacocks." He describes a dreamlike landscape; there is no

4.2. William Macready Jr., illustration for Robert Browning's "The Pied Piper of Hamelin; A Child's Story" (1842). Armstrong Browning Library, Baylor University, Waco, Texas.

copying from nature here as the child reorders the known and observable world to describe winged horses and stingless bees. Like one of Richardson's students, this child has heard and imagined a story told by an adult guide—although certainly the Piper's intentions are more malicious than Richardson's—and suspended that image in his mind, fully formed, to reproduce it in his own manner.

Macready, in turn, illustrates the legend of the piper in a manner that draws on but departs from Browning's narration, and his four drawings might challenge our assumptions about the child artist and, in a larger context, how children respond to and co-create children's literature.[18] While Browning baited Macready's pencil with fleet-footed dogs and eagle-winged horses, subjects later adult illustrators greedily took up, the young artist responded not to the fantastic but to the civic and pastoral elements of Browning's poem: the piper entering a crowded council chamber, a meadow carpeted with rats, a landscape that would be serene if its edge did not reveal a mob of doomed children, and a quiet scene in which a townsperson paints a memorial to the lost young people of Hamelin.[19] Like Willie's illustrations for "The Cardinal and the

4.3. William Macready Jr., illustration for Robert Browning's "The Pied Piper of Hamelin; A Child's Story" (1842). Armstrong Browning Library, Baylor University, Waco, Texas.

Dog," described in my introduction, these drawings are infused with the visual rhetoric of the stage, emphasizing that the particularities of Willie's experience, especially his time growing up as the son of a famous actor, is a more powerful influence on his art than anything else, including the assumption that children possess fantastic imaginations. In these drawings, Willie is both an imitator and an inventor. Like all illustrators, he practices careful scene selection, choosing those elements of the story he finds most amenable to his pencil. And notably, he plays with imitation and invention in the manner of a literary adaptation; he reproduces elements of the theater—carefully arranged scenery in the style of set designs, dramatic entrances and exits, even a version of a proscenium arch in his depiction of the council chamber—in order to reinvent the poem as play, both make-believe and dramatic (Figures 4.2 and 4.3).

The documents that describe the Browning-Macready collaboration reveal that the adult-child partnership at the heart of "The Piped Piper" is multigenerational as well as multimedia; it stretches forward, through subsequent generations, and backward, into Browning's familial history.

For instance, Browning ends the poem with a quatrain, a moral tag that speaks to the young artist's influence:

> So, Willy, let me and you be wipers
> Of scores out with all men—especially pipers!
> And, whether they pipe us free from rats or mice,
> If we've promised them aught, let us keep our promise! (219)

The phrase "me and you" suggests collective action and, perhaps, control over the course of the tale, whether or not the piper is paid. The final two lines look forward, implying that the partnership is not yet over. Moreover, the creative partnership between Browning and Willie began, perhaps, before Willie was born, when Browning first encountered the legend of the Pied Piper in his childhood. As Forest D. Burt notes, Browning's father kept in his library Nathaniel Wanley's *The Wonders of the Little World* (1678), a text his father loved that contains the piper legend. "In selecting Wanley as a source for these poems," Burt contends, "Browning was in many ways reaching back into his own childhood and empathizing with young Willie Macready's wish. The poet could no doubt recall Wanley with fondness since his father often read to his children from this work and made illustrations from it" (32). Browning Sr. began a versification of the Pied Piper himself but, upon learning that his son was composing a poem on the legend, stopped work. Browning Jr. seems much happier to accommodate—really, encourage—an intergenerational treatment of the subject. Browning's father was both author and illustrator; Browning himself shared these duties with the young Willie.

Because Willie's illustrations were unpublished, his ownership of the poem remains relatively invisible, existing only in the private relationship between poet and child artist. A few decades later, however, Margaret Gatty, with her own domestic circle of collaborators, would use her periodical *Aunt Judy's Magazine* (1866–1885) to make visible such private collaborations. Through innovative family-oriented features, the magazine would, in a sense, mass-produce the sort of collaboration between adult writer and child artist Browning and Willie used to create "The Pied Piper," offering ready-made instructions to help readers reproduce similar intergenerational collaborations. In other words, while the adult-child collaboration behind "The Pied Piper" is an evocative but ultimately short-lived example of a child artist's collaboration with an adult author, *Aunt Judy's Magazine* demonstrates how such collaborations might have occurred in households across England. The magazine was, in the words of U. C. Knoepflmacher, "a journal that openly proclaimed its identity as a Gatty family enterprise" ("*Aunt*" 152). While it is best known for its publication of writers such as Hans Christian Andersen and Lewis Carroll, all members of the Gatty family contributed to its text and illustrations. Knoepflmacher describes how Gatty and her daughter Juliana, who would herself earn acclaim as an author for children as Juliana Ewing, worked with friends and family to design features—such as correspondence columns, contests, and games—that reproduce, in the lives of their young readers, the familial collaboration they found so productive in the Gatty home. Susan Drain, in her publishing history of *Aunt Judy's Magazine*, singles out regular elements in the periodical that endorse such partnerships, such as "Nights at the Round Table," which "presented stories within a family network of teller and listeners" (14). The round table image, Drain argues, signals equal participation among all members of the family, suggesting "all children were equally welcome to participate, according to their abilities, in the family activities" (14).

The magazine provides opportunities for intergenerational partnerships forged not only through storytelling but also through the collaborative potential of illustration and its play between imitation and invention. In 1869 Gatty introduced a new feature: a series of short narratives called "Nursery Nonsense." Gatty explains that these brief stories

> are intended to serve a double purpose—to be read to the *very* little ones . . . and also to give the young artists of a family an opening for the exercise of their talent, while at the same time it is devoted to the use and benefit of the domestic circle. In these days artistic talent of a greater or less extent is by no means uncommon, and wherever it shows itself it is, as a general rule, cultivated. Let some of our young artistic friends, then, turn the accomplishment to the practical use proposed, which will, we are satisfied, win them golden opinions from younger brothers and sisters as well as from papa and mamma. (183)

These initial instructions are followed by a simple story, told in eight numbered scenes, describing the adventures of a young girl named Barbara, her mother, and her nurse. The feature continued for seven installments, each consisting of a narrative of up to fifteen scenes that follow Barbara through adulthood and showcase other characters, especially her cousin

Charlie and Uncle Charles. Drain points to this feature as a particularly apt example of activities Gatty designed to encourage the readership of *Aunt Judy's Magazine* to mimic the familial collaboration that produced the periodical. Parents contribute through narration; the youngest members of the family enjoy a story; and child artists illuminate the narrative, creating illustrations that please the entire family. "Nursery Nonsense," then, allowed adults to collaborate with child artists. Like Macready, whose creativity provided the occasion for Browning's composition of "The Pied Piper," the child readers of *Aunt Judy's Magazine* led Gatty to accommodate the talents of child artists—talents that are "by no means uncommon"—and to write stories as material for their illustration—to provide an "opening for the exercise of their talent."

However, Drain's account of the intergenerational partnerships enabled through such features is too static. The collaboration Gatty introduces in her "Nursery Nonsense" feature is shifting and complex; in her instructions and throughout the stories she offers for illustration, Gatty (who signed this feature simply as "Editor") imagines and reimagines sometimes contradictory relationships between parents and children, both the real children listening to Barbara's story and the fictional children in the stories themselves. In particular, Gatty negotiates multiple paradigms of childhood and multiple approaches to the child artist, recognizing both what I describe as the imitative child artist—the young illustrator in need of guidance in his or her maturation toward sophisticated draftsmanship—as well as the inventive child artist—whose work is worthy of celebration according to its own norms and values. This instability translates to adult-child relationships both imagined, in the fictions of "Nursery Nonsense," and real, encouraged among its readership, that sometimes follow familiar patterns of adult authority, sometimes foster respectful partnerships between generations, and sometimes put forward the possibility that children, as creative agents, can challenge the assumptions of adult authority that underpin much children's literature and art instruction.

The more directive elements of "Nursery Nonsense" recall earlier modes of art education in which the child is imagined as an inept artist striving toward adult mastery. For example, Gatty's instructions, pointedly directed to the parents of young artists and not to the family as a whole, frame this feature as an opportunity for adults to teach children the "proper" way to draw. Gatty suggests that, in preparation for "Nursery Nonsense," a little study of Fröhlich's beautiful illustrations of 'Mdlle. Lili's Journée,' will show [children] the sort of thing that is wanted. ... One cannot become a Fröhlich at once, but one may charm the nursery spectators, and be crowned with drawing-room laurels for the attempt, however defective. If mamma or papa are artists too, or an uncle or friend who is visiting at the home, wonders may be done in guiding the first attempts at this sort of designing. (183)

Gatty does not criticize what she understands to be the mistakes children inevitably will make in their artwork but instead assures that even flawed children's drawings may "be crowned with drawing-room laurels" simply for "the attempt." However, it is undeniable that, in the context of "Nursery Nonsense," any exercise of children's talents is in service to an assumed teleology of aesthetic education, part of a creative progression from "defective" to "the sort of thing that is wanted." Gatty assures parents that "little ones will be charmed to sit at the table or on the floor in the proper positions" (182). The format of the attached narrative is also instructive; Gatty breaks the story into scenes, each a few sentences in length, and those breaks are meant to determine which elements of a story the child will illustrate. Now and then she nudges the listening artist in a particular creative direction—noting, for example, when her characters strike a particularly evocative tableau. "Charlie puts one arm around [Barbara's] waist, and doubles the first of the other in the air," she writes in one installment. "It is a position for an artist" (250). It appears at first, then, that the collaboration enabled through "Nursery Nonsense" is limited: Gatty provides a framework for familial partnerships based on the interaction of text and image, but these collaborations prioritize the norms and values of adults' art and education over any contribution the child could make.

However, amid this at times heavy-handed artistic instruction, Gatty registers her respect for the child artist—allowing, for instance, a degree of creative license when she suggests that the narrating adult should let children "try sketches of these scenes either in pencil or colours—either serious or grotesque" (183). Her privileging of the young artist's point of view is more apparent in the fictions she wrote for "Nursery Nonsense"; like Browning, she includes in her stories child characters who are artists in their own right, in particular storytellers and poets. Notably, Barbara and her cousin Charlie understand children's ability to appropriate, critique, and even dismiss the stories adults tell to them. For example, in "Mr. Manners' Last Piece," Charlie turns author, writing his own narrative *within* Gatty's, and imagines the backstory of his mother's persistent dictum that he should always leave the last tartlet at dinner or toast at tea for "Mr. Manners." "Once upon a time there was Mr. Manners," Charlie writes. "Some people will call him *Good*, but I don't. I call him *Bad*, because he was so greedy he ate the last piece of everything off all the dishes. . . . His name was *Shocking Bad Manners*, I believe" (314). Shocking Bad Manners crowns himself king and demands that his subjects save him the last serving at every meal or face beheading. In imaginatively appropriating authorship of this "Nursery Nonsense" tale, Charlie transforms Mr. Manners, the epitome of Victorian table etiquette, into an evil despot, reinterpreting the disciplined child into an oppressed subject who, empowered by a sense of injustice, rightfully demands redress.[20] The children listening to their parents read "Mr. Manners' Last Piece" from the pages of *Aunt Judy's Magazine* are invited to illustrate not only this challenge to authority but also, in Charlie's frame story, the figure of the child author. While Charlie's father finds his son's decision to become a writer a "very good joke," young Barbara "can see nothing funny about it" (313). Charlie's story about Mr. Manners is part of a larger reconsideration of children's and adults' power that weaves throughout "Nursery Nonsense." In the feature's second installment, titled "Bogy Will Fetch You," Barbara and Charlie attempt to discover the truth behind the Bogy story Barbara's nurse uses to frighten her into obedience. The children illustrating the story are asked to depict scenes that challenge adult authority: for example, one in which Barbara and Charlie ask their nurse suspicious questions about the Bogy's appearance, clothing, and preferred diet, and another in which they learn that it is not, in fact, a monster that devours the bones Charlie leaves in the basement as Bogy-bait but instead their pet dog Sancho.

Gatty does not allow the possibility of subversive childhood to stand uncontested, and both stories end with adults recapturing creative power. "Bogy Will Fetch You" concludes when Barbara's father dispels the Bogy myth. While the children have already determined that the Bogy is a flimsy scare tactic, their discovery is reiterated—and substantiated—when an adult agrees. "Papa explains . . . that there are no Bogies in cellars," the narrator notes. "Also that children need fear nothing so much as the evil tempers of their own hearts. The children are greatly comforted, though they look a little grave of having to be afraid of themselves" (250). The child who undermines adult discipline apparently is the true villain of this story. Charlie's story about Mr. Manners is similarly co-opted:

> Uncle Charles says he doesn't think Charlie has written the *moral*, and offers to do it for him. . . . They watch Uncle Charles print MORAL very big underneath—"Bad examples should be avoided, not followed. *So don't take the last piece off the dish, my dears, like Mr. Shocking Bad Manners.*" It was not exactly the conclusion Charlie had intended perhaps, but Uncle Charles seemed to think it such a *very* good joke, the children thought they must think so too. And they think so still. (314)

Once again, an adult figure snatches creative authority from the child artist. Here, however, the conclusion seems to give Uncle Charles's pretension a sideways glance. His unsolicited appropriation of his son's story, the "very big" letters he uses, and the incongruence of the appended moral and Charlie's intentions might signal not his authority but instead his inflated ego (and his propensity for getting a laugh at his son's and niece's expense). In fact, one could read the conclusion of the story as a critique of adults' (often incorrect) interpretations and uses of child art, or their eagerness to translate children's creative expression into forms and narrative patterns that align with adult values.

Gatty, in encouraging child artists' efforts through storytelling, engages in a pattern of listening and response that was a hallmark of adult-child collaboration throughout the nineteenth century. As noted above, educational theorists such as Cizek and Richardson created curricula that capitalized upon the child's ability to transform adult narration into art. Such curricula provided child artists with material to encourage their inventive faculties rather than visual models for imitation, and authors for children who sought to collaborate with young artists, such as Gatty, often employed similar strategies. Contemporary readers can only speculate about how children might have illustrated Gatty's stories; because the work of the young artists inspired by Barbara's adventures was never published, we don't know if these children followed Gatty's advice to become little Fröhlichs or if they drew in a manner quite their own. However, my next example—American author David Starr Jordan's *The Book of Knight and Barbara, Being a Series of Stories Told to Children, Corrected and Illustrated by the Children* (1899)—allows readers to see how young artists responded to told tales.[21] The title of the book, in its repetition of "children" and its recognition to two of its primary contributors—Jordan's son Knight and daughter Barbara—emphatically registers the role of young artists in the published text.

The book includes nearly fifty short narratives: original tales Jordan told to his children as well as some humorous adaptations of myths and fairy tales, accompanied by line drawings. Jordan, like Browning and Gatty before him, credits the composition of the book to the encouragement of young listeners who enjoyed his stories and to the inspiration of child artists who created illustrations to illuminate his narrative. The dedication to the book reads, "To the many children of California, who, with Knight and Barbara, have given this little volume 'its best excuse for being'" (iii). This dedication, and the preface that follows, make clear that from the start Jordan imagined *The Book of Knight and Barbara* as a collaboration with children, and primarily child artists. He notes that the "pictures made by the children," in addition to justifying the book's publication, "have been found to interest deeply other children, a fact which gives them a certain value as original documents in the study of the working of the child-mind" (vi). Jordan's reference to "the child-mind" indicates that this book is part of the common Child Study practice, discussed above, of compiling and publishing examples of children's drawings for comparison and analysis. Jordan did, in fact, publish *The Book of Knight and Barbara* at the encouragement of two graduate students in Child Study working at Stanford University: Louise Maitland, who had already begun to publish on child art, and Harriet Hawley.[22] Maitland and Hawley recommended that Jordan circulate his stories widely as material that could inspire child art for further study. Hawley recorded the stories in shorthand, and Maitland shared them with children in schools in Palo Alto, Oakland, Santa Cruz, and Washington, DC, selecting those that appear in the published volume from the hundreds of drawings young people produced in response. Jordan supplemented these drawings with a selection of drawings by university students, which, he notes, appear primarily in the later pages of the book and are "intended to assist the imagination of child-readers" (vi).[23]

However, Jordan amended the Child Study approach to child art, revising its practices of compilation and analysis and, in the process, transforming his collection of children's drawings into a creative, intergenerational collaboration. Jordan seems less interested in scientific analysis and the manner that child art mimics primitive art than in the pleasures of crafting stories in partnership with inventive child artists and editors. Notably, the design of *The Book of Knight and Barbara* obscures distinctions between child art and adult art, child text and adult text, and therefore dismantles the usual hierarchies of adult and child contributors. Certainly some reviewers described the child illustrations included in the volume in condescending language—the *New York Mail and Express* notes that the book's "crude drawings" are "remarkably interesting" (D. Appleton)—but Jordan notably does *not* do this, despite the widespread practice in the 1890s of describing child art as quaint, primitive, or rudimentary. He simply notes in his preface that schoolchildren provided "illustrative pictures, after their fashion" (v). Jordan's unwillingness to assign lesser value to child art or storytelling carries through the ensuing text, in which he provides few textual or visual cues to help the reader disentangle the contributions of the children and adults who participated in the book's composition. He includes occasional subtitles referring to the originals from which his stories are adapted—"With acknowledgments to Jacob Grimm" (88), for example, or "After an Ancient Document" (134)[24]—but only one story is attributed to a child: "Una's Children and the Lion" is described as "Dictated and Illustrated by Barbara," who was seven or eight years old at the time of the book's publication. Only twice is a story is interrupted by footnotes attributed in direct speech to Jordan's children; for example, Knight, ten or eleven at the book's publication, interrupts "The Head and the Snakes," the beginning of a Medusa story, to defend the name of one of the story's primary characters: "'Quicksilver is the same as Mercury and sounds better' (*Knight*). Hawthorne has made a similar observation" (117). The note both acknowledges Knight's contribution and supports his opinion with that of an established author.

Aside from these infrequent gestures, however, the many artists, storytellers, transcribers, and editors behind the production of *The Book of Knight and Barbara* are concealed by an outwardly seamless text.[25] Admittedly, in much of the text it appears simple to identify a drawing as belonging to a child. The illustrations for "The Little Legs that Ran Away" (9–11), for example, exhibit features commonly associated with young children's drawings, including a house with transparent walls, an out-of-perspective bedstead, and human figures with splayed, twig-like fingers. However, this is not always the case. Readers—alert to Jordan's caveat that some drawings were contributed by university students—find themselves hyperaware of the sometimes arbitrary standards by which we judge children's versus adults' art. A drawing of the Castle of Heidelberg

The Castle of Heidelberg.

4.4. Unattributed illustration for "The Otto-Heinrich Tower" in David Starr Jordan's *The Book of Knight and Barbara, Being a Series of Stories Told to Children, Corrected and Illustrated by the Children*. New York: D. Appleton, 1899, 96.

in the story "The Otto-Heinrich Tower," for example, seems somewhat sophisticated for child art, but its inclusion relatively early in the volume would suggest that it is the work of a young artist (92). An emblematic illustration of a cat grappling with a turkey buzzard in "The Strange Rabbit" could be the work of either an elementary school student or of a much older artist mimicking a medieval manuscript or engaging in the flattened and naïve styles popular at the end of the nineteenth century (Figures 4.4 and 4.5). This confusion of contributors is particularly pronounced in the text, which is professedly narrated by Jordan, transcribed by Hawley, and edited by children. The stories are uniformly childlike in tone and language, and therefore—aside from those moments when Barbara's and Knight's interjections are clearly footnoted—it is nearly impossible for a reader to determine if, or where, a child editor intervened. When, in the story "How Barbara Came to Escondité," the heroine kills a coyote and then "washed the coyote-stuff all off from the floor," are we to suspect a child's voice, or an adult mimicking a child? (6).

Jordan, in fact, seems determined not only to obscure the precise moments when an adult or child is narrating or drawing but also to minimize his role in assembling the book. At times, the result is an account of the book's publication that seems to assign its authorship to no one at all. In his memoir, for example, Jordan notes that the collection was "ready for publication without my ever having written a line of it" and that the volume "built itself up" (*Days* 568–69). At other moments, it seems that Jordan minimizes his role and the interventions of Maitland and Hawley in order to celebrate instead his child collaborators. In his preface, he admits that "several of the stories, especially the classical travesties,

4.5. Unattributed illustration for "The Strange Rabbit" in David Starr Jordan's *The Book of Knight and Barbara, Being a Series of Stories Told to Children, Corrected and Illustrated by the Children.* New York: D. Appleton, 1899, 49.

would not be printed were it not for the children's drawings," and years later he contended that "its interest [laid] as much in the pictures as in my fantastic text" (vi, *Days* 569).[26] In consequence of Jordan's evasiveness about which parts of the book belong to whom and his unusual account of the book's origins, readers are obliged to scrutinize each sentence and illustration, evaluating what is "childlike" or sophisticated about particular words or images. They entertain the possibility that adults can be inept imitators while children can be surprisingly inventive and artistic. After all, Jordan's "travesties"—his perversions of well-known stories about Diogenes or Odin—can be read as quite clumsy adaptations while the accompanying illustrations can delight in their vibrant depictions of the described scenes.

A better-known text that, according to its author, arose from an intergenerational collaboration between adult storyteller and child listeners and artists is Rudyard Kipling's *Just So Stories for Little Children*. Kipling published the collected twelve stories—including interspersed poems and his own illustrations—in 1902, but he composed the tales and released them in *St. Nicholas Magazine*, *Ladies' Home Journal*, and *Pearson's Magazine* between 1897 and 1902. Contemporary scholars frequently describe the *Just So Stories* as collaborative, imagined jointly between Kipling and his daughter, Effie. Linda M. Shires, for example, argues that "the narrator engages adult and child listener-readers as indispensable coinventors" (194), and nearly every critical account of the collection references as evidence of its intergenerational authorship Kipling's introduction in *St. Nicholas Magazine* to the first *Just So* tale: "In the evening there were stories meant to put Effie to sleep," Kipling writes, "and you were not allowed to alter those by one single little word. They had to be told just so; or Effie would wake up and put back the missing sentence" (89). While he acknowledges that "little people are not alike," he insists that "if you catch some Effie rather tired and rather sleepy at the end of the day, and if you begin in a low voice and tell the tales precisely as I have written them down, you will find that Effie will presently curl up and go to sleep" (89). As these remarks suggest, Kipling invited his readers to reproduce in their own homes the parent-child relationship he'd built with Effie, and he remained committed to this project even after the emotional devastation of Effie's death at age six in 1899. The result is an uneasy collaboration with both real and imagined children; Kipling represents Effie, U.C. Knoepflmacher argues, as "an undying fictional Other who was his personal Best Beloved as well as a universal Every-child" ("Kipling's" 31). Direct addresses to that Every-child weave throughout the *Just So Stories* in narrative asides that anticipate questions a child might ask, for example, and in onomatopoeic phrases (such as the "ooshy-skooshy" sea in "How the Whale Got His Throat") that replicate oral narration to a child audience (8).

These collaborations are not only multigenerational but also multimedia, relying on image as much as text; like Darwin's son Francis, the real children listening to the *Just So Stories* and the imagined children inside the tales use art to collaborate with the adults around them. For example, in the stories scholars have dubbed the Taffy tales—"How the First Letter Was Written" and "How the Alphabet Was Made"—father-daughter partners Tegumai and Taffy collaborate over the pictograms Taffy carves onto a piece of birch bark. Knoepflmacher calls these pictograms the "child-artist's story" and documents the vital role they play in the narrative; over the course of two tales, her symbols evolve into the Roman alphabet.[27] Kipling publishes his fictional child's art just as Jordan published the drawings of real children; he "lovingly reproduces—within the text and without a caption—Taffy's own drawing," Knoepflmacher writes. "The efforts of a paternal artist-writer are required to supplement the budding creative powers of a . . . child," and the adult "defers to the nascent achievements of young artists-to-be" ("Kipling's" 38). Knoepflmacher and many others interpret Tegumai and Taffy as the fictional counterparts of Kipling and Effie, but Taffy as a child artist also is the fictional counterpart of the child artists listening to or reading the *Just So Stories*—those other Effies that Kipling alludes to in his *St. Nicholas* introduction to the *Just So Stories*. Kipling addresses those living children in the rambling, witty captions attached to each full-page illustration in the story collection—captions Brian Alderson calls "the most famous and distinctive feature" of the *Just So Stories* images ("Just So" 159). These captions often invite the child audience to color or otherwise alter the existing illustrations. For example, the caption for an illustration for "How the Leopard Got His Spots" reads, in part, "This is wise Baviaan, the dog-headed Baboon, Who is Quite the Wisest Animal in All South Africa. I have drawn him from a statue that I made up out of my own head. . . . I should like to paint him with paint-box colours, but I am not allowed" (36).

Such invitations recall the growing recognition of children as inventive artists documented in the previous section of this chapter and temporarily subvert adult authority over childhood through the possibility of creative mischief. The narrator of the *Just So Stories* is, for the most part, a storytelling adult who entertains the younger Best Beloved, but here that narrator becomes, briefly, the child; his regret that he is "not allowed" to paint this portrait of Baviaan reframes him as a young person expected to submit to parental discipline.[28] Narrator and reader momentarily exchange positions, allowing the storyteller to empathize with child listeners whose experiences with illustrated books are policed by adults and who, perhaps, are exhorted to handle such volumes carefully, with clean hands. No painting boxes allowed. Moreover, when this caption is read in relationship with the illustration of Baviaan, it seems likely that Kipling, through the narrator's voice, is representing the "correct" manner to interact with an illustration only to invite children to challenge that order, implicitly asking them to flout the conventions of accepted behavior with their creativity. Kipling, in a very practical way, was *not* allowed to paint his illustrations, which were printed in black and white, but when he represents Baviaan, he does so in a simple line drawing with large, open spaces that tempt a child's paintbrush. Lamenting he cannot color this drawing, Kipling implies that the child holding the book, in fact, could. Children, through their imagined potential for misbehavior—their subversive and sometimes destructive play, their insistence in doing what is "not allowed"—can enliven the image of Baviaan in a way that Kipling, an adult, cannot.

The narrator's explanation of the origins of the Baviaan illustration—his note that the image is "drawn . . . from a statue" that he "made up out of [his] own head"—also registers the tensions between imitation and invention that characterized art education in the years when Kipling was writing "How the Leopard Got His Spots." The first half of this statement, the narrator's assertion that Baviaan is "drawn from a statue," recalls imitative methods of art education that required students to copy existing artwork as accurately as possible; the narrator, like the child artists copying Fröhlich prints as they listen to Gatty's "Nursery Nonsense," refers to a model before rendering the dog-headed baboon. However, the second half of this statement undercuts the first, for the statue is imaginary, "out of [the narrator's] own head." This phrase evokes methods of art education that appreciate the lines, colors, and forms children produce independent of models and guides. The caption to Baviaan, then, ultimately privileges an artistic imagination that is purely inventive rather than imitative. Illustration and representation, Kipling implies, need not answer to the conventions of the rational world, and the children inspired to paint the illustrations of the *Just So Stories* should feel free to choose their colors as they please, disregarding adults' disapproval at altering the book and the colors and the forms and artistic conventions found in the model prints set before them in art classes.

The narrator makes similar suggestions for artistic collaboration in many of the captions in *Just So Stories*. Commenting upon an image from "The Sing-Song of Old Man Kangaroo," for instance, the narrator informs the child reader that "Yellow-Dog Dingo is drawn black, because I am not allowed to paint these pictures with real colours out of the paint-box," and in the caption describing an illustration from "The Elephant's Child," the narrator notes, "This is just a picture of the Elephant's Child going to pull bananas off a banana-tree after he had got his fine new long trunk. I don't think it is a very nice picture; but I couldn't make it any better, because elephants and bananas are hard to draw. . . . I think it would look better if you painted the banana-tree green and the Elephant's Child red" (64). By conceding that the picture isn't very good and admitting that "elephants and bananas are hard to draw," Kipling sympathizes with child listeners who have perhaps experienced similar difficulties in their own artistic attempts, and by inviting those children to alter the picture, to paint the banana-tree and the elephant, the narrator invites collaboration and validates the contributions of a child artist.

AS A CHILD WOULD DRAW UPON A SLATE

The multiple opportunities for collaboration in the *Just So Stories* are, undoubtedly, a manifestation of a collaboration that is simultaneously real and imagined; these are part of Kipling's efforts to represent and reflect upon his relationship with his daughter. However, Kipling's interactions with his child audience, and in particular the dialogue he develops in the captions quoted above, also reflect a growing array of art materials and illustrations available for young people—materials and illustrations that reflected new ideas about art education. In this final section, I will identify how books and activities marketed to young people in the latter half of the nineteenth century not only offer the opportunity for children to draw *like children* (rather than like aspiring adult artists) but also celebrate the naïve styles of child artists alongside, and perhaps in spite of, a growing attention to refined and sophisticated children's book illustration.

For instance, Kipling's line drawing of Baviaan, with its empty spaces perfect for "paint-box colours," transforms the published volume of *Just So Stories* into a painting book. By the 1880s, painting books designed for children were widely available and, judging by the proliferation of advertisements for them, quite popular. The concept of the child's painting book was popularized by *The "Little Folks" Painting Book, A Series of Outline Engravings for Watercolour Painting* (1884), which contains over one hundred black-and-white outlines of illustrations by Kate Greenaway drawn from a number of her picture books: *Under the Window, Birthday Book, A Day in a Child's Life,* and *Mother Goose*. According to the author of "Art in the Nursery," the *"Little Folks"* painting book was "a book for wear and tear—a common, every-day delight; it contains some of the artist's most amiable work, it should be popular all the world over" (257). This painting book's success hinged on its association with the popular *Little Folks* magazine, and it was followed with other titles connected to that periodical, including the *"Little Folks" Proverb Painting Book* and *Fruits and Blossoms for "Little Folks" to Paint*. Other publishers followed suit. In fact, Hodder and Staughton, perhaps inspired by Kipling's cheeky captions, transformed four individual tales from Kipling's *Just So Stories* into painting books between 1922 and 1923: *The Elephant's Child, The Sing-Song of Old Man Kangaroo, How the Rhinoceros Got His Skin,* and *How the Alphabet Was Made.* These books followed what became a familiar formula: outline images interspersed with text from the stories.[29]

These painting books, usually sold for one shilling, were on the surface meant to be educational, published to instruct children in the placement and harmony of colors and in moral and cultural norms, communicated in didactic stories and verses. The editors of the *"Little Folks" Painting Book*, for example, note that it "is, of course, apparent that, in a book of this description, the talents of young artists must be chiefly directed to the fitting choice of colours, and their harmonious arrangement" (vii). Child artists are instructed to find, in the final pages of the book, directions for mixing colors, particularly adapted for the use of the Little Folks Fine Art Moist Colour Box. To emphasize the merits of determining "fitting" colors and their "harmonious" placement, the *Little Folks* book and similar productions include, alongside black-and-white outlines meant for children to paint, full-color versions of the same images. Yet while didactic in tone, painting books also offer children a degree of artistic agency. First, as more painting books were published based on the illustrations of popular artists, child artists were invited to collaborate, albeit in a mediated way, with some of the most recognizable children's book illustrators of the nineteenth century, from Greenaway to Walter Crane to Randolph Caldecott.[30] Moreover, the artists and publishers who produced these painting books could not control how children used the blank spaces on their pages. These books are potentially opportunities for children to contribute their point of view, to align their artwork with the examples and instructions publishers offer, conforming to the norms of art and even the rational world, or to break off in original, imaginative directions. As painting books developed as a form into the early twentieth century, in fact, publishers regularly provided opportunities for young artists to draw their own images. In 1927, for example, the *Bookman* reviewed *The Covent Garden Painting Book*, which features "several pages left to the discretion of the children." These blank pages seemed to make the reviewers nervous. Children, "if they are wise," the reviewer notes, "will leave these till last, when they have gained all the experience they can" from those pages that offer guidance through outlines and colored model plates (*Covent*). While painting books attempted to encourage young people in certain habits of taste and to educate them in particular habits of artistic expression—the epitome of art education through imitation—the blank spaces included in these books invite invention. The subversive potential of the painting and coloring books was realized in the twentieth century with the rise of the activity book, a genre that seeks to foster free-form drawing, imaginative play, and individual creativity.[31]

This trend in children's painting books was anticipated by Sir Henry Cole, who published under the pseudonym Felix Summerly *The Little Painter's Portfolio*, a collection of ten colored and four outline pictures, sold alongside a "Colour Box for Little Painters" (Cole 162). The painting book was part of a series of books and toys for children, titled The Home Treasury, that Cole released between 1841 and 1849 with publisher Joseph Cundall. Throughout the series, which features titles from *Reynard the Fox* to *Beauty and the Beast* to *Alphabets of Quadrupeds*, Cole was attentive to illustration and visual design; the subtitle of the series notes that it is "purposed to cultivate the Affections, Fancy, Imagination, and Taste of Children"—and taste was of utmost importance (160). Cole, who was involved with England's schools of design beginning in 1848 and who helped organize the Great Exhibition of 1851, sought to use his Home Treasury to raise what he considered to be the appalling standards of children's book illustration. "All [the books in the series] will be illustrated," he writes, "but not after the usual fashion of children's books, in which it seems to be assumed that the lowest kind of art is good enough to give first impressions to a child. In the present series, though the statement may perhaps excite a smile, the illustrations will be selected from the works of Raffaelle, Titian, Hans Holbein, and other old masters. Some of the best modern Artists have kindly promised their aid in creating a taste for beauty in little children" (161). Artists such as Charles West Cope and William Mulready contributed illustrations, and the Home Treasury was well received by critics such as William Thackeray, who praised the series in *Fraser's Magazine*, writing under his Michael Angelo Titmarsh pseudonym. Thackeray agreed that, in previous years, "picture-books . . . were illustrated with the most shameful, hideous, old wood-cuts" and that their "painted pictures . . . [were] almost all of the very worst kind." However, "the mere sight of the little books published by Mr. Cundall . . . is as good as a nosegay. Their actual covers are as brilliant as a bed of tulips, and blaze with emerald, and orange, and cobalt, and gold, and crimson. . . . What a library!—what a picture-gallery!" ("On Some" 496–97).

Plenty of such picture galleries were available for the Victorian child's library. The mid-nineteenth century witnessed the rise of engravers such as William James Linton and the Dalziel brothers as well as artists such as Richard Doyle, John Tenniel, and the famous triumvirate working under Edmund Evans: Caldecott, Crane, and Greenaway. Many critics and essayists, enamored with this embarrassment of riches, adopted as Thackeray did the language of fine art and picture galleries to describe children's books. William Henley, in 1880, praised the work of Caldecott, for example, by writing that "under his sway, Art for the nursery has become Art indeed" ("Randolph" 212). In 1883 a reviewer wrote in "Art in the Nursery" that "nothing is too pretty or too good for our little ones, as there was nothing too cheap and too bad for the little ones of a century ago. They . . . rejoice in colour-printing that gives their books a claim to be considered as works of art; they are deluged with examples of taste and skill" (128–29). The child "may be said to be something of an art critic ere he leaves his cradle, and an adept in style ere he sees fit to abandon long garments for short. . . . It is his own fault if he be not, for his aesthetic opportunities are innumerable, and the matter produced for the gratification of his pampered appetite is perhaps the daintiest ever seen" (128).

Such critics measure the success of children's book illustrations by their ability to elevate the form to high art. While Cole—who imagined his Home Treasury as an imaginative response to purely educational children's literature—would chafe against the idea, these new standards in children's book design were a reworking of the didactic tendencies of the genre under a new guise. As the author of "Art in the Nursery" blithely notes, improved illustrations for children were intended to transform the young into educated appreciators and consumers of the arts, and the right illustrations were meant to exert a positive if passive influence on children's creative sensibilities. Mark Girouard calls these illustrated texts "secret persuaders," arguing that "dedicated aesthetes . . . fell upon them with delight as a means of conditioning their children" (139). Some publishers and educators were less subtle regarding their agenda. In 1883, for example, Mary Elizabeth Christie—with the assistance of a litany of notables in the art and literary world, including John Ruskin, Matthew Arnold, Robert Browning, William Morris, and Sidney Colvin—established the Art for Schools Association, tasked with providing quality prints of the "finest creations of art" to England's classrooms, "not merely [for] decoration, but education" ("Art for Schools" 185). The assumed value of high art on the child's bookshelf and in the classroom suggests that

Victorians' views on appropriate art for children were connected to their views on children as artists. Just as many art educators contended that children needed an artistic education in the norms and values of art *production*, an education best accomplished through exercises in imitation and line, many Victorians thought that children, as viewers and future consumers of art, needed an education in taste. This was best achieved by surrounding children not with art they might recognize as their own but instead, in the words of Cole, the work of the "old masters" and the "best modern artists." Both theories of art education and standards of children's book illustration, then, often constructed children as inhabiting a particular stage on a narrative of increasing artistic accomplishment and sophistication.

Joining, or perhaps upsetting, the ranks of artists such as Greenaway, Crane, and Caldecott was Edward Lear, who began publishing illustrated books for children in 1846 with his *Book of Nonsense*. His childlike drawings feature uneven perspectives, imprecise forms, and lopsided figures balanced in impossible poses, and they are anomalous when examined alongside the works of his contemporaries. He is a jester in a court of royals. By the time Lear published this first volume of limericks and drawings, he was an accomplished artist whose work, in many ways, depended on extraordinary accuracy; he had earned acclaim for his studies of birds, which he drew almost entirely from nature (paying careful attention to all details of feather and color), and critics have noted Lear's preoccupation with realism—sometimes with admiration, sometimes with disdain. For example, in "Appreciation of Lear as a Painter," Henry Strachey writes, "one is sometimes tempted to think that when Lear painted an olive-tree ... he counted the leaves" (xxxvii). Such attention to detail puts into relief the chaotic energy of his nonsense drawings. Not everyone appreciated Lear's nonsense style—some of the artist's contemporaries would not allow their children to look at Lear's work "for fear of the precious infants' 'sense of the beautiful' might be damaged" (Davidson 187)—but most applauded Lear's cartoonish designs, remarking what skill the artist must possess to produce such unskilled work. As one reviewer writes in 1867, Lear's sketches "are drawn as a child would draw upon a slate. This may appear an easy thing to do; but let the reader who thinks so try it, and we will be bound to say that the first child will detect the imposture" (A.W. 27). Edmund Strachey published a similar assessment in "Nonsense as a Fine Art" (1888): "Only an artist could have given with such a free hand all the grotesque forms in which he pretends to emulate the awkward scrawls of the school-boy on his slate" (139). A critic in *The Saturday Review* wrote in that same year, "The drawings very cunningly combine the clumsy conventions dear to children with the types and expressions that display real artistic knowledge and observation" ("Lear's Book" 361). Almost forty years after Lear's death, Emile Cammaerts—in his landmark study *The Poetry of Nonsense* (1925)—would write that Lear's art is "at once childish, deliberately exaggerated and irresistibly funny," and that "no artist or connoisseur will question the intentional character of these 'mistakes'" (67).[32]

These assessments of Lear's work upend traditional hierarchies of aesthetic value, and they do so by adopting the language of imitation and invention that was at the center of discourses of art education. Critics found the drawings in Lear's nonsense books admirable not because he supplies young readers with models of fine art (which is how they evaluated many other titles published for children) but because he reflects back to children their own forms. And because Lear is an adult creating work in a childlike style, he also is the quintessential imitative artist. Rather than modeling for young readers "proper" modes of representation, and rather than taking the successful work of his contemporaries in the children's book trade as his own models, he copies the scrawls of a schoolboy's slate, and the public finds his reproductions pitch perfect. Lear's childlike errors are intentional mistakes, and his style is one that "may appear an easy thing to do" but is, instead, an ingenious "idealization of the efforts of a clever child" ("Lear's Nonsense" 1251). In evaluating Lear's nonsense drawings, then, reviewers reverse the narrative of artistic education—the movement from simplistic and flawed to sophisticated and polished. If Crane, Caldecott, and Greenaway appealed to those who considered children impressionable artists in training, then Lear perhaps won over those who were beginning to pay attention to and admire the chaotic lines and palpable energy of children's drawings.

Despite these reviewers' insistence that Lear's work is a remarkable imitation of child art, he did not, in the strictest sense, collaborate with children.[33] However, his work demonstrates how the burgeoning cultural interest in child art began to infiltrate the world of children's book illustration and even suggests an intergenerational collaboration, albeit a purely fictional one, between adult and child forms. As the reviews above suggest, the critical tradition surrounding Lear not only celebrates the childlike qualities of his drawings but also frames them as a partnership between sophisticated draftsmanship and naïve modes of representation.

In other words, Lear's nonsense (like Francis Darwin's fantastic drawings) marries professional practices and childlike style, and his nonsense, like many of the examples of intergenerational partnerships explored throughout this project, suggests the creative potential of this blending of adults' and children's ways of representing the world. Ann Colley, for example, identifies in her study of Lear's limericks the visual threads that connect his professional bird illustrations and the more ridiculous, childlike drawings of birds that appear throughout his nonsense, arguing that readers should "regard Lear's limericks not only as antitheses of the serious pieces but also as inversions of them. It is as if Lear, when composing his limericks, took his daily 'academic' work and turned it upside down and inside out" ("Edward Lear's" 285).[34] Vivien Noakes similarly argues that Lear's landscapes and natural history monographs influence his nonsense and vice versa—that "the various threads of his life and creativity interweave and overlap" (189). I would expand upon Colley's and Noakes's arguments to contend that Lear capitalizes on the connection between his "academic" work, which is often read as sophisticated and "adult," and his nonsense drawings, which are read as crude and childlike, by imitating in his nonsense adult modes of representation for the purposes of childlike invention. Much of Lear's nonsense models for young readers how children can attain creative agency by reiterating but transforming forms associated with professional, sophisticated art. In other words, a childlike artist can transform imitation *into* invention.

The best examples of this practice are found in those sketches that display (and also defy) their ties to the artist's work in natural history. Such nonsense is a negotiation between, on the one hand, imitation—figured through the conventions of ornithological and natural history drawings, which demand accuracy—and invention—the power of creating something new and original, that derives but departs from the known world, often troped as childlike. Lear's colored bird books, for example, are part of his nonsense works but immediately recall Lear's sophisticated studies of birds, such as his *Illustrations of the Family Psittacidæ, or Parrots* (1832). Evelyn Baring, the Earl of Cromer, describes the genesis of one such nonsense bird book in his introduction to *Queery Leary Nonsense* (1911). "When my eldest son was about three years old," he writes, "his mother expressed a wish that he should acquire some knowledge of colour. Lear, with his usual kindness, at once sent twenty drawings of birds of various colours.... I had these bound in a book" (18).[35] Thomas Byrom calls these books "some of Lear's most delightful works—half-cartoons, half-formal"

(41). The hybridity Byrom detects here is particularly striking when these watercolors are examined next to Lear's professional bird lithographs. The "Dark Blue Bird" published in *Queery Leary Nonsense*, for example, is a simplified mirror image of the *Hyacinth Macaw*, published in his study of parrots. But Lear builds such correspondences between his colored birds and the carefully categorized birds of his ornithological studies only to break that pattern. Interspersed between birds of expected colors—the "Light Red Bird," the "Black Bird"—Lear included the "Scroobious Bird," a disproportionate creature with an enormous head and multicolored plumage, and the "Runcible Bird," a long-legged creature with stripes of blue, pink, and gold (28–29). These nonsense birds, presented as single specimen drawings on a field of white, use the form of the nature study to imagine beyond existing species, lampooning artistic, etymological, and biological modes of classification and encouraging viewers to recognize the limits of the systems that organize the way we understand and represent the world.

Some of Lear's most vibrant bird drawings appear in his examples of nonsense botany: the *Cockatooca Superba*, for instance, in which a single bird emerges from a graceful stem like an avian lily, or *Pollybirdia Singularis*, in which Lear replaces a flower's petals with a cluster of tiny parrots (*Complete* 251, 253). Unlike Lear's colored birds, the nonsense botany drawings, published between 1871 and 1877 in three different nonsense collections, represent *only* nonsense plants: comic transformations of the scientific taxonomy and specimen drawings used by the Linnaean Society (of which Lear was an associate).[36] Theories of nonsense from the Victorian period to the present often comment upon the necessary relationship between sense and nonsense—nonsense, contend Celia Catlett Anderson and Marilyn Fain Apseloff, is "not the absence of sense but a clever subversion of it that heightens rather than destroys meaning" (5)—but Lear's botanies root such inversions in particular modes of representation and forms of artistic expression. These drawings represent not only the interplay of scientific norms of imitation and accuracy and childlike imaginative invention but also how these two discourses can be mutually transformative. A review titled "The Science of Nonsense," published in *The Spectator* in 1870, makes clear that interpreting these nonsense plants requires recognizing textual and visual scientific forms as well as acknowledging their transformation. The reviewer contends, for example, that Lear's "picture of 'the Bottleforkia Spoonifolia' is one which would make Dr. Hooker roar; the thing looks so like a new botanical genus, with its bottle-shaped calyx, and fork-shaped stamens, and spoon-shaped leaves, and sounds so like a true genus as well" (1505).[37]

Scientific categories, when refracted through nonsense, accommodate new forms rather than simply replicate the order of the established world, suggesting that the imaginative play associated with childlike invention is akin to scientific discovery. The act of discovery requires the ability to see beyond the expected and to alter one's assumptions about what is possible—to recognize new varieties of life, such as the Runcible Bird or the *Cockatooca Superba*—and this seems to be a quality Lear found particularly childlike, aptly represented by the naïvetés of nonsense. Lear's first foray into nonsense botany was, in fact, framed as an act of discovery; while he was sketching his first nonsense specimens in 1870, he wrote to friend Mrs. Ker, "As I know how fond you & Mr Ker are of flowers, I have looked out carefully for any new ones all about the Grasse Hills, & have been fortunate enough to find 9 sorts:—they are all very rare, & only grow about here, & in the Jumbly islands, where I first saw them long ago" (*Complete* 511). A similar sense of childlike discovery is legible in an earlier letter, a message Lear wrote in 1860 to his friend and mushroom enthusiast George Grove, in which Lear explains that "in a wood very near here, there are Toadstools of the loveliest and most surprising colour and form:—orbicular, cubicular and squambingular" (*Complete* 155). The accompanying illustration, in Lear's nonsense style, depicts a perfectly spherical Lear, balanced on tiptoe, his arms thrown directly backward in happy surprise, encountering an equally delighted personified mushroom.

Not many illustrators contemporary to Lear adopted a childlike aesthetic similar to that found in these nonsense books. The exception, perhaps, is Basil T. Blackwood, an artist most famous for his illustrations for Hillaire Belloc's satires, including *The Bad Child's Book of Beasts* (1896), *More Beasts (For Worse Children)* (1897), and *Cautionary Tales for Children, Designed for the Admonition of Children between the Ages of Eight and Fourteen Years* (1908). Blackwood's dynamic images recall Lear's in their simple lines, multiplied figures that seem to dance off the floor, and humanoid animals (and animal-like humans). Lear, however, was a bellwether, and in the ensuing decades more illustrators would turn to self-consciously childlike styles. William Steig does so in *Shrek!* (1990), for example, and Quentin Blake does the same, especially in his well-known illustrations for Roald Dahl. Blake, like Lear, seems to use these childlike styles to suggest reversals of power between adults and children: the tiny Matilda facing down a monstrous Trunchbull, the ridiculous adults visiting Willy Wonka's chocolate factory. Today, childlike illustrations in children's books are commonplace and extraordinarily popular, as evidenced by Mo Willems's pigeon books, such as *Don't Let the Pigeon Drive the Bus* (2003), and Oliver Jeffers's flat-perspectived, colorful creations, such as *The Day the Crayons Quit* (2013). The rise of childlike illustrations in children's books suggests the scales have tipped regarding what is considered "appropriate" art for children. If, in the nineteenth century, the tastefully decorated interiors in Crane's picture books and the daintily watercolored, mob-capped children in Greenaway's were "secret persuaders," and the work of Lear could be potentially dangerous to a child's "sense of the beautiful," then in the twentieth the art of the nursery is, in the most literal sense, children's art.

CONCLUSION

In 1888, the year Lear died, Princess Louise founded the Royal Drawing Society, an organization to promote education through art with attention to developing the child's perception and memory. The society included in its membership respected figures in art and in children's literature—such as Tenniel, Carroll, Edward Burne-Jones, and John Everett Millais—and was headed by Ablett, the educator who delighted Cooke at the International Conference on Education in 1884. Two years after the society's founding, Ablett worked in conjunction with the princess to produce a professional display of the work of young artists that Louise's husband, the Duke of Argyll, dubbed "The Children's Royal Academy." In his history of art education, Stuart MacDonald notes that "the Victorian public, familiar with the child worlds created by Kate Greenaway, Tenniel, and Carroll, were enthusiastic about the annual exhibitions of the Society. ... In [1892] Princess Louise made her own contribution to the recognition of child art by purchasing 'Babyland,' a watercolour consisting of 112 figures, exhibited by a girl of twelve years" (327). The few scholars who have written about the Children's Royal Academy (including MacDonald) tend to consider it either a means to reinforce among young artists Victorian norms of representation and beauty or part of Victorians' love for idealized childhood.

However, the princess's purchase is an apt conclusion to an examination of Victorians' changing ideas about art created by and for children. The Children's Royal Academy not only recognizes children as artists but also situates them in a tradition of illustration for children, begun by

Golden Age artists such as Greenaway and Tenniel; the sale of a twelve-year-old girl's painting demonstrates that the boundary between adult artists for children and their audiences was, by the end of the nineteenth century, permeable, able to be traversed by the artistic efforts of the young themselves. Larger changes were to come. For example, the year after Princess Louise purchased *Babyland*, Joan Miró was born—an artist who, alongside Wassily Kandinsky, Paul Klee, and Pablo Picasso, would appropriate the rough forms and naïve perspectives of children's art. And the society's first exhibition anticipates Roger Fry's publication of "Children's Drawings" (1917)—an article published upon his own exhibition of art by children under twelve; there, Fry takes child artists quite seriously, noting that "if nothing is put in the way to hinder its expression, the child translates [its] vivid visual perceptions with an extreme directness and simplicity, whereby it manages to convey to the spectator something of the emotional forces of its own perceptions" (268). As evidence, he reproduces a painting of a snake by a nine-year-old boy, claiming that "no one can miss the intensity with which the boy has realized the snakiness of a snake" (268), that superlative phrase recalling the nonsense of Lear or, perhaps, anticipating the antics of Seuss. The Children's Royal Academy, in fact, lasted through high modernism, when the child artist would be widely recognized as muse, collaborator, and genius.

CONCLUSION

Mentors and Muses
Why the Collaborative Child Matters

Many of the authors included in the preceding chapters were well practiced in collaboration. Margaret Gatty, editor of *Aunt Judy's Magazine*, and Charles Dickens, editor of *Household Words* and *All the Year Round*, were attuned to how content and form are shaped by the give-and-take of contributors, illustrators, printers, and readers. Robert Louis Stevenson wrote extensively on his reluctant partnerships with publishers and booksellers, noting the unavoidable and at times damaging influence those collaborators exerted on the content and production of his work.[1] J. M. Barrie's *Peter Pan* responded to countless creative partners between the initial appearance of its title character in *The Little White Bird* (1902), its first performance in 1904, and the script's eventual publication in 1928. Before it was resigned to print, the play, like Peter himself, was protean, shape-shifting according to the collaborative dynamics of the stage. Recent work by book historians and literary scholars in children's literature and beyond has revealed how even those authors who seem to stand aloof were necessarily implicated in a web of collaborators and creative partners—the complex network required to transmit an idea to print and to circulate it among readers. As Brian Alderson argues, "Almost every book is a collaboration. Each possesses a private history of its own, a study which will reveal its dependence on influences operating outside the control of its originator" ("Making" 38).[2]

However, as my work in *Between Generations* has made clear, what is missing from most studies of children's literature—including examinations of the collaborative nature of books for young readers—is the real child collaborator. This elision is due, in part, to the legacy of Jacqueline Rose's *The Case of Peter Pan, or, The Impossibility of Children's Fiction* and to those who have taken up that book's critical assumptions. This scholarly tradition holds that knowledge of real young people inevitably is obscured by adults' investment in children as idealized others.[3] Yet critics who write about multiple authorship know that such blind spots are not unusual in the larger purview of literary studies. Jack Stillinger, in *Multiple Authorship and the Myth of Solitary Genius*, writes that "the collaborative authorship of writings that we routinely consider the work of a single author" is "quite common" and that examples of unidentified or under-recognized collaboration "can be found virtually anywhere we care to look in English and American literature of the last two centuries" (22). Studies on authorship that dismantle the myth of the solitary writer tend to overlook collaborators whose subject positions might seem to preclude their participation in literary production—especially, I would argue, children. In other words, those who do not conform to our expectations about the social actors who can contribute to a text often remain outside authorship paradigms forwarded by book history or are demoted to roles as readers and consumers, their influence on the market limited or tangential. These silent partners are obscured by subjects more formally and unproblematically recognized as actors in the literary marketplace, or they are overlooked due to the biases of writers, publishers, or readers.[4] Marjorie Stone and Judith Thompson recognize collaboration's entanglement with these larger systems of identity and power, writing that "the coupling together of writers and their texts—by the writers themselves, their publishers, or their readers—is inflected by ideologies of gender and race, generic constraints and opportunities, political concerns ('collaborations' of another kind), and by changing cultural and historical circumstances" (15). Work on collaboration involving such assumedly vulnerable subjects, then, is often work of recovery, intent on identifying those whose names do not appear on the title page and revealing the cultural and critical machinery that celebrates some authors while relegating others to the margins. By focusing not simply on unrecognized collaborators but on child collaborators, *Between Generations* challenges definitions of authorship and paradigms of childhood that collectively eclipse the role young people play in children's literature and culture and, in turn, distort our understanding of children's literary history.

While professional norms and publishing practices make some creative partners invisible—especially those, such as children, who are considered passive, powerless, or otherwise unable to access creative authority—multiple authorship can comment on those very disappearances. Authors working in collaboration, in other words, might reflect on their own process; while they may be caught in the biases underpinning access to creative authority, they can recognize and disrupt those systems of power inside their work and in the documents recording their creative practices. As I have shown, Golden Age writers often turned to collaboration as a means to reflect self-consciously on the writing process, and adult-child partnerships in particular can translate the critical self-consciousness latent in multiple authorship into a recognition of child agency. For example, as I discuss in Chapter Three, Barrie explains the authorship of *Peter Pan* by introducing a number of possible authors, and the conflicts and companionships among these authors signify his complex relationship with the children, real and imagined, who surround, inhabit, and author the play. Barrie's decision to represent his most famous play as a collaboration is not, as many would argue, a manifestation of his nostalgia for his own or the Llewelyn Davies brothers' childhoods or an instance of playful evasiveness meant, ultimately, to lead back to his own role as author. Instead, Barrie shares his claim with a series of child authors because, as a playwright, he is familiar with the way multiple authorship works: its ability to foreground the roles of otherwise invisible actors in the production of literature and culture. Robert Browning, whom I consider in the introduction and in Chapter Four, similarly rehearses the complicated power dynamics of intergenerational collaboration in "The Pied Piper of Hamelin" through real collaborations and fictional adult-child partnerships. He corresponded with the real Willie Macready, whose request for verses to illustrate inspired the poet's work, and reproduced in the poem a boy storyteller who, while tempted by the seductive power of the adult piper, could not march into obscurity with the other children of Hamelin. Attention to the composition narratives beyond *Peter Pan* and "The Pied Piper" reveals that collaboration provided a critical lens through which a range of Victorian authors navigated the tricky terrain of child agency.

I have argued throughout *Between Generations* that the nineteenth and early twentieth centuries were characterized by shifting views of childhood and children's literature that provided authorial access to the collaborative child. However, a cultural investment in children as creative actors working alone, with one another, or alongside adults persists long past the nineteenth century. An exploration of the post-Victorian exploits of the intergenerational partnerships invites not only discussions of the role of children, real and imagined, in the literary and cultural movements of the twentieth century but also reassessments of the origins of twentieth-century literature for both adults and children, canonical and critically neglected. While I have sought to join a body of scholarship working to recognize the agency of real children by tracing what I consider the origins of adult-child collaborations, I invite other scholars to recover the work of other child collaborators, contemporary and historical. Many of these creative children are hiding in plain sight; others have received little or no attention, and their work is ripe for critical consideration. Kenneth Grahame's 1908 *The Wind in the Willows*, for example, famously originated in letters to Grahame's son Alistair, affectionately known as Mouse—a boy who, according to Grahame, selected the cast of characters in his father's "stories about moles, giraffes & water-rats" (Dingley). The modernist experimentation in visual and literary cultures in the first decades of the twentieth century transformed popular understanding of children's perspectives, and the archive of the playful Bloomsbury Group reveals a subversive network of adult-child partnerships, from domestic theatricals featuring child and adult actors to *The Charleston Bulletin Supplements*, a family newspaper written by Virginia Woolf and illustrated by her nephew Quentin Bell that lampooned the serious work of elite writers and artists.[5] J. R. R. Tolkien narrated early versions of *The Hobbit* (1937) to his children and, more than fifty years later, J. K. Rowling lulled her daughter to sleep with stories about a young wizard, tales that would ensure Rowling's meteoric rise upon the 1997 publication of *Harry Potter and the Philosopher's Stone* (Duriez).

Each new iteration of the collaborative child is inflected by its particular cultural moment and by its contemporary ideas about creative agency and childhood. However, many of the adult-child partnerships established in the years following the Victorian period also bear traces of the origins of intergenerational collaboration in the Golden Age; these more recent collaborations reproduce, in the creative dynamics they establish between generations and in their uneasy interplay between real children and powerful constructs of childhood, the same self-consciousness about child agency expressed in the composition narratives that surround many Victorian texts. In other words, later collaborations do not entirely abandon the nineteenth century as their originary moment, and while the continuing tradition of adult-child collaboration continues to shift and transform with our understanding of child life, the young people who participate in this tradition have much in common with the young artists and authors I've explored throughout *Between Generations*. I will demonstrate the persistence of the collaborative child by considering in detail two examples of adult-child collaboration selected from the rich array of such partnerships: one a literary collaboration forged in England and one a partnership based in visual culture that took place in the United States. I have chosen partnerships that epitomize the tenacity of intergenerational collaboration as a creative practice that accommodates shifting paradigms of childhood across time and place; these two case studies, therefore, demonstrate the critical possibilities of intergenerational collaboration as an analytic through which we can understand adult-child relationships through the twentieth century and to the present day.

THE FAR-DISTANT OXUS, 1937

Arthur Ransome's well-loved series of children's novels, Swallows and Amazons, depicts the thrill of child adventure free from adult supervision, a celebration of child independence and creativity that is reinforced in his documented indebtedness to child-friends in composing those books.[6] However, Ransome's respect for capable children who make their way in the world with or without adults' assistance is perhaps most apparent in his relationship with young authors Pamela Whitlock and Katharine Hull. Early in 1937, the girls, aged fifteen and sixteen, sent Ransome a full manuscript of their novel *The Far-Distant Oxus*, accompanied by a cover letter. "We enclose a manuscript of a book we have been writing together," they begin. "We don't want to bother you with it if you are busy with other things, but we are not quite sure what to do with it and we thought you might help us" (Ransome vii). While the girls' tone is timid, signaling their trepidation in approaching such a well-known author, their work was not nearly so meek. Ransome describes the manuscript as a "colossal, orderly bulk." He was taken aback by its size—most child writers, he argues, do not finish their manuscripts—and suspected that the book was a hoax, written by "some wretched grown-up masquerading behind them." However, he notes that his suspicions were "entirely unjustified" (ix–x). The book, a novel about a group of children adventuring among the ponies in Exmoor, delighted Ransome, and he set to helping the authors publish. He presented the manuscript to his own publisher, Jonathan Cape, and advised the girls through the processes of book design and revision. Accompanied by Whitlock's illustrations, *The Far-Distant Oxus* was a success, although it is difficult to determine how far the girls' authorial aspirations would have gone without the assistance of Ransome, who introduced the novel to Cape in glowing terms: "I've got this year's best children's book under my arm" (xi).

The coauthors relied on Ransome for more than his connections to the publishing world. Those who have written on *The Far-Distant Oxus* frame it as a novel in Ransome's style, obviously and unabashedly inspired by the Swallows and Amazons series. For example, Hugh Brogan, in his biography of Ransome, argues that Whitlock and Hull's talent "might have taken years to express itself, if it had ever done so, without its discovery of the literary form invented by Arthur Ransome" (351). He catalogues a number of similarities between *Oxus* and Ransome's novels: the girls' use of imaginative fantasy blended with everyday life on the English countryside, for example, and their depiction of middle-class children on summer holidays. Victor Watson notes that *Oxus* resembles Ransome's novels in form as well as content—they "were published in a format identical to that of Swallows and Amazons, but in a different colour"—and that they were certainly in the vein of Ransome, though not as accomplished. "The novels are as absorbing as Ransome at his best, with liveliness, a fast plot and frequent touches of lyrical descriptive prose," he notes, "but without the adult writer's greater psychological depth" (*Far-Distant*). Humphrey Carpenter compares the book to Ransome's series three times in one short paragraph, noting that *Oxus* "is a novel written in imitation of the *Swallows and Amazons* stories of Arthur Ransome," that "Whitlock illustrated it in the Ransome style," and that the book "has all the features of a typical Swallows and Amazons adventure" (182).

Ransome, on the contrary, insisted on Whitlock and Hull's originality. He understood them as readers who "are not content to adopt my stories, but go a stage further. It was "not for them to act over again the adventures of others. They had to invent something new for themselves. Now, from thus using the grown-up author as a springboard from which to leap upward into original invention, it is only one step to doing without the grown-up author altogether and WRITING new stories instead of merely playing them" (viii). Ransome's somewhat contradictory depiction of Whitlock and Hull registers simultaneously the possibility of child agency and what he sees as the inherent limits of even the most precocious child's abilities. He wavers between extolling their individual, childlike genius—they do not "act over again the adventures of others"—and trivializing their work by emphasizing their temporary dependence on the "springboard" of established adult authors—soon they will not be "merely playing" but will be "WRITING." Some contemporary readers, perhaps less invested in the genius of Whitlock and Hull, similarly suggest that *The Far-Distant Oxus* was "something new," departing in important ways from Ransome's style. Brogan, for example, notes "an authenticity about their tale which makes it in some ways the most searching critique that the Swallow books have ever received" (352), and Carpenter argues that "Ransome's plain style is ably imitated, perhaps even improved upon" (182). And it was Ransome, more than any other reader, who championed *Oxus*, noting, "even if Miss Hull and Miss Whitlock had done their very best to imitate, originality would have come breaking through all over the place. These two could not be copyists if they wished" (xiv). Here, as in many moments of Ransome's introduction to the published novel, he describes the young authors in language adopted from a Romantic idealization of childhood. "They are not old enough to be afraid of their youth," he writes. "We elders look back to a world that once was young. For them the dew is still on the grass" (xiv). The coauthors are not "dull grown-ups" but fresh-faced and fresh-sighted young people whose "youth gives them an advantage over all grown-up authors whomsoever" (xiv).[7]

Ransome balances this idealization with respect for the girls as writers who have developed savvy and professional authorial practices. While at times he characterizes the girls' success as a product of their youthful natures—they seemed, he notes, "to have an *instinctive* knowledge of how a book should be written" (x, emphasis added)—his portrait of the girls at work characterizes them as serious, well-read, and practiced in the methods of the book trade. "They have read your books, my books, and the books of everybody else who manages to find his way into school libraries," he writes, "and, young themselves, dissatisfied with our elderly efforts, have struck out on their own to show us what our books should be" (xiv). The sense that these child authors have much to teach the professional world reappears throughout Ransome's introduction. For example, he admires the girls' detailed plans for editing their manuscript, a process that is far removed from the spontaneous creativity often aligned with childhood; they carry out their revisions according to merciless editorial practices that, Ransome notes, "might serve as a model to be followed by much more experienced writers" (xii). Whitlock and Hull were strict with themselves, eliminating "any parts which were misleading or didn't fit into the story," "any unnecessary and driveling descriptions," "all useless words," "any words we disliked," and "all the passages we loathed but which somehow managed to squirm their way in." Notably, one of the words they banished from the manuscript was "children" (Ransome xii). Having provided a studied account of the girls' craft, Ransome is still careful to note that *Oxus* is not a child's book in the vein of Daisy Ashford's *The Young Visiters*—not a charming example of the humorous ways the young mangle language; "its readers will not find themselves laughing at quaint spellings," he warns, "or making any kind of allowances on account of its authors' ages" (xiii).

Ransome's relationship with Whitlock and Hull is not very far removed chronologically from the Golden Age collaborations I trace throughout *Between Generations*, and in many ways it resembles those earlier intergenerational partnerships. Critics' characterizations of the girls' work as responsive to or dependent upon Ransome's fiction suggest the collaborative strategies of Victorian writers for children such as Gatty, who sought to provide children with similar "springboards" to creativity in the "Nursery Nonsense" feature in *Aunt Judy's Magazine*, which I describe in Chapter Four. The stories she included in that column were designed "to give young artists of a family an opening for the exercise of their talent" (183), just as reviewers imagined that Ransome's fiction gave Whitlock and Hull inspiration for their own novel. Yet Ransome and others recognized that these young writers were not mere imitators, and the Victorians also rejected the notion that children were destined to merely repeat the work of adults; Child Study scholar James Sully, whose theories of language acquisition are outlined in Chapter Two, insisted that the "little linguist" moved "beyond servile imitation of our conventional sounds" to new and often more poetic or logical forms of expression (*Studies* 144), just as Ransome and more contemporary critics applauded the ways *The Far-Distant Oxus* deviated from rather than simply replicated the plots from the Swallows and Amazons series. Most notably, however, Whitlock and Hull, as savvy authors and editors, recall the young Lloyd Osbourne, seriously entering the literary market by calculating the potential profits of a collection of Stevenson poems printed on his toy press, or the young respondents to Edward Salmon's survey of child readers for *Juvenile Literature As It Is* (1888). It seems Whitlock and Hull took up the challenge of one of those young readers, who disparaged the "milk-and-watery sorts of stories that we could generally write better ourselves" (29). Like these precocious book critics, Whitlock and Hull do not conform to assumptions about the spontaneous creativity of the imaginative child and instead fill more practical, rational, and even professional roles.

But the collaboration that produced *The Far-Distant Oxus* does not easily fit into the parameters of an intergenerational collaboration, despite the flexibility of that authorial model. Ransome obviously enjoyed working with Whitlock and Hull, and yet the adult's role in this creative partnership is limited: a guiding hand meant to leave no evidence of its intervention. When Whitlock and Hull sent their manuscript to Ransome, they may not have imagined the mentor-mentee collaboration critics of *Oxus* assume but instead an equal partnership with one another, aided by external advice from an established author. In his correspondence with the girls, Ransome suggests he imagined them as equals rather than endearing child-writers. His salutation was "My dear Fellow-authors," and his sign-off was "your respectful colleague" (Brogan). In many ways, the girls' partnership was single- rather than intergenerational, and they adopted a slogan that rejects the importance of adults in their enterprise: "By children, about children, for children ... do without the grown-ups altogether" (Watson).[8] Ransome echoes this sentiment in his introduction, which seems to both recognize and dismiss his role in the publication of *Oxus*. "It really is about children, for children, and *by* children," he writes. "I have spoken of using the grown-up author as a spring-board, and then of doing without him altogether. That is what has happened here" (xiii). It seems that, once introduced to a publisher and established as authors, Whitlock and Hull did not work as closely with Ransome. They did, however, continue to collaborate with one another, publishing two sequels—*Escape to Persia* (1938) and *Oxus in Summer* (1939)—and later, after World War II, a fantasy novel, *Crowns* (1947). By the time they published this final novel, Whitlock was twenty-five and Hull was twenty-six. However, their impulse to throw off the conventions of adulthood is evident in the plot, in which a group of cousins fashion a world according to their imaginative desires.

ECHOLILIA, 2010

Timothy Archibald, a contemporary American editorial and commercial photographer, is interested in those imaginative worlds of childhood and how to access them. In 2010, over seventy years after the publication of Whitlock and Hull's final collaborative novel, Archibald published *Echolilia: Sometimes I Wonder*. The volume features forty-three images, mostly photographs of Archibald's son, Elijah (called Eli)—a boy who was five years old when Archibald was beginning his project and soon to be diagnosed as having autism—as well as scans of materials and objects related to Eli's life at home. The book is a portrait of Eli's world. We see him in a sunny room, shirtless and wearing a dented mesh trash can on his head as a space helmet. A crumpled piece of notebook paper, scrawled with Archibald's notes on his son's diagnosis, alongside a bloody bandage, the remnant of a scraped knee. Eli standing in the middle of an empty suburban street on a foggy day, dwarfed by his father's black hooded sweatshirt and dangling a baby doll by its leg. Archibald printed a limited number of copies of *Echolilia*, but the project earned national recognition when it was featured in a number of high-profile venues, including *Time* magazine, *National Geographic*, and *Lens*—the *New York Times* blog on photography, video, and visual journalism.

Archibald describes *Echolilia* as a project created in collaboration with Eli, contending that each photograph is the product of mutual decision making. "I'd kind of initiate [the photograph] with some direction, [and] he'd do something that seemed unexpected . . . something I'd never have been able to think of," Archibald explains. "We'd look at the images together on the digital camera and try to refine them . . . try to improve them, try to take them in other directions. The idea of turning the creative control over to a child, while I operated the camera, allowed me to make images that seemed to have this sense of discovery to me" (Archibald, "*Echolilia* Interview," ellipses in original). Each session with the camera, Archibald notes, lasted about five to ten minutes, the limit of Eli's attention span. While at times Archibald would suggest that they take a photograph in a particular place or request that Eli adjust his pose, he insists that Eli directed the shoots. For example, Eli's fascination with the ways sound travels through a vacuum hose led to the photograph Archibald titled "Closed System," in which a reclining Eli blows into one end of the hose and listens to the swooshing sound of his breath through the other. It was Archibald, however, who recommended that they move their shoot to the backyard to create a stark contrast between his pale skin and the dirt ground. Despite Archibald's occasional directions, however, Eli "really didn't have interest in just being the subject"; instead, "he needed to be involved," and their images arise from the complicated relationship among "him, myself, and then all that is shared," what Archibald at times calls their "collective creative brain" (Pantall). As photography writer Conor Risch notes, "Archibald had to get used to the idea that 'you can't really tell a five-year-old what to do.'" As the project progressed, Eli began not only to determine the content of the photographs but also to commandeer the camera, creating images of Archibald inspired by the photographs they had previously created together (Risch). While so often scholarship on adult-child relationships focus on how adults frame children, here Eli frames his adult father, reversing the hierarchy often assumed to underpin images of childhood.

The book is an intimate portrait of Eli, inescapably inflected by the details of his relationship with his father, their life in twentieth-century California, and Archibald's career as a professional photographer. But the process and product of *Echolilia* resonates with the Victorian collaborations I discuss in previous chapters. Like authors and artists such as Dickens, Matthew Arnold, or Browning, Archibald is attentive to what he considers to be the child's creative power. The model of collaboration behind *Echolilia* does not merely solicit Eli's input; it subordinates Archibald's control as a photographer to Eli's creative whims—to his imaginative and often idiosyncratic way of seeing the world of objects around him. Some similarities between Victorian collaborations and Archibald's more contemporary project are small. For instance, the Echo Press that published *Echolilia*—not a press at all, Archibald explains, but "just me and Eli"—finds its twin in the Davos Press of Stevenson and his stepson Osbourne: another small, private press venture that enabled inversions of adult-child power relationships. Osbourne's jubilation that Davos Press editions of Stevenson's poems earned him two or three dollars is reiterated in Eli's excitement at the prospect of "signing the books, [and] making a buck" from each copy of *Echolilia* (Hart 31; Pantall). Moreover, the title *Echolilia*—a play on the term echolalia, which refers to the manner in which some children with autism mimic language and sounds—recalls the storyteller-auditor collaborations and the theories of children's language acquisition outlined in Chapter One, both of which recognize how children's repetition and transformation of sound and language might exemplify creative power. Archibald himself is preoccupied with how the images in *Echolilia* and even Eli himself reproduce but transform the world in a manner that forces adults to reconsider their place in the world. "I liked the idea of it: photography is a form of copying," Archibald muses, reflecting on the title of his book. "Kids are a form of repetition. And looking at my kid with photography allowed me to see myself anew" (Archibald, "Photographic Conversation").

Most notably, Archibald's partnership with Eli resembles in more important ways the creative dynamic between Barrie and the Llewelyn Davies brothers, which I discuss in Chapter Three. It is not difficult to detect the similarities between *Echolilia* and Barrie's photo-essay *Boy Castaways of Black Lake Island*, which was created in collaboration the brothers. Barrie expresses a stronger desire than Archibald for control over his subjects; while Archibald relishes "the idea of turning the creative control over to a child, while I operated the camera," Barrie admits bitterly but playfully that the brothers "were always off doing the wrong things when I pressed the button" (*Peter Pan* 81). However, both the Edwardian Barrie and the contemporary Archibald credit their images to the boy (or boys) in the photograph, presenting the inversion of the adult-child hierarchy in terms that stress the young's creative potential. Both contend, for example, that the finished product of their collaborations—*Peter Pan* and *Echolilia*, respectively—would never have come to fruition, would never have been within the creative power of the adult, without the child's intervention. Barrie calls the Llewelyn Davies brothers "the Five without whom [Peter] never would have existed" (*Peter Pan* 75), and Archibald, looking at some images in this collection, muses, "It just seems like I never made a photo like that," that there "was no way [I] could come up with some of the interesting things Eli would do." This "freshness," he admits, was only possible because he relinquished control to Eli (Risch).

Perhaps most strikingly, however, Archibald replicates through his consideration of the father-son dyad, and how that relationship is transformed through Eli's life with autism, the project of Child Study scholars. In many ways, Archibald joins those Child Study scholars who felt intensely a separation from childhood and who sought to remedy that separation by exploring child life, often with the assistance of children themselves. Current scholarship in disability studies has challenged the assumption, popularized by researchers such as Simon Baron-Cohen, that those with autism are unable to empathize with others—that they are systematizers rather than empathizers, because they lack theory of mind.[9] However, while scholars seek to dislodge these essentializing theories about the experiences of those with autism as well as the ableist assumptions about neurotypicality that underpin them, autism as a diagnosis still carries with it for many the assumption of emotional separation, and many do experience challenging interpersonal relationships with children with autism. Collaboration, on the other hand, holds out the possibility of connection, both creative and affective. Archibald's *Echolilia*, and his commentary on the project, expands upon that possibility. "I knew he was tuned differently," Archibald explains to *New York Times* blogger Jane

Gross, "and I needed to build a bridge, get inside his head, learn what made him tick."

Like Child Study scholars before him, Archibald responded to this need to understand the child by creating a cache of materials on childhood—an archive of Eli. He notes that, at the beginning of the project, he dealt with his feelings of alienation from his son by "taking photographs of things he created, photographs of him, of the evidence of him and his behavior around our house. I thought maybe I'd see something or get at something" (Pantall). Concentrating on materials that spoke to his son's mind, body, and means of expression, Archibald works to depict Eli's way of seeing the world, and it is perhaps for this reason that so many of Archibald's photographs reveal, in the most literal way, how Eli *looks* at things, how he sees: through the warped glass of a bubble gum machine, into the tapering end of a plastic funnel, between the scissor-cut slits of a white paper mask. We're looking at Eli, considering how Eli looks. It is as if Archibald shares Child Study scholar Blanche Dismore's desire that the opacity of a child's interiority could be somehow resolved, that their minds could operate instead like magic lanterns, able to be project their thoughts onto the wall (43–44). Archibald suggests that the closest the adult can get to seeing *like* a child is to see *with* a child—in this case, through a camera lens.

Moreover, like the work of the Child Study movement, the images in *Echolilia* recognize but complicate dominant paradigms of childhood that took root in the Romantic period. Archibald suggests that Eli, by virtue of both his childhood and his place on the autism spectrum, is in some ways socially separate from both his father and the world around him. While this separation, in its sometimes painful emotional charge, is perhaps at odds with the heavenly childhood championed by the Romantics, this construction of childhood surfaces in Archibald's photographs in similar visual language. In the photograph "Elijah in a Fairy Tale," for example, Eli curls inside a clear plastic tub, nude, his eyes closed beatifically—an image that Archibald notes was inspired by the idea of his son curled inside an egg. In "Screen Door," Eli leans his head against a mesh window, doubly framed by the scalloped edges of the door and the green backyard. Archibald admits that, despite his intention of allowing Eli creative freedom, he did know when elements of an image detracted from the idea of the child he was depicting: a universal child who, in some ways, resembles the Wordsworthian boy, close to nature. "I really think of these images trying to be archetypal," he argues. "I want the feral child to be there. I don't want to see a logo, a style, a t-shirt with a ninja turtle on it. And then he's in his school uniform alot [*sic*], so it helps the idea of this looking like the child in someone's brain or memory" (Archibald, "*Echolilia* Interview"). Archibald is looking to find an image of his son that is intentional, metaphorical, somehow arising from our collective memory just as the photographs in *Echolilia* emerge from the collective creative brain of Eli and his father.

But the perfection of that image is bound to fail. Viewers have responded to those images they find idyllic, suggesting that they are a misrepresentation of childhood and in particular of life with a child with autism; their criticisms led Archibald to reflect upon the impulse behind picturing Eli this way. "The story of a dad building an emotional bridge to his autistic son is a very attractive one, but the reality of the relationship, how challenging it is on a daily basis, how it can still drive me crazy, is something I wish the project acknowledged a little more," Archibald admits. "The other week things were really challenging at home with Eli, and I found myself telling my wife that I wanted it to be more like the photographs were: dreamy, romantic, quiet, poetic, organic, this whole inner emotional journey where I was in control and he and I were equals.... She laughed and reminded me that it never really was like that" (Pantall, ellipses in original). Scholars of childhood and children's literature such as Rose, James Kincaid, and Catherine Robson have documented similar patterns of wish fulfillment and representations of children throughout the nineteenth century, and the inclination to idealize childhood, especially recalcitrant childhood, is still powerful today, as Archibald's comments show. But Archibald captures in his project not only idealistic images of childhood but also their breakdown, creating a more complex view of child life, in *Echolilia* and elsewhere. Known in part for his portraits of young people, Archibald considers carefully what he wants to communicate about the young. As Risch notes, "since having children (Archibald and his wife have two sons), Archibald has tried in his commercial and editorial photographs of kids not to 'shortchange their complexity' [and] in his work he's made an effort 'to enter their secret world a little bit and give them a full range of emotions.'" That desire to know the "secret world" of a child recalls, again, the work of Child Study scholars; many in this movement, from James Sully to Alexander Chamberlain, considered the child's imagination as a territory to be discovered, their languages as tongues forgotten by and inaccessible to adults. Archibald's commitment to this view of childhood is apparent in those images that might unsettle viewers, challenging them to redefine what a child is, how a child behaves. Eli wearing a thick rubber band around his head, his features warped. Eli with the red plastic handle of a pair of pliers in his mouth, the pointed tips dangling into the center of the frame. Archibald likes the latter image, Risch notes, because it suggests danger and tension.

Archibald's collaboration with Eli reiterates and exaggerates the cultural and historical circumstances that led Victorian writers and artists to partner with the young. He shares the nineteenth-century impulse to explore child life outside of the adult's imagination—to consider, in the words of Oscar Chrisman, the possibility that "we do not know our children" (55). Archibald himself combats stereotypes of the child with autism as incapable of building affective connections with others. He is clear, when discussing *Echolilia*, that Eli is "a real communicator," and that exploring his relationship with his son is simply another way to examine, through collaboration, the difficulty of any parent-child or adult-child relationship. Some might argue that autism makes that difficulty particularly apparent, but Archibald's photographs are not only unsettling but also familiar, communicating the distance between adult and child in a striking way. "When I started shooting . . . we didn't know Eli was on the Autistic Spectrum," Archibald explains, "we just knew he was different and there was a mystery, a conflict, a question I was trying to figure out. What was the question? I guess it was 'What is up with my kid?' or 'How do I relate to this kid?' or something like that. . . . I don't really care about Autism. I care about relationships, individuals, personal connections" (Pantell). Answering those questions is challenging, and Archibald staged through collaboration with his son a means to look for answers. While Eli's vulnerability is vivid in Archibald's work, his bare skin soft and pale against rough, dark surfaces—dirt in the backyard, the hard metal of pliers protruding from his mouth, the angular corner of a dented waste basket—the narrative surrounding the photographs' creation emphasizes Eli's control. *Echolilia* is a collaborative text that is seamless, bound between covers, but polyvocal, allowing Archibald's and Eli's voices to speak separately and together.

COLLABORATIVE PRACTICES

Adult-child creative partnerships, not only Golden Age collaborations but also more contemporary relationships, dislodge the entrenched assumption that, in Robin Bernstein's words, "constructed childhood and juvenile humans exist in tension with if not in opposition to one another" (*Racial* 22). Whitlock and Hull, as they are legible in the publication history of *The Far-Distant Oxus*, are both poetic naïfs and disciplined editors, those two roles inextricably intertwined. The Eli pictured in *Echolilia* is at times the ideally framed dreamlike child, but he is also an unknowable and sometimes unsettling boy, and his father knows him as an exacting art director; the photobook that father and son created together, in fact, can be read as a negotiation of the many parts Eli can play. These case studies demonstrate that collaboration as a material practice and a theorized relationship is well situated to deconstruct that tension between real and imagined children—and that is largely because the recognition of and interplay between two opposing states is central to the practice of multiple authorship. As James S. Leonard and Christine E. Wharton argue, in collaborative works, "original singleness of vision is neither possible nor sought . . . [but a] certain achievement of 'unitary thought' is worked out: a relatively seamless fabric of textual logic, the effect of a single voice speaking. But significantly, here the effect is professedly a simulated one. It cannot be imagined otherwise without denying the collaborative process altogether" (32–33). Collaborative writing is not the opposite of sole authorship but instead a mode of composition that maintains both polyvalence and unity. It recognizes simultaneously two opposing textual states, a harmony of voices and their discord, just as many artifacts of children's literature and culture recognize both the child-figure and real children who may align with, complicate, or subvert adult desire. Collaborative partnerships differ in the degree to which they allow discord to exist inside a text; the collaborations I have focused on throughout this book are best characterized as what Andrea A. Lunsford and Lisa Ede call dialogic collaborations. In dialogic collaborations, "one person may occupy multiple and shifting roles as a project progresses," and "those participating . . . generally value the creative tension inherent in multivoiced and multivalent ventures" (133). They "can in some circumstances be deeply subversive" because the voices of vulnerable subjects who may be silenced by the unifying forces of the text (such as children) remain audible even when—perhaps especially when—those voices create contradictions or tensions within the text (133).

 I have turned to the flexibility of dialogic collaboration because it offers insight into the ways Golden Age authors negotiated issues of child agency and provides, for present-day scholars of the Victorian period and of childhood more generally, new tools for writing about real children. In particular, this model of multiple authorship suspends in productive dialogue the tension between real children and figurations of childhood. Because in dialogic collaborations "one person may occupy multiple and shifting roles as a project progresses," these partnerships adapt to many and sometimes divergent configurations of creative authority; child and adult occupy various positions in relationship to a literary or cultural text throughout its production. Consider the children who collaborated with David Starr Jordan to produce *The Book of Knight and Barbara*, which I explore in Chapter Four. Those children were creative authorities, invited by Jordan to act as illustrators, storytellers, and editors; however, their work also was examined as evidence of the workings of the child mind by scholars of Child Study, a field inflected by Romantic and evolutionary models of childhood that could both foreclose and accommodate children's creative expression. Such shifts in authority also can occur across an extended adult-child partnership. In Chapter Two, I trace how Stevenson's relationship with Osbourne shifted as the younger partner matured from a boy interested in toy presses and pirate tales into a professional author—changes registered in the texts they produced, from "Not I" to *Treasure Island* to *Ebb-Tide*. The elasticity of dialogic collaboration allowed Osbourne, as an enterprising amateur small press printer, to carve out opportunities for creative agency in the roles of publisher and distributor and then, as he grew through adolescence and toward his own career as a professional author, to devise new strategies to manage his father's substantial reputation—for example, by narrating the genesis of *Treasure Island* in a manner that emphasizes his instrumentality in composing that adventure tale. As the volatile relationship between Jim Hawkins and his adult shipmates in *Treasure Island* makes clear, in many cases authors created fictions that comment on the creative negotiations that produced them. These examples demonstrate that, while the play of agency between adults and children varies over time within a particular adult-child relationship or within the culture at large—and, as I have demonstrated throughout *Between Generations*, the Victorian period witnessed reconsiderations of children as artistic agents on many fronts—modes of collaboration can also adjust and stretch. The recovery of authorial practices, then, often corresponds with the recovery of child agency.

Like Golden Age authors before us, scholars working in children's literature studies are faced with the challenge of parsing the place of the child's voice as a force that sometimes submits to, sometimes inspires, and sometimes informs the direction of texts for young people. I propose the model of dialogic collaboration as an exceptionally apt analytic for critics engaging in such negotiations. It maintains a crucial awareness that adult-child relationships are usually unequal partnerships, as adults possess cultural capital that children may not be able to access, and that any representation of the child is susceptible to the influence of figurations of childhood generated by adult desire. As Marah Gubar makes clear, "if we as scholars want to claim that children have agency . . . we must concede that the kind of agency that they have is not synonymous with autonomy" ("Hermeneutics" 293). However, considering adult-child relationships as dialogic collaborations acknowledges the potentially powerless or passive roles children might occupy without reading them as all-encompassing narratives of childhood; those roles instead exist as some of the many shifting positions children fill in the discursive field of children's literature and culture. This recognition is vital for those examining childhood and children's literature of the Victorian period. For many, the nineteenth century continues to be characterized as a cultural moment so steeped in the construction of the ideal child that any other paradigm of child life, and in particular any model that makes room for agentic childhood, seems impossible. The framework of dialogic collaboration allows us to approach both constructions of the child and real young people through one critical project. A turn to dialogic collaboration as a paradigm for understanding adult-child relationships—real and fictive, inside and outside of texts—can therefore answer the call of scholars such as Gubar, Bernstein, Rachel Conrad, and others who encourage scholars to find ways to talk about real children, despite a critical tradition that insists we conceive of the child as other, alien, or inescapably tied to adult desire.[10]

Gubar and Bernstein use performance and reception studies to theorize the real children who exist alongside, complicate, and negotiate the child-figure. In *Between Generations*, however, I have turned instead to publication history—a methodology that has the potential to alter the critical practice of scholars in children's literature and Victorian studies. First, attention to publication history challenges us to expand the roster of who contributes to literature and culture by defamiliarizing the parameters of authorship—even those boundaries we find most natural or incontestable, such as the form authorship can take or the ways an author's age allows for or precludes her participation in professional literary culture. Scholars such as Laurie Langbauer, Angela Sorby, Christine Alexander, and Juliet McMaster have begun to document the role young people have played and continue to play in literary history. As Alexander and McMaster explain, "the child as creator of culture has been subsumed within the child as mere consumer," and yet "the child's expression of his or her own subjectivity is there and available for us, if we will only take the time to pay attention" (1). What is remarkable about this body of scholarship is its intent to move beyond the critical frame of juvenilia, a term that suggests the immature work of writers who later establish themselves as well-known authors, to consider instead a "juvenile tradition" (to use Langbauer's phrase) that "recasts literary history," requiring us to recognize previously understudied forms and redefine seemingly well-known literary movements and periods (3–4). Recovering a tradition of intergenerational collaboration, as I do here, not only contributes to that project by demonstrating the rewards of locating and seriously examining the work of young authors but also recognizes the spectrum of ways young people acted as creators of culture: as artists, critics, and amateur journalists, for example, and as the not-always-facile students or subjects of Child Study. The Golden Age of children's literature and, in fact, the Victorian period itself are in turn transformed into a volatile and plastic moment in the history of childhood that produced a cultural field in which both young and old participate.

A focus on collaboration not only reframes the Victorian period and the Golden Age—redefining the roles adults and children might fulfill in the creation of children's literature and indeed in the construction of childhood—but also expands how scholars might think about adult-child relationships writ large. As the previous chapters demonstrate, if we commit to exploring the cultural work of real children not in spite of but in dialogue with social constructs of the child, then we are emboldened to reconsider, perhaps radically, the types of connections children did, and can, form with adults. In *Between Generations*, then, I model a departure from a long-held critical investment in examining adults' relationships with young people as mediated primarily by desire (on the part of the adult) or dependency (on the part of the child), especially in studies of the nineteenth century. Rose takes this approach, as does Kincaid, who asserts that for the Victorians and for adults in the present (the inheritors of Victorian constructs of childhood and desire), "a child is not, in itself, anything. Any image, body, or being we can hollow out, exalt, abuse, and locate sneakily in a field of desire will do for us as a 'child'" (*Child-Loving* 5).[11] This erotic emptiness frames the "postromantic child" as both desirable and vulnerable to that desire, and childhood "has come to be largely a coordinate set of *have nots* . . . Its liberty, however much prized, is a negative attribute, as is its innocence and purity" ("Producing" 10). Mavis Reimer and charlie peters cite Kincaid's work in their outline of the "two dominant theoretical frameworks through which 'the child' is conceptualized" in Western societies: "the ignorant child who develops into the rational adult and the innocent child who is corrupted by entry into the adult world" (89, 97). While scholars have identified both as constructions, those constructions have persisted from at least the seventeenth century to the present, and both assume, to some degree, the inferiority or vulnerability of the child subject. Even scholarship that seeks to pluck at the seams that hold these constructs together reifies the fact that they constitute the two most familiar modes of discussing adult-child relationships.

Scholarship, such as *Between Generations*, that focuses on real children despite the challenges of doing so puts pressure on these models of desire and vulnerability, requiring us to imagine adult-child relationships that account for both the demands adults place on the child and how the child responds. Some critics already have considered how models of childhood that seem to rob real young people of agency might, in fact, provide them access to self-definition. In *Dependent States: The Child's Part in Nineteenth-Century American Culture* (2005), Karen Sánchez-Eppler uses a range of documents written not only about but also by children (in particular children's diaries) to redefine dependency, one of the most common and naturalized words associated with childhood, "as an issue both of personal agency and of national and institutional relationships" (xiv). Others explore how focusing on the bodies of children can reconfigure our understanding of intergenerational relationships. Robson does so in *Heart Beats: Everyday Life and the Memorized Poem* (2012), where she is attentive to the children tasked with reciting poetry in nineteenth- and twentieth-century classrooms—young people who experienced the nervous or excited palpitations of performance and sometimes the sting of a birch when a recitation went awry. While she recognizes "the route pioneered by such critics as James R. Kincaid and Eve Sedgwick who . . . intimate that when beating, children, and literature are present, then sexual excitement must be there too—whether in the person or persons of the flogger, the floggee, or the gentle reader," Robson focuses on a different set of relationships, including not only the power dynamics between adult listener and child orator but also the sympathetic bond between teacher and pupil "exploring a work together" (112, 183). I am inspired by such research into children's writings and experiences and its potential to reconfigure critical accounts of adult-child relationships, and in the preceding chapters I expand the reach of this work. By taking on texts and discourses that seem to epitomize adult authority over or idealizations of children—such as Golden Age children's literature or scientific studies of child life—and revealing the unexpected paradigms of collaboration that underpin them, I establish that it is our critical perspective, and not necessarily the realities of child life, that have made sympathetic, friendly, or even professional relationships between generations invisible.

In other words, paying attention to the collaborative child, as I have throughout *Between Generations*, addresses directly the paucity of models we have for adult-child connections that accommodate child agency by uncovering a series of intergenerational partnerships that exceed adult desire or child dependency—partnerships that often occur in cultural arenas assumed to be ruled by adult authority. Consider the empathic and respectful relationships between adults and children suggested by William Brighty Rands, who calls for adults to approach children "in willing sympathy, treating them as we do our equals in noble friendship" ("Children" 465). Stevenson and Osbourne—that "American gentleman" with "classic taste"—forged a relationship grounded both in play and professionalism. Shifting our focus way from adults' investments in children as objects of desire or dependency and considering alternative connections between generations transforms the types of questions we ask when considering real and fictive children. Rather than asking how a child, in books or in life, behaves in ways that reinscribe, reinforce, or passively conform to the adult imagination, we can ask what new paradigms of child life might be at work and what is at stake in those paradigms, including questions of age or competency. Reframing our inquiries about Victorian childhood, or childhood in general, in this manner reveals that often young people were instrumental rather than docile subjects who participated alongside adults in shaping discourses about childhood in, for example, literary culture, the visual arts, education, and science.

As this range of discourses suggests, and as I have demonstrated throughout the previous chapters, adult-child collaborations occur not only as authorial practice but also in the spaces and institutions where children and adults interact, including classrooms, libraries, art galleries, and even laboratories. Turning to collaboration as a structuring paradigm for relationships between real young people and adults, therefore, can inspire expansive and complex interdisciplinary methodologies.

Between Generations, in fact, might be better characterized as scholarship in childhood studies rather than children's literature studies, in that throughout I am invested in determining how children's participation and representation in literary culture is entangled with other ways of approaching child life, from medicine to education to library science. This multifaceted approach is central to the practice of childhood studies, an interdisciplinary field that, in the words of Anna Mae Duane, "defies the easy divisions of biology and culture, body and book" and deconstructs the seemingly contradictory approaches of the humanities and the sciences. The "integrative approaches" of childhood studies, Conrad notes, "take into account conceptions of childhood, cultural representations of children, and lived experiences of children" (126). Some of the most provocative work on childhood and children's literature published in recent years—Sally Shuttleworth's *The Mind of the Child: Child Development in Literature, Science, and Medicine* (2010), Kenneth Kidd's *Freud in Oz: At the Intersections of Psychoanalysis and Children's Literature* (2011), and Jessica Straley's *Evolution and Imagination in Victorian Children's Literature* (2016), for example—considers the ways a range of disciplines mutually constitute childhood. I have incorporated similar multifaceted approaches to childhood in *Between Generations* in part to make the case that childhood studies' interdisciplinary approach is one of the most promising means for scholars to pursue a criticism that not only deals with figures of childhood but also continually seeks out ways to ethically and usefully account for the lived experiences of real young people.[12]

The examples of intergenerational collaboration I include throughout this book, after all, illuminate how perceptions of childhood in one cultural arena resonate in another. Theories of language acquisition developed by Child Study scholars, with their attention to patterns of repetition and revision, resurfaced in Golden Age authors' scenes of storytelling. The curricula developed by nineteenth-century art educators signal shifts in the valuation of child art that found expression in children's book illustration and in the creative work of young artists such as Willie Macready and Francis Darwin. Librarians' attempts to gauge the reading habits of young people and school inspectors' attention to the well-being of children's bodies and minds granted an authority to young people's perspectives that was exaggerated in the topsy-turvy plots of children's fiction and poetry by authors such as Charles Dickens and Rands. For scholars who are writing from a literary studies perspective, the interdisciplinary approaches provided by childhood studies are not a replacement or substitute for our own disciplinary commitments, but they do illuminate the relevance of literary and visual culture for real, embodied subjects, and they suggest opportunities for collaboration with scholars in history, medicine, sociology, anthropology, psychology, the fine arts, philosophy, and linguistics.

If the field of childhood studies holds out the promise of interdisciplinary collaboration, then adult-child collaboration proposes similar bonds between young people and the writers, teachers, parents, and other adults they encounter. Children's literature criticism in past decades has emphasized the alienation between adult and child and the various forms that separation might take in literature and culture, exploring adults' colonization, idealization, or objectification of young people. However, as this study has demonstrated, Golden Age literature and culture does not support such separations. Victorian children's literature and culture reveals instead a lively practice of adult-child collaborations—partnerships that provide creative thresholds where both adults and children can meet. Even when child and adult seem most isolated from one another, in fact, Victorians found the means to recognize that separation while building bridges to traverse it. Child Study scholars adopted theories of recapitulation that divided the child savage from the civilized adult with years of evolution and development, and yet G. Stanley Hall praised Child Study as a field that "helps to break down to some extent the partitions between grades of work, so that the kindergartner and university professor can cooperate in the same task" (700). Storytelling practices situated adults as tellers and children as listeners, but Mary Molesworth solicited the opinions, critiques, and interruptions of her young auditors. When toy press companies divided boys and men into amateurs and professionals, Osbourne and Stevenson ignored their advice and went into business together—and when the younger partner printed the older writer's poetry, he concluded the small pamphlet with an image of two hands clasping. *Not I*, the title proclaimed, but we. If we pay attention to that plural pronoun and similar rejections of the sole author, we can discern that adults and children, from the nineteenth century to the present, build collaborative relationships that span generations.

Notes

INTRODUCTION: A CHILD'S STORY

1. Some accounts of Browning's relationship with Willie Macready—including that by Browning's sister Sarianna, included in note 2 below—state that Browning wrote "The Cardinal and the Dog" for Willie. However, this is unlikely. There is a draft of the poem in the margins of Browning's copy of Nathaniel Wanley's *The Wonders of the Little World* dated February 27, 1841, which predates Willie's illness and correspondence with Browning. See Kelley and Hudson, 330.

2. Macready Sr. and Browning exchanged letters frequently, beginning soon after their first meeting in November 1835. Macready's diary reveals that he was never fully satisfied with Browning's work, and Browning's letters suggest the poet's eagerness for Macready's approval. Macready staged and even performed in some of Browning's plays—including *Strafford*, staged in 1837 at Covent Garden with Macready in the lead role, and *A Blot in the 'Scutcheon*, staged in 1843 at Drury Lane, where Macready was the manager. However, the two quarreled over the latter play—a fight that signaled the end of their friendship. Browning was writing poetry for Willie Macready, then, as his friendship with Macready Sr. was deteriorating. This has led some scholars to suspect the poet's partnership with the young artist was a ploy to remain in the actor's good graces. Stefan Hawlin, for instance, notes that while Browning was pressing Macready Sr. to approve of *Blot in the 'Scutcheon*, he was also "charming him with two poems for his little son William" (14–15).

3. The drawings and letters are held in the Armstrong Browning Library in Waco, Texas. Sarianna's note on the exterior of this envelope reads as follows: "In May, 1842, Macready's eldest little boy was confined to the house by a cough. To amuse him, Robert wrote two poems which the child was to illustrate—'Crescentius, the pope's Legate' and the 'Pied Piper'—At first, there was no thought of publishing them, but I copied the Pied Piper and showed it to Alfred Dommett who was so much pleased with it that he persuaded Robert to include it in the forthcoming number of Bells and Pomegranates—'Crescentius,' he did not publish till the last, in Asolando—These are the boy's illustrations" (Kelley and Hudson 350). There are two probable inaccuracies in Sarianna's account. The first I explain in note 1. Second, Sarianna probably did not show "The Pied Piper" to Dommett, at least not when she claims to have done so. Dommett

sailed for New Zealand before Willie's correspondence with Browning began. However, "The Pied Piper" indeed was published in *Dramatic Lyrics*, the third number of *Bells and Pomegranates* (Kelley and Hudson). Browning did not intend to include "The Pied Piper" but did so at the request of his publisher, Edward Moxon, who needed more copy to fill the volume; the poem therefore appears in the second, but not the first, proof of that collection (Woolford, Karlin; Phelan 172).

4. I use the term *Golden Age* throughout this book to signal the boom in children's literature and culture that occurred from the mid-nineteenth to the early twentieth centuries in England. While the idea of a "Golden Age" of children's literature is a construction, and while some contest its dates and character as deployed by critics, the phrase remains for me a useful shorthand for an important epoch in the history of children's literature and childhood.

5. Attaching a date to *Peter Pan* is, as many scholars have already noted, a tricky prospect. This 1904 date refers to the first staging of the play, but its script was not published until 1928. See Stirling for an account of the many origin texts of *Peter*.

6. I focus primarily on British attitudes toward childhood and children's literature, but there are moments in the chapters that follow when a more transatlantic lens is necessary. For instance, I frequently discuss discourses of child life—such as education, Child Study, and librarianship—that were Continental or transatlantic in scope.

7. Most editions of Browning's "Pied Piper" for children bear little trace of Macready's participation, aside from his name in the poem's final quatrain, which I will discuss in more detail in Chapter 4; that quatrain appears consistently, despite no other mention of Macready in the poem. I have located thus far only two editions of Browning's "Pied Piper" that do, in more substantial ways, recognize Macready. An 1889 edition published by Harry Quilter and richly illustrated by Mary Quilter includes a dedication to the couple's children, calling the poem a "child's story written by a great poet for the son of a famous actor." Because this reference does not name Macready or describe his role in the creation of "The Pied Piper"—and because Browning, in this dedication, is "great" and Macready Sr. "famous"—Willie seems rather unimportant. I find more interesting the 1912 J. M. Dent edition illustrated by Margaret W. Tarrant, which includes Browning's dedication to Willie—"written for, and inscribed to, W. M. the Younger"—on the book's title page, directly below Browning's name. This is an anomaly in editions of Browning's poem for children; all other editions I have found delete the dedication entirely, and here its placement in such close proximity to Browning's might evoke, in some ways, collaboration.

8. Others have taken Rose's thesis even further, in particular Karín Lesnik-Oberstein and the critical tradition rooted at the University of Reading. Lesnik-Obserstein's scholarship often focuses on how children's literature criticism is based upon assumptions about real childhood in ways that undermine its project as a whole. For example, in her opening essay to *Children in Culture: Approaches to Childhood* (1998), she contends that "children's literature critics depend upon, and exist for, an essentialist 'real child': their entire endeavor is self-defined as the effort to define and find the good book for the child" (19).

9. The Nodelman and Flynn essays I cite here are part of a forum on child agency published in the Summer 2016 issue of *Jeunesse*. The forum also includes position pieces by Sarah L. Schwebel and Marah Gubar, both of whom I cite in this introduction.

10. David Goslee, near the end of his consideration of the play of childhood and adulthood in "The Pied Piper," notes that Browning considered his poem "only as a written vehicle for Willie Macready's pictures" but later reduces him to passive listener—Browning's "juvenile audience-of-one" (50, 51). Mary S. Pollock, considering connections between the "Piper" and Browning's religious poetry, states briefly and cagily that Browning "evidently considered 'The Pied Piper' a collaboration with Willie" (141). Browning considers the poem a collaboration, Pollock implies, but she is not so sure.

11. In her book *Artful Dodgers*, Gubar offers an alternative reading of the creative child as that figure appears in Golden Age children's literature. She posits that while Victorians often warned against the risks of child precocity, they also often characterized such precocity, including creativity, "in positive terms" (35). See, for example, her reading of Sara Crewe from *A Little Princess* (37–38). I discuss Gubar's *Artful Dodgers* in more detail later in this introduction.

12. Ogata, like Parkes, draws compelling connections between the figure of the creative child and adults' economic and political ends. In *Designing the Creative Child: Playthings and Places in Midcentury America*, Ogata cites Jacqueline Rose's work in theorizing her approach to the child as construct (27) and describes the creative child as a product of systems of education, art and architecture, consumer goods, parenting, and psychology that work toward political, social, and economic ends. Ogata acknowledges the real child as a potentially creative subject but does not take that real child as a subject of her study: "Rather," she writes, "I argue that 'real' children are implied in the schemes that parents and other adults have created, but that they are nonetheless strongly idealized interpretations" (xvi).

13. Here, I primarily will refer to the work of Knoepflmacher and Myers. For Beckett on cross-writing, see *Crossover Fiction: Global and Historical Perspectives* (2009) and her entry on "crossover literature" in *Keywords for Children's Literature* (2011).

14. For Rose's reading of *Peter Pan*'s performances and the spectacle of the child, see Chapter Four of *The Case of Peter Pan*, "Peter Pan and the Commercialisation of the Child: Children Are a Good Sell," particularly 97–99.

15. This scholarship is particularly productive in its attention to forms that have, until now, remained outside the purview of children's literature studies. See, for example, Katharine Capshaw's *Civil Rights Childhood: Picturing Liberation in African American Photobooks* (2014), in particular her analysis of child poet Kali Grosvenor at 169–83; Catherine Tosenberger's and Sara K. Day's work on fanfiction; and scholarship on children's writing in periodicals by Anna Redcay and Rebecca Onion.

16. My methodology of composition narratives is indebted to Gérard Genette's concept of paratexts. As Genette argues, a text "is rarely presented in an unadorned state, unreinforced and unaccompanied by a certain number of verbal or other productions, such as an author's name, a title, a preface, illustrations" (1). These paratexts, as Genette makes clear, are "thresholds" to a text and as spaces of transaction between text and

reader (2). While for the most part, Genette focuses on how paratexts transform a text's life beyond publication, I consider composition narratives a means to read backward to a text's production to recuperate evidence of collaborative authorship that might otherwise remain hidden.

17. My focus on corroborative evidence aligns with Gubar, who deploys similar methods in her examination of children's theater. She writes that "in making claims about whether specific dramas were aimed at and enjoyed by children, we must try to collate different kinds of corroborative evidence, even as we acknowledge that our conclusions can only ever be tentative, since our knowledge is inevitably fractional, incomplete" ("*Peter*" 479). In gathering and reinforcing evidence in this manner, I also hope to address, at least in part, critical concerns about archived materials by children, which are often influenced by adults and social institutions, such as schools, and preserved according to adults' systems of value. For more on the difficulties of accessing archives of children's reading experiences in particular, see Schwebel.

18. While this book has fallen into obscurity, it was popular upon publication and ended the holiday season second in sales only to George du Maurier's *Trilby*. It went through three editions in four months ("Books for Young People" 380; Avery 176).

19. Crockett later published a sequel to *Sweetheart Travellers* titled *Sweethearts at Home* (1912), a volume that collects more stories about the adventures of his children. Crockett claims that this volume, published when Maisie was twenty-four years old, is even more "hers," purportedly excerpted from her diaries and edited by her father.

20. There are many comprehensive studies of Romantic childhood and its influence on past and current figures of childhood. See, for example, James Holt McGavran Jr.'s *Romanticism and Children's Literature in Nineteenth-Century England* (1991) and *Literature and the Child: Romantic Continuations, Postmodern Contestations* (1999), Judith Plotz's *Romanticism and the Vocation of Childhood* (2001), and Alan Richardson's *Literature, Education, and Romanticism: Reading as Social Practice, 1780–1832* (2004).

21. Critics disagree about the nature of Edgeworth's collaboration with her father. See, for example, Grathwol (75) and Gallagher (274).

22. Mitzi Myers acknowledges the collaborative impulse in Edgeworth's work apart from the influence of the author's father. For example, Myers, describing stories in *Early Lessons*, writes that the author "speaks through the tale's adult educators to constitute the story as a parable for the parents who buy the book and may also read it to their children. The tale packs manifest and latent lessons into small space" ("Reading" 63).

23. Barbauld's brother, John Aikin, encouraged his sister to publish her poetry, and the siblings, as adults, actively collaborated on at least two projects: John Aikin's 1772 *Essays on Song-Writing*, which included six songs by his sister, and a volume of essays titled *Miscellaneous Pieces in Prose* in 1773. Two years later, in 1775, Barbauld wrote to her brother of the small pieces of fiction and drama both had composed, suggesting that they "must some day sew all [their] fragments together, and make a *Joineriana* of them" (*Works* 9). The siblings never pieced together that *Joineriana*.

24. The word *budget* appears frequently in the titles of children's periodicals and books and, according to its simplest definition, implies a "collection" or "stock."

However, the word's financial overtones imply that the stories in a "budget" act as a guide for how children should use their creative resources. The phrase "to open one's budget," obscure today but in circulation at the writing of *Evenings*, means "to speak one's mind." This could suggest that the authors of such collections were communicating their ideas on early education, often spoken or read aloud. But possibly—when modified by the adjective "juvenile," as in *Juvenile Budget Opened*—the word *budget* communicates the possibility that children, the juveniles in question, can speak their own minds.

25. Another tale, "The Boy Without a Genius," similarly presents conflicting theories of education. The story reproduces the letters between the angry father of an underachieving student and a schoolteacher. By the end of the tale, the boy is thriving and the schoolmaster sends a scathing letter to the father, whose unrealistic expectations were the true problem. The story's moral is directed not to the child but to the parent.

26. Barbauld's texts were reprinted, reformulated, excerpted, and illustrated throughout the eighteenth and nineteenth centuries, in both England and America. *Lessons for Children* was particularly popular abroad. While, as Sarah Robbins notes, "Barbauld herself had refrained from claiming . . . to be offering a female teaching model intended for widespread replication in other middle-class homes, her later editors consistently characterized her text and its implied program as such," and Barbauld "was constantly being appropriated and reshaped throughout the nineteenth century by Anglo-American promoters of the ethos of domestic didacticism" ("Lessons" 135–36). The editors and authors who appropriated and reworked *Lessons*, aided by the absence of international copyright law, found a way to collaborate with Barbauld, reshaping her text through revisions and illustrations to fit the particular needs and methods of American maternal pedagogy ("Remaking" 158).

CHAPTER ONE
ACTIVE LISTENERS: CHILD AUDITORS AS CREATIVE COLLABORATORS

1. Doyle created the woodcut of Thackeray and Story discussed above to accompany Locker-Lampson's poem, which was published in *A Selection from the Works of Frederick Locker-Lampson* (London, 1865).

2. For an exploration of the ways Victorian novels for adults recognize and complicate the tensions between oral and written culture, see Ivan Kreilkamp, *Voice and the Victorian Storyteller*.

3. The exception to Rousseau's rejection of books for his pupil is, famously, *Robinson Crusoe*, which in the words of Rousseau is the "one book which, to [his] thinking, supplies the best treatise on an education according to nature" (176). For a discussion of how *Robinson Crusoe* operates in *Émile*, see Flanders.

4. It is likely that Rousseau is using the word *inarticulate* to denote speech that is, as the Oxford English Dictionary defines, "not consisting of distinct parts having each a definite meaning."

5. The schoolteachers were Margaret A. Clapperton, Mary E. Crees, and Mary Louch, who would later become editor of the Child Study Association's journal, the *Paidologist*. In histories of the Child Study movement, in particular earlier histories written at the beginning of the twentieth century, Hall is remembered as the originator of the Child Study Association, and American organizations inquiring into child life are represented as the true beginnings of the movement. D. E. Bradbury, for example, notes that "only in America" did Child Study "have a widespread popular appeal," largely due to the work of Hall (21). Kate Stevens, secretary of the London branch of the British Child Study Association in 1906, agrees. "The Child Study movement in Great Britain owes its inception and much of its progress to American psychology," she writes, "since the inspiration which led to the founding of the British Child Study Association was given by Dr. G. Stanley Hall" (245). It is important to note, however, that while Hall's influence was unmatched by any Child Study expert in England, the movement was international in nature, including perspectives of childhood in Britain and throughout Europe. Hall, in a short 1900 article on Child Study, notes that he knows of periodicals in various countries with sections devoted to the movement: "three journals in Germany, two in France, one each in England, Italy, Japan, Russia, and Spain" (688).

6. Sally Shuttleworth argues that Preyer's text "was to become the definitive work" of Child Study for two decades, and she notes that Preyer compiled his study self-consciously as "high science," systematically observing his son three times daily for three years ("Inventing" 145).

7. The volume of literature produced during the Child Study movement is overwhelming. In 1900 Hall claims that the movement is "represented by a bibliography of some two thousand titles, including only the books and articles well worth reading, and not comprising the yet larger mass of chaff" (688).

8. While Blackford notes a tension between children and the ability to "look within," there was, at the end of the nineteenth century, a growing association between childhood and interiority. Carolyn Steedman notes that

> long established associations between littleness and interiority and between history and childhood were theorized in emergent psychoanalysis between about 1895 and 1920. In establishing psychoanalysis as a body of theory and as a cognitive form, Sigmund Freud worked with the imaginative legacy of cell theory, that is to say with notions of littleness, of entities composed of smaller parts, and with the idea of the smallest possible entity as the birthplace, or progenitor, of memory and consciousness of time. (77)

9. Henry James, five years earlier, employed a similar but inverted simile that draws on the correspondences between imagining, "picturing," and interpretation in his novel *What Maisie Knew* to articulate the confusion children experience when attempting to understand adults' minds. Maisie, subject to the manipulations of her divorcing parents, "was taken into the confidence of passions on which she fixed just the stare she might have had for images bounding across the wall in the slide of a magic lantern"

(17). James was connected to the Child Study movement through his brother, William James, who encouraged him to write about the implications of Child Study in a fictional form. For an account of the influence of Child Study on Henry James and in particular on *Maisie*, see Levander.

10. Taine himself was inspired by Max Müller's 1873 series of articles in *Fraser's Magazine* in 1873, Lectures on Mr. Darwin's Philosophy of Language. See Shuttleworth, *Mind of the Child*, 258–59.

11. Scholars during the Child Study movement were conscious of their debt to Rousseau. Drummond, for example, writes that "there were great educators before Rousseau, yet to Rousseau, in spite of all his vagaries, exaggerations, and paradoxes, we owe many of the doctrines which in our own day are becoming dogmas of the New Education" (14). A. Tolman Smith, while critical of the movement, notes that "the study of children" is largely indebted to *Émile* (238).

12. Recapitulation theory, in its first manifestations, dealt primarily with the physical development of the embryo, but sociologists and anthropologists soon applied the assumptions behind the theory to cultural, social, and linguistic development. Wooldridge argues that it was the Child Study movement's reliance on the recapitulation theory that contributed largely to the theory's decline in the early twentieth century. Growing criticism of the aims and methods of the movement in both America and Europe "coincided with a demolition of . . . the recapitulation theory in the technical literature," writes Wooldridge. "The rise of experimental biology made the theory unfashionable" (45). Wooldridge also, however, defends the choice experts in Child Study made to rely on the recapitulation theory, noting that while it lost currency in scientific communities, some of the most important figures in psychology, including Piaget and Freud, were recapitulationists.

13. Chamberlain notes that Psammetichus "came to the conclusion that the oldest language on the face of the earth was Phrygian, because two children, isolated by his orders, spoke first the word *bekos*, which in that language signified 'bread'" (114). He and other writers like him demonstrate how the language of Child Study scholars is saturated with the motif of origins. Not only do children recapitulate the origins of language, but also studies of children's language recapitulate the origin of language studies, which even in antiquity "turned to childhood" (113).

14. There are a few Child Study scholars who disagree, claiming instead that children's sense of hearing is not fully developed. Tracy, for example, claims that the child's sense of hearing is "imperfect, both in structure and functioning." He therefore understands "the initial babbling of the infant, and . . . its marvelous flexibility, and the enormous variety of its intonations and inflections" not as evidence of the child's acute hearing but instead as proof that "the child has come into the world already possessing a considerable portion of the equipment by which he shall in after years give expression to his feelings and thoughts" (120–21). F. H Champneys, in "Notes on an Infant" (1881), also contends that the sense of hearing is "late" in appearance (106).

15. Shuttleworth also cites Sully's and Taine's accounts of children's language acquisition to demonstrate how these two scholars were "keen to emphasize . . . the creative use of language of the child" (*Mind* 285).

16. Today this is sometimes called idioglossia. There are quite a few studies of secret languages developed between young twins in particular, a phenomenon with the separate name cryptophasia, sometimes more casually called twin talk or twin speak. Contemporary discussions of cryptophasia tend to dwell on the potentially negative effects of twins' secret languages on their cognitive and language development. For an example of recent research into twins' secret languages, see Thorpe, Greenwood, Eivers, and Rutter.

17. Hun insists that the girl's invented vocabulary shows little trace of words formed by imitation, and that while a few of her words resemble French, he was not sure that the child had ever heard that language spoken (526).

18. The practice of offering adults glossaries to understand the language of young people, and the contention that adults do not "know" their children, continued through the twentieth century and persists in the present day. See in particular the glossaries of adolescent slang that accompanied the social invention of the teenager in the 1950s and 1960s; Harrison E. Salisbury provides such a glossary in his book *The Shook-Up Generation* (1958), for example, that defines words such as "bop" ("to fight"), "dig" ("to understand"), and "grind" ("an erotic dance, similar to the fish") (ix). More recent glossaries aim to help parents understand their tech-savvy children's text-speak (Cohen). Often these glossaries are couched in alarmist language about child and teen delinquency, as parents are warned that their children can communicate about dangerous or illegal activities in ways that deliberately exclude adults.

19. I have chosen to discuss the Grimms in this chapter and not other fairy tale collectors and writers, such as Charles Perrault and Hans Christian Andersen, because the Grimms' collections had particularly far-reaching influence in England, especially after Edgar Taylor's 1823 translation, *German Popular Stories*, illustrated by George Cruikshank.

20. All references to the Grimms' collections are cited from *The Annotated Brothers Grimm*. I have cited the Grimms by edition, volume, and page number in the *Annotated* edition. "Grimm 1.2.410," then, indicates the first edition, second volume of the *KHM*, printed on page 410 in the *Annotated* edition.

21. The critical tradition that surrounds the *KHM* often focuses on whether or not the Grimms were collectors of truly oral tales or if their claimed role as recorders of the spoken word was a constructed one. However, whether the Grimms were, in the words of Siegfried Neumann, "intent upon tales issuing genuinely from the oral folk tradition" or if they were, in the words of Donald Ward, actually collectors of "a mixture of oral texts with those taken from printed sources," while important, matters less to me. I am interested instead how the Grimms set forth to prove the "genuineness" of tales they collected by recording their "contamination," how they were rewritten as they passed from teller to audience and from teller to teller (Neumann 27; Ward 17). Jack Zipes dubs the Grimms "the greatest contaminators of fairy tales in the nineteenth century," a claim meant not to challenge the validity of the Grimms' work but instead to insist upon the nature of told tales as always contaminated. "Contamination can be an enrichment process; it can lead to the birth of something unique and genuine in its own

right," writes Zipes. "In fact, it is practically impossible to avoid contact with foreign substances" (79). Moreover, some recent fairy tale scholarship, discussing the Grimms in the wider context of fairy tale collection and publication, argues for a history of the genre based in written rather than oral texts. See Bottigheimer.

22. See Maria Tatar, "Sex and Violence: The Hard Core of Fairy Tales," in *The Hard Facts of the Grimms' Fairy Tales*, expanded 2nd ed. (Princeton, NJ: Princeton University Press, 2003).

23. As Caroline Sumpter points out in *The Victorian Press and the Fairy Tale*, Victorian readers "would have been familiar with scientific models that explicitly linked the fairy tale to childhood"—in particular recapitulation; "children became psychologically analogous to early man," Sumpter writes, "both groups existing in a state of mental immaturity that was adapted to the creation and reception of simple art forms such as the fairy tale" (41).

24. Rowe also notes the printed text in Cruikshank's first frontispiece and the absence of text in the second. She, however, draws a different conclusion, interpreting the book as "perhaps an indication of a disparity in literacy, but also a subtle testament to the literary appropriation of the female voice practice by the brothers Grimm and [Charles] Perrault" (68). This interpretation grants Cruikshank a greater regard for the authority of female storytellers than is practiced by other male figures associated with the Grimms' collections.

25. See Schacker. Moreover, the transformation of fairy tales into children's literature—and authors' and collectors' editorial decisions to that end—led many writers to consider fairy tales a genre that fosters adult-child relationships. Consider the nineteenth-century champions of the "pure," traditional tale, from Charles Dickens to Andrew Lang, who railed against what they perceived as unnecessary meddling in the stories of their childhood. Much of their vitriol was directed at Cruikshank, who in 1852 began publishing a series of fairy tales promoting a particular moral agenda, emphasizing most notably the evils of alcohol. Dickens responded in his famous essay "Frauds on the Fairies" (1853): "We have lately observed, with pain, the intrusion of a Whole Hog of unwieldy dimensions into the fairy flower garden. The rooting of the animal among the roses would in itself have awakened in us nothing but indignation; our pain arises from his being violently driven in by a man of genius, our own beloved friend, Mr. George Cruikshank" (97). Assaults on moralizing tales like Cruikshank's were joined by protests against modernized tales in general. In his introduction to the 1868 edition of *German Popular Stories*, for example, Ruskin condemns the "licentious change and retouching of stories to suit particular tastes, or inculcate favourite doctrines" (x). In their call to preserve fairy tales for children, these authors suggest that the vivid imaginations of the young do not separate adults from childhood but instead make possible sympathy between generations. In protecting the imaginative lives of the young from undue interference, adults have the opportunity to reconnect with children in unexpected partnership, and essays addressing the value of fairy tales often glance timidly toward this possibility. Dickens, for instance, notes that fairy tales have "greatly helped to keep us, in some sense, ever young, by preserving through our worldly ways

one slender track not overgrown with weeds, where we may walk with children, sharing in their delights" (97). In fulfilling their obligation to protect the imaginative lives of young people and their literature, in recognizing and taking that "slender track" amid the weeds, adults preserve the possibility of reconnecting with previous generations.

26. Taylor was the primary translator. As Blamires notes, "Translators" is plural here to indicate "others in [Taylor's] immediate circle of family and acquaintances" who assisted with the project ("Early" 165).

27. While Taylor frames Gammer Grethel as a character based on Viehmann, it is possible that Viehmann herself is also a fiction, although she is presented by the Grimms as an authentic source. See Schacker, 41.

28. Hunt's translation is based on the final German edition of *KHM*, published in 1857. Early editions of Taylor's *German Popular Stories* and *Gammer Grethel* include Hansel and Gretel stories but do not include a scene in which Gretel pushes the witch into an oven. The variant in *German Popular Stories* recounts how Hansel shifts shapes from boy to deer and how Gretel protects him during a king's hunting expedition. The variant in *Gammer Grethel* includes the familiar plotting witch and gingerbread house before a series of magical transformations; brother and sister, for example, transform into a lake and a swan, Gretel becomes a daisy, and Hansel again becomes a deer. In this story, the siblings flee without killing their captor.

29. In *Kipling's Children's Literature*, Walsh argues that scholarship that "implies a belief in the possibility of accessing and identifying [a] 'pure' reality" has dominated interpretations of Rudyard Kipling's *Just So Stories* and his later Taffy tales in particular (96). She offers an alternative reading: "In contrast to extant critical assessments of the *Just So Stories* as exemplarily 'oral,'" she argues that Kipling "problematiz[es] the notion of 'orality' and its supposed privileged relationship to the 'real'" (99).

30. Kit's stories are indeed "strange," presented as his true adventures but including supernatural or fantastic elements. Mr. and Mrs. Swallow, in the book's opening chapter, discuss the nature of Kit's stories. Mr. Swallow is nervous about the influence of a teller who "has a spice of romance in him that . . . has led him to see all his adventures with a fanciful eye" (9). Mrs. Swallow responds with a short lecture on the merits of imaginative literature for children when properly balanced with serious study.

31. See also Nelson, *Boys Will Be Girls*, and Robson, *Men in Wonderland*.

32. Susan Drain notes that an aunt figure is in a privileged position to mediate between adults and children, initiating familial collaboration. The aunt, notes Drain, "is outside the strict hierarchy of parent and child, having the authority of an adult, but not that of a parent; she is associated with a relaxation of discipline . . . and she provides an occasion or even a catalyst for family interaction" (10).

33. I discuss William Brighty Rands's *Lilliput Levee* in more detail in Chapter Three.

34. One of Gatty's children, Alfred Alexander, was born in 1847 but died in infancy. Her last son, Horatio Nelson, would be born in 1855 but would also die in infancy.

35. Maxwell cites a somewhat scathing letter by Gatty in which, confronted by a schoolroom stocked with the "instructive" books of Jane Marcet, she calls such an author a "great bore" and expresses her preference for more imaginative fare. She "cared

for nothing but buying Grimms and Andersens" for her own children, and she would later favorably review Andersen, as well as other imaginative authors such as Lewis Carroll, in the early numbers of her periodical *Aunt Judy's Magazine* (94, 149). It was, in part, the fairy tale's appeal to the child's imagination that inspired Gatty.

36. "Cook Stories" is a lesson against the biting condescension of the upper class, although the moral—"to make allowances, and not expect more from people than what they've had opportunity for"—in some ways enacts the arrogance it disclaims (75).

37. It is useful to compare Gatty's representation of storytelling circles—and in particular this model of the "black bag"—to Anna Laetitia Barbauld's in *Evenings at Home*, which I discuss in my introduction.

38. The black bag—both the original in the Gatty household and its fictional counterpart in *Aunt Judy's Letters*—is said to be made out of the funeral cloak of Lord Nelson. Gatty's father was chaplain to Nelson.

39. I discuss the "Nursery Nonsense" feature of *Aunt Judy's Magazine* in more detail in Chapter Four.

CHAPTER TWO
FAMILY DYNAMICS: THE STRANGE CASE OF
ROBERT LOUIS STEVENSON AND LLOYD OSBOURNE

1. Portions of this chapter were published in vol. 35, no. 1 of *Children's Literature Association Quarterly* as "Toy Presses and Treasure Maps: Robert Louis Stevenson and Lloyd Osbourne as Collaborators."

2. See Stevenson's essays in particular. "A Humble Remonstrance" (1884) is Stevenson's response in *Longman's* magazine to an earlier piece by Henry James about the purpose of fiction and its relationship to life, and "Letter to a Young Gentleman who Proposes to Embrace the Career of Art" (1888) is a treatise on both the joys and challenges of the literary profession. He also published a number of studies of individual authors, including Robert Burns (1879) and Walt Whitman (1878).

3. Samuel Lloyd Osbourne is the full name of Fanny's son. In childhood, he was called Sam, after his father. Stevenson called him Sam and Lloyd by turns and eventually Lloyd almost exclusively. See Hart 4.

4. The size of small presses varied. In *The Boy and His Press*, Elizabeth Harris describes the small presses displayed at the Smithsonian's National Museum of American History's Hall of Graphic Arts. The measurements of the models' chases (the frames that hold type) vary from 1 x 2.5 inches to 11.5 x 13 inches.

5. The small press produced by the American company J. W. MacDonald in 1867, for example, is described in its patent as "adapted to the wants of the mercantile and manufacturing community in printing cards, circulars, &c., as they may be required, without the delays attendant upon sending to and from a regular printing office, and at much less expense" (Harris 10). From the early to the mid-nineteenth century, American printers "had been taunted, and perhaps bruised, by do-it-yourself office printing systems specifically designed to cut out the printer" (Hart 10).

6. Girls certainly participated in small-scale printing, but the presses were not initially marketed to a female audience. Thomas G. Harrison, in *The Career and Reminiscences of an Amateur Journalist, and a History of Amateur Journalism* (1883), suggests that girls did not want to participate. "It has always been a hard matter to induce young ladies to enter the ranks of Amateur Journalism, the work apparently not being congenial," he writes, "and in the sarcastic language of one journal . . . 'it is only occasionally a girl can be found who is sensible enough to forsake her mirror and fashion book long enough to pay attention to Amateur Journalism'" (64). By 1900 toy presses "were advertised for girls as much as for boys" (Harris 25).

7. Profits were insignificant for most child printers. H. L. Mencken, who owned a small press as a boy, noted, "So far as I can remember, my father was my only customer'" (Harris 9). Even those amateur journalists who circulated their work in larger numbers likely did not make much money. Harrison argues that these papers are not published for profit but instead "for the benefit of receiving exchanges and for *Ambition and Fame*" (16). "Amateur Journalists are not capitalists," he writes, "the majority of them being youths of small pecuniary means" (76).

8. "Qlease [sic] do not mind my very bad printing," wrote Daniel in a letter to his father, "for when any one looks on any part of it, it is really immensely, terribly, and dreadfully horrible" (Madan 69–70). Harris quotes a boy with even more fundamental problems with his venture. "L. H. Gray wrote back to Kelsey for more instructions: 'I received my press and like it very much the only thing that I do not understand is the setting of type'" (8).

9. Much of the hostility on the part of professional printers was directed not at children but at advertisements that downplayed the expertise required by the printing trade. William H. Bushnell, in "The Curse of Amateurism," cites an advertisement that guarantees a child can learn to use a small press in a mere three hours. "The statement is unmitigated trash," Bushnell concludes, "and all parties connected with it ought to be ashamed of themselves; at least all but the boy should. He ought to be sent to school to complete the rudiments of education, and early put to bed, for meddling with matters he could not by any possibility know anything about" (79).

10. For more information on children's manuscript magazines, see Bell and Bell.

11. Spencer and Harrison both include accounts of the political side of amateur journalism among boys in the United States. These histories describe the numerous conventions of amateur journalists in the late nineteenth and early twentieth centuries and chronicle the elections and power struggles that often characterized meetings.

12. As Hart notes, "It is not certain who gave [Osbourne] the wonderful present." While the critical consensus seems to be that the press was a gift from Stevenson, Hart notes that "perhaps it came from the father who was about to lose his son, a boy for whom he cared enormously and to whom . . . he gave other cultural presents" (4–5).

13. According to Hart, Osbourne clipped an advertisement for the Model press for a scrapbook, but the press he used "differed slightly" from this press "and its maker has not been identified by either of two major manufacturers of printing presses whose history goes back beyond 1880" (5).

14. See Stevenson's essay "A Penny Plain and Twopence Coloured" and the final installment of Osbourne and Stevenson's Letters to Young Friends in *St. Nicholas Magazine*.

15. The word "unindent-ed" refers both to Osbourne's struggles to achieve correct spacing—see the disjointed word "taper" in this poem—and the fact that he is not indentured—that is, working without the aid of professional guidance.

16. Hart notes, "Nowhere did it describe itself simply as the Davos Press, although that is a name often given to it by chroniclers of Stevenson. The name seems improper in that it tends to isolate one period too much from another in the continuing career of a boy whose presswork originated in California and was yet to travel on to Scotland, even though the high point of his activities occurred in [his] second winter in Switzerland" (24).

17. Osbourne's press was broken in transit from Davos to Kingussie, Scotland, and could not be repaired, a quite literal breakdown of the press ventures. *The Graver and the Pen*, then, was printed in fact by a Mr. Crerar, who had a press in the local general store (Hart 42).

18. A number of nineteenth-century critics, writers, and publishers initiated a countermovement of morally upright boys' literature. The Religious Tract Society, for example, initiated the *Boy's Own Paper* specifically to counteract the unsavory influence of such literature. However, the influence of the penny dreadful became entrenched in daredevil characters such as Jack Harkaway (Nelson 126).

19. The Society for Promoting Christian Knowledge published a number of books of instruction in this model, including *Natural History of Quadrupeds* and the *Life of Nelson and Mungo Park's Travels*, and the Religious Tract Society followed suit with a series that included titles such as "The Animalcule" and "The Ant" (Bratton 103). J. M. Barrie parodies this instructional, scientific tone in *Boy Castaways of Black Lake Island* (1901), when young George encounters a tree that he "at once recognised . . . to be the Mango (*Mangifera Indica*) by its lancet-shaped leaves and the cucumber-shaped fruit."

20. Children adopted a range of adventure tales as their own, regardless of the authors' intentions. In *Juvenile Literature As It Is* (1888), Edward Salmon ranked boys' and girls' favorite books and authors based on the responses of 790 children. The boys' top authors include Charles Dickens, Kingston, Scott, Jules Verne, Marryat, Ballantyne, and—further down the list—Kingsley. Girls' top authors include some of the same writers, namely Dickens, Scott, Verne, Kingston, and Kingsley. For a reproduction of Salmon's rankings, see Jonathan Rose. I discuss Salmon's work in more detail in Chapter Three. Later, in April 1908, the periodical *The Captain: A Magazine for Boys and Old Boys*, published a survey of 800 readers that ranks the twelve best boys' books ever published. *Treasure Island* earns second place, followed by *Robinson Crusoe* and *Westward Ho!* by Kingsley. *King Solomon's Mines*, *Coral Island*, *Last of the Mohicans*, and Marryat's *Mr. Midshipman Easy* also appear (Richards 8).

21. For different perspectives on the success of the serialized *Treasure Island*, see David Angus, who notes that the "young folks in question . . . were neither entertained nor amused, and said so" (83). Also see Jason A. Pierce, who argues that after initial

negative reactions by young readers in the correspondence section of *Young Folks*, endorsements of the story-in-progress by editors and reviewers illustrated "the editorial staff's enthusiasm for the story and the readers' changing attitudes" (363).

22. *Treasure Island* was not Stevenson's first book. "But I am well aware," he writes, that "the great public, regards what else I have written with indifference, if not aversion" ("First" 277). Before *Treasure Island*, Stevenson published a number of books, including his travel memoirs: *An Inland Voyage* (1878) and *Travels with a Donkey in the Cévennes* (1879), as well as some essay collections.

23. For a discussion of the influence of popular boys' stories on *Treasure Island*, see Watson or Hardesty and Mann.

24. Osbourne, who would struggle with not wholly positive reviews of his own fiction, writes that his stepfather, before *Treasure Island*, "was an unknown and unsuccessful author . . . who wrote books that never passed beyond one small edition, and whose gay acquiescence in failure cost me many a childish pang" ("Note" ix).

25. Amy Wong also examines the collaborative storytelling scenes at Braemar, focusing on the co-creative dynamics of what she calls Stevenson's poetics of talk. For an extensive treatment of how Stevenson's writing, including *Treasure Island* but especially *Strange Case of Dr. Jekyll and Mr. Hyde*, was affected by his relationship with his father, see Beattie.

26. It is interesting to note two additional maps. The first Stevenson created when the original was lost on its way to the publisher. Stevenson notes that this replacement "somehow was never *Treasure Island* to me," lamenting that "it is one thing to draw a map at random, set a scale in one corner of it at a venture, and write up a story to the measurements. It is quite another to have to examine a whole book, make an inventory of all the allusions contained in it, and with a pair of compasses painfully design a map to suit the data" ("First" 282–83). The second is an edited map Livesey gives Silver on their approach to the island so the sea cook can help steer the ship ashore—a document that does not include directions to the treasure. These maps, I argue, are robbed of their narrative possibility because they are not collaborative; the multiple hands of both are replaced by a single hand.

27. This quotation comes from Letters to Young Friends, a series of stories about Samoa by Stevenson published in *St. Nicholas* between December 1895 and February 1896, after the author's death—another example of the pair's collaboration (in this case posthumous). Osbourne edited the letters, wrote an introduction, and included commentary throughout.

28. Stevenson reproduces this vacillation between adult and child in the narrative structure of *Treasure Island*, a story split between the narration of Jim, who recounts the bulk of the tale, and Livesey, who intervenes to narrate chapters sixteen through eighteen. Livesey's narration creates a disruption in the text; a reader grown accustomed to Jim's narration—who for fifteen chapters has read the "I" as belonging to the boy—must self-consciously redefine the first person as the adult doctor. Indeed, this confusion is present throughout the text, even in those early chapters told by Jim. His narration is similarly divided between adult and child, for while he relates an adventure

he experienced as a boy, he does so from the position of an adult remembering his youth. Jim is, as Fiona McCulloch notes, "a [child] hero who is, in effect, a masquerading adult" (75). For a different perspective on the split narration of *Treasure Island*—and in particular the conflict between the child Jim and the "cruel, greedy, emotionless, and quick to punish" adulthood represented by Dr. Livesey (3)—see Valint.

29. Huish is referring to *Ministering Children: A Tale Dedicated to Childhood* (1854), by Maria Louisa Charlesworth. It is a pious book meant to teach young people sympathy for the poor.

30. Vanessa Smith similarly notes the failure of collaboration between Herrick, Huish, and Davis at the beginning of *The Ebb-Tide*, noting that "the types of narration and writing in which the three beachcombers . . . engage fail to achieve authority, and are fragmentary and self-enclosed" (272).

31. This *Saturday Review* piece is, however, more circumspect than other reviews in that the critic is not quick to dismiss Osbourne and valorize Stevenson. "Mr. Stevenson's writings have accustomed us to a standard of excellence which few living writers of fiction can be said to have attained," the reviewer writes. "Of Mr. Lloyd Osbourne, as a writer, we know nothing, except in the elusive conditions presented by his association now and previously with Mr. Stevenson. He is therefore, possibly, placed at a disadvantage. . . . Mr. Osbourne . . . may conceivably be in some danger of being credited with Mr. Stevenson's lapses" (330).

32. Despite such comparisons and scathing reviews—the *Critic*, for example, found nothing kind to say about *Baby Bullet* apart from noting it contains "a great many exclamation points" (579)—Osbourne was a moderately successful author, and some commentators in his lifetime suspected that his relationship with Stevenson obscured the younger writer's talents. "It is difficult to estimate the place in literature of one whose connections are so distinguished," notes the *National Cyclopaedia of American Biography* in 1910. "In this instance, mention of Mr. Osbourne inevitably suggests Stevenson, and brings to memory that master's witchery of style" ("Osbourne" 459).

33. Years later, in 1949, Morley would call Osbourne an "unspoiled little innocent" and claim he was "perhaps the greatest American boy (barefoot, with cheek) since Whittier and Mark Twain" (89–90). Obviously, Osbourne's reputation as a child persisted long after Stevenson claimed he had lost his youthfulness.

34. The typescript is held at the Robert Louis Stevenson Museum in St. Helena, California. It includes the script and set designs for four of the five acts. The third act does not include an illustrated set design. Perhaps Strong did not include a design for this act, but it seems more likely that this illustration is missing.

35. Strong later would establish a career as a playwright on Broadway. He is most known for his play *Seventh Heaven*, which was adapted into a film starring Simone Simon and James Stewart.

36. I presume the small notations are Strong's because the handwriting in this marginalia matches the signatures and dates included under his set design illustrations.

37. For a discussion of illustrations of Stevenson's *Treasure Island*, and the manner in which illustrated editions of the novel borrow both from one another and from earlier texts about pirates, see Eidam.

38. In the typescript, the name "Ruth" in this sentence was not in the original typed dialogue but instead added in pen above a dash.

39. The pair possibly collaborated on a third play titled *The Drums of Oude*. Scripts of this play feature only Strong's name as author; however, Strong mentions in an interview that he wrote the play with Osbourne ("Chat" X1).

CHAPTER THREE
COLLABORATING WITH THE AUTHORITIES:
CHILDREN AS AUTHORS, EXPERTS, AND CRITICS

1. For examples of scholars' responses to Hunt's childist criticism at the time of its publication in the early 1980s, see Kelly-Byrne and Schmidt. For more recent responses, see Nodelman's *The Hidden Adult* (esp. 84–85), Chapleau, and the introduction to Nikolajeva's *Power, Voice, and Subjectivity in Literature for Young Readers*.

2. Hunt concedes that "simply to invite adults to read as children is scarcely novel, and is likely to revive all the old prejudices. Rather, we have to challenge all our assumptions very thoroughly" (45).

3. For an example of how sentimentality and nostalgia creep into Craik's essay, consider her conclusion, which is a mourning for lost youth: "The season is gone by, for us grown people at least, when glamour was over all the world," she writes, "when everybody seemed so good and so beautiful, and from others as well as from ourselves we expected the noblest deeds" ("Age" 163).

4. Nikolajeva's study is wide-ranging, incorporating children's texts from all over the world, both historic and contemporary. She does discuss some Victorian and Edwardian authors, in particular George MacDonald, E. Nesbit, and Lewis Carroll, whose *Alice's Adventures in Wonderland*, she writes, "is one of the rare texts [in Western children's literature] that, instead of empowering the fictional child through displacement in an alternative world, explicitly disempowers and even humiliates her" (33).

5. Claudia Nelson explores age inversion plots in detail in *Precocious Children and Childlike Adults: Age Inversion in Victorian Literature*.

6. *Holiday Romance* ran from January through May 1868, during the latter part of Dickens's 1867–1868 American tour. The February 1868 number of *Our Young Folks* did not include a segment of *Holiday Romance*, which was published in four parts. Dickens had published only one text written specifically for children: *A Child's History of England*, an ambitious project published in *Household Words* between January 1851 and December 1853 that children have never enjoyed according to Gillian Avery, because "it is too complicated for recreational reading . . . and too subversive (and inaccurate) to be prescribed by pedagogues" (xxiv). *The Life of Our Lord*, which Dickens wrote in 1848 for his own children, was not intended for circulation and was published posthumously in 1934.

7. In each installment, the header "By Charles Dickens" appears below the title, but that name is always followed by a second attribution—for example, "Romance. From

the Pen of Miss Nettie Ashford"—which includes an asterisk indicating the author's age—in this case, "half-past six."

8. Alice Rainbird's fairy tale has earned more favor among the critics; it has been reprinted in anthologies of Victorian fantasy literature as "The Magic Fish-Bone" and rewritten in more contemporary literature for children. Nicole Bacile di Castiglione is more forgiving and calls *Holiday Romance* a "final witty ploy in an engaging battle in favour of imagination and of a healthy use of fantasy" (154).

9. Dickens was particularly enamored with Redforth's pirate adventure. "You must try to like the pirate story," he writes to John Forster, "for I am very fond of it" (*Letters* 11.387). He expressed similar favoritism to James Fields: "I should like to be beside you when you read . . . the Pirate's story. It made me laugh to that extent that my people thought I was out of my wits, until I gave it to them to read—when they did likewise" (*Letters* 11.403).

10. Barrie uses the phrase "at last" here because *Peter Pan*, while first performed onstage in 1904, was not printed in script form until 1928. Barrie novelized the story as *Peter and Wendy*, published in 1911. For a concise textual history of the Peter Pan story, see Hollindale's introduction, x–xiii.

11. Leonée Ormond notes Barrie "was always prepared to listen to the actors, and, if appropriate, to change his mind. A Barrie play was a collaboration among cast, director and playwright: never finally completed, the texts were always open to revision" (Hollindale x). Critics have noted Barrie's aptitude at collaboration; Hollindale, for example, notes that "Barrie was a highly professional dramatist, for whom the collaborative nature of theatrical performance was one of the attractions which drew him to it from the novel" (x).

12. Barrie is the subject of a critical tradition that celebrates his childlike spirit; for example, Max Beerbohm's 1905 review of *Peter* in *The Saturday Review* calls Barrie "a child who, by some divine grace, can express through an artistic medium the childishness that is in him" (13). However, despite a widespread celebration of Barrie's youthful nature, there is evidence that he felt keenly a separation from his own boyhood and youth in general. A number of elements of Barrie's biography contribute to this sense of isolation. Much has been made, for example, of the early death of Barrie's brother, David, at the age of thirteen. David is an early inspiration for the character of Peter, and many of Barrie's works can be read as an attempt to recapture the boyhood of David, who became increasingly distant as Barrie aged. See Birkin, Chapter 1. Moreover, Barrie's desire for child companionship was thwarted by his childless marriage, and he tried to reconnect with the child world by intruding upon the Llewelyn Davies family. This isolation from childhood works on a larger, cultural scale as well. Critics have long noted how Barrie's works are variations upon this theme of lost childhood. Kincaid argues that *Peter Pan* is "usually received as a bittersweet piece of nostalgia, a self-protective lament for the remoteness of the child that creates that very distance" (*Child-Loving* 279).

13. Hollindale, for example, reads the dedication as one of a series of "disingenuous hide-and-seek games of an author who was never able to conceal himself," a "mock

self-abnegation" that ultimately fails, as Barrie "remains a strong, ostensibly self-denying, but actually conspicuous intermediate persona between his creation and their audience" (xviii). And Rose, of course, uses Barrie's squeamishness about *Peter*'s authorship as the centerpiece of her famous study about children's literature as a product of adult desire.

14. Gubar's *"Peter Pan* as Children's Theatre: The Issue of Audience" is an important exception (see esp. 483). Stirling also considers the ways Barrie references the collaborative nature of *Peter Pan* in the play and its paratexts, writing that, for Barrie, "storytelling is a communal rather than an individual action, that stories cannot exist until they have been told and retold, with the listener participating as actively as the teller" (14).

15. Charles Turley Smith once wrote to Barrie, "'I am always glad to see your writing tho' I cannot read it.'" Barrie frequently chuckled at his horrible penmanship; in a 1918 letter to his godson Peter Scott, Barrie jokes, "Your mother thinks I do not write clearly, but I expect this is jealousy" (*Letters* 67, 50).

16. Birkin reproduces this contact on p. 99 of *J. M. Barrie and the Lost Boys*, and Barrie references it in his dedication: "You watched . . . my next play with peeled eyes, not for entertainment but lest it contained some chance witticism of yours that could be challenged as collaboration; indeed I believe there still exists a legal document, full of the Aforesaid and Henceforward to be called Part-Author, in which for some such snatching I was tied down to pay No. 2 one halfpenny daily throughout the run of the piece" (77).

17. In 1929 Barrie donated the rights of *Peter Pan* to London's Great Ormond Street Hospital, which holds them and benefits from the popularity of the play to date. In 1987, fifty years after Barrie's death, the copyright expired, but former prime minister Lord Callaghan amended the Copyright Designs and Patents Act of 1988 to grant *Peter Pan* a unique, extended copyright in perpetuity. In the United States, the play is under copyright until 2023.

18. The image appears again in *Peter and Wendy* (1911), the prose version of *Peter*, in which a grown-up Wendy considers Peter "no more than . . . a little dust in the box in which she kept her toys" (220).

19. *Boy Castaways* records the adventures of three brothers: George, Jack, and Peter, Nos. 1, 2, and 3, respectively. Michael, No. 4, is quite young in the summer of 1901, having been born in June 1900, and No. 5, Nico, was not born until 1903.

20. I am restricting my analysis to Barrie's dedication and similar texts *about* the play. However, *Peter Pan* itself exhibits similar ambivalence about the creative child—Peter himself. Peter, like the Llewelyn Davies brothers, is a child adept at seizing adult authority. He can imitate any noise, including Hook's voice. See act 2, scene 1, in which Peter, ventriloquizing Hook, convinces pirates Smee and Starkey that the real Captain Hook is nothing but a codfish. Peter's ability to seize adult authority, in fact, ends the play; his triumph in the final battle is signaled by his definitive appropriation of Hook's command. The battle ends, and *"the curtain rises to show Peter a very Napoleon on his ship,"* note the stage directions. *"It must not rise again lest we see him on the poop in Hook's hat and cigars, with a small iron claw"* (226–28). Many performances and film

adaptations stage this scene despite the narrator's instructions to hide Peter's transformation. In fact, in *Peter and Wendy*, Peter's metamorphosis is much more extensive. Peter asks Wendy to make him a set of clothes "out of some of Hook's wickedest garments," and it is rumored that Peter "sat long in the cabin with Hook's cigar-holder in his mouth and one hand clenched, all but the forefinger, which he bent and held threateningly aloft like a hook" (206–7). See also Hsiao, who reads the battle between Peter and Hook as a conflict between Peter as a character associated with orality and Hook as "an obsessively literate character" (156).

21. For more child responses to *Peter Pan*, see *Peter Pan's Postbag* (1909), by Pauline Chase.

22. To be fair, any critic, young or old, is subject to outside influence, although admittedly the power dynamics of adult-child relationships exacerbate the problem. In fact, in "Among the Toys," a critic in the *Examiner and London Review* recognizes that his wariness about the judgment of child reviewers extends to grown people as well, writing that the "multitude of the young can no more than the multitude of their elders be permitted to give the word of command to literature" (307).

23. Large sections of *Juvenile Literature As It Is* appeared previously in Salmon's essays for popular periodicals, including *The Fortnightly Review*, *The Nineteenth Century*, and *Atalanta*. See Carrington.

24. Salmon, then, takes the approach that Gubar recommends to contemporary scholars of childhood and children's literature: one of "cautious humility" that recognizes the limitations of what we can know about children's experiences but does not allow the inevitable tentative and fractional nature of our knowledge to paralyze inquiry (*Peter* 479).

25. Jackie Horne concludes her book *History and the Construction of the Child in Early British Children's Literature* with a consideration of Salmon's study and especially the girl readers' results. She pays attention to the types of "boys' books" female readers listed as favorites, noting the absence of robinsonades and the prevalence of historical romance. "Did the lack of female characters in the typical Victorian robinsonade, in contrast to their common presence in the historical romance (at least as love interests, if not as adventurers themselves) contribute to this difference?" (243).

26. In 1906 Florence B. Low published in *The Nineteenth Century* a survey that resembles Salmon's titled "The Reading of the Modern Girl." Low sent surveys to "some two hundred girls, between fifteen and eighteen years of age, who attend secondary schools in different parts of England." Low takes some precautions against bias that Salmon does not; she notes that the responses "may be regarded as genuine expressions of opinion, for the papers sent in were accompanied by no names, and the girls were told that their own teachers would not read the lists" (279). However, unlike Salmon, Low includes only four open-ended questions (such as "Which are your favorite novels?" and "Do you read magazines? If so, which?"). The remaining questions, which ask the young women to reveal if they've read the work of particular authors (such as Dickens, Jane Austen, Elizabeth Gaskell, and William Thackeray) are extremely directive and reveal the questioner's standards of literary value.

27. Under Hewins's leadership, the Hartford Public Library was the first in the United States to feature separate reading rooms for children. For a description of the opening of these rooms in 1904, as well as an account of Hewins's efforts to improve resources and services for children at the library, see her article "How Library Work with Children Has Grown in Hartford and Connecticut." See also Lundin and Vandegrift.

28. Hewins also cites an example of consulting child critics in "How Library Work with Children Has Grown in Hartford and Connecticut." There, she describes how she directed a curious patron to "the records kept for years by the North School children of books which they have read, and sent to the librarian to be commented on and criticized in an hour's friendly talk in the school room" (94).

29. The schools that HMIs inspected served primarily poor and working-class students. Therefore, these reports, for the most part, do not account for the educational experiences of the upper classes. However, the reports I cite in this chapter do account for a variety of institutions and students: male and female students in both coed and single-sex learning environments, rural and urban schools, and those affiliated with the Church of England and a spectrum of other religious institutions. From this point forward, as I mention individual inspectors, I will include endnotes indicating the schools they were responsible for examining.

30. Attaching critical government funding to attendance was particularly trying in the 1860s, because attendance would not even begin to become compulsory until the Elementary Education Act of 1870. Therefore, many students, especially those whose income or domestic work was necessary for their family's survival, attended school only sporadically.

31. The government had begun funding education in the 1830s. Prior to this funding, schools operated on donations and voluntary support (Tollers 108). Collins William Lucas, describing in January 1862 the growing expense of educating the poor in particular, noted that if "the present system ... goes on, it will amount in the course of time to—nobody knows what; two millions, three millions" (78).

32. Brookfield was responsible for inspecting the Church of England schools in the counties of Kent, Surrey, Sussex, and the Channel Islands. Additional subjects were added to examinations in subsequent codes. From 1867, for example, subjects such as geography and history were included (Rose, *Erosion* 119).

33. Many, but not all, HMIs opposed the Code. They were particularly angry that Lowe did not take into account their experiences in the schools while formulating his policy. See Horn, "Robert Lowe and the HM Inspectorate."

34. Coleridge's essay recalls Edgar Taylor's preface to *German Popular Stories*, which argues for admitting fairy tales into children's nurseries that otherwise have, under the influence of reason, produced "lisping chemists and leading-string mathematicians" (iv).

35. Alderson was responsible for the British and other Protestant schools not connected with the Church of England in the counties of Bedford, Cambridge, Derby, Huntingdon, Leicester, Lincoln, Norfolk, Northampton, Nottingham, and Suffolk. Arnold was responsible for the British and other schools not connected with the

Church of England in the counties of Berks, Bucks, Essex, Herts, Kent, Middlesex, and Oxford.

36. The bursting Tomtoddies reflect a fear in the final decades of the 1800s that working-class children were dying of overpressure from the stress of their studies. See "Education and Insanity" for a contemporary view of overpressure. Galbraith also discusses the phenomenon in Chapter 7 of *Reading Lives*. The parallel becomes even clearer in the epitaph one of the fairies in *The Water-Babies* composes for a burst Tomtoddy:

> Instruction sore long time I bore,
> And cramming was in vain;
> Till heaven did please my woes to cease,
> With water on the brain. (305)

37. Stokes was responsible for the Roman Catholic schools in the counties of Chester, Cumberland, Derby, Flint, Lancaster, Salop, and Stafford.

38. Lionel Rose outlines "the absurdities inflicted by the worst kind of inspectors, who seemed to enjoy catching children out," noting in particular an inspector in the 1880s who "dictated to infants a passage beginning 'While Hugh was culling yew, his ewes...'" (124).

39. Bellairs was responsible for the Church of England schools in the counties of Gloucester, Hereford, Monmouth, Oxford, Warwick, and Worcester.

40. Much of Catherine Robson's compelling study *Heart Beats: Everyday Life and the Memorized Poem* (2012) is dedicated to parsing schoolchildren's lived and embodied experiences of reciting poetry in classrooms in the United States and England in the nineteenth and twentieth centuries. She mines autobiographies, textbooks, educational history, and fiction for evidence of those experiences and considers both reluctant and eager young orators. On the one hand, for the nervous student, "the anticipation, and then the actuality, of performance would likely be attended by the fear, or at least the anxiety, of failure—and thus palpitations, clammy palms, shaking legs, and pounding hearts were part and parcel of the genre in a testing environment" (112). The relationship between pupil and teacher in this case was largely antagonistic, perhaps, and shadowed by the threat of corporal punishment. Others remember childhood recitations fondly as opportunities to luxuriate in poetic language and demonstrate academic achievement. In either case, recitation, Robson contends, is "an educational praxis that made a profound physical and emotional connection between the literature it assigned and the bodies that read that literature" (95).

41. Gordon was responsible for schools connected with the Church of Scotland and other schools in the counties of Ayr, Dumfries, Kirkbudbright, Lanark, Renfrew, and Wigton. Wilson visited schools connected with the Free Church and other schools inspected in the west of Scotland and in the Western Isles. Stewart inspected the Church of England schools in the counties of Bedford, Buckingham, Cambridge, Hertford, and Huntington.

42. The Elementary Education Act of 1870 was written by William Forster, Arnold's brother-in-law. The voluntary and religious societies that sponsored the majority of schools throughout England in the early nineteenth century were given six months to supply the "deficiency in school places" before a school board would be established to build board schools in their district (Rich 90). The Act also instituted what Eric E. Rich calls "permissive powers of compulsion" (93). School boards were not required to formulate bylaws requiring attendance, and if they did, such requirements could neither override the balance of work and half-time schooling mandated by the Factory Acts nor, assumedly, trump family obligations, such as girls' responsibilities to tend to younger siblings. Many argued for adjusting the ages stated in compulsory education policies so children would be required to stay in school longer; however, the Earl of Shaftesbury amended the bill to allow the partial exemption even of children over the age of ten who achieved a certain standard of education. "Thus," notes Rich, "after the age of ten, education was subordinated to the demands of employers and the needs of parents for their children's wages" (94). While this attendance policy may seem permissive, "this was by design," argues Nigel Middleton, "for Forster had framed a deceptively mild measure, so that he could introduce the tip of the wedge of universal compulsory education" (172). Complete compulsory education in England would be established in 1880.

43. For Rands on compulsory education, see his essay "School Board Comedies" (1873), written under the pseudonym Angelo Merritt Gray. There, he worries that such policies have a disproportionate impact on the poor, who need the income of children, and signals undue government intervention into family life. "It is, indeed, desirable that every child should be well taught," he writes, "but not at the cost of sending the policeman into every home, and setting magistrates to flog little boys and girls who play truant. . . . Hadn't you better take children from their parents altogether, and feed, clothe, and educate them by Act of Parliament from first to last? That is what it must come to, if we go on like this" (292–93).

CHAPTER FOUR
PICTURES OF PARTNERSHIP: ART EDUCATION,
CHILDREN'S LITERATURE, AND THE RISE OF THE CHILD ARTIST

1. See the American Museum of Natural History's digital Darwin Manuscripts Project. The online archive provides access to a range of manuscript and published materials relating to Darwin and his family, including digital scans of Darwin's manuscripts and journals as well as many drawings by his children.

2. Darwin himself often wrote on the reverse sides of his notes and manuscript pages, a practice Francis laments. "He had a pet economy in paper," Francis writes, "but it was rather a hobby than a real economy. All the blank sheets of letters received were kept in a portfolio to be used in making notes; it was his respect for paper that made him write so much on the backs of his old MS., and in this way, unfortunately, he destroyed large parts of the original MS of his books. His feeling about paper extended

to wastepaper, and he objected, half in fun, to the habit of throwing a spill into the fire after it had been used for lighting a candle" (121).

3. The Darwin Manuscript Project's curators have labeled this piece "Drawing: Aubergine and Carrot Cavalry."

4. Francis records at least one instance of this in *The Life and Letters of Charles Darwin*. He notes that his father "was fond of quoting the saying of one of his little boys, who, having found a grass that his father had not seen before, had laid it by his own plate during dinner, remarking, 'I are an extraordinary grass-finder!'" (94). The Darwin children were, moreover, scientific subjects. Darwin carefully observed his growing sons and daughters as he formulated his theory of evolution. See Keynes, *Darwin, His Daughter, and Human Evolution*.

5. As many art historians and other scholars have noted, the phrase "child art" is relatively modern. Many—including Wilhelm Viola, Arthur D. Efland, and Donna Darling Kelly—credit Franz Cizek, whom I discuss later in this chapter, with coining the phrase. For ease of reference, I often use this phrase in its simplest sense to refer to art by children. However, others are more exacting. Viola, for example, writes, "The term 'Child Art' itself is very young. Two generations ago nobody dreamt that every child is born an artist, which does not mean that every child should or could become an artist. The discovery of Child Art is parallel with, or perhaps a consequence of, the discovery of the child as a human being with his own personality and his own particular laws" (7).

6. Francis would later enter the natural sciences himself and collaborate with Darwin as a botanist. Beginning in his mid-twenties, in 1874, he spent eight years as an assistant and secretary to his father. In 1880 the two published the results of some of their work together as *The Power of Movement in Plants*; the title page reads "By Charles Darwin assisted by Francis Darwin." See Junker.

7. I agree with Sutton that Rousseau's work was, in many ways, prophetic of upcoming changes in art education. However, as the remainder of this section will demonstrate, I believe Rousseau's more visionary ideas would begin to resurface in the 1890s, earlier than Sutton suggests.

8. Wealthier children—especially boys attending public schools such as Eton, Charterhouse, Harrow, and Rugby—experienced a different sort of art education. At those institutions, drawing usually consisted of lessons in landscapes and perspective and was considered an "extra," taught by a resident teacher. Some of these schools, however, adopted the design- and industry-focused methods of middle-class schools. Shrewsbury, for example, encouraged boys with hopes of a career in engineering or surveying by excusing them from some of their schoolwork so they could attend the School of Design, where linear and geometric methods dominated art pedagogy. See Sutton, 86–89.

9. Kelly describes new approaches to child art in the latter half of the nineteenth century and the beginning of the twentieth as the Mirror paradigm, in which children's drawings are understood primarily as clues to the young artist's psychology, and the Window paradigm, in which child art is appreciated aesthetically. While these

paradigms are useful in considering changing attitudes toward young artists, I do not see their boundaries as firmly as Kelly suggests they are.

10. In his list of occupations, Froebel explains that in "pea work" students use "small pointed sticks" to join "soaked and softened peas, to form skeleton three-dimensional constructions" (Lawrence 239).

11. Werner Hofmann points out that a similar position is articulated in the eighteenth century by Sir Joshua Reynolds in his third discourse on art (6). Reynolds argues that artists

> must have recourse to the Ancients as instructors. It is from a careful study of their works that you will be enabled to attain to the real simplicity of nature.... And, indeed, I cannot help suspecting, that in this instance the Ancients had an easier task than the moderns. They had, probably, little or nothing to unlearn, as their manners were nearly approaching to this desirable simplicity; while the modern artist, before he can see the truth of things, is obliged to remove a veil, with which the fashion of the times has thought proper to cover her. (49)

12. The *Alternative Syllabus* is usually attributed to Cooke, although it was published by the Science in Art Department. How much of the syllabus and the drawing exercises and examples included in its pages were truly the work of Cooke is debated and, as far as I can discover, undetermined. See Sutton, 153.

13. For a summary of each speaker's contribution, see Kelly, Chapter 7, and Carline, Chapter 11.

14. Ricci's work was translated by Louise Maitland as "The Art of Little Children" and published, in part, in the 1894 volume of *Pedagogical Seminary*.

15. Barnes was an American Child Study scholar, serving for a time as head of the Department of the History and Art of Education at Stanford University. However, ideas in this field circulated transatlantically.

16. Child Study scholars make similar observations about imitation and invention regarding children's language acquisition. See Chapter 1.

17. Wilhelm Viola, in his published work on child art and Franz Cizek, produces what he claims to be transcribed dialogues between Cizek and the pupils of the Juvenile Art Class. These conversations betray art lessons that are sometimes laissez-faire, sometimes directive.

18. Macready's illustrations are archived in the Armstrong Browning Library at Baylor University in Waco, Texas, and reprinted in that library's catalogue of its Pied Piper holdings. See Herring.

19. For examples of later printings of Browning's "The Pied Piper" in which adult illustrators represent the fabulous land where the Piper leads Hamelin's children, see Kate Greenaway's illustrations for the 1888 edition for Routledge, which includes a famous image of the Piper playing for white-robed children as they dance around a flowering tree, an image later used for the cover of an edition published by Frederick Warne. Hope Dunlap's illustrations for a 1910 Rand McNally edition include interior

illustrations of this scene as well as an illustration of children riding winged horses in its endpapers. Margaret W. Tarrant's illustrations for a 1912 edition published by J. M. Dent include children chasing after "sparrows . . . brighter than peacocks."

20. This story, in rewriting the disciplined child as oppressed subject, resembles "The Little Victims," a story included in Gatty's *Aunt Judy's Tales* (1859) and discussed in Chapter 1. Gatty's daughter Juliana Ewing similarly would use her own literature for children to foster children's knowledge of the adult project of storytelling and the potential for children's agency through appropriation, revision, and narration. See Marah Gubar, "Revising the Seduction Paradigm: The Case of Ewing's *The Brownies*" (*Children's Literature* 30).

21. While Jordan is an American author, his representations of child art are relevant to my discussion of the same phenomenon in the United Kingdom. While I have not been able to locate any reviews of Jordan's book in British periodicals, it was published in the United Kingdom and is referenced in *British Books in Print*. (British Periodicals did, however, review Jordan's writings in science and politics.) Moreover, in a general sense, Child Study—a field important to the book's publication—was a transatlantic (and, really, an international) endeavor.

22. Jordan had the opportunity to meet Maitland and Hawley because in 1891 he was appointed the first president of Stanford University, where the two women were studying; he would serve in that office until 1913. Maitland's publications on child art include her much-cited translation of Corrado Ricci's *L'arte dei Bambini* in *Pedagogical Seminary* in 1894; "Children's Drawings" (1895), published in the *Pacific Education Journal*; and "What Children Draw to Please Themselves" (1895), published in *The Inland Educator*.

23. The Child Study community was eager to investigate these drawings. Before *The Book of Knight and Barbara* was published, Barnes reproduced one of Jordan's stories, "Perseus and Medusa," and its accompanying illustrations in *Studies in Education*, appending to the story "commentary and questions by the editor," including, "What light do these drawings . . . throw upon the impression made upon her mind by the story?" (343). Some reviews of Jordan's book echo Barnes's questions almost verbatim; for example, one reviewer in the *New York Mail and Express* writes, "some of these crude drawings are remarkably interesting for the light they throw upon the young mind and its workings" (D. Appleton).

24. Jordan acknowledges Grimm in his story "How the Prince Learned Something New," which is an adaptation of "The Story of the Youth Who Went Forth to Learn What Fear Was," and he acknowledges an "Ancient Document" in his poem "How We Captured Troy."

25. While Jordan does not include much information about individual contributors in *The Book of Knight and Barbara* itself, at times other sources that comment upon that book offer clues as to the identities of its artists and writers. For example, Earl Barnes, in his commentary in *Studies in Education* before the publication of Jordan's book, identifies the artist of the illustrations and captions for the Perseus and Medusa story as "a girl of twelve, who had no teaching in drawing, but who had drawn and read

a good deal" (342). In his memoir—*The Days of a Man, Being Memories of a Naturalist, Teacher and Minor Prophet of Democracy*—Jordan notes that "the quaintest sketches were largely by [John Lord] Jenkins' daughter Alice; the most finished, by Seward Wrathburn, son of my old friend at the Smithsonian" (569). However, read independently of these sources, *The Book of Knight and Barbara* is mute on the names and ages of its child artists.

26. In his memoir, Jordan continued his interest in young people's reactions to his stories. There, he includes a few snippets of child readers' purported assessments of *The Book of Knight and Barbara*. "A little girl at Edmonton, Alberta, declared the collection to be 'perfectly jake, perfectly peachy,'" he writes. "But the little daughter of a Boston friend remarked 'What a pity they let those California children spoil this nice book!' And a Chicago child, still more critical, asked if 'Dr. Jordan spent his time thinking up such things as that!'" (569–70). Adult critics and reviewers tended to receive the book very well, and it remained in print until at least 1929.

27. For a consideration of the relationship between image and text in the *Just So Stories*, see Liu. For a critique of Knoepflmacher's reading of the Taffy tales, see Walsh, Chapters 3 and 4.

28. Such moments of childlike adulthood are not unique to the captions of the *Just So Stories*, in which the boundaries of adulthood and childhood are porous. The Mariner in "How the Whale Got His Throat," for example, "had his Mummy's leave to paddle, or else he would never have done it, because he was a man of infinite-resource-and-sagacity" (2–3). Shires also comments on the narrator's complex childlike/adult position in these captions. See 198.

29. For bibliographic information on these painting books and other illustrated adaptations of Kipling's *Just So Stories*, see Alderson.

30. Routledge published *Walter Crane's Painting Book* in 1880. Caldecott's illustrations were transformed into outlines and posthumously published by Warne in at least three series under the title *Randolph Caldecott's Painting Book* (1901–1902).

31. An extreme example of the activity book's ability to inspire invention rather than imitation is Susan Striker's Anti-Coloring Book series, which she began publishing in 1978. Striker claims that traditional coloring books "inhibit a child's natural inventiveness with drawings that simply require him or her to color within the lines someone else has drawn," and she created her series, full of books comprised of blank or sparsely illustrated pages accompanied by prompts meant to encourage children to invent their own drawings ("Anti"). Striker's series, and her attitudes toward child art, provide one interesting endpoint to the history of Victorian ideas about children's art outlined in this chapter. For more information about nineteenth-century art materials and painting books, see Menefee, "Art and Data," and Smith, "Art Critics in the Cradle."

32. Nineteenth-century reviewers made similar comments on the challenge of the *textual* aspects of Lear's nonsense. A reviewer for *The Times* wrote in 1871 that "nothing is more difficult" than to write nonsense, and another in the 1876 volume of the *Examiner* argues that a "'great many attempts have been made to imitate what seems

to be so easy' and have failed" (Colley, *Critics* 3). Contemporary scholars also comment upon the studied childlike character of Lear's nonsense drawings. See Richard Dalby, who calls Lear's work "deceptively simple," with a "childish spontaneity" (19); Herman W. Liebert, who notes these drawings are "like the work of a gifted child" (22); and Lisa Ede, who argues that the illustrations' "apparent naiveté mask an underlying design of great subtlety" and that "it is a sign of his success that his illustrations are often compared to children's drawings" (113).

33. However, Lear did create many of his nonsense alphabets, limericks, stories, and drawings for particular children. For example, he composed the first *Book of Nonsense* for the children at Knowsley, the estate of the Earl of Derby, where he was commissioned to create an accurate visual record of the birds and animals in the estate's menagerie. Lear recognizes that first audience in the dedication to the 1861 edition, which was published under his own name (rather than under his pseudonym Derry Down Derry). The time that had elapsed since his stay at Knowsley in the 1830s required that he address the family's subsequent generations: "To the great-grandchildren, grand-nephews, and grand-nieces of Edward, 13th Earl of Derby, this book of drawings and verses (The greater part of which was originally made and composed for their parents,) is dedicated by the author, Edward Lear." He composed his most famous poem, "The Owl and the Pussycat," for Janet Symonds, the daughter of John Addington Symonds, and gave three fair copies to other children. And Margaret Terry Chanler—who befriended Lear as a child when her family was traveling in San Remo—remembers how Lear left her and her brother letters for a nonsense alphabet on their plates at luncheon, which they then assembled into a book (Chanler 29–30).

34. For example, Colley argues that looking at Lear's professional painting of a spectacled owl alongside the owlish "Old Person of Crowle" in *More Nonsense, Pictures, Rhymes, Botany, Etc.* (1872) reveals both the "human quality that lurks within the bird's face" in the former and the "half-human appearance" of the latter; each image illuminates the implicit quality of the other ("Edward Lear's" 288–89).

35. The birds created for Baring's son were also published on their own as *The Lear Coloured Bird Book for Children* in 1912, and they were only one series of such drawings. Lear made three similar sets of colored birds: one in 1863 for Mary de Vere, one in 1880 for "the little Fentons," and another in 1880 for Charles Geffrard Pirouet.

36. Lear's nonsense botany was published in *Nonsense Songs, Stories, Botany, and Alphabets* (1871); *More Nonsense Pictures, Rhymes, Botany, Etc.* (1872); and *Laughable Lyrics: A Fourth Book of Nonsense Poems, Songs, Botany, Music, &c.* (1877). His nonsense trees, which are similar drawings of nonsense specimens that do not include Linnaean names but do include paragraph-long descriptions—were included in the posthumously published *Teacups and Quails*, edited by Angus Davidson and Philip Hofer in 1953.

37. The reviewer is referring to Sir Joseph Dalton Hooker, a famous Victorian botanist, close friend of Charles Darwin, and director of the Royal Botanical Gardens, Kew.

CONCLUSION

MENTORS AND MUSES: WHY THE COLLABORATIVE CHILD MATTERS

1. See, for example, Stevenson's essays "A Chapter on Dreams" and "Authors and Publishers," reproduced in *The Lantern-Bearers and Other Essays*, ed. Jeremy Treglown.

2. For examples of book-length analyses on the impact of collaborators such as publishers and editors on children's literature, see Lissa Paul's *The Children's Book Business: Lessons from the Long Eighteenth Century* (2010), which examines how models of the thinking, reasoning child worked in tandem with publishing trends to transform the market in children's literature at a pivotal moment in its history, and Caroline Sumpter's *The Victorian Press and the Fairy Tale* (2008). Sumpter dedicates her second chapter to a consideration of fairy tales' transformation into children's literature in children's periodicals.

3. See the introduction to this book, pp. 8–12.

4. Some of the most innovative work on unseen collaborators unites book history and gender and sexuality studies to consider, for example, the female collaborators often obscured by a male writer presented as sole author. See Marjorie Stone and Judith Thompson's *Literary Couplings: Writing Couples, Collaborators, and the Construction of Authorship* (2007) and Jane Aaron's *A Double Singleness: Gender and the Writings of Charles and Mary Lamb* (1991).

5. In the preface to her novel *Orlando*, published in 1928, Woolf would call her nephew Quentin Bell, then eighteen years old, "an old friend and collaborator in fiction" (6). Some interpret *The Charleston Bulletin Supplements* as a descendent of the *Hyde Park Gate News*, the family newspaper Virginia Woolf, then Virginia Stephen, wrote with her siblings. *The Charleston Bulletin Supplements* were published in 2013 by the British Library, edited and introduced by Claudia Olk and with a preface by David Bradshaw. See also Olk's "The Art of 'Scene-Making' in the *Charleston Bulletin Supplements*."

6. See Lynch, who notes that the characters in Ransome's Swallows and Amazons series were inspired by the Altounyan and Collingwood children. Lynch notes, for example, that while he was writing *Peter Duck*, Ransome read parts of the novel to Titty and Roger Altounyan, who also helped with the illustrations. Consider also the Captain Flint character in the series, an adult who collaborates with and makes possible the adventures of the child protagonists.

7. As evidence of the girls' innocence, Ransome excerpts the novel itself, a passage in which characters Peter, Jennifer, and Bridget observe the landscape. While Peter and Jennifer speculate about what verses and paintings they could create in response to the landscape if they were poets and artists, Bridget reflects, "But as we aren't . . . we look and see it all just like an artist, and look and feel it all like a poet—and just do nothing but think about it" (xv). Ransome suggests that Whitlock and Hull, like the characters in their book, are "alive . . . with looking and seeing and feeling" (xv).

8. I do wonder if Whitlock and Hull purposefully (and perhaps strategically) fostered and maintained a public identity attached to childhood. Their motto "by children, for

children, about children" situates the authors as children themselves, even though—by the time they published *Oxus* in 1937—they were both in their mid-teens and the term "adolescence" was already in circulation. G. Stanley Hall published his benchmark study *Adolescence* in 1904.

9. Many have challenged Baron-Cohen's theories, especially his argument that those with autism exhibit an "extreme male brain" in their supposed lack of empathy (in *The Essential Difference*) and the parallels he draws between what he considers behaviors associated with autism with cruelty or even evil (in *The Science of Evil*). For important challenges to Baron-Cohen's work and similar research, see Jordynn Jack, *Autism and Gender: From Refrigerator Mothers to Computer Geeks*; Stuart Murray, *Representing Autism: Culture, Narrative, Fascination*; and Marion Quirici, "Geniuses without Imagination: Discourses of Autism, Ability, and Achievement."

10. For a discussion of Gubar, Bernstein, and others who advocate for developing methodologies to talk about real children in scholarship on children's literature and culture, see the introduction to this book, pp. 13–20.

11. Certainly Kincaid does not neglect the lived realities of children, both Victorian and present day; in fact, he argues that his exploration of the roots of our modern eroticization of childhood—and the denial of that desire—is in service to living children, who are the "chief casualties" of freighted figures of childhood. "Needing the *idea* of the child so badly," he writes, "we find ourselves sacrificing the bodies of children for it" (*Child-Loving* 6).

12. For an early reflection on this type of scholarship, see Flynn, "The Intersection of Children's Literature and Childhood Studies."

Works Cited

Aaron, Jane. *A Double Singleness: Gender and the Writings of Charles and Mary Lamb.* Oxford: Clarendon Press, 1991. Print.
Alderson, Brian. "Just-So Pictures: Illustrated Versions of *Just So Stories for Little Children.*" *Children's Literature* 20 (1992): 147–74. Print.
———. "The Making of Children's Books." In *The Cambridge Companion to Children's Literature*, edited by M. O. Grenby and Andrea Immel, 35–54. Cambridge: Cambridge University Press, 2009. Print.
———. "The Spoken and the Read: *German Popular Stories* and English Popular Diction." In *The Reception of Grimms' Fairy Tales: Responses, Reactions, Revisions*, edited by Donald Haase, 59–77. Detroit: Wayne State University Press, 1993. Print.
Alexander, Christine, and Juliet McMaster. *The Child Writer from Austen to Woolf.* Cambridge: Cambridge University Press, 2010. Print.
"Among the Toys." *The Examiner and London Review* 3198 (May 15, 1869): 307–8. *British Periodicals.* Web. 9 August 9, 2015.
Anderson, Celia Catlett, and Marilyn Fain Apseloff. *Nonsense Literature for Children: Aesop to Seuss.* Hamden, CT: Library Professional Publications, 1989. Print.
Angus, David. "Youth on the Prow: The First Publication of *Treasure Island.*" *Studies in Scottish Literature* 25 (1990): 83–99. Print.
Anstey, F. *Vice Versâ; or, A Lesson to Fathers.* 3rd ed. New York: D. Appleton, 1882. *HathiTrust.* Web. August 18, 2015.
"The Anti-Coloring Book." *Susan Striker.* Web. July 18, 2015.
Archibald, Timothy. "*Echolilia*: A Father's Photographic Conversation with His Autistic Son." *Time Photos.* Time Inc. Web. May 25, 2013.
———. "The *Echolilia* Interview/100 Eyes." *Timothy Archibald.* June 24, 2009. Web. May 24, 2013.
———. *Echolilia: Sometimes I Wonder.* San Francisco: Echo Press, 2010. Print.
Arnold, Matthew. *Reports on Elementary Schools, 1853–1882.* New ed. Edited by F. S. Marvin. London: Her Majesty's Stationery Office, 1908. *HathiTrust.* Web. August 25, 2015.
"The Art for Schools Association." *The Academy* 593 (September 15, 1883): 185–86. *British Periodicals.* Web. July 12, 2015.

"Art in the Nursery." *Magazine of Art* 6 (1883): 127–32. *British Periodicals*. Web. July 12, 2015.

Avery, Gillian. Introduction to *A Holiday Romance and Other Writings for Children*. Edited by Gillian Avery and Michael Slater, xix–xxviii. London: J. M. Dent, 1995. Print.

———. *Nineteenth-Century Children: Heroes and Heroines in English Children's Stories, 1780–1900*. London: Hodder and Stoughton, 1965. Print.

A.W. "Nursery Tales and Toy Books." *Once a Week*, n.s. 3 (January 5, 1867): 25–27. *Google Books*. Web. July 12, 2015.

Bailey, Henry T. *A First Year in Drawing*. Boston: Educational Publishing, 1894. *Internet Archive*. Web. June 7, 2015.

Balfour, Graham. *The Life of Robert Louis Stevenson*. New York: Scribners, 1901. Print.

Ballantyne, R. M. *The Coral Island*. London: Thomas Nelson and Sons, 1960. Print.

Barbauld, Anna Letitia, and Lucy Aikin. *The Works of Anna Lætitia Barbauld, with a Memoir*. 2 vols. London: Richard Taylor, 1825. *Google Books*. Web. September 9, 2015.

Barnes, Earl, ed. *Studies in Education: A Series of Ten Numbers Devoted to Child-Study and the History of Education*. Stanford, CA: Stanford University, 1897. *Google Books*. Web. June 7, 2015.

Baron-Cohen, Simon. *The Essential Difference: Male and Female Brains and the Truth about Autism*. New York: Basic Books, 2003. Print.

———. *The Science of Evil: On Empathy and the Origins of Cruelty*. New York: Basic Books, 2011. Print.

Barrie, J. M. *The Boy Castaways of Black Lake Island, Being a Record of the Terrible Adventures of the Brothers Davies in the Summer of 1901, Faithfully Set Forth by Peter Llewelyn Davies*. Published by J. M. Barrie in the Bloucester Road, 1901. Beinecke Rare Book and Manuscript Library. Yale University, New Haven, CT. Web. August 19, 2015.

———. *Letters of J. M. Barrie*. Edited by Viola Meynell. London: Peter Davies, 1942. Print.

———. *The Little White Bird; or, Adventures in Kensington Gardens*. Vol. 11 of *The Novels, Tales, and Sketches of J. M. Barrie*. New York: Charles Scribner's Sons, 1912. Print.

———. *Peter and Wendy: Peter Pan in Kensington Gardens and Peter and Wendy*. Edited by Peter Hollindale. Oxford and New York: Oxford University Press, 1991. 67–226. Print.

———. *Peter Pan: Peter Pan and Other Plays*. Edited by Peter Hollindale. Oxford and New York: Oxford University Press, 1995. 73–154. Print.

———. "To the Five: A Dedication." *Peter Pan and Other Plays*. Edited by Peter Hollindale. Oxford: Oxford University Press, 1995. 75–86. Print.

Beattie, Hilary H. "Father and Son: The Origins of *Strange Case of Dr. Jekyll and Mr. Hyde*." *The Psychoanalytic Study of the Child* 56 (2001): 317–60. Print.

Beckett, Sandra L. *Crossover Fiction: Global and Historical Perspectives*. New York and London: Routledge, 2009. Print.

———. "Crossover Literature." In *Keywords for Children's Literature*, edited by Philip Nel and Lissa Paul, 58–61. New York and London: New York University Press, 2011. Print.

Beerbohm, Max. "The Child Barrie." *The Saturday Review* 99, no. 2567 (1905): 13–14. *British Periodicals*. Web. August 19, 2015.

———. "Mr. Martin Harvey at S. Helena." *The Saturday Review* 95 (May 16, 1903): 615–16. *Google Books*. Web. September 17, 2015.

Bell, Olivia, and Alan Bell. "Children's Manuscript Magazines in the Bodleian Library." In *Children and Their Books: A Celebration of the Work of Iona and Peter Opie*, edited by Gillian Avery and Julia Briggs, 399–412. Oxford: Clarendon Press, 1989. Print.

Bernstein, Robin. "Children's Books, Dolls, and the Performance of Race; or, the Possibility of Children's Literature." *PMLA* 126, no. 1 (January 2011): 160–69. *Project Muse*. Web. May 17, 2016.

———. *Racial Innocence: Performing Childhood and Race from Slavery to Civil Rights*. New York: New York University Press, 2011. Print.

———. "Toys Are Good for Us: Why We Should Embrace the Historical Integration of Children's Literature, Material Culture, and Play." *Children's Literature Association Quarterly* 38, no. 4 (Winter 2013): 458–63. *Project Muse*. Web. July 26, 2016.

Biber, Edward. *Henry Pestalozzi, and His Plan of Education; Being an Account of His Life and Writings; with Copious Extracts from His Works, and Extensive Details Illustrative of the Practical Parts of His Method*. London: John Souter, School Library, 1831. *HathiTrust*. Web. May 23, 2015.

Birkin, Andrew. *J. M. Barrie and the Lost Boys: The Real Story Behind Peter Pan*. New Haven, CT, and London: Yale University Press, 2003. Print.

Blackford, Holly. "Apertures into the House of Fiction: Novel Methods and Child Study, 1870–1910." *Children's Literature Association Quarterly* 32, no. 4 (Winter 2007): 368–89. Print.

Blamires, David. "The Early Reception of the Grimms' *Kinder- und Hausmärchen* in England." In *The Translation of Children's Literature: A Reader*, edited by Gillian Lathey, 163–74. Topics in Translation. Clevedon, UK: Multilingual Matters, 2006. Print.

———. "A Workshop of Editorial Practice: The Grimms' *Kinder- und Haudmärchen*." In *A Companion to the Fairy Tale*, edited by Hilda Ellis Davidson and Anna Chaudhri, 71–83. Woodbridge, Suffolk, UK: D. S. Brewer, 2006. Print.

"Books for Babes." *The Saturday Review*, supplement 2250, no. 86 (December 10, 1898): 761–62. *Google Books*. Web. August 9, 2015.

"Books for the Young." *The Saturday Review* 66, no. 1725 (November 17, 1888): 575–76. *British Periodicals*. Web. August 2, 2015.

"Books for Young People." *Literary News* (December 1896): 374–84. *Google Books*. Web. September 9, 2015.

Bottigheimer, Ruth B. *Fairy Tales: A New History*. Albany: State University of New York Press, 2009. Print.

Bradbury, D. E. "The Contributions of the Child Study Movement to Child Psychology." *Psychological Bulletin* 34, no. 1 (January 1937): 21–38. *PsycNET*. American Psychological Association. Web. September 16, 2015.

Bratton, J. S. *The Impact of Victorian Children's Literature*. London and Sydney: Croom Helm, 1981. Print.

Brogan, Hugh. *The Life of Arthur Ransome*. London: J. Cape, 1984. Print.

Brown, Elmer. *Notes on Children's Drawings*. Berkeley, CA: Berkeley University Press, 1897. *Google Books*. Web. June 4, 2015.

Browning, Robert. "The Cardinal and the Dog." In *Asolando: Fancies and Facts*. 6th ed, 40–41. London: Smith, Elder, 1890. *HathiTrust*. Web. July 26, 2016.

———. "The Pied Piper of Hamelin; A Child's Story." In *Dramatic Lyrics, Dramatic Romances, Christmas-Eve and Easter-Day*, 209–19, edited by Charlotte Porter and Helen A. Clarke. New York: Thomas Y. Crowell, 1898. *HathiTrust*. Web. June 25, 2015.

———. *The Pied Piper of Hamlin: A Child's Story*, Illustrated by Margaret W. Tarrant. London: J. M. Dent, 1912. *HathiTrust*. Web. July 26, 2016.

———. *The Pied Piper of Hamelin: A Child's Story, Set Forth in a Series of Designs and Decorative Borders by Harry Quilter, W. J. Barrister-at-Law and Written in Ornamental Text by Mary His Wife*. London: Harry Quilter, 1898. *University of Florida Digital Collections*. Web. July 26, 2016.

"budget, n." *OED Online*. Oxford University Press, September 2015. Web. September 9, 2015.

Burgess, Gelett. "Some Phases of Primitive Art." *The Lark* 1, no. 1 (May 1895): [6–8]. Print.

Burt, Forrest D. "Browning's 'Pied Piper of Hamelin: A Child's Story' and 'The Cardinal and the Dog': Considering the Poet's Early Interest in Drama and Art." *Studies in Browning and His Circle* 16 (1988): 30–41. Print.

Bushnell, William H. "The Curse of Amateurism." *The Inland Printer* 5 (1887): 78–80. Print.

Byrom, Thomas. *Nonsense and Wonder: The Poems and Cartoons of Edward Lear*. New York: E. P. Dutton, 1977. Print.

Cammaerts, Emile. *The Poetry of Nonsense*. New York: Dutton, 1926. Print.

Capshaw, Katharine. *Civil Rights Childhood: Picturing Liberation in African American Photobooks*. Minneapolis: University of Minnesota Press, 2014. Print.

Capshaw Smith, Katharine. *Children's Literature of the Harlem Renaissance*. Bloomington and Indianapolis: Indiana University Press, 2004. Print.

Carline, Richard. *Draw They Must: A History of the Teaching and Examining of Art*. London: Edward Arnold, 1968. Print.

Carpenter, Humphrey, and Mari Prichard. "*The Far-Distant Oxus* (1937)." In *The Oxford Companion to Children's Literature*, 182. Oxford and New York: Oxford University Press, 1984. Print.

Carrington, Bridget. *"Juvenile Literature As It Is."* In *Oxford Encyclopedia of Children's Literature*, edited by Jack Zipes. Oxford: Oxford University Press, 2006. *Oxford Reference*. Web. August 2, 2015.

Castiglione, Claudia Bacile di. "'Holiday Romance': Children's Dreams of Omnipotence in Dickens's Last Fiction." In *Dickens: The Craft of Fiction and the Challenges of Reading, Proceedings of the Milan Symposium, Gargnano, September 1998*, edited by Rossana Bonadei, Clotilde Stasio, Carlo Pagetti, and Alessandro Vescovi, 153–65. Milan: Unicopli, 2000. Print.

Chamberlain, Alexander F. *The Child: A Study in the Evolution of Man*. London: Walter Scott, 1900. *HathiTrust*. Web. September 16, 2015.

Champneys, F. H. "Notes on an Infant." *Mind* 6, no. 21 (January 1881): 104–7. *Oxford University Press Humanities Archive*. Web. September 16, 2015.

Chanler, Margaret Terry. *Roman Spring: Memoirs*. Boston: Little, Brown, 1934. *HathiTrust*. Web. July 15, 2015.

Chapleau, Sebastien. "Children's Literature, Issues of Definition: The 'Why?' and 'Why Not?' of Criticism." *L'esprit Createur* 45, no. 4 (Winter 2005): 10–19. Print.

Chase, Pauline, Max Beerbohm, and Albert Rutherston. *Peter Pan's Postbag: Letters to Pauline Chase*. London: Heinemann, 1908. Print.

"A Chat with Austin Strong." *New York Times*, October 27, 1907, X1. *Proquest Historical Newspapers*. Web. August 30, 2014.

"Children Admirers Routed Peter Pan: Miss Adams Showered with Confetti at Her Last Matinee." *New York Times*, June 10, 1906, 9. *ProQuest Historical Newspapers*. Web. August 28, 2015.

"Children's Books." *The Leader* 4, no. 196 (December 24, 1853): 1245. *British Periodicals*. Web. August 16, 2015.

"Children's Books." *The London Review* 13, no. 337 (December 15, 1866): 665–66. *British Periodicals*. Web. August 4, 2015.

Chrisman, Oscar. "The Secret-Language of Childhood." *Century Magazine* 56, no.1 (May 1898): 54–58. *Google Books*. Web. September 16, 2015.

———. "The Secret Languages of Children." *North-western Monthly* 8 (1897–1898): 187–93, 375–79, 649–61. *Google Books*. September 16, 2015.

Clarke, Mary Cowden. *Kit Bam's Adventures; Or, The Yarns of an Old Mariner*. Illustrated by George Cruikshank. 1849. Reprint, Boston: Ticknor and Fields, 1856. *HathiTrust*. Web. September 16, 2015.

Cohen, Elizabeth. "Parents, do you know what these texts mean?" *CNN*. Turner Broadcasting System, Inc., August 26, 2010. Web. August 4, 2016.

Cole, Sir Henry. "Felix Summerly's Home Treasury of Books, Pictures, Toys, Etc., Edited by Felix Summerly, Proposed to Cultivate the Affections, Fancy, Imagination, and Taste of Children." In *Fifty Years of Public Work of Sir Henry Cole, K.C.B., Accounted for in His Deeds, Speeches, and Writings*. Vol. 2, 160–62. London: George Bell and Sons, 1884. *HathiTrust*. Web. July 11, 2015.

Coleridge, Hartley. "A Nursery Lecture Delivered by an Old Bachelor." *Essays and Marginalia by Hartley Coleridge, Edited by His Brother*. 2 vols. London: Edward Moxon, 1851. 1:301–7. *Google Books*. Web. August 26, 2015.

Colley, Ann. *Edward Lear and the Critics*. Literary Criticism in Perspective. Columbia, SC: Camden House, 1993. Print.

——. "Edward Lear's Limericks and the Reversals of Nonsense." *Victorian Poetry* 26, no. 3 (Autumn 1988): 285–99. Print.

Conrad, Rachel. "'We Are Masters at Childhood': Time and Agency in Poetry by, for, and about Children." *Jeunesse* 5, no. 2 (Winter 2013): 124–50. Project Muse. Web. July 13, 2016.

Cooke, Ebenezer. "The Basis and Beginnings of Brushwork." In *The Book of School Handwork: An Encyclopaedia of Educational Handwork Subjects, Methods, Materials, Tools, Organisation, etc.*, vol. 1, edited by H. Holman, 92–108. London: Caxton, 1913. *HathiTrust*. Web. May 27, 2015.

——. "Our Art Teaching and Child Nature." In *Transactions of the Education Society, 1884-5*, 65–91. London: William Rice, 1885. Google Books. Web. June 7, 2015.

Cooper, Jane. *Mrs. Molesworth: A Biography*. Crowborough, East Sussex, UK: Pratts Folly Press, 2002. Print.

Cosslett, Tess. "Child's Place in Nature: Talking Animals in Victorian Children's Fiction." *Nineteenth-Century Contexts* 23, no. 4 (2001): 475–95. Print.

——. *Talking Animals in British Children's Fiction, 1786–1914*. London: Ashgate, 2006. Print.

Coward, Seth. "Brushwork in an Elementary School (with Illustrations)." *Special Reports on Educational Subjects, 1896–7*. 101–14. London: Printed for Her Majesty's Stationery Office by Eyre and Spottiswoode, 1897. Google Books. Web. June 2, 2015.

Craik, Dinah Maria Mulock. "The Age of Gold." *Macmillan's Magazine* 4 (February 1860): 293–304. *British Periodicals*. Web. August 16, 2015.

——. "Want Something to Read." *Chambers's Journal of Popular Culture* 227 (May 8, 1858): 289–92. *British Periodicals*. Web. August 18, 2015.

Crockett, S[amuel] R[utherford]. *Sweetheart Travellers: A Child's Book for Children, for Women, and for Men*. Illustrated by Gordon Browne and W. H. C. Groome. 2nd ed. New York and London: Frederick A. Stokes, 1895. Print.

Cromwell, Archibald. "S. R. Crockett and His Stories." *Windsor Magazine* 3 (January–June 1896): 494–98. Google Books. Web. July 26, 2016.

Dalby, Richard. *The Golden Age of Children's Book Illustration*. London: Michael O'Mara Books, 1991. Print.

D. Appleton and Co's New and Recent Juvenile Books. Advertisement. *Plain Dealer* (Cleveland, OH), December 15, 1900: 10. *America's Historical Newspapers*. Web. July 4, 2015.

Darnton, Robert. "What Is the History of Books?" *Daedalus* 111, no. 3 (Summer 1982): 65–83. Print.

Darton, F. J. Harvey. *Children's Books in England: Five Centuries of Social Life*. Cambridge and New York: Cambridge University Press, 1932. Print.

Darwin, Charles. "A Biographical Sketch of an Infant." *Mind* 2, no. 7 (July 1877): 285–94. Google Books. Web. September 16, 2015.

———. *The Life and Letters of Charles Darwin, Including an Autobiographical Chapter.* Edited by Francis Darwin. Vol. 1. London: John Murray, 1888. *HathiTrust.* Web. 3 vols. April 8, 2015.

Darwin Manuscripts Project. American Museum of Natural History, New York, NY, n.d. Web. May 31, 2015.

Davidson, Angus. *Edward Lear, Landscape Painter and Nonsense Poet.* London: J. Murray, 1938. Print.

Davidson, Guy. "'Ancient Appetites': Romance and Desire in Robert Louis Stevenson." *Australasian Victorian Studies Journal* 3, no. 1 (December 1997): 60–70. Print.

Day, Sara K. "Pure Passion: The *Twilight* Saga, 'Abstinence Porn,' and Adolescent Women's Fan Fiction." *Children's Literature Association Quarterly* 39, no. 1 (Spring 2014): 28–48. *Project Muse.* Web. July 26, 2016.

De-B.W., Baron. "Our Booking-Office." *Punch* 103 (July 30, 1892): 48. *Google Books.* Web. September 17, 2015.

Deane, Bradley. "Imperial Boyhood: Piracy and the Play Ethic." *Victorian Studies* 53, no. 4 (Summer 2011): 689–714. Print.

"Delightful Mischief." *The Outlook* 4, no. 97 (December 9, 1899): 626. *British Periodicals.* Web. August 16, 2015.

Dickens, Charles. "Frauds on the Fairies." *Household Words* (October 1, 1853): 97–100. *British Periodicals.* Web. September 16, 2015.

———. *Hard Times.* Edited by Frank Kaplan and Sylvère Monod. 3rd ed. New York and London: Norton, 2001. Print.

———. *A Holiday Romance and Other Writings for Children.* Edited by Gillian Avery and Michael Slater. London: J. M. Dent, 1995. Print.

———. "Infant Gardens." *Household Words* 11, no. 278 (July 21, 1855): 577–82. *British Periodicals.* Web. May 23, 2015.

———. *The Letters of Charles Dickens.* Edited by Madeline House, Graham Storey, and Kathleen Tillotson. 11 vols. Pilgrim ed. Oxford: Clarendon Press, 1965–2002. Print.

Dingley, R. J. "Kenneth Grahame." *British Children's Writers, 1880–1914.* Edited by Laura M. Zaidman. Detroit: Gale Research, 1994. Dictionary of Literary Biography, vol. 141. *Literature Resource Center.* Web. June 8, 2013.

Dismore, Blanche. "How Words Get Content." *Studies in Education* 2 (1902): 43–61. *Google Books.* Web. September 16, 2015.

Donaldson, Islay Murray. *The Life and Work of Samuel Rutherford Crockett.* Aberdeen, Scotland: Aberdeen University Press, 1989. Print.

Drain, Susan. "Family Matters: Margaret Gatty and *Aunt Judy's Magazine.*" *Publishing History* 61 (2007): 5–45. Print.

Drummond, W. B. *The Child: His Nature and Nurture.* London: J. M. Dent, 1901. *HathiTrust.* Web. September 16, 2015.

Duane, Anna Mae. Introduction. In *The Children's Table: Childhood Studies and the Humanities*, edited by Anna Mae Duane, 1–14. Athens: University of Georgia Press, 2013. Print.

Dundes, Alan. "Texture, Text, and Context." In *Interpreting Folklore*, 20–32. Bloomington and London: Indiana University Press, 1980. Print.

Duriez, Colin. "J(ohn) R(onald) R(euel) Tolkien." In *British Children's Writers, 1914–1960*, edited by Donald R. Hettinga and Gary D. Schmidt. Detroit: Gale Research, 1996. Dictionary of Literary Biography Vol. 160. *Literature Resource Center*. Web. June 8, 2013.

E.C. "The Child and the Poets." *The Speaker* 6 (May 24, 1902): 230–31. *Google Books*. Web. August 4, 2015.

Ede, Lisa S. "Edward Lear's Limericks and Their Illustrations." In *Explorations in the Field of Nonsense*, edited by Wilm Tigges, 103–16. Amsterdam: Rodopi, 1987. Print.

Edgeworth, Maria. *The Parent's Assistant, or, Stories for Children*. Illustrated by H. W. Herrick. New York: Hurd and Houghton, 1869. *Google Books*. Web. September 9, 2015.

"Education and Insanity." *The Saturday Review* 1447 (July 21, 1883): 74–75. *British Periodicals*. Web. August 26, 2015.

Efland, Arthur D. *A History of Art Education: Intellectual and Social Currents in Teaching the Visual Arts*. New York and London: Teachers College Press, 1990. Print.

Eidam, Laura. "Reexamining Illustration's Role in *Treasure Island*: Do Images Pirate Texts?" *English Literature in Transition, 1880–1920* 55, no. 1 (2012): 45–68. Print.

Ewing, Juliana Horatia. *Six to Sixteen: A Story for Girls*. Boston: Little, Brown, 1902. *Google Books*. Web. August 5, 2016.

Flanders, Todd R. "Rousseau's Adventure with Robinson Crusoe." *Interpretation: A Journal of Political Philosophy* 24, no. 3 (Spring 1997): 319–37. Print.

Flynn, Richard. "'Affirmative Acts': Language, Childhood, and Power in June Jordan's Cross-Writing." *Children's Literature* 30 (2002): 159–85. *Project Muse*. Web. July 12, 2016.

———. "The Intersection of Children's Literature and Childhood Studies." *Children's Literature Association Quarterly* 22, no. 3 (Fall 1997): 143–45. *Project Muse*. Web. August 20, 2016.

———. "What Are We Talking about When We Talk about Agency?" *Jeunesse* 8, no. 1 (Summer 2016): 254–65. *Project Muse*. Web. August 20, 2016.

French, John. "Victorian Responses to Children's Art." *College Art Journal* 15, no. 4 (Summer 1956): 327–33. Print.

Froebel, Friedrich. *Education by Development, the Second Part of the Pedagogics of the Kindergarten*. Translated by Josephine Jarvis. International Education Series. New York: D. Appleton, 1899. *Google Books*. Web. May 24, 2015.

———. *The Education of Man*. Translated and annotated by W. N. Hailmann. New York: D. Appleton, 1906. *Google Books*. Web. May 23, 2015.

Fry, Roger. "Children's Drawings." In *A Roger Fry Reader*, edited by Christopher Reed, 266–70. Chicago: University of Chicago Press, 1996. Print.

Galbraith, Gretchen R. *Reading Lives: Reconstructing Childhood, Books, and Schools in Britain, 1870–1920*. New York: St. Martin's Press, 1997. Print.

Gallagher, Catherine. "The Changeling's Debt: Maria Edgeworth's Productive Fictions." In *Nobody's Story: The Vanishing Acts of Women Writers in the Marketplace, 1670–1820*, by Catherine Gallager, 257–327. Berkeley: University of California Press, 1994. Print.

Gatty, Mrs. Alfred [Margaret]. *Aunt Judy's Letters*. Illustrated by Clara S. Lane. London: Bell and Daldy, 1862. *Google Books*. Web. September 16, 2015.

———. *Aunt Judy's Tales*. Illustrated by Clara S. Lane. London: Bell and Daldy, 1859. *Google Books*. Web. September 16, 2015.

———. *Domestic Pictures and Tales*. London: Bell and Daldy, 1866. *Google Books*. Web. September 16, 2015.

———. *The Fairy Godmothers, and Other Tales*. London: George Bell, 1851. *Google Books*. Web. September 16, 2015.

———. "Nursery Nonsense." *Aunt Judy's Magazine* 6 (1869): 183–85, 248–50, 313–15, 375–76; 7 (1869): 56–58, 248–50, 375–77. *Google Books*. Web. September 18, 2015.

Girouard, Mark. "Picture-books." In *Sweetness and Light: The 'Queen Anne' Movement, 1860–1900*, 139–51. Oxford: Clarendon Press, 1977. Print.

Genette, Gérard. *Paratexts: Thresholds of Interpretation*. Translated by Jane E. Lewin. Cambridge: Cambridge University Press, 1997. Print.

Godley, Eveline C. "A Century of Children's Books." *The National Review* 47 (May 1906): 437–49. *Google Books*. Web. August 3, 2015.

Goslee, David. "Paying Browning's Piper." *Studies in Browning and His Circle* 16 (1988): 42–51. Print.

Grathwol, Kathleen B. "Maria Edgeworth and the 'True Use of Books' for Eighteenth-Century Girls." In *New Essays on Maria Edgeworth*, edited by Julie Nash, 73–91. Aldershot, UK: Ashgate, 2006. Print.

Green, Roger Lancelyn. *Mrs. Molesworth*. London: The Bodley Head, 1961. Print.

Grimm, Jacob, and Wilhelm Grimm. *The Annotated Brothers Grimm*. Translated and edited by Maria Tatar. Introduction by A. S. Byatt. New York and London: W. W. Norton, 2004. Print.

———. "Tom Thumb." In *German Popular Stories, Translated from the Kinder und Haus Marchen, collected by M. M. Grimm from Oral Tradition*, illustrated by George Cruikshank, 57–68. Facsimile of the 1823 edition published in London by C. Baldwyn. Menston, UK: Scolar Press, 1971. Print.

Gross, Jane. "Son and Father Pierce Autism's Veil." *Lens: Photography, Video and Visual Journalism. The New York Times*, November 5, 2010. Web. May 24, 2013.

Gubar, Marah. *Artful Dodgers: Reconceiving the Golden Age of Children's Literature*. Oxford: Oxford University Press, 2009. Print.

———. "The Hermeneutics of Recuperation: What a Kinship-Model Approach to Children's Agency Could Do for Children's Literature and Childhood Studies." *Jeunesse* 8, no. 1 (Summer 2016): 266–77. *Project Muse*. Web. August 20, 2016.

———. "Introduction: Children and Theatre." *The Lion and the Unicorn* 36, no. 2 (April 2012): v–xiv. *Project Muse*. Web. July 26, 2016.

———. "*Peter Pan* as Children's Theatre: The Issue of Audience." In *The Oxford Handbook of Children's Literature*, edited by Julia Mickenberg and Lynne Vallone, 475–96. Oxford: Oxford University Press, 2011. Print.

———. "Revising the Seduction Paradigm: The Case of Ewing's *The Brownies*." *Children's Literature* 30 (2002): 42–66. *Project Muse*. Web. May 12, 2016.

———. "Risky Business: Talking about Children in Children's Literature Criticism." *Children's Literature Association Quarterly* 38, no. 4 (Winter 2013): 450–57. Print.

Haggard, H. Rider. *King Solomon's Mines*. Edited by Gerald Monsman. Orchard Park, NY: Broadview, 2002. Print.

Hale, Horatio. *The Origin of Languages, and the Antiquity of Speaking Man. An Address Before the Section of Anthropology of the American Association for the Advancement of Science, At Buffalo, August, 1886*. Cambridge MA: John Wilson and Son University Press, 1886. *HathiTrust*. Web. September 16, 2015.

Hall, A. Neely. *The Boy Craftsman: Practical and Profitable Ideas for a Boy's Leisure Hours*. Illustrated by A. Neely Hall and Norman P. Hall. Boston: Lothrop, Lee & Shepard, 1905. *Internet Archive*. Web. September 17, 2015.

Hall, G. Stanley. "Child Study and Its Relation to Education." *The Forum* 29 (August 1900): 688–702. American Periodicals, Series III. Web. September 16, 2015.

Hardesty, William H. III, and David D. Mann. "Stevenson's Method in *Treasure Island*: 'The Old Romance, Retold.'" *Essays in Literature* 9, no. 2 (Fall 1982): 180–93. Print.

Harman, Claire. *Robert Louis Stevenson: A Biography*. Hammersmith, UK: Harper Collins, 2005. Print.

Harris, Elizabeth. *The Boy and His Press: An Exhibition in the Hall of Graphic Arts, National Museum of American History*. Washington, DC: Smithsonian Institution, 1992. Print.

Harrison, Thomas G. *The Career and Reminiscences of an Amateur Journalist, and a History of Amateur Journalism*. Indianapolis, IN: Thomas G. Harrison, Publisher and Printer, 1883. *Google Books*. Web. September 17, 2015.

Hart, James D. *The Private Press Ventures of Samuel Lloyd Osbourne and R. L. S., With Facsimiles of their Publications*. San Francisco: Book Club of California, 1966. Print.

Hawlin, Stefan. *The Complete Critical Guide to Robert Browning*. London and New York: Routledge, 2002. Print.

[Henley, W. E.]. Review of *Treasure Island*, by Robert Louis Stevenson. *The Saturday Review* 56 (December 8, 1883): 737–38. *British Periodicals*. Web. September 17, 2015.

———. "Randolph Caldecott." *The Art Journal*, new ser., 7 (July 1881): 208–12. *Google Books*. Web. July 11, 2015.

Herring, Jack W. *The Pied Piper of Hamelin in the Armstrong Browning Library, Baylor University, Waco, Texas: A Catalogue of Materials Related to Browning's Poem, Including a List of Items on Exhibit in the Library During January and February, 1969*. Baylor University Browning Interests 20. Waco, TX: Baylor University Press, 1969. Print.

Hewins, Caroline M. *Books for Boys and Girls: A Selected List*. 2nd ed., rev. [Boston]: Library Bureau, 1904. *HathiTrust*. Web. August 5, 2015.

———. "Books That Children Like." In *Transactions of the Second International Library Conference, Held in London, July 13–16*. London: Morrison and Gibb, 1898. *Google Books*. Web. August 5, 2015.

———. "How Library Work with Children Has Grown in Hartford and Connecticut." *Library Journal* 39, no. 2 (February 1914): 91–99. *Google Books*. Web. August 5, 2015.

———. "Report on List of Children's Books with Children's Annotations." *Library Journal* 27 (1902): 79–82. *Google Books*. Web. August 5, 2015.

Hofmann, Werner. "The Art of Unlearning." In *Discovering Child Art: Essays on Childhood, Primitivism, and Modernism*, edited by Jonathan Fineberg, 3–14. Princeton, NJ: Princeton University Press, 1998. Print.

Hollindale, Peter. "Introduction." In *Peter Pan and Other Plays*, edited by Peter Hollindale, vii–xxv. Oxford and New York: Oxford University Press, 1995. Print.

Horn, Pamela. "Robert Lowe and the HM Inspectorate, 1859–1864." *Oxford Review of Education* 7, no. 2 (1981): 131–43. Print.

———. *The Victorian and Edwardian Schoolchild*. Gloucester, UK, and Wolfeboro, NH: Alan Sutton, 1989. Print.

Horne, Jackie C. *History and the Construction of the Child in Early British Children's Literature*. Farnham, UK, and Burlington, VT: Ashgate, 2911. Print.

Hsiao, Irene. "The Pang of Stone Words." In *J. M. Barrie's Peter Pan In and Out of Time: A Children's Classic at 100*, edited by Donna R. White and C. Anita Tarr, 155–71. Children's Literature Association Centennial Studies Series 4. Lanham MD: Scarecrow Press, 2006. Print.

Hun, E. R. "The Singular Development of Language in a Child." *Quarterly Journal of Psychological Medicine & Medical Jurisprudence* 2, no. 3 (1868): 525–28. American Antiquarian Society Historical Periodicals Collection, Series 5. Web. September 16, 2015.

Hunt, Peter. "Childist Criticism: The Subculture of the Child, the Book, and the Critic." *Signal* 43 (1984): 42–59. Print.

"Inarticulate." Def. 2a. *The Oxford English Dictionary Online*. Web. February 13, 2009.

Jack, Jordynn. *Autism and Gender: From Refrigerator Mothers to Computer Geeks*. Urbana, Chicago, and Springfield: University of Illinois Press, 2014. Print.

James, Henry. *What Maisie Knew*. 1897. Introduction by Penelope Lively. London: J. M. Dent, 1997. Print.

———. *William Wetmore Story and His Friends, from Letters, Diaries, and Recollections*. 2 vols. Boston: Houghton and Mifflin, 1903. *Google Books*. Web. September 16, 2015.

Johnston, Charles. "The World's Baby-Talk, and the Expressiveness of Speech." *The Fortnightly Review* 60, no. 358 (October 1896): 494–505. *British Periodicals*. Web. September 16, 2015.

Jordan, David Starr. *The Book of Knight and Barbara, Being a Series of Stories Told to Children, Corrected and Illustrated by the Children*. New York: D. Appleton, 1899. Print.

———. *The Days of a Man: Being Memories of a Naturalist, Teacher, and Minor Prophet of Democracy*. Vol. 1, *1851–1899*. Yonkers-on-Hudson, NY, and New York: World Book Company, 1922. *Google Books*. Web. June 30, 2015.

Junker, Thomas. "Darwin, Sir Francis (1848–1925)." In the *Oxford Dictionary of National Biography*. Oxford: Oxford University Press, September 2014. Web. April 7, 2015.

Kelley, Philip, and Ronald Hudson. *The Brownings' Correspondence*. Vol. 5. Winfield, KS: Wedgestone Press, 1987. Print.

Kelly, Donna Darling. *Uncovering the History of Children's Drawing and Art*. Publications in Creativity Research. Westport, CT, and London: Praeger, 2004. Print.

Kelly-Byrne, Diana. "The 1984 Conference of the Children's Literature Association, Charlotte, North Carolina, May 24–27: A Participant's Response." *Children's Literature Association Quarterly* 9, no. 4 (Winter 1983–1984): 195–98. Print.

Keynes, Randal. *Darwin, His Daughter, and Human Evolution*. New York: Riverhead Books, 2002. Print.

Keynes, Randal, and David Kohn. "*On the origin of species*, 1859: Surviving Manuscript Leaves." American Museum of Natural History, New York, NY. Darwin Manuscripts Project. Web. February 13, 2015.

Kidd, Kenneth. *Freud in Oz: At the Intersections of Psychoanalysis and Children's Literature*. Minneapolis: University of Minnesota Press, 2011. Print.

Kincaid, James R. *Child-Loving: The Erotic Child in Victorian Culture*. New York: Routledge, 1992. Print.

———. "Producing Erotic Children." In *Curiouser: On the Queerness of Children*. Minneapolis and London: University of Minnesota Press, 2004. 3–16. Print.

Kingsley, Charles. *The Water Babies: A Fairy Tale for a Land Baby*. Illustrated by J. Noel Paton. Boston: T.O.H.P. Burnham, 1864. Google Books. Web. August 26, 2015.

Kipling, Rudyard. *Just So Stories for Little Children*. 1902. Reprint, New York: Gramercy Books, 2003. Print.

———. "The 'Just-So' Stories ['How the Whale Got His Throat']." *St. Nicholas* 25 (December 1897): 89–93. Google Books. Web. July 8, 2015.

Knoepflmacher, U. C. "*Aunt Judy's Magazine* and the Uses of Collaboration." *Princeton University Library Chronicle* 67 (2005–2006): 146–55. Print.

———. "Kipling's 'Just-So' Partner: The Dead Child as Collaborator and Muse." *Children's Literature* 25 (1997): 24–49. Print.

———. *Ventures into Childland: Victorians, Fairy Tales, and Femininity*. Chicago and London: University of Chicago Press, 1998. Print.

Knoepflmacher, U. C., and Mitzi Myers. "From the Editors: 'Cross-Writing' and the Reconceptualizing of Children's Literature." *Children's Literature* 25 (1997): vii–xvii. Project Muse. Web. July 26, 2016.

Kreilkamp, Ivan. *Voice and the Victorian Storyteller*. Cambridge: Cambridge University Press, 2005. Print.

Lamb, Charles. Letter to William Godwin, March 10, 1808. In *The Works of Charles and Mary Lamb: Letters, 1796–1820*, edited by E. V. Lucas, 387–89. Vol. 6. London: Methuen, 1905.

[Lang, Andrew]. Review of *Treasure Island*, by Robert Louis Stevenson. *Pall Mall Gazette* 38 (December 15, 1883): 4–5. Google Books. Web. August 18, 2016.

Langbauer, Laurie. *The Juvenile Tradition: Young Writers and Prolepsis, 1750–1835*. Oxford: Oxford University Press, 2016.

———. "Prolepsis and the Tradition of Juvenile Writing: Henry Kirke White and Robert Southey." *PMLA* 128, no. 4 (October 2013): 888–906. Print.

Lawrence, Evelyn. *Friedrich Froebel and English Education*. New York: Philosophical Library, 1953. Print.

Lear, Edward. *A Book of Nonsense*. London: Routledge, 1862. *Google Books*. Web. July 15, 2015.

———. *Edward Lear: The Complete Verse and Other Nonsense*. Edited by Vivien Noakes. New York: Penguin, 2002. Print.

———. *Queery Leary Nonsense: A Lear Nonsense Book*. Compiled by Lady Constance Strachey. Introduced by Evelyn Baring, Earl of Cromer. London: Mills and Boon, 1911. Florida State University Digital Library. Web. July 15, 2015.

"Lear's Book of Nonsense." *The Saturday Review* 65, no. 1691 (March 24, 1888): 361–62. *British Periodicals*. Web. July 12, 2015.

"Lear's Nonsense Books." *The Spectator* (17 September 1887): 1251–52. *Google Books*. Web. July 17, 2015.

Leeds, Jo Alice. "History of Attitudes toward Children's Art." *Studies in Art Education* 30, no. 2 (Winter 1989): 93–103. Print.

Leonard, James S., and Christine E. Wharton, eds. *Author-ity and Textuality: Current Views of Collaborative Writing*. West Cornwall, CT: Locust Hill Press, 1994.

Lesnik-Obserstein, Karín. "Childhood and Textuality: Culture, History, Literature." In *Children in Culture: Approaches to Childhood*, edited by Lesnik-Obserstein, 1–28. Houndsmills, UK: Macmillan, 1998. Print.

Levander, Caroline. "'Informed Eyes': The 1890s Child Study Movement and Henry James's *The Turn of the Screw*." *Critical Matrix* 12, nos. 1–2 (2001): 8–25. Print.

Levy, Michelle. "Family, Nation, and the Radical Education of Anna Barbauld and John Aikin." In *Family Authorship and Romantic Print Culture*, by Michelle Levy, 20–44. Palgrave Studies in the Enlightenment, Romanticism and Cultures of Print. Basingstoke, Hampshire, UK: Palgrave Macmillan, 2008. Print.

"Librarians at Play." *The Speaker* 18 (October 22, 1898): 485–87. *British Periodicals*. Web. August 6, 2015.

Liebert, Herman W. *Lear in the Original: Drawings and Limericks*. New York: H. P. Kraus, 1975. Print.

The "Little Folks" Painting Book: A Series of Outline Engravings for Water-Colour Painting. By Kate Greenaway, with Descriptive Stories and Verses by George Weatherley. London, Paris, and New York: Cassell, Petter, and Galpin, 1884. Print.

Liu, Yin. "Text as Image in Kipling's *Just So Stories*." *Papers on Language and Literature* 44, no. 3 (June 2008): 227–49. Print.

Locker-Lampson, Frederick. "The Rose and the Ring, Christmas, 1854, and Christmas, 1863." 1864. In *London Lyrics*, introduction by Austin Dobson, 146–47. London: Macmillan, 1904. *HathiTrust*. Web. September 16, 2015.

Low, Florence B. "The Reading of the Modern Girl." *The Nineteenth Century and After* 348 (February 1904): 278–87. *Google Books*. Web. August 10, 2015.

Lucas, Collins William. "The Poor and Their Public Schools: The New Minute." *Blackwood's Edinburgh Magazine* 91, no. 555 (January 1862): 77–102. *British Periodicals.* Web. August 25, 2015.

Luckey, G. W. A. "Child Study Department." *North-western Monthly: A Magazine Dedicated to the Correlation of Educational Forces* 8, no. 4 (November 1897): 243–61. *Google Books.* Web. September 16, 2015.

Lukens, Herman T. "A Study of Children's Drawings in the Early Years." *Pedagogical Seminary* 4 (1896): 79–110. Print.

Lundin, Anne. "A Delicate Balance: Collection Development and Women's History." *Collection Building* 14, no. 2 (1995): 42–46. Print.

Lunsford, Andrea A., and Lisa Ede. "New Beginnings." In *Singular Texts/Plural Authors: Perspectives on Collaborative Writing,* by Andrea A. Lunsford and Lisa Ede, 130–43. Carbondale and Edwardsville: Southern Illinois University Press, 1990. Print.

Lynch, Catherine M. "Arthur (Michell) Ransome." In *British Children's Writers, 1914–1960,* edited by Donald R. Hettinga and Gary D. Schmidt. Detroit: Gale Research, 1996. *Dictionary of Literary Biography,* vol. 160. *Literature Resource Center.* Web. June 10, 2013.

MacDonald, George. "The Imagination: Its Functions and Its Culture." In *A Dish of Orts: Chiefly Papers on the Imagination and on Shakespeare,* illustrated by Cyrus Cuneo and G. H. Evison, 1–42. London: E. Dalton, 1908. Print.

Macdonald, Stuart. *History and Philosophy of Art Education.* New York: American Elsevier Press, 1970. Print.

Macready, William Charles, Jr. "To Robert Browning." [May 1842]. In *The Brownings' Correspondence,* edited by Philip Kelley and Ronald Hudson. Vol. 5. 329–30. Winfield, KS: .Wedgestone Press, 1987. Print.

———. "To Robert Browning." May 18, 1842. In *The Brownings' Correspondence,* edited by Phillip Kelley and Ronald Hudson, Vol. 5. 350. Winfield KS: Wedgestone Press, 1987. Print.

Madan, Falconer. *The Daniel Press: Memorials of C. H. O. Daniel, With a Bibliography of the Press, 1845–1919.* Oxford: Printed on the Daniel Press in the Bodleian Library, 1921. Print.

Maitland, Louise. "Children's Drawings." *Pacific Education Journal* 11, no. 9 (September 1895): 413–17. *Google Books.* Web. June 30, 2015.

———. "What Children Draw to Please Themselves." *The Inland Educator* 1, no. 2 (September 1895): 77–81. *Google Books.* Web. June 30, 2015.

Malarte-Feldman, Claire L. "Thumbling, Tom Thumb." In *The Greenwood Encyclopedia of Folktales and Fairy* Tales. Volume 3: *Q–Z,* edited by Donald Haase, 969. Westport, CT: Greenwood Press, 2008. Print.

Malvern, S. B. "Inventing 'Child Art': Franz Cizek and Modernism." *British Journal of Aesthetics* 35, no. 3 (July 1995): 262–72. Print.

Marryat, Captain [Frederick]. *The Settlers in Canada.* London: Frederick Warne and Co. and George Bell and Sons, 1886. *Internet Archive.* Web. September 17, 2015.

Maxwell, Christabel. *Mrs. Gatty and Mrs. Ewing.* London: Constable Publishers, 1949. Print.

McCulloch, Fiona. "'Playing Double': Performing Childhood in *Treasure Island*." *Scottish Studies Review* 4, no. 2 (Autumn 2003): 66–81. Print.

McDowell, Katie. "Children's Voices in Librarians' Words, 1890–1930." *Libraries and the Cultural Record* 46, no. 1 (2011): 73–101. Print.

McGavran, James Holt, Jr. *Literature and the Child: Romantic Continuations, Postmodern Contestations.* Iowa City: University of Iowa Press, 1999. Print.

———. *Romanticism and Children's Literature in Nineteenth-Century England.* Edited by James Holt McGavran Jr. Athens: University of Georgia Press, 1991. Print.

Menefee, Joan. "Art and Data: Children's Mark-Making and Modernity." *The Lion and the Unicorn* 36, no. 3 (September 2012): 225–44. Print.

Middleton, Nigel. "The Education Act of 1870 as the Start of the Modern Concept of the Child." *British Journal of Educational Studies* 18, no. 2 (June 1970): 166–79. Print.

Molesworth, Mary Louisa [Ennis Graham, pseud]. *Tell Me a Story.* London: Macmillan, 1875. *HathiTrust.* Web. September 16, 2015.

Molesworth, Mrs. [Mary Louisa]. *An Enchanted Garden: Fairy Stories.* Illustrated by W. J. Hennessy. London: T. Fisher Unwin, 1892. *Internet Archive.* Web. September 16, 2015.

———. "On the Art of Writing Fiction for Children." *Atalanta* 6 (May 1893): 183–86. Reprinted in *A Peculiar Gift: Nineteenth Century Writings on Books for Children*, edited by Lance Salway, 340–46. Harmondsworth, UK: Kestrel Books, 1976. Print.

———. "Story-Reading and Story-Writing." *Chambers's Journal* 1, no. 49 (November 5, 1898): 772–75. *British Periodicals.* Web. September 16, 2015.

Moran, James. "Miniature, 'Toy,' Amateur and Card Presses." In *Printing Presses: History and Development from the Fifteenth Century to Modern Times*, by James Moran, 227–47. Berkeley and Los Angeles: University of California Press, 1973. Print.

Morley, Christopher. *The Ironing Board.* Freeport, NY: Books for Libraries Press, 1949. Print.

Mosley, James. "The Press in the Parlour: Some Notes on the Amateur Printer and His Equipment." *The Black Art* 2, no. 1 (Spring 1963): 2–16. Print.

Moss, Anita. "Varieties of Children's Metafiction." *Studies in the Literary Imagination* 18, no. 2 (Fall 1985): 79–92. Print.

Murray, Stuart. *Representing Autism: Culture, Narrative, Fascination.* Liverpool, UK: Liverpool University Press, 2008. Print.

Myers, Mitzi. "Reading Rosamund Reading: Maria Edgeworth's 'Wee-Wee Stories' Interrogate the Canon." In *Infant Tongues: The Voice of the Child in Literature*, edited by Elizabeth Goodenough, Mark A. Heberle, and Naomi B. Sokoloff, 57–79. Detroit: Wayne State University Press, 1994. Print.

Nelson, Claudia. *Boys Will Be Girls: The Feminine Ethic and British Children's Fiction, 1857–1917.* New Brunswick, NJ: Rutgers University Press, 1991. Print.

———. *Precocious Children and Childlike Adults: Age Inversion in Victorian Literature.* Baltimore: Johns Hopkins University Press, 2012. Print.

Neumann, Siegfried. "The Brothers Grimm as Collectors and Editors of German Folktales." In *The Reception of Grimms' Fairy Tales: Responses, Reactions, Revisions*, edited by Donald Haase, 24–40. Detroit: Wayne State University Press, 1993. Print.

Nikolajeva, Maria. *Power, Voice, and Subjectivity in Literature for Young Readers*. New York and London: Routledge, 2010. Print.

Noakes, Vivien. *Edward Lear, 1812–1888*. Introduction by Sir Steven Runcimen and essay by Jeremy Maas. New York: Harry N. Abrams, 1986. Print.

Nodelman, Perry. *The Hidden Adult: Defining Children's Literature*. Baltimore: Johns Hopkins University Press, 2008. Print.

———. "The Hidden Child in *The Hidden Adult*." *Jeunesse* 8, no. 1 (Summer 2016): 266–77. Project Muse. Web. August 20, 2016.

———. "The Other: Orientalism, Colonialism, and Children's Literature." *Children's Literature Association Quarterly* 17, no. 1 (Spring 1992): 29–35. Print.

Norquay, Glenda. "Trading Texts: Negotiations of the Professional and the Popular in the Case of *Treasure Island*." In *Robert Louis Stevenson: Writer of Boundaries*, edited by Richard Ambrosini and Richard Dury, 60–69. Madison: University of Wisconsin Press, 2006. Print.

Ogata, Amy F. *Designing the Creative Child: Playthings and Places in Midcentury America*. Minneapolis: University of Minnesota Press, 2013. Print.

Olk, Claudia. "The Art of 'Scene-Making' in the *Charleston Bulletin Supplements*." *Literature Compass* 4, no. 1 (2007): 252–62. Print.

Ong, Walter J. *Orality and Literacy: The Technologizing of the Word*. London and New York: Methuen, 1982. Print.

Onion, Rebecca. "Writing a 'Wonderland' of Science: Child-Authored Periodicals at the Brooklyn Children's Museum, 1936–1946." *American Periodicals* 23, no. 1 (2013): 1–21. Project Muse. Web. July 26, 2016.

"Osbourne, Lloyd." In *The National Cyclopaedia of American Biography, Being the History of the United States as Illustrated in the Lives of the Founders, Builders, and Defenders of the Republic, and of the Men and Women who are Doing the Work and Moulding the Thought of the Present Time*, edited by "Distinguished biographers, selected from each state and revised and approved by the most eminent historians, scholars, and statesmen of the day," 459. New York: James T. White, 1910. Print.

Osbourne, Samuel Lloyd. *Davos News*. Davos-Platz, Switzerland. Reprinted in *The Private Press Ventures of Samuel Lloyd Osbourne and R. L. S., With Facsimiles of their Publications*, edited by James D. Hart. San Francisco: Book Club of California, 1966. Print.

———. *An Intimate Portrait of R.L.S., by His Stepson*. New York: Scribner's, 1924. Print.

———. "Note by Lloyd Osbourne." In *Treasure Island and Prince Otto*. Vol. 5 of *The Works of Robert Louis Stevenson*, ix–xi. Vailima ed. New York: Charles Scribner's Sons, 1922. Print.

———. Preface. In *Moral Emblems & Other Poems, Poems Written and Illustrated with Woodcuts*, v–xviii. New York: C. Scribner's Sons, 1921. Print.

———. *The Surprise.* 1880. Reprinted in *The Private Press Ventures of Samuel Lloyd Osbourne and R. L. S., With Facsimiles of their Publications*, edited by James D. Hart. San Francisco: Book Club of California, 1966. Print.

Osbourne, [Samuel] Lloyd, and Austin Strong. *Treasure Island: A Melodrama in Five Acts.* June 18, 1902. Typescript, Robert Louis Stevenson Museum, St. Helena, CA.

Pantall, Colin. "An Interview with Timothy Archibald." *Colin Pantall's Blog.* November 30, 2010. Web. May 24, 2013.

Parkes, Christopher. *Children's Literature and Capitalism: Fictions of Social Mobility in Britain, 1850–1914.* Critical Approaches to Children's Literature. Houndsmills, UK: Palgrave Macmillan, 2012. Print.

Patrick, G. T. W. "Should Children Under Ten Learn to Read and Write?" *Popular Science Monthly* 54 (January 1899): 382–92. *Google Books.* Web. September 16, 2015.

Patten, Robert L. *George Cruikshank's Life, Times, and Art,* Vol. 1, *1792–1835.* New Brunswick NJ: Rutgers University Press, 1992. Print.

Paul, Lissa. *The Children's Book Business: Lessons from the Long Eighteenth Century.* Hoboken, NJ: Taylor and Francis, 2010. Print.

Perez, Bernard. *The First Three Years of Childhood.* Edited and translated by Alice M. Christie. Introduction by James Sully. London: Swan Sonnenschein, 1889. *HathiTrust.* Web. September 16, 2015.

Peterson, William S., ed. *Browning's Trumpeter: The Correspondence of Robert Browning and Frederick J. Furnivall, 1872–1889.* Washington DC: Decatur House Press, 1979. Print.

Pierce, Jason A. "The Belle Lettrist and the People's Publisher: or, The Context of 'Treasure Island's' First Publication." *Victorian Periodicals Review* 31, no. 4 (Winter 1998): 337–68. Print.

Plotz, Judith. *Romanticism and the Vocation of Childhood.* New York and Basingstoke, UK: Palgrave, 2001. Print.

Pollock, F. "An Infant's Progress in Language." *Mind* 3, no. 11 (July 1878): 392–401. *Oxford University Press Humanities Archive.* Web. September 16, 2015.

Pollock, Mary S. "'Undue Levity': The Moral Complexity of Browning's 'Pied Piper.'" *Children's Literature Association Quarterly* 24, no. 3 (Fall 1999): 141–47. Print.

Pratt, Linda Ray. "Passionate Reporting: Arnold on Elementary Schools, Teachers, and Children." *Nineteenth-Century Prose* 34, nos. 1–2 (Spring–Fall 2007): 25–57. Print.

Quirici, Marion. "Geniuses without Imagination: Discourses of Autism, Ability, and Achievement." *Journal of Literacy and Cultural Disability Studies* 9, no. 1 (2015): 71–88. *Project Muse.* Web. August 18, 2016.

[Rands, William Brighty]. "Children and Children's Books." *Argosy* 2, no. 12 (November 1866): 464–69. *British Periodicals.* Web. August 12, 2015.

———. *Lazy Lessons and Essays on Conduct.* Edited by R. Brimley Johnson. London: James Bowden, 1897. Print.

———. *Lilliput Lectures.* London: Strahan, 1871. *HathiTrust.* Web. August 14, 2015.

———. *Lilliput Levee: Poems of Childhood, Child-Fancy, and Childlike Moods.* Illustrated by John Everett Millais and G. J. Pinwell. London: Alexander Strahan, 1864. *HathiTrust.* Web. August 14, 2015.

———. "The Nurture of Children." In *Alexandra: A Gift Book to the Alexandra Orphanage for Infants, Hornsey Rise*, edited by Thomas Archer, 119–38. London: James Clarke, 1869. *Google Books*. Web. August 14, 2015.

———. [Angelo Merrit Gray]. "School Board Comedies." *St. Paul's Magazine* 12 (March 1873): 290–95. *Google Books*. Web. August 28, 2015.

Ransom, Will. "What Is a Private Press?" In *Books and Printing: A Treasury for Typophiles*, by Will Ransom, 175–81. Cleveland and New York: World Publishing Company, 1951. Print.

Ransome, Arthur. Introduction to *The Far-Distant Oxus*, by Katharine Hull and Pamela Whitlock. New York: Macmillan, 1938. Print.

Ray, Gordon Norton. Introduction to *The Rose and the Ring, Reproduced in Facsimile from the Author's original illustrated manuscript in the Pierpont Morgan Library*, by William Makepeace Thackeray. New York: Pierpont Morgan Library, 1947. Print.

———. *Thackeray: The Age of Wisdom, 1847–1863*. 2 vols. New York: McGraw-Hill, 1955. Print.

Redcay, Anna M. "'Live to learn and learn to live': The Saint Nicholas League and the Vocation of Childhood." *Children's Literature* 39 (2011): 58–84. *Project Muse*. Web. July 26, 2016.

Reimer, Mavis, and charlie peters. "Ignorant and Innocent: The Childs of Common Cultural Discourses." *Jeunesse* 3, no. 2 (2011): 88–99. *Project Muse*. Web. August 18, 2016.

Report for the Committee of Council on Education, with Appendix, 1862–3, Presented in Both Houses of Parliament by Command of Her Majesty. London: Printed by George E. Eyre and William Spottiswoode, for Her Majesty's Stationery Office, 1863. *Internet Archive*. Web. August 25, 2015.

Review of *Ackermann's Juvenile Forget-Me-Not*, ed. Frederick Shoberl. *Eclectic Review* (December 1830): 561–69. *Google Books*. Web. August 9, 2015.

Review of *The Adventurer*, by Lloyd Osbourne. *Nation* 85 (1907): 518. *Google Books*. Web. September 17, 2015.

Review of *Baby Bullet*, by Lloyd Osbourne. *Critic* 47 (1905): 579. *Google Books*. Web. September 17, 2015.

Review of *The Child and His Book*, by E. M. Field. *Edinburgh Review* 194, no. 398 (October 1901): 414–37. *British Periodicals*. Web. August 16, 2015.

Review of *Covent Garden Painting Book, Easy Painting Book (Waterside)*, and *Easy Painting Book (Landscapes)*. *The Bookman* 73, no. 435 (December 1927): 14. *British Periodicals*. Web. October 4, 2014.

Review of *The Ebb-Tide, A Trio and a Quartette*, by Robert Louis Stevenson and Lloyd Osbourne. *The Saturday Review* 78 (September 22, 1894): 330. *British Periodicals*. Web. September 17, 2015.

Review of *The Ebb-Tide*, by Robert Louis Stevenson and Lloyd Osbourne. *The Speaker* 10 (September 19, 1894): 362–63. *British Periodicals*. Web. September 17, 2015.

Review of *Juvenile Literature As It Is*, by Edward Salmon. *Journal of Education* 10 (December 1, 1888): 597. *HathiTrust*. Web. August 2, 2015.

Review of *A Person of Some Importance*, by Lloyd Osbourne. *National Magazine* 36 (1912): 241. *Google Books*. Web. September 17, 2015.

Review of *Treasure Island*, by Robert Louis Stevenson. *Academy* 604 (December 1, 1883): 362.

Review of *Treasure Island*, by Robert Louis Stevenson. *Graphic* 38 (December 15, 1883): 599. *Google Books*. Web. September 17, 2015.

Reynolds, Sir Joshua. "Discourse III: Delivered to the Students of The Royal Academy, on the Distribution of Prizes, December 14, 1770." In *Discourses on Art*, edited by Robert R. Wark, 39-53. New Haven, CT, and London: Yale University Press, 1997. Print.

Ricci, Corrado. "The Art of Little Children" ("L'arte des bambini"). Translated by Louise Maitland. *Pedagogical Seminary* 3 (1894): 302–7. Print.

Rich, Eric E. *The Education Act of 1870: A Study of Public Opinion*. London and Harlow, UK: Longmans, 1970. Print.

Richards, Jeffrey, ed. *Imperialism and Juvenile Literature*. Manchester, UK, and New York: Manchester University Press, 1989. Print.

Richardson, Alan. *Literature, Education, and Romanticism: Reading as Social Practice, 1780–1832*. Cambridge Studies in Romanticism. Cambridge: Cambridge University Press, 2004. Print.

Richardson, Marion. *Art and the Child*. Introduction by Sir Kenneth Clark. Peoria, IL: Chas. A. Bennett, 1948. Print.

Risch, Conor. "Family Business." *Photo District News, Eastern Edition* 30, no. 9 (September 2010): 92, 94, 96. Print.

Robbins, Sarah. "Lessons for Children and Teaching Mothers: Mrs. Barbauld's Primer for the Textual Construction of Middle-Class Domestic Pedagogy." *Lion and the Unicorn* 17, no. 2 (December 1993): 135–51. Print.

——. "Re-Making Barbauld's Primers: A Case Study in the Americanization of British Literary Pedagogy." *Children's Literature Association Quarterly* 21, no. 4 (Winter 1996): 158–69. Print.

Robson, Catherine. *Heart Beats: Everyday Life and the Memorized Poem*. Princeton, NJ, and Oxford: Princeton University Press, 2012. Print.

——. *Men in Wonderland: The Lost Girlhood of the Victorian Gentleman*. Princeton, NJ: Princeton University Press, 2001. Print.

Rose, Jacqueline. *The Case of Peter Pan, or, The Impossibility of Children's Fiction*. London and Basingstoke, UK: Macmillan, 1984. Print.

Rose, Jonathan. "How Historians Study Reader Response: Or, What Did Jo Think of *Bleak House*?" In *Literature in the Marketplace: Nineteenth-Century British Publishing and Reading Practices*, edited by John O. Jordan and Robert L. Patten, 195–212. Cambridge Studies in Nineteenth-Century Literature and Culture. Cambridge: Cambridge University Press, 1995. Print.

Rose, Lionel. *The Erosion of Childhood: Child Oppression in Britain, 1860–1918*. London and New York: Routledge, 1991. Print.

Rousseau, Jean-Jacques. *Émile*. 1762. Translated by Barbara Foxley. Introduction by P. D. Jimack. London: J. M. Dent, 1993. Print.

Rowe, Karen E. "To Spin a Yarn: The Female Voice in Folklore and Fairy Tale." In *Fairy Tales and Society: Illusion, Allusion, and Paradigm*, edited by Ruth B. Bottigheimer, 53–74. Philadelphia: University of Pennsylvania Press, 1986. Print.
Rowe, Richard. *A Child's Corner Book: Stories for Boys and Girls*. London and Edinburgh: William P. Nimmo, 1876. *Google Books*. Web. August 9, 2015.
Rudd, David. "Theorising and Theories: The Conditions of Possibility in Children's Literature." In *International Companion Encyclopedia of Children's Literature*, edited by Peter Hunt, 29–43. London: Routledge, 2004. Print.
Ruskin, John. *The Elements of Drawing; In Three Letters to Beginners*. New York: John Wiley and Sons, 1883. *HathiTrust*. Web. May 23, 2015.
———. "Fairy Stories." 1868. Reprinted in *Fantastic Literature: A Critical Reader*, edited by David Sandner, 59–63. Westport, CT: Praeger, 2004. Print.
Salisbury, Henderson E. *The Shook-Up Generation*. New York: Harper and Row, 1958. Print.
Salmon, Edward. *Juvenile Literature As It Is*. London: Henry J. Drane, 1888. *HathiTrust*. Web. August 4, 2015.
Sánchez-Eppler, Karen. *Dependent States: The Child's Part in Nineteenth-Century American Culture*. Chicago: University of Chicago Press, 2005. Print.
Schacker, Jennifer. "The Household Tales in the Household Library: Edgar Taylor's *German Popular Stories*." In *National Dreams: The Remaking of Fairy Tales in Nineteenth-Century England*, by Jennifer Schacker, 13–45. Philadelphia: University of Pennsylvania Press, 2003. Print.
Schmidt, Gary D. "Questions of Power." *Children's Literature* 21 (1993): 167–73. Print.
Schwebel, Sara L. "The Limits of Agency for Children's Literature Scholars." *Jeunesse* 8, no. 1 (Summer 2016): 266–77. *Project Muse*. Web. August 20, 2016.
"The Science of Nonsense." *The Spectator* (December 17, 1870): 1505–6. *Google Books*. Web. July 17, 2015.
"Sheet from Darwin's 'On the origin of Species' manuscript on display for first time." *The Telegraph*. The Telegraph Media Group, July 3, 2009. Web. February 15, 2015.
Sherard, Robert H. "Notes from Paris." *The Author* 6, no. 1 (June 1, 1895): 8–10. *British Periodicals*. Web. September 9, 2015.
Shires, Linda M. "Mutual Adaptation in Rudyard Kipling's Letters to His Children and *Just So Stories*." *Children's Literature* 43 (2015): 182–207. Print.
Shuttleworth, Sally. "Inventing a Discipline: Autobiography and the Science of Child Study in the 1890s." *Comparative Critical Studies* 2, no. 2 (2005): 143–63. Print.
———. *The Mind of the Child: Child Development in Literature, Science, and Medicine, 1840–1900*. Oxford: Oxford University Press, 2010. Print.
Smith, A. Tolman. "Browning's 'Sordello': A Study in the Psychology of Childhood." *Poet Lore* 6, no. 5 (1894): 238–43. *Google Books*. Web. September 16, 2015.
Smith, Vanessa. "Piracy and Exchange: Stevenson's Pacific Fiction." *Robert Louis Stevenson*. Edited by Harold Bloom. Bloom's Modern Critical Views. Philadelphia: Chelsea House, 2005. 261–306. Print.
Smith, Victoria Ford. "Art Critics in the Cradle: Fin-de-Siècle Painting Books and the Move to Modernism." *Children's Literature* 43 (2015): 161–81. Print.

———. "Toy Presses and Treasure Maps: Robert Louis Stevenson and Lloyd Osbourne as Collaborators." *Children's Literature Association Quarterly* 35, no. 1 (Spring 2010): 26–54. *Project Muse*. Web. August 18, 2016.

Sorby, Angela. *Schoolroom Poets: Childhood, Performance, and the Place of American Poetry, 1865–1917*. Lebanon: University of New Hampshire Press, 2005. Print.

Sparkes, J. "On the Teaching of Drawing and of Colouring as a Preparation for Designing and Decorative Work." In *Proceedings of the International Conference on Education, London, 1884*, 2 vols., edited by Richard Cowper, 2:200–208. London: William Clowes and Sons, 1884. *Internet Archive*. Web. May 28, 2015.

"Special Art Competition—Children's Story—Debate—Results of October Competitions." *Quiver* (January 1920): 301–3. *British Periodicals*. Web. August 28, 2015.

Spencer, Truman J. *The History of Amateur Journalism*. New York: The Fossils, 1957. Print.

Squibbler. "Hengler's and Horsier." *Punch* 90 (February 13, 1886): 73. *Google Books*. Web. August 4, 2015.

———. "Something Like a Drama!" *Punch* 90 (February 20, 1886): 93. *Google Books*. Web. August 4, 2015.

Stayner, McKenna. "Darwinian Doodles." *The New Yorker*. February 9, 2015. Web. March 30, 2015.

Steedman, Carolyn. *Strange Dislocations: Childhood and the Idea of Human Interiority, 1780–1930*. London: Virago Press, 1995. Print.

Stephens, W. B. *Education in Britain: 1750–1914*. Basingstoke, UK, and London: Macmillan, 1998. Print.

Stevens, Joan. "A Fairy Tale Mishandled, *The Rose and the Ring*." *AUMLA: Journal of the Australasian Universities* 23 (May 1965): 5–23. Print.

Stevens, Kate. "Child Study in Great Britain." *Pedagogical Seminary* 13 (1906): 245–49. *Google Books*. Web. September 16, 2015.

Stevenson, Fanny Van de Grift. "Prefatory Note." In *Treasure Island* and *Prince Otto*. Vol. 5 of *The Works of Robert Louis Stevenson*, xii–xvii. Vailima ed. New York: Charles Scribner's Sons, 1922. Print.

Stevenson, Robert Louis. "Authors and Publishers." In *The Lantern-Bearers and Other Essays*, edited by Jeremy Treglown, 259–64. New York: Cooper Square Press, 1988. Print.

———. *Catriona*. London and Edinburgh: Thomas Nelson & Sons, 1892. *HathiTrust*. Web. September 17, 2015.

———. "A Chapter on Dreams." In *The Lantern-Bearers and Other Essays*, edited by Jeremy Treglown, 216–25. New York: Cooper Square Press, 1988. Print.

———. "Child's Play." *Virginibus Puerisque*. Vol. 2 of *The Works of Robert Louis Stevenson*, edited by Will D. Howe and Lloyd Osbourne, 168–83. 26 vols. New York: Scribner's Sons, 1921. Print.

———. "A Gossip on Romance." In *The Lantern-Bearers and Other Essays*, edited by Jeremy Treglown, 172–82. New York: Cooper Square Press, 1988. Print.

———. *The Graver & The Pen, Or, Scenes from Nature with Appropriate Verses*. Illustrated by Robert Louis Stevenson. Edinburgh: S. L. Osbourne & Company, n.d. Reprinted in *The Private Press Ventures of Samuel Lloyd Osbourne and R. L. S., with Facsimiles of their Publications*. Edited by James D. Hart. San Francisco: Book Club of California, 1966. Print.

———. "A Humble Remonstrance." In *The Lantern-Bearers and Other Essays*, edited Jeremy Treglown, 1992–201. New York: Cooper Square Press, 1988. Print.

———. *The Letters of Robert Louis Stevenson*. Edited by Bradford A. Booth and Ernest Mehew. 8 vols. New Haven, CT, and London: Yale University Press, 1994. Print.

———. "Letter to a Young Gentleman Who Proposes to Embrace the Career of Art." In *The Lantern-Bearers and Other Essays*, edited by Jeremy Treglown, 244–50. New York: Cooper Square Press, 1988. Print.

———. *Letters to Young Friends*. Introduction and notes by S. L. Osbourne. *St. Nicholas Magazine* 23, nos. 2–4 (December 1895), (January 1896), and (February 1896). American Periodicals Series III. September 17, 2015.

———. "My First Book." *The Lantern-Bearers and Other Essays*. Edited by Jeremy Treglown, 277–84. New York: Cooper Square Press, 1988. Print.

———. *Not I and Other Poems*. Davos: S. L. Osbourne, 1881. Reprinted as *The Private Press Ventures of Samuel Lloyd Osbourne and R. L. S., With Facsimiles of their Publications*. Edited by James D. Hart. San Francisco: Book Club of California, 1966. Print.

———. "A Penny Plain and Twopence Coloured." In *Memories and Portraits*. Vol. 12 of *The Works of Robert Louis Stevenson*, 169–70. Vailima ed. New York: Scribner's, 1923. Print.

———. "The Persons of the Tale." In *Juvenilia, Moral Emblems, Fables, and Other Papers*. Vol. 25 of *The Works of Robert Louis Stevenson*, 183–87. Vailima ed. New York: Scribner's, 1923. Print.

———. "The Reader." In *Juvenilia, Moral Emblems, Fables, and Other Papers*. Vol. 25 of *The Works of Robert Louis Stevenson*, 213–14. Vailima ed. New York: Scribner's, 1923. 213–14. Print.

———. *Treasure Island*. Edited by Wendy R. Katz. Centenary ed. Edinburgh: Edinburgh University Press, 1998. Print.

Stevenson, Robert Louis, and [Samuel] Lloyd Osbourne. *The Ebb-Tide: A Trio & Quartette*. Edited by Peter Hinchcliffe and Catherine Kerrigan. Centenary ed. Edinburgh: Edinburgh University Press, 1995. Print.

Stillinger, Jack. *Multiple Authorship and the Myth of Solitary Genius*. Oxford: Oxford University Press, 1991. Print.

Stirling, Kirstin. "Origins and Storytelling." In *Peter Pan's Shadows in the Literary Imagination*, 7–25. Children's Literature and Culture 83. New York: Routledge, 2012. Print.

Stone, Marjorie, and Judith Thompson, eds. *Literary Couplings: Writing Couples, Collaborators, and the Construction of Authorship*. Madison: University of Wisconsin Press, 2006. Print.

Story, Edith [La Marchesa Peruzzi de Medici]. "Thackeray, My Childhood's Friend." *Cornhill Magazine*, n.s. 31 (July–December 1911): 178–81. *HathiTrust*. Web. September 16, 2015.

[Strachey, Edmund]. "Nonsense as a Fine Art." *The Quarterly Review* 167 (October 1888): 335–65. *Google Books*. Web. July 12, 2015.

Strachey, H[enry]. "Appreciation of Lear as a Painter." In *Letters of Edward Lear, Author of the "Book of Nonsense," to Chichester Fortescue and Frances Countess Waldegrave*, edited by Lady [Constance] Strachey, xxxvi–xl. London: T. Fisher Unwin, 1907. *Google Books*. Web. July 17, 2015.

Straley, Jessica. *Evolution and Imagination in Victorian Children's Literature*. Cambridge Studies in Nineteenth-Century Literature and Culture. Cambridge: Cambridge University Press, 2016. Print.

Sully, James. *Studies of Childhood*. 1895. New York and London: D. Appleton, 1914. *HathiTrust*. Web. September 16, 2015.

Sumpter, Caroline. *The Victorian Press and the Fairy Tale*. Palgrave Studies in Nineteenth-Century Writing and Culture. New York: Palgrave Macmillan, 2008. Print.

Sutherland, John. "R[obert] M[ichael] Ballantyne." In *The Stanford Companion to Victorian Fiction*, 39–40. Stanford, CA: Stanford University Press, 1989. Print.

Sutton, Gordon. *Artisan or Artist? A History of the Teaching of Art and Crafts in English Schools*. Oxford: Pergamon Press, 1967. Print.

Taine, Hippolyte. "On the Acquisition of Language by Children." *Mind* 2 (1877): 252–59. *Google Books*. Web. September 16, 2015.

Tatar, Maria. *The Hard Facts of the Grimms' Fairy Tales*. Expanded 2nd ed. Princeton, NJ: Princeton University Press, 2003. Print.

Taylor, Edgar. "Preface." In *German Popular Stories and Fairy Tales, as Told by Gammer Grethel, from the Collection of MM. Grimm*, by Jacob and Wilhelm Grimm, translated by Edgar Taylor, iii–vii. 1839. London: Bell and Daldy, 1872. *Google Books*. Web. September 16, 2015.

[Taylor, Edgar]. "Preface." In *German Popular Stories, Translated from the Kinder und Haus Marchen, collected by M. M. Grimm from Oral Tradition*, illustrated by George Cruikshank, iii–xii. Facsimile of the 1823 edition published in London by C. Baldwyn. Menston, UK: Scolar Press, 1971. Print.

Thackeray, William Makepeace [Michael Angelo Titmarsh]. "On Some Illustrated Children's Books." *Fraser's Magazine* 33 (April 1846): 495–502. *Google Books*. Web. July 11, 2015.

———. *The Rose and the Ring; Or, The History of Prince Giglio and Prince Bulbo. A Fire-Side Pantomime for Great and Small Children*. New York and London: J. P. Putnam's Sons, 1854. *HathiTrust*. Web. September 16, 2015.

Thorpe, Karen, Rosemary Greenwood, Areana Eivers, and Michael Rutter. "Prevalence and Developmental Course of 'Secret Language.'" *International Journal of Language and Communication Disorders* 36, no. 1 (January–March 2001): 43–62. *Wiley Online Library*. Web. August 4, 2016.

Tollers, Vincent L. "A Working Isaiah: Arnold in the Council Office." *Essays and Studies* 41 (1988): 108–24. Print.
Tosenberger, Catherine. "Mature Poets Steal: Children's Literature and the Unpublishability of Fanfiction." *Children's Literature Association Quarterly* 39, no. 1 (Spring 2014): 4–27. *Project Muse.* Web. July 26, 2016.
Tracy, Frederick. *The Psychology of Childhood.* 1894. Boston: Heath, 1909. *HathiTrust.* Web. September 16, 2015.
Trimmer, Sarah. *An Easy Introduction to the Knowledge of Nature, and Reading the Holy Scriptures, Adapted to the Capacities of Children.* 10th ed. London: Longman, 1799. *Google Books.* Web. September 9, 2015.
"Unindented." *Oxford English Dictionary Online.* Web. August 16, 2008.
Valint, Alexandra. "The Child's Resistance to Adulthood in Robert Louis Stevenson's *Treasure Island*: Refusing to Parrot." *English Literature in Transition, 1880–1920* 58, no. 1 (2015): 3–29. Print.
Vandegrift, Kay E. "Female Advocacy and Harmonious Voices: A History of Public Library Services and Publishing for Children in the United States." *Library Trends* 44, no. 4 (Spring 1996): 638–718. Print.
Vanpée, Janie. "Reading Lessons in Rousseau's *Émile, ou de l'éducation*." *Modern Language Studies* 20, no. 3 (Summer 1990): 40–49. Print.
Viola, Wilhelm. *Child Art.* 2nd ed. Peoria, IL: Chas. A. Bennet, 1944. Print.
Walsh, Sue. *Kipling's Children's Literature: Language, Identity, and Constructions of Childhood.* Ashgate Studies in Childhood, 1700 to Present. Burlington, VT: Ashgate, 2010. *Proquest ebrary.* Web. June 25, 2016.
Ward, Donald. "The German Connection: The Brothers Grimm and the Study of 'Oral' Literature." *Western Folklore* 53, no. 1 (January 1994): 1–26. Print.
Watson, Harold Francis. *Coasts of Treasure Island: A Study of the Backgrounds and Sources for Robert Louis Stevenson's Romance of the Sea.* San Antonio, TX: Naylor, 1969. Print.
Watson, Victor. "By children, about children, for children." In *Where Texts and Children Meet*, edited by Eve Bearne and Victor Watson, 51–67. London and New York: Routledge, 2000. Print.
———. "The Far-Distant Oxus." In *Cambridge Guide to Children's Books in English*, edited by Victor Watson, 255. Cambridge: Cambridge University, Press, 2001. *Gale Virtual Reference Library.* Web. June 7, 2013.
Watts, Mrs. Alaric, ed. *The New Year's Gift; and, Juvenile Souvenir.* London: Longman, Rees, Orme, Brown, and Green, 1831. *Google Books.* Web. August 9, 2015.
"What the Audience Thinks: 'Mary Rose' and "Peter Pan' Prize Competitions Results." *The Bookman* 59, no. 351 (December 1920): 114–22. *British Periodicals.* Web. August 28, 2015.
White, Daniel E. "The 'Joineriana': Anna Barbauld, the Aikin Family Circle, and the Dissenting Public Sphere." *Eighteenth-Century Studies* 32, no. 4 (Summer 1999): 511–33. Print.
Whiting, Lilian. *The Golden Road.* Boston: Little, Brown, 1918. *Google Books.* Web. September 16, 2015.

Wilson, Francesca. *A Class at Professor Cizek's; Subject—"Autumn."* [London]: Children's Art Exhibition Fund, 1921. *HathiTrust*. Web. June 10, 2015.

———. *A Lecture by Professor Cizek*. [London]: Children's Art Exhibition Fund, 1921. *HathiTrust*. Web. June 10, 2015.

Wong, Amy. "The Poetics of Talk in Robert Louis Stevenson's *Treasure Island*." *SEL: Studies in English Literature, 1500–1900* 54, no. 4 (Autumn 2014): 901–22. Print.

Wooldridge, Adrian. *Measuring the Mind: Education and Psychology in England, 1860–1990*. Cambridge and New York: Cambridge University Press, 1994. Print.

Woolf, Virginia. "Preface." In *Orlando: A Biography*, 5–7. San Diego, New York, and London: Harcourt, 1956. Print.

Woolf, Virginia, and Quentin Bell. *The Charleston Bulletin Supplements*. Edited by Claudia Olk. London: The British Library, 2013. Print.

Woolford, John, and Daniel Karlin, eds. *The Poems of Robert Browning*. Vol. 2, *1841–1846*. London and New York: Routledge, 2014. Print.

Wordsworth, William. "Ode: Intimations of Immortality from Recollections of Early Childhood." In *The Complete Poetical Works of William Wordsworth*, edited by Henry Reed, 470–73. Philadelphia: Portman and Coates, 1851.

Zipes, Jack. "The Contamination of the Fairy Tale; Or, The Changing Nature of the Grimms' Fairy Tales." *Journal of the Fantastic in the Arts* 11, no. 1 (2000): 77–93. Print.

Index

Aaron, Jane, 290n4
Ablett, T. R., 204, 237
adolescence, 106–7, 125, 255, 270n18, 291n8
adult-child collaboration: adults and child artists, 35, 89, 192–94, 196, 198–99, 202–3, 207, 209–10, 211–30, 238; adults and child reviewers and experts, 143–46, 163–78; and adventure fiction, 71, 274n20; Barrie and the Llewelyn Davies brothers, 6, 24, 157, 158–59, 160–62, 241, 249–50, 280n16; beyond Victorian period, 35–36, 241–53; Browning and Macready, 3–6, 8–9, 12–13, 211–15, 217, 241, 263nn1–3, 264n7, 265n10; Carroll and Liddell sisters, 6, 16; Clarke and children, 33, 43, 71–74, 93; in classrooms, 185–87, 188, 202–3, 208–10; critical neglect of, 6, 8–12, 239–40; and cross-writing, 14–16; fictive, 7, 22, 34, 35, 116, 118, 125, 146, 152, 157–58, 163, 256; Gatty and children, 6, 33, 35, 43, 78–90, 93, 215–20, 246; hybrid, 22, 23–26, 40, 49, 76, 82, 94, 107, 125, 157, 179, 192; Jordan and children, 6–7, 35, 220–24, 255; Kipling and children, 6, 12, 15, 22, 23, 224–28; and language acquisition, 43, 49–54, 57–58, 249; Molesworth and children, 33, 43, 75–78, 90; Rands and children, 34, 152–55, 187, 259; real, 22–23, 34–35, 116, 144, 152, 241; recuperating evidence of, 7, 13–24; reproduction of, 39–40, 78, 89, 154, 225; Stevenson and young Osbourne, 7–8, 23, 33–34, 93–94, 101–7, 113–14, 116–19, 246, 249, 255; storytellers and auditors, 6, 33, 37–43, 58–91, 93, 249, 261; Taylor and children, 43, 65–68; Thackeray and children, 6, 21, 33, 37–42, 90; types of, 22–26; and underexamined forms, 13, 16–17
adventure fiction, 71, 275n20; as amenable to adult-child collaboration, 16, 33–34, 93; didacticism in, 108–9; as imperialist, 33–34, 109–10; intergenerational audience, 108–14; negotiating tradition of, 114, 117; and Stevenson, 107, 111–24, 138–39
Adventurer, The (Osbourne), 132
aetonormativity (Nikolajeva), 145, 152
Aikin, John, 29–32, 266n23
Alderson, Brian, 67, 226, 239, 288n29
Alexander, Christine, 256–57
Alice's Adventures in Wonderland (Carroll), 6, 278n4
All the Year Round, 146, 239
amateur journalism, 98–99, 100, 274n6, 274n11
Andersen, Hans Christian, 39, 71, 154, 216, 270n19, 273n35
Anderson, Celia Catlett, 235
Angus, David, 275n21

Anstey, F., 145–46
Anti-Coloring Book series (Striker), 288n31
Apseloff, Marilyn Fain, 235
Archibald, Timothy, and son Elijah, 35, 247–54
Arnold, Matthew, 249; and Art for Schools Association, 231; as school inspector, 34, 179–80, 182, 184–87, 282n35
Art and the Child (Richardson), 210
art education, 35, 193, 195–204, 212, 227, 228, 260, 285n8; and Cizek, 35, 193, 208–9, 220, 285n5, 286n17; collaborative models, 8, 202–3, 208–10; and Cooke, 201–4, 207, 237; and Froebel's kindergarten, 193, 199–200, 201, 202, 204, 286n10; and Pestalozzi, 197–98, 199, 200, 201, 202; and Richardson, 209–10, 213, 220; and Rousseau, 35, 193, 194–97, 198, 200, 208, 285n7; and Ruskin, 200–201; and taste, 231–32, 233, 237; valuing accuracy and imitation, 195–97; valuing children's forms alongside imitation, 198–204; as vocational, 194, 197, 204
Art for Schools Association, 231
Artful Dodgers: Reconceiving the Golden Age of Children's Literature (Gubar), 16–18, 22, 110, 147, 151, 265n11
Ashford, Daisy, 246
Aunt Judy's Letters (Gatty), 88–90, 273n38
Aunt Judy's Magazine, 88–89, 215–16, 239, 273n35; "Nursery Nonsense" feature, 216–20, 227, 246, 273n39
Aunt Judy's Tales (Gatty), 6, 33, 81–88, 273n36, 287n20
autism, 248, 249, 250–51, 252, 253, 291n9

Bad Child's Book of Beasts (Belloc), 236
Bailey, Henry T., 207
Ballantyne, R. M., 108; *Coral Island*, 108, 109, 110, 275n20; included in surveys of young readers, 275n20; as inspiration for Stevenson, 111–12, 113

Barbauld, Anna Laetitia, 29–32, 33, 266–67nn23–26, 273n37
Barnes, Earl, 205–6, 286n15, 287n23, 287n25
Baron-Cohen, Simon, 250, 291n9
Barrie, J. M., 132, 144, 163, 181; *The Boy Castaways of Black Lake Island*, 160–61, 250, 275n19, 280n19; general comments on writing and authorship, 157, 279n11, 280n15; *Little Mary*, 158; *The Little White Bird*, 157–58, 239; and Llewelyn Davies brothers, 6, 24, 34, 157, 158–59, 160–62, 241, 249–50, 280n16; *Peter and Wendy*, 162, 178, 279n10, 280n18, 281n20; *Peter Pan*, authorship of, 6, 24, 34, 155–62, 239, 241, 250, 264n5, 279n10, 279–80nn12–14; *Peter Pan*, general references to, 162–63, 178, 265n14, 280n17, 280–81nn20–21; *Sentimental Tommy*, 158
Baxter, Charles, 140
Beattie, Hilary H., 276n25
Beckett, Sandra L., 14, 254n13
Beerbohm, Max, 140, 279n12
Bell, Quentin, 242, 290n5
Belloc, Hilaire, 236
Bernstein, Robin, 256, 281n10; on children as embodied vs. abstract, 19, 22, 23, 254; on children's toys and play, 18–20
"Biographical Sketch of an Infant, A" (Darwin), 47, 49
biography as evidence: suspicion toward, 9, 11–12; utility of, 12–13, 21–22, 211
Birkin, Andrew, 158, 279n12, 280n16
Blackford, Holly, 48, 268n8
Blackwood, Basil T., 236
Blake, Quentin, 236–37
Blamires, David, 61, 272n26
Book of Knight and Barbara, The (Jordan), 6–7, 194, 220–24, 255, 287–88nn23–26
Book of Nonsense (Lear), 232, 289n33
Bourdieu, Pierre, 176

Boy Castaways of Black Lake Island, The (Barrie), 160–61, 250, 275n19, 280n19
boyhood, constructions of, 73–74, 95, 109–10, 112
Boy's Own Paper, The, 169, 170, 171, 275n18
Bradbury, D. E., 268n5
Bratton, J. S., 108, 110, 275n19
Brodie, Warren J., 99
Brogan, Hugh, 244, 245, 247
Brophy, A. F., 204
Brown, Elmer, 205
Browne, Frances, 72–73
Brownies, The (Ewing), 81, 287n20
Browning, Robert, 35, 39, 218, 221, 249; and Art for Schools Association, 231; "The Cardinal and the Dog," collaboration with Willie Macready, 3–4, 211, 213–14, 263n1, 263n3; "The Pied Piper of Hamelin," collaboration with Willie Macready, 4–6, 9, 12–13, 21, 193–94, 211–15, 217, 241, 263n3, 264n7, 265n10, 286n18; "Pied Piper," illustrated editions of, 286n19; "Pied Piper," published in *Dramatic Lyrics*, 5, 8; "Pied Piper," relationship with father, 215; relationship with William C. Macready Sr., 263n2
Browning, Robert, Sr., 215
Browning, Sarianna, 5, 211, 263n1, 263n3
Bunyan, John, 27
Burgess, Gelett, 207
Burne-Jones, Edward, 237
Burnett, Frances Hodgson, 14, 16, 265n11
Burt, Forest D., 215
Bushnell, William H., 274n9

Caldecott, Randolph, 229, 231, 232, 233, 288n30
Cammaerts, Emile, 233
Capshaw, Katharine, 15, 265n15
"Cardinal and the Dog, The" (Browning), 3–4, 211, 213–14, 263n1, 263n3
Carline, Richard, 199, 286n13
Carpenter, Humphrey, 244, 245

Carroll, Lewis, 6, 16, 216, 237, 273n35, 278n4
Case of Peter Pan: Or, The Impossibility of Children's Fiction (Rose), 9–10, 44, 81, 155, 239–40, 265n14, 280n13
Chamberlain, Alexander Francis, 252; on children and art, 205, 208; on children and language acquisition, 50–51, 52, 54, 56, 269n13
Champneys, F. H., 269n14
Charleston Bulletin Supplements (Woolf and Bell), 242, 290n5
Charlie and the Chocolate Factory (Dahl), 237
child, construct and real, considering together, 8, 11–14, 16, 19, 22–24, 70, 194, 242, 254–56, 260, 291n11
child, construct vs. real debate, 8–20, 256–61, 264n8, 291nn10–11
child, embodied: and childhood studies, 260–61; in classrooms, 179, 182–84, 202–3, 207, 258, 283n40; and imagination, 115, 120–24; theorizing, 14, 19, 142–44, 152–54
child, real or actual: critical skepticism of, 8–12, 239–40; and cross-writing, 15–16; as embodied (see child, embodied); influence as readers and audiences, 43, 61–62, 76, 82, 156, 176–78; participant in literature and culture, 6–8, 146, 152; recuperating evidence of, 13–24, 142–44, 256–57, 291n10
child agency: and child artists, 35, 192, 194, 209, 211, 217, 229, 234; and child listeners, 33, 43, 65, 70; in classrooms, 35, 179, 181, 203; critical conversation surrounding, 10, 13–20, 143, 265n9; critical neglect of, 7, 8–12, 239–40; and cross-writing, 15–16; in Enlightenment children's literature, 27–32; and language acquisition, 51–58; and modes of authorship and collaboration, 5, 21, 24, 26, 35, 36, 241, 242, 254–59; and play, 18–20; and power disparities or reversals, 124,

145, 244; revising ideas of childhood, 20, 91, 189
child art: and child psychology, 198, 204, 210, 285n9; and Child Study, 193, 198, 201–2, 204–8, 209, 210, 212, 221, 287n23; and Cizek, 35, 193, 208–9, 220, 285n5, 286n17; and Cooke, 201–4, 207, 237; defining, 285n5; by Francis Darwin, 190–92, 193, 225, 234, 260, 285n3; and Froebel's kindergarten, 193, 199–200, 201, 202, 204, 286n10; in galleries and exhibitions, 237–38; and imitation or accuracy, 191–94, 195, 197–99, 201, 204–7, 209, 214–17, 220, 227, 230; and invention or creativity, 192–94, 199–204, 206–10, 211, 214, 216, 217, 220, 226; and Jordan, 35, 194, 220–24, 226, 255, 287nn21–23, 287n25; and Pestalozzi, 197–98, 199, 200, 201, 202; and recapitulation, 192, 205–6; and Richardson, 209–10, 213, 220; and Rousseau, 35, 193, 194–97, 198, 200, 208, 285n7; as vocational, 194, 197, 204; by Willie Macready, 3–6, 8–9, 12–13, 193–94, 211–15, 217, 241, 260, 263nn1–3, 286n18
child author, fictive: in Barrie, 34, 160–61; in Dickens, 16, 34, 146–50, 166, 178, 183, 278–79nn5–9; in Gatty, 218–20
child author, real, 15–16, 172; Hull and Whitlock, 34, 243–47, 254, 290nn7–8
child narrators, 16; in Dickens, 146–50; in Stevenson, 276n28
child reviewers and experts, 34–35, 143–44, 151–52, 162–78, 281nn21–23, 281nn25–26, 282n28, 288n26; difficulty representing, 168–71, 174–76; fictive, 165–66; reader surveys, 34–35, 169–78, 246, 275n20, 281nn23–26; skepticism toward, 163–64, 170–71, 177–78, 281n22
Child Study, 20, 250, 261; and child art, 193, 198, 201, 204–8, 210, 221; and child imagination, 72, 252; and language acquisition, 8, 33, 43, 46, 48–58, 70, 83, 93, 246, 252, 260, 269n10, 269nn13–15; origins of, 46–48, 268nn5–7

child voices and perspectives: adopting, 142–44, 154–55; and child art, 8, 192, 194, 198, 200, 201, 238, 242; in classrooms, 181, 184–85, 188; and cross-writing, 14–15; difficulty representing, 7, 8, 34–35, 48, 168–71, 174–76; reader surveys, 34–35, 169–78, 246, 275n20, 281nn23–26; representations in children's literature, 31–32, 148, 222–23. *See also* child narrators; child reviewers and experts
childhood studies, 48, 143, 260–61, 291n12
childist criticism, 142–43, 278nn1–2
Child-Loving: The Erotic Child in Victorian Culture (Kincaid), 10, 257, 279n12, 291n11
children's periodicals: *Aunt Judy's Magazine*, 88–89, 215–20, 227, 239, 246, 273n35, 273n39; *The Boy's Own Paper*, 169, 170, 171, 275n18; *The Girl's Own Paper*, 170; *Kingston's Magazine for Boys*, 110; *Our Young Folks*, 146, 278n6; *Quiver*, 163; *St. Nicholas Magazine*, 96, 225, 226, 275n14, 276n27; *Young Folks*, 110, 119, 169, 276n21; *Youth's Companion*, 96
children's theater, 16–17, 18, 22, 162, 266n17
Chrisman, Oscar, 55–58, 90, 253
Cizek, Franz, 35, 193, 208–9, 220, 285n5, 286n17
Clarke, Mary Cowden, 22, 33, 43, 71–74, 78, 93, 272n30
Cole, Sir Henry, 230, 231, 232
Coleridge, Hartley, 182, 282n34
collaboration, 239, 290n2, 290n4; among adults and children (*see* adult-child collaboration); among adults in

children's literature, 28–32; among children, 54–57, 98–99, 243–47, 290n8; Barrie and adults, 156, 279n11; dialogic, 105, 254–56; Osbourne and Strong, 22, 33, 134–41, 278n39; Stevenson and adults, 118–19, 125–27, 130–34, 255
Colley, Ann, 234, 288n32, 289n34
coloring books. *See* painting books
Colvin, Sidney, 119, 130, 131, 231
composition narratives, 33, 35; as evidence of child collaborator, 21–22, 241, 242, 265n16; of particular texts, 24, 25, 40–41, 107, 135
Conrad, Rachel, 15–16, 20, 256, 260
Continuation of Early Lessons (Edgeworth), 29
Cooke, Ebenezer, 201–2, 237; *Alternative Illustrated Syllabus of Instruction in Drawing in Elementary Schools*, 203, 286n12; "The Basis and Beginnings of Brushwork," 202–3; and collaborative art instruction, 202–4; and freehand drawing vs. stricter art exercises, 202; "Our Art Teaching and Child Nature," 204, 207
Cooper, James Fenimore, 108, 275n20; and Stevenson's *Treasure Island*, 111–12, 113
Cooper, Jane, 76
Coral Island, The (Ballantyne), 108, 109, 110, 275n20
Cosslett, Tess, 31, 32, 46
Craik, Dinah Mulock, 147–48, 152; "The Age of Gold," 143–44, 185, 188, 278n3
Crane, Walter, 231, 232, 233, 237; frontispiece for *Tell Me a Story* (Molesworth), 76–78; and painting books, 229, 288n30
Crockett, Maisie, 24–26, 266n19
Crockett, Samuel Rutherford, 24–26, 266nn18–19
cross-writing, 14–16, 114, 265n13

Crowns (Whitlock and Hull), 247
Cruikshank, George: and fairy tales, 271n25; frontispieces for *German Popular Stories* (Taylor), 62–65, 76, 77, 270n19, 271n24; frontispiece for *Kit Bam's Adventures* (Clarke), 71–74, 85

Dahl, Roald, 236–37
Dalby, Richard, 289n32
Dalziel brothers, 231
Daniel, C. H. O., 97, 274n8
Darnton, Robert, 176
Darton, J. Harvey, 79, 109, 110, 148
Darwin, Charles, 289n37; "A Biographical Sketch of an Infant," 47, 49; relationships with children, 190–92, 284nn1–2, 285n4, 285n6
Darwin, Francis: adult collaboration with Charles Darwin, 285n6; childhood art, 190–92, 193, 225, 234, 260, 285n3; remembrances of Charles Darwin, 284n2, 285n4
Davidson, Angus, 232
Davidson, Guy, 109–10, 289n36
Day, Sara K., 265n15
Day the Crayons Quit, The (Jeffers), 237
de Medici, Marchesa Peruzzi. *See* Story, Edith
Deane, Bradley, 109
Defoe, Daniel, 108, 115, 135, 169, 267n3, 275n20
dialogue (as a form): in Barbauld, 29–32; in Cizek, 286n17; in Rands, 155
Dickens, Charles, 144, 163, 239, 249, 260; *A Child's History of England*, 278n6; on fairy tales, 271n25; *Hard Times*, 31, 181; *A Holiday Romance*, 16, 34, 146–50, 166, 178, 183, 278–79nn6–9; in *Juvenile Literature As It Is* (Salmon), 169, 170, 171, 275n20; on kindergarten, 200; *The Life of Our Lord*, 278n6
Dismore, Blanche, 48, 251
Domestic Pictures and Tales (Gatty), 79–81

Don't Let the Pigeon Drive the Bus
   (Willems), 237
Doyle, Richard, 37–38, 231, 267n1
Drain, Susan, 88–89, 216, 217, 272n32
Dramatic Lyrics (Browning), 4, 5–6, 8,
   212, 264n3
Drummond, W. B., 47, 269n11
Duane, Anna Mae, 260
Dundes, Alan, 59
Dunlap, Hope, 286n19

Early Lessons (Edgeworth), 29, 266n22
*Easy Introduction to the Knowledge of
   Nature* (Trimmer), 28
Ebb-Tide, The (Stevenson and Osbourne),
   34, 125, 126, 127–31, 255, 277nn29–30
Echolilia: Sometimes I Wonder
   (Archibald), 35, 247–53, 254
Ede, Lisa, 105, 254, 289n32
Edgeworth, Maria, 27, 28–29, 32, 163,
   266nn21–22
Edgeworth, Richard, 27, 29, 266nn21–22
education: collaboration in, 185–87,
   188, 202–3, 208–10; compulsory
   attendance, 46, 187, 188, 282n30,
   284nn42–43; cramming and overpressure, 180–84, 283n36; Forster Act
   (Elementary Education Act of 1870),
   187–88, 282n30, 284n42; payment by
   results, 179–80, 181, 182, 184; poetry
   recitation in schools, 185–86, 258–59,
   283n40; reports of Her Majesty's
   Inspectorate (HMI), 179–82, 184–87,
   260, 282n29, 283n38; Revised Code of
   1862, 178–87, 188, 282n33. *See also* art
   education
Efland, Arthur D., 198, 203, 209, 285n5
Elementary Education Act of 1870
   (Forster Act), 187–88, 282n30, 284n42
Elements of Drawing (Ruskin), 200–201
Émile, or On Education (Rousseau), 56,
   269n11; art education in, 194–97;
   print culture vs. children's spoken
   language in, 42, 43–46, 86, 267nn3–4

Enlightenment child, 27–32
Escape to Persia (Whitlock and Hull), 247
Evans, Edmund, 231
*Evenings at Home, or, The Juvenile Budget
   Opened* (Aikin and Barbauld), 29–32,
   266–67nn24–25, 273n37
Ewing, Juliana Horatia, 75, 81–82, 171,
   216, 287n20
Exile, The (Osbourne and Strong), 140

Fairy Godmothers, and Other Tales, The
   (Gatty), 78–79
fairy tales, 43, 70–71, 74, 78–79, 90;
   as children's literature, 27, 61–66,
   271n23, 271n25, 282n34; Grimms,
   58–62, 71, 79, 80, 86, 270–71nn19–21;
   translations of Grimms, 63–69,
   270n19, 272nn26–28. *See also* story
   collections for children
Far-Distant Oxus, The (Hull and
   Whitlock), 35, 243–47, 254, 290nn7–8
Field, E. M., 176
Finley, Martha, 163–64
First Year of Drawing, A (Bailey), 207
Flynn, Richard, 10, 15, 265n9, 291n12
Folks at Home, 110
Forster Act (Elementary Education Act
   of 1870), 187–88, 282n30, 284n42
French, John, 207–8
Froebel, Friedrich, 193, 199–200, 201,
   202, 204, 286n10
Fry, Roger, 238
Furnivall, Frederick James, 4, 5, 211

Galbraith, Gretchen, 187, 283n36
*Gammer Grethel; or German Fairy
   Tales, and Popular Stories, from
   the Collection of MM Grimm, and
   Other Sources* (Taylor), 43, 66–68, 71,
   272nn27–28
Gatty, Margaret, 35, 43, 91, 93, 221, 239,
   272nn34–35; *Aunt Judy's Letters*,
   88–90, 273nn37–38; *Aunt Judy's
   Magazine*, 88–89, 215–16, 239,

273n35; *Aunt Judy's Magazine* feature "Nursery Nonsense," 216–20, 227, 246, 273n39; *Aunt Judy's Tales*, 6, 33, 81–88, 273n36, 287n20; and the collaborative Gatty household, 75, 78, 82, 87–88, 89–90, 216; *Domestic Pictures and Tales*, 79–81; *The Fairy Godmothers, and Other Tales*, 78–79
Genette, Gérard, 265n16
German Popular Stories, translated from the Kinder und Haus Märchen, collected by M. M. Grimm, from Oral Tradition (Taylor), 43, 65–66, 67, 80, 270n19, 271n25, 272n28, 282n34; Cruikshank's frontispieces for, 62, 63, 64–65, 76
girls' literature, 169, 170–72, 177, 281n26
Girl's Own Paper, The, 170
Girouard, Mark, 231
Godley, Eveline C., 163–65, 170
Golden Age of children's literature, 212, 238, 255, 259, 260; and child agency, 21, 124, 242–43, 254, 257; definition of, 264n4; Gubar on, 16, 81, 151, 265n11; histories and origins of texts, 5–7, 18, 22, 257; and idealized children, 12, 70; and real child collaborators, 12, 18, 27, 32, 246, 253, 261
Golden Road, The (Whiting), 37
Goslee, David, 265n10
Gosse, Edmund, 93, 103, 119
Graham, Ennis. *See* Molesworth, Mary Louisa
Grahame, Alistair, 242
Grahame, Kenneth, 242
Green, Roger Lancelyn, 75–76
Greenaway, Kate, 231, 232, 233, 237–38; illustrations as basis for painting books, 228, 229; illustrations for "The Pied Piper," 5, 212, 286n19
Grimm, Jacob and Wilhelm, 80, 222, 270n19, 271n22, 271n24, 273n35, 287n24; as fairy tale collectors, 58–59, 272n27; *Kinder- und Hausmärchen*, 43, 59–62, 71, 79, 80, 86, 270nn20–21, 272n28; translations of, 63–69, 270n19, 272nn26–28
Grimms' Household Tales (Hunt), 68, 272n28
Gubar, Marah: on adventure fiction, 110, 123; *Artful Dodgers: Reconceiving the Golden Age of Children's Literature*, 16–18, 22, 110, 147, 151, 265n11; on child narrators, 16; on child precocity, 265n11; on child reviewers, 162; on children as creative agents and collaborators, 13, 16, 20, 81, 147, 151, 256, 265n9, 287n20; on children's theater, 16–17, 20, 280n14; on evidence of real children, 18, 266n17, 281n24; "The Hermeneutics of Recuperation: What a Kinship-Model Approach to Children's Agency Could Do for Children's Literature and Childhood Studies," 13, 18, 256; on kinship model of childhood, 17–18, 151–52, 187; "Risky Business: Talking about Children in Children's Literature Criticism," 13, 17–18, 151–52
Gulliver's Travels (Swift), 174

Haggard, H. Rider, 109, 110
Hale, Horatio, 54–55
Hall, A. Neely, 96
Hall, G. Stanley, 47–48, 54, 261, 268n5, 268n7, 291n8
"Hansel and Gretel," 68, 272n28
Hard Times (Dickens), 31, 181
Harman, Claire, 93
Harris, Elizabeth, 94, 96–98, 273–74nn4–8
Harrison, Thomas G., 99, 274nn6–7, 274n11
Harry Potter and the Philosopher's Stone, 242
Hart, James D.: on Osbourne's small press, 99–100, 102, 121, 125, 249,

273n3, 274nn12–13, 275nn16–17; on small presses in general, 95, 273n5
Hawley, Harriet, 221, 223, 287n22
Hawlin, Stefan, 263n2
Hawthorne, Nathaniel, 174, 222
Henley, W. E., 93, 111, 231
Henty, G. A., 108, 174
Hewins, Caroline: *Books for Boys and Girls: A Selected List*, 172–73, 174; *Books for the Young: A Guide for Parents and Children*, 172; "Books That Children Like," 173–74; "How Library Work with Children Has Grown in Hartford and Connecticut," 173, 282n27; "Report on [the] List of Children's Books with Children's Annotations," 174–76; on representing child readers' voices, 34, 173–76, 177, 178, 187, 282n28
Hidden Adult: Defining Children's Literature, The (Nodelman), 10, 13, 278n1
Hobbit, The (Tolkien), 242
Hofmann, Werner, 195, 286n11
Hogg, W. Dods, 99
Holiday Romance, A (Dickens), 16, 34, 146–50, 166, 178, 183, 278–79nn6–9
Hollindale, Peter, 279n10, 279n13
Holyoake, Maltus Questell, 74
Home and Colonial School Society, 198
Horn, Pamela, 180, 282n33
Horne, Jackie, 281n25
Household Words, 200, 239, 278n6
How Gertrude Teaches Her Children (Pestalozzi), 197–98
Hsiao, Irene, 281n20
Hull, Katharine, 35, 243–47, 254, 290nn7–8
Hun, E. R., 54–55, 270n17
Hunt, Margaret, 68, 272n28
Hunt, Peter, 142–43, 144, 278nn1–2

illustration: of *Aunt Judy's Tales*, 85–87, 88; of "The Cardinal and the Dog," 3–4, 211, 213–14, 263n3; of *German Popular Stories* (Taylor), 62–65, 76, 271n24; of *Just So Stories* (Kipling), 23, 225–28, 229, 288nn27–29; of *Kit Bam's Adventures*, 71–73, 85; picture books, 192–93, 230–32, 237; of "The Pied Piper," 4–6, 8–9, 193–94, 211–15, 263n3, 264n7, 286nn18–19; of *Rose and the Ring*, 37–38, 41, 267n1; of *Tell Me a Story*, 76–78
imagination, child's: and Child Study, 72, 252; children constructed as imaginative, 13–14, 179–81, 188–89, 265nn11–12; gendered, 72–75; Stevenson on, 115–16, 120–22; and visualization, 72
imitation: in child art, 35, 191–94, 195, 197–99, 201, 204–7, 209, 214–17, 220, 227, 230; in children's language acquisition, 33, 49–52, 54–55, 56, 246, 249, 260
imperialism, 33–34, 109–10
intergenerational collaboration. *See* adult-child collaboration
Intimate Portrait of R.L.S., A (Osbourne), 126, 132, 135

Jack, Jordyn, 291n9
James, Henry: biography of William Wetmore Story, 37, 39, 40; and Robert Louis Stevenson, 102, 273n2; *What Maisie Knew*, 268n9
Japp, Alexander, 119
Jeffers, Oliver, 237
Johnston, Charles, 51
Jordan, David Starr, 35, 226, 255, 287nn21–22; *The Book of Knight and Barbara*, 6–7, 194, 220–24, 255, 287–88nn23–26
Jordan, June, 15
Just So Stories (Kipling), 22, 73, 272n29; illustrations as invitation for collaboration, 23, 225–28, 288nn27–28; influence of Josephine Kipling, 6, 12,

15, 224–25, 226, 228; painting books based on, 228–29, 288n29
Juvenile Literature As It Is (Salmon), 169–72, 177–78, 246, 275n20, 281nn23–25

Kandinsky, Wassily, 238
Kelly, Donna Darling, 195, 200, 285n5, 285n9, 286n13
Keynes, Randal, 190, 285n4
Kidd, Kenneth, 260
Kincaid, James, 10, 252, 257–58, 279n12, 291n11
Kinder- und Hausmärchen (Grimms), 43, 59–62, 71, 79, 80, 86, 270nn20–21, 272n28
kindergarten, 187, 199–200, 204
King Solomon's Mines (Haggard), 109, 110, 275n20
Kingsley, Charles, 108, 135, 169, 275n20; *The Water-Babies: A Fairy Tale for a Land-Baby*, 182–84, 186, 283n36
Kingston, W. H. G., 110, 111, 112, 113, 169, 275n20
Kingston's Magazine for Boys, 110
kinship model of childhood (Gubar), 17–18, 151–52, 187
Kipling, Josephine, 6, 12, 15, 224–25, 226, 228
Kipling, Rudyard, 73, 272n39; illustrations of *Just So Stories* as invitation for collaboration, 23, 225–28, 288nn27–28; influence of Josephine Kipling on *Just So Stories*, 6, 12, 15, 224–25, 226, 228; painting books based on *Just So Stories*, 228–29, 288n29
Kit Bam's Adventures; or, The Yarns of an Old Mariner (Clarke), 22, 33, 71–74, 85, 272n30
Klee, Paul, 238
Knoepflmacher, U. C.: on cross-writing, 14–15, 113–14, 265n13; on fairy tales, 74; on Gatty, 75, 88, 216; on Kipling,

15, 22, 225–26, 288n27; on Thackeray, 38, 40
Kohn, David, 190, 191
Kreilkamp, Ivan, 267n2

Lamb, Charles, 164, 290n4
Lane, Clara S., 85–87, 88
Lang, Andrew, 111, 271n25
Langbauer, Laurie, 27, 256, 257
language acquisition, 249, 260; and adult-child collaboration, 43, 49–54, 57–58, 249; imitation and, 191–94, 195, 197–99, 201, 204–7, 209, 214–17, 220; secret languages of children, 18, 54–58, 90, 252, 270nn16–18; theorized by Child Study scholars, 8, 33, 43, 46, 48–58, 70, 83, 93, 246, 252, 260, 269n10, 269nn13–15; theorized by Rousseau, 42–46, 86
Last of the Mohicans (Cooper), 108, 109, 275n20
Lazy Lessons (Rands), 188
Lear, Edward: *Book of Nonsense*, 232, 289n33; childlike style of nonsense art, 35, 194, 232–34, 236–37, 288n32; drawings of birds, 193, 234–35, 289nn34–35; limericks and textual nonsense, 234, 238, 288n32; nonsense botany, 235–36, 289n26; *Queery Leary Nonsense*, 234–35; as realistic painter, 232, 234; relationships with children, 234, 289n33
Leeds, Jo Alice, 208
Leonard, James S., 254
Lesnik-Oberstein, Karín, 264n8
Lessons for Children (Barbauld), 267n26
Levy, Michelle, 29
librarians, 172, 260, 282n27; surveying child readers, 34–35, 173–76, 272n28
Liddell sisters, 6
Liebert, Herman W., 289n32
Lilliput Lectures (Rands), 154–55
Lilliput Levee (Rands), 34, 78, 150–54, 166, 178, 188, 272n33

Linton, William James, 231
Little Father of the Wilderness (Osbourne and Strong), 140
"Little Folks" Painting Book, The, and related titles, 228–29
Little Mary (Barrie), 158
Little Pretty Pocket-Book (Newbery), 28
Little Princess, A (Burnett), 14, 265n11
Little White Bird, The, 157–58, 239
Llewelyn Davies brothers, 11, 279n12, 280n16, 180n20; *The Boy Castaways of Black Lake Island*, 160–61, 249–50, 275n19, 280n19; as collaborators with Barrie, 6, 24, 34, 157, 158–59, 162, 241, 250
Locke, John, 27, 31, 44
Locker-Lampson, Frederick, 21, 41–42, 43, 267n1
Longfellow, Henry Wadsworth, 115
Low, Florence B., 281n26
Lowe, Robert, 179–80, 282n33
Luckey, G. W. A., 58
Lukens, Herman T., 207
Lunsford, Andrea, 105, 254
Lynch, Catherine M., 290n6

MacDonald, George, 188–89, 278n4
MacDonald, Stuart, 237
Macready, William Charles, Jr. (Willie), 11, 260; "Cardinal and the Dog," collaboration with Browning, 3–4, 211, 213–14, 263n1, 263n3; "Pied Piper of Hamelin," collaboration with Browning, 4–6, 8–9, 12–13, 21, 193–94, 211–15, 217, 241, 263n3, 264n7, 265n10, 286n18; as son of Macready Sr., 263n2, 264n7
Macready, William Charles, Sr., 3, 211, 263n2
Maitland, Louise, 221, 223, 286n14, 287n22
Malvern, S. B., 209
Manual for Drawing from Models (Williams), 197

Marryat, Captain Frederick, 108, 115, 275n20
Masterman Ready, or the Wreck of the Pacific (Marryat), 114, 117
Matilda (Dahl), 236
Maxwell, Christabel, 78–79, 81–82, 88, 272n25
McCulloch, Fiona, 277n28
McGavran, James Holt, Jr., 266n20
McMaster, Juliet, 256–57
Memories of Vailima (Osbourne), 132
Mencken, H. L., 274n7
Middleton, Nigel, 284n42
Millais, John Everett, 237
Milne, A. A., 6
Milne, Christopher Robin, 6
Mind of the Child, The (Preyer), 47, 268n6
Miró, Joan, 238
modernism, 8, 192, 193, 196, 210, 238, 242
Molesworth, Mary Louisa, 33, 43, 91; collaborating with child auditors, 75–78, 168, 261; *An Enchanted Garden*, 90; "On the Art of Writing Fiction for Children," 75–76, 168; "Story-Reading and Story-Writing," 75; *Tell Me a Story*, 76–78, 90
Moore, Anne Carroll, 174–75
Moral Tales for Young People (Edgeworth), 29
More Beasts (For Worse Children) (Belloc), 236
Morris, William, 231
Moss, Anita, 148
Mother Bunch's Fairy Tales (Harris), 71
multiple authorship. *See* collaboration
Murray, Stuart, 291n9
Myers, Mitzi, 14, 15, 113–14, 265n13, 266n22

Nelson, Claudia, 95, 108, 110, 272n31, 275n18, 278n5
Nesbit, E., 14, 166, 278n4
Neumann, Siegfried, 270n21
Newbery, John, 28

Nikolajeva, Maria, 145, 150, 152, 278n1, 278n4
Noakes, Vivian, 234
Nodelman, Perry, 10, 13, 14, 15, 17, 19, 265n9, 278n1
nonsense, 193, 232–37, 238, 288–89nn32–36
Norquay, Glenda, 114
nostalgia, 60, 111, 143, 177, 287n3; and Barrie, 157, 241, 279n12; and language, 57, 90
Notes on Children's Drawings (Brown), 205

Ode: Intimations of Immortality (Wordsworth), 26–27
Ogata, Amy F., 14, 265n12
Old and Young, 110
On the Origin of Species manuscript (Darwin), 190–92
Ong, Walter, 42, 61
Osbourne, Samuel Lloyd, 11, 273n3, 276n24, 277nn32–33; *The Adventurer*, 132; *Baby Bullet*, 277n32; collaboration with Stevenson (general), 23, 33–34, 93–94, 107, 121–22, 124–26, 132, 135, 255, 259; collaboration with Strong, 23, 33, 134–41, 278n39; *The Ebb-Tide*, 34, 125, 127–31, 277nn29–30; *The Exile*, 140; *An Intimate Portrait of R.L.S.*, 126, 132, 135; *Letters to Young Friends*, 275n14, 276n27; *Little Father of the Wilderness*, 140; *Memories of Vailima*, 132; *A Person of Some Importance*, 132; reviews of novels coauthored with Stevenson, 131–34, 277n31; small press printing, 23, 33–34, 93, 94, 99–107, 125, 134, 246, 249, 261, 275n13; and *Treasure Island*, 7–8, 34, 93, 107, 113–14, 116–19, 125, 126, 135; *Treasure Island: A Melodrama in Five Acts*, 23, 134–40, 277n34, 277n36, 278n38; *The Wrecker*, 125, 126–27, 132; *The Wrong Box*, 125

Our Uncle the Traveller's Stories (Browne), 72–73
Our Young Folks, 146, 278n6
Oxus in Summer (Whitlock and Hull), 247

painting books, 13, 18, 228–30, 288nn29–31
paratexts, 265n16; in adventure fiction, 110; of children's literature, 13, 28; of *Peter Pan*, 280n14; of story collections, 74, 86; of *Sweetheart Travellers*, 25; of *Treasure Island*, 111–14
Parent's Assistant, The (Edgeworth), 29
Parkes, Christopher, 14, 265n12
Patrick, G. T. W., 51
Patten, Robert L., 64
Paul, Lissa, 27–28, 290n2
Perez, Bernard, 49
Perrault, Charles, 270n19, 271n24
Person of Some Importance, A (Osbourne), 132
Pestalozzi, Johann, 197–98, 199, 200, 201, 202
Peter and Wendy (Barrie), 162, 178, 279n10, 280n18, 281n20
Peter Pan (Barrie): authorship of, 6, 24, 34, 155–62, 239, 241, 250, 264n5, 279n10, 279–80nn12–14; general references to, 162–63, 178, 265n14, 280n17, 280–81nn20–21
peters, charlie, 258
photography, 265n15; in Archibald, 35, 247–53, 254; in Barrie, 160–61; in Crockett, 26
Picasso, Pablo, 238
picture books, 192–93, 230–32, 237
"Pied Piper of Hamelin; A Child's Story" (Browning): collaboration with Willie Macready, 4–6, 8–9, 12–13, 21, 193–94, 211–15, 217, 241, 263n3, 264n7, 265n10, 286n18; illustrated editions of, 286n19; as published in *Dramatic Lyrics*, 5, 8; relationship with Browning's father, 215

Pierce, Jason A., 275n21
Pilgrim's Progress from This World to That Which Is to Come, The (Bunyan), 27
play, 183; as child agency, 18–20; and kindergarten, 200
Plotz, Judith, 266n20
Pollock, F., 49
Pollock, Mary S., 265n10
power, adult and child: and child art, 193, 194, 199–200, 203–4, 208–10, 226–27, 236–37; in classrooms, 178–89; imbalance, 10, 30, 33, 117, 123–24; reconsidered in children's literature and culture, 34–35, 68, 81, 144–59, 249–50; re-theorizing adult-child power relationships, 17–20, 240–41, 255–60; topsy-turvy plots, 34, 144–52, 154, 157, 203, 260
Practical Education (Edgeworth), 29
Prelude, or Growth of a Poet's Mind, The (Wordsworth), 27
Preyer, William T., 47, 268n6
Princess Louise, 237–38
publication history. *See* composition narratives
Punch, 132–34, 165–66

Quiller-Couch, Arthur, 158
Quiller-Couch, Bevil, 158
Quilter, Harry and Mary, 264n7
Quirici, Marion, 291n9
Quiver, 163

Rackham, Arthur, 5, 212
Rands, William Brighty, 144, 181, 260; "Children and Children's Books," 153–54, 155, 259; on collaborative partnership with children, 152–55, 187, 259; on compulsory school attendance, 284n43; *Lazy Lessons*, 188; *Lilliput Lectures*, 154–55; *Lilliput Levee*, 34, 78, 150–54, 166, 178, 188, 272n33; "The Nurture of Children," 152–53

Ransom, Will, 94–95
Ransome, Arthur, 35, 243–47, 290nn6–7
recapitulation theory, 14, 261, 269n12, 271n23; and art, 192, 205–6; and language acquisition, 44–45, 50–51, 56, 70
Redcay, Anna, 265n15
Reid, Captain Mayne, 108
Reimer, Mavis, 258
Religious Tract Society, 275nn18–19
Revised Code of 1862, 178–83, 184–87, 188, 282n33
Reynolds, Sir Joshua, 198, 286n11
Ricci, Corrado, 205, 286n14, 287n22
Rich, Eric E., 284n42
Richards, Jeffrey, 109, 275n20
Richardson, Alan, 266n20
Richardson, Marion, 209–10, 213, 220
Robbins, Sarah, 267n26
Robinson Crusoe (Defoe), 108, 114, 115, 117, 169, 187, 267n3, 275n20
Robson, Catherine, 10–11, 27, 252, 258, 272n31, 283n40
Romantic ideal of childhood, 208, 245, 251–52, 266n20; as contradictory construct, 24–25, 26–27, 255; as imaginative, 14; relationship to language, 45–46, 91
Rosamund: A Sequel to Early Lessons (Edgeworth), 29
Rose, Jacqueline, 81, 155, 280n13; on child actors, 17, 265n14; on child and language, 44, 45, 70; on child as construct, 9–10, 19, 252, 257; influence on later scholars, 11, 14, 22, 239–40, 264n8, 265n12
Rose, Lionel, 180, 181, 282n32, 283n38
Rose and the Ring, The (Thackeray), 6, 21–22, 33, 37–42
Rousseau, Jean-Jacques, 27; and art education, 35, 193, 194–97, 198, 200, 208, 285n7; on children and language, 42–46, 60, 70, 86, 155, 267nn3–4;

influence on the Child Study movement, 49, 50–51, 53, 56, 269n11
Rowe, Karen E., 64–65, 74–75, 271n24
Rowe, Richard, 166
Rowling, J. K., 242
Royal Drawing Society, 237–38
Rudd, David, 11, 13
Ruskin, John, 231; *Elements of Drawing*, 200–201; on fairy tales, 65, 271n25

Salisbury, Harrison E., 270n18
Salmon, Edward, 34, 187, 281n26; *Juvenile Literature As It Is*, 169–72, 177–78, 246, 275n20, 281nn23–25; *Juvenile Literature* compared to Hewins study, 172, 173, 174, 175, 178
Sánchez-Eppler, Karen, 258
Schacker, Jennifer, 61, 271n25, 272n27
Schwebel, Sarah L., 265n9, 266n17
Scott, Sir Walter, 108, 169, 170, 171, 275n20
secret languages of children, 18, 54–58, 90, 252, 270nn16–18
Sentimental Tommy (Barrie), 158
Settlers in Canada, The (Marryat), 108–9
Shaftesbury (Lord Ashley; Anthony Ashley-Cooper), 284n42
Shires, Linda M., 225, 288n28
Shook-Up Generation, The (Salisbury), 270n18
Shrek! (Steig), 236
Shuttleworth, Sally, 260, 269n10; on Child Study, 46, 48, 268n6; on children's imaginations, 14; on children's language acquisition, 269n10, 269n15
Six to Sixteen (Ewing), 75
small presses: and amateur journalism, 98–99, 100, 274n6, 274n11; and child agency, 18–20; as educational tool, 33–34, 93, 96–98, 274nn6–9; history of, 94–96, 273nn4–5; and Osbourne, 99–101, 274n13, 275n15; and Osbourne with Stevenson, 23, 33, 99, 101–7, 113, 125, 134, 246, 249, 255, 261, 274n12, 275nn15–17

Smith, A. Tolman, 269n11
Smith, Vanessa, 130, 277n30
Society for Promoting of Christian Knowledge, 275n19
Sorby, Angela, 256
Sparkes, J., 204
Spencer, Herbert, 202
Spencer, Truman J., 96, 98–99, 100, 274n11
St. Nicholas Magazine, 96, 225, 226, 275n14, 276n27
Steedman, Carolyn, 268n8
Steig, William, 236
Stephens, W. B., 180
Stevens, Joan, 41
Stevens, Kate, 268n5
Stevenson, Fanny, 93, 119, 134, 135, 273n3
Stevenson, Robert Louis: "Authors and Publishers," 93, 103, 290n1; on authorship and the book trade, 92–94, 103, 120–21, 127, 239, 273n2; *Catriona*, 140–41; "A Chapter on Dreams," 93, 112, 290n1; *A Child's Garden of Verses*, 116, 125; "Child's Play," 115–16, 120–21; collaboration with Osbourne (general), 33–34, 93–94, 125–27, 131–32, 140–41, 255, 259, 276n27, 277nn31–32; *The Ebb-Tide*, 34, 125, 126, 127–31, 255, 277nn29–30; "A Gossip on Romance," 102, 112; "A Humble Remonstrance," 273n2; *An Inland Voyage*, 276n22; *Kidnapped*, 125, 169; "Letter to a Young Gentleman," 273n2; *Letters to Young Friends*, 121, 275n14, 276n27; "My First Book," 93, 114–16, 117–19, 120, 126, 276n22, 276n26; "A Penny Plain and Twopence Coloured," 275n14; small press printing with Osbourne, 23, 33, 99, 101–7, 113, 125, 134, 246, 249, 255, 261, 274n12, 275n16; *Strange Case of Dr. Jekyll and Mr. Hyde*, 93, 125, 127, 276n25; toy theater, soldiers, and other games, 102, 121–22, 135; *Travels*

with a Donkey in the Cévennes, 276n22; *Treasure Island* (general), 7, 92–93, 107, 122–25, 137–38, 139, 169, 275–76nn20–22, 276nn25–26, 276n28, 277n37; *Treasure Island* as adventure fiction, 110–13, 114–16, 135, 139; *Treasure Island* as collaboration with Osbourne, 7–8, 34, 93, 107, 113–14, 116–19, 126, 135, 255; *The Wrecker*, 125, 126, 132–33; *The Wrong Box*, 125
Stevenson, Thomas, 119
Stillinger, Jack, 240
Stirling, Kristin, 264n5, 280n14
Stone, Marjorie, 240, 290n4
Story, Edith, 6, 21–22, 37–39, 40, 41–42, 90, 267n1
story collections for children: eighteenth-century collections, 28–32, 266–67nn24–26; fairy tale collections, 22, 43, 58–70, 270n19; Golden Age collections, 6, 22, 24–26, 71–91, 221–28
Strachey, Edmund, 232–33
Strachey, Henry, 232
Straley, Jessica, 50–51, 184, 260
Striker, Susan, 288n31
Strong, Austin, 23, 134–38, 140–41, 277nn34–36, 278n39
Studies in Education (Barnes), 205, 206, 287n23, 287n25
Studies of Childhood (Sully), 47; on children as artists, 205, 206; on children's imaginations, 72; on children's language acquisition, 49, 50, 52–53, 55, 246
Sully, James, 47, 91; on children as artists, 202, 205, 206; on children's imaginations, 72, 252; on children's language acquisition, 49, 50, 52–53, 55, 83, 246, 269n15
Sumpter, Caroline, 89, 271n23, 290n2
surveys of child readers, 34–35, 169–78, 246, 275n20, 281nn23–26
Sutton, Gordon, 195, 197, 285nn7–8

Swallows and Amazons series (Ransome), 243, 244, 246, 290n6
Sweetheart Travellers: A Child's Book for Children, for Women, and for Men (Crockett), 24–26, 266nn18–19
Sweethearts at Home (Crockett), 266n19
Swiss Family Robinson (Wyss), 169
sympathy between adults and children, 82, 145; in classrooms, 187, 194, 200, 202–3, 209, 258–59; in Rands, 153–54

Taine, Hippolyte, 49, 52, 53, 91, 269n10, 269n15
Tanglewood Tales (Hawthorne), 174
Tarrant, Margaret W., 264n7, 287n19
Tatar, Maria, 59, 62, 271n22
Taylor, Edgar, 43, 63–68, 71, 80, 89–90, 270n19, 272nn26–28, 282n34
Tell Me a Story (Molesworth), 76–78, 90
Tenniel, John, 231, 237–38
Thackeray, Anny and Minny, 6, 39
Thackeray, William Makepeace, 33; on picture books, 230, 231; relationship with Edith Story, 6, 21, 37–40, 41–42, 90, 267n1; *The Rose and the Ring*, 6, 21–22, 33, 37–42
Thompson, Judith, 240, 290n4
Tolkien, J. R. R., 242
Tom Thumb, 66, 68–70
topsy-turvy plots, 34, 144–52, 154, 157, 203, 260
Tosenberger, Catherine, 266n15
toy presses. *See* small presses
toys and games: and child agency, 18–20; toy theaters, 102, 135; war games, 102, 121–22
Tracy, Frederick, 51–52, 83, 269n14
Treasure Island (Stevenson), 7, 92–93, 107, 122–25, 137–38, 139, 169, 275–76nn20–22, 276nn25–26, 276n28, 277n37; as adventure fiction, 110–13, 114–16, 135, 139; as collaboration with Osbourne, 7–8, 34, 93, 107, 113–14, 116–19, 126, 135, 255

Treasure Island: A Melodrama in Five Acts (Osbourne and Strong), 23, 134–40, 277n34, 277n36, 278n38
Treasure Seekers, The (Nesbit), 14, 166
Treatise on the Education of Children and Youth (Watts), 28
Trimmer, Sarah, 28, 32

Valint, Alexandra, 277n28
Vanpée, Janie, 44, 45
Verne, Jules, 275n20
Vice Versâ; or, A Lesson to Fathers (Anstey), 145–46
Viehmann, Dorothea, 67–68, 272n27
Viola, Wilhelm, 209, 285n5, 286n17

Walsh, Sue, 12, 15, 22, 70, 272n29, 288n27
Wanley, Nathaniel, 215, 263n1
Ward, Donald, 270n21
Water-Babies: A Fairy Tale for a Land-Baby, The (Kingsley), 182–84, 186, 283n36
Watson, Victor, 244, 247, 276n23
Watts, Isaac, 28, 31
Watts, Mrs. Alaric, 166
Westward Ho! (Kingsley), 169, 275n20
Wetherell, Elizabeth, 169
Wharton, Christine E., 254
Wheeler, Edward J., 132–34
White, Daniel E., 29
Whiting, Lilian, 37
Whitlock, Pamela, 35, 243–47, 254, 290nn7–8
Wide, Wide World (Wetherell), 169
Wilde, Oscar, 110
Willems, Mo, 237
Williams, C. E. Butler, 197, 198
Wind in the Willows, The (Grahame), 242
Winnie-the-Pooh (Milne), 6
Wollstonecraft, Mary, 27
Wonder Tales (Hawthorne), 174
Wonders of the Little World, The (Wanley), 215, 263n1
Wong, Amy, 276n25
Wooldridge, Adrian, 46–47, 49, 50, 269n12
Woolf, Virginia, 242, 290n5
Wordsworth, William, 26–27, 154
Wrecker, The (Stevenson and Osbourne), 125, 126, 132–33
Wrong Box, The (Stevenson and Osbourne), 125
Wyss, Johann David, 169

Young Folks, 110, 119, 169, 276n21
Young Visiters, The (Ashford), 246
Youth's Companion, 96

Zipes, Jack, 270n21

www.ingramcontent.com/pod-product-compliance
Lightning Source LLC
Chambersburg PA
CBHW030606230426
43661CB00053B/1857